MW00696103

GLOBALIZING MOROCCO

GLOBALIZING MOROCCO

*Transnational Activism and
the Postcolonial State*

David Stenner

Stanford University Press
Stanford, California

Stanford University Press
Stanford, California

© 2019 by the Board of Trustees of the Leland Stanford Junior University.
All rights reserved.

No part of this book may be reproduced or transmitted in any form or
by any means, electronic or mechanical, including photocopying and
recording, or in any information storage or retrieval system without the
prior written permission of Stanford University Press.

Printed in the United States of America on acid-free, archival-quality paper

Library of Congress Cataloging-in-Publication Data

Names: Stenner, David, author.
Title: Globalizing Morocco : transnational activism and the post-colonial
    state / David Stenner.
Description: Stanford, California : Stanford University Press, 2019. |
    Includes bibliographical references and index.
Identifiers: LCCN 2018060887 (print) | LCCN 2019000801 (ebook) |
    ISBN 9781503609006 (electronic) | ISBN 9781503608115 |
    ISBN 9781503608115 (cloth : alk. paper) | ISBN 9781503608993
    (pbk. : alk. paper)
Subjects: LCSH: Nationalism—Morocco—History—20th century. |
    Anti-imperialist movements—Morocco—History. | Political
    activists—Morocco—History—20th century. | Moroccans—Social
    networks—History—20th century. | Morocco—Foreign public
    opinion—History—20th century. | France—Colonies—Africa—
    Foreign public opinion. | Morocco—History—1912-1956.
Classification: LCC DT324 (ebook) | LCC DT324 .S74 2019 (print) |
    DDC 964/.04—dc23
LC record available at https://lccn.loc.gov/2018060887

Typeset by Motto Publishing Services in 10.5/15 Adobe Garamond Pro
Cover photo by Aboubakr Bennouna. Members of the Moroccan Office
of Information and Documentation at the UN, 1952.
Cover design by Rob Ehle.

To Vianney, who traveled with me

CONTENTS

ACKNOWLEDGMENTS

A great many individuals and institutions have contributed to the making of this book. A Mellon Fellowship from the Council on Library and Information Resources (CLIR), a grant from the France-Berkeley Fund, and the continuous support of the Department of History at UC Davis financed the necessary archival research; a fellowship from the Mabelle McLeod Lewis Memorial Fund permitted me to write unfettered by any teaching obligations; and my tenure as the Sultan Visiting Scholar in Arab Studies at UC Berkeley's Center for Middle Eastern Studies allowed me to make significant progress on the manuscript. This project also benefited from lessons learned during the Summer Institute for Conducting Archival Research organized by the Institute for European, Russian, and Eurasian Studies at The George Washington University as well as during the 2012 American Institute for Maghrib Studies (AIMS) Writing Workshop at UCLA. Finally, the Department of History at Christopher Newport University made a generous contribution to the production of the book.

The complicated research process benefited from the invaluable help of countless individuals. Nonetheless, I need to highlight a few of them: Aboubakr Bennouna most generously shared his family papers with me; Kenza Torres helped me navigate Tetouan's archival landscape on several occasions; Robert E. Rodes V sent me sources about his grandfather; the chief librarian of the Allal al-Fassi Foundation, Ustadh Amin, granted me access to important documents previously unavailable to researchers; Mostafa Bouaziz provided information about the Moroccan activists in Paris; Maâti Monjib explained Moroccan politics; María Rosa de Madariaga mentored me with regard to the Spanish archives; Jocelyne Dakhlia introduced me to French academia; Jamaâ Baïda's advice during my first summer in Morocco laid the foundation for the entire project; and Mohammed Larbi Messari and M'hammad Boucetta shared some important historical insights during private conversations. In addition, I need to thank the archivists and librarians at the numerous repositories I visited during the course of my research, whether in Nantes, London, Rabat, Alcalá de Henares, or elsewhere. I would like to extend special thanks to the staff of the Centre d'Etudes et de Recherches Mohamed Bensaid Aït Idder in Casablanca, the Holt-Atherton Special Collections at the University of the Pacific in Stockton, the Special Collections Research Center at Syracuse University, the Centre François Mauriac in Saint-Maixant, and the Tangier American Legation Institute for Moroccan Studies. These individuals made my visits particularly successful for a variety of reasons.

Several colleagues have helped me turn my ideas into an intelligible manuscript. Kate Wahl's generous critique at an early stage allowed me to structure the text more coherently. The comments made by Cyrus Schayegh and an anonymous reviewer enabled me to improve its content. Moreover, I would like to thank Eric Calderwood, Chris Silver, R. Joseph Parrot, Aomar Boum, and the participants of a workshop on Moroccan history at Cambridge University in May 2013, all of whom provided invaluable feedback at different stages of the project.

My greatest debts, however, are to those who helped me become a scholar of the modern Arab world. First and foremost, I would like to thank my mentor, Susan Gilson Miller, who introduced me to the historian's craft as well as all things North African. Her generous support has no limits. Suad Joseph showed me how to dissect any argument before reassembling it into clear and concise prose; Omnia El Shakry made me realize the importance of concepts and ideas; Baki Tezcan taught me how to survive academia through efficiency; and Edward Dickinson provided a rigorous introduction to the art of writing publishable scholarly articles. Yet before I ever arrived in California, many others had already made significant contributions to my intellectual development. Dr. Lederbogen awakened my interest in classical philology. Mohamed Ansary helped me improve my Arabic skills during my stays in Egypt. Jonas Tallberg guided me through the writing of my first research paper with his emphasis on methodology. Last but not least, I need to mention the faculty of the Institution för lingvistik och filologi at Uppsala University, especially Anette Månsson, Gail Ramsay, Jonathan Morén, Sina Tezel, Mats Eskhult, and Ablahad Lahdo, who provided me with the rigorous language training necessary for becoming a historian of the Arab world.

Finally, I would like to thank my wife, Vianney, for traveling with me to North Africa and Europe while always showing great patience for my intellectual endeavors. And my parents, Andrea and Reinhard, who have taught me more than all of my teachers combined.

ABBREVIATIONS

AEMNA	*Association des étudiants musulmans nord-africains*
AFL	American Federation of Labor
AMB	*Association marocaine de bienfaisance*
ATA	American Trade Association
BBC	British Broadcasting Corporation
BDIPI	*Bureau de documentation et d'information du Parti de l'Istiqlal*
CFM	*Comité France-Maghreb*
CGT	*Confédération générale du travail*
CIA	Central Intelligence Agency
CIO	Congress of Industrial Organizations
FLN	*Front de Libération Nationale*
ICFTU	International Confederation of Free Trade Unions
ICJ	International Court of Justice
MAP	*Maghreb Agence Presse*

MOID	Morocco Office of Information and Documentation
MRP	*Mouvement Républicain Populaire*
MUP	Moroccan Unity Party; *Hizb al-Wahda al-Maghribiyya*
NAACP	National Association for the Advancement of Colored People
NATO	North Atlantic Treaty Organization
NSA	National Security Agency
OMB	*Oeuvre marocaine de bienfaisance*
OSS	Office of Strategic Services
PCF	*Parti communiste français*
PDI	Party for Democracy and Independence; *Hizb al-Shura wa-l-Istiqlal*
PLO	Palestine Liberation Organization
PNR	Party of National Reform; *Hizb al-Islah al-Watani*
RCC	Revolutionary Command Council
RPF	*Rassemblement du Peuple Français*
SFIO	*Section Française de l'Internationale Ouvrière*
UGSCM	*Union générale des Syndicats confédérés du Maroc*
UGTT	*Union générale tunisienne du travail*
UMT	*Union Marocain du Travail*
UN	United Nations
UNFP	*Union nationale des forces populaires*
USIS	United States Information Service
WFTU	World Federation of Trade Unions

NOTE ON TRANSLITERATION

For Arabic words, I have generally followed the transliteration system of the *International Journal of Middle East Studies*, excluding diacritical marks except for ʿayn (ʿ) and hamza (ʾ). But some exceptions apply. Most of the North Africans discussed in this book spelled their own names in accordance with French orthographic conventions, and I always use the spelling adopted by the individual in question. Thus, for example, I write "Mehdi Bennouna" rather than "al-Mahdi Binnūna." For place names, such as Tangier and Tetouan, I use the standard spelling found in English-language maps and guides.

GLOBALIZING MOROCCO

NETWORKED ANTICOLONIAL ACTIVISM

I N   N O V E M B E R   1 9 5 2 ,   a group of Moroccan anti-colonial activists gathered in New York to advocate before the United Nations for their country's independence from French and Spanish colonial rule. They had come to receive the global body's approval of their demands less than a decade after the formation of the Moroccan nationalist movement during World War II. Notwithstanding the dark suits and leather briefcases that made them look like regular diplomats, they had no legal standing in the new headquarters of international diplomacy due to their country's colonial status. But the representatives of several sovereign states offered their assistance and provided the nationalists with passports that identified them as members of the Saudi, Indonesian, Pakistani, Iraqi, or Yemeni delegations. They could thus attend committee meetings dealing with colonial affairs. Pakistan's eloquent foreign minister at the time, Mohammed Zafrullah Khan, threw the full weight of the Islamic world behind their demands during a debate in the UN General Assembly on the situation in North Africa. Despite considerable French efforts to keep the Moroccan question off the agenda, the nationalists gained a partial victory when the gathered delegates adopted a resolution confirming "the fundamental liberties of the people of Morocco."[1] From the nationalist viewpoint, "the very fact . . . [that] the UN considered itself competent to deal with the Moroccan problem and pass a resolution" constituted a "victory" for their cause, even though the declaration had failed to explicitly condemn France.[2]

Many of their compatriots back home followed the campaign in New York with great excitement. A close confidant of Sultan Mohammed ben Youssef informed the activists of the "delight of our Excellency about the presentation of the [Moroccan] case [abroad]";[3] poets recited verses in praise of the UN;[4] and a nationalist communiqué celebrated the fact that "our brothers in America issue a weekly news publication every Friday [which] is distributed to . . . public and university libraries . . . and important personalities who follow our case."[5] The anticolonial weekly al-Istiqlal frequently published articles and editorials from US newspapers to keep its readership informed about "the reactions of American [public] opinion."[6] As one nationalist informed his brother in New York, "The people here pay a lot of attention to the news and we often hear the details in the street before we read them in the newspapers, all of which comes from listening to the various radio stations. . . . They follow the situation in America and the people here attach great hope [to it]."[7]

The Moroccan struggle for independence had gone global. But how exactly did the nationalists internationalize their case so successfully that even the UN eventually deliberated the issue? How did they communicate their message abroad given that almost none of them spoke any English? Why did the international media eventually engage with the demands of activists from a somewhat obscure kingdom in northwestern Africa as an Iron Curtain descended over Europe and the ensuing tensions threatened to drag the entire planet into yet another world war? While certainly impressive in hindsight, the eventual success of their anticolonial campaign had not been predetermined when it began in the immediate aftermath of World War II. Few contemporary observers would have anticipated that the Moroccan question might soon attract considerable international attention.

To overcome the obstacles in their path, the Moroccans adopted an innovative strategy that positioned them in the vanguard of worldwide anticolonial movements, many of which would emulate them in future decades. They succeeded by creating a network of sympathizers that enabled them to raise global awareness for their case. Former intelligence agents, British journalists, Asian diplomats, Egyptian Islamists, Coca-Cola executives, Western labor activists, Catholic intellectuals, French socialists, a Nobel laureate, a US Supreme Court judge, Chilean businessmen, a former American First Lady, and many others supported their efforts. These allies not only translated the nationalists' demands into their specific cultural contexts but also legitimized the calls for an independent Morocco among their compatriots by speaking out against colonial rule in the Maghrib. The result was an international alliance that spanned across four continents and successfully brought the nationalists' case to the attention of world public opinion. Ultimately, it even convinced the UN General Assembly to address the status of the North African kingdom.

This diplomatic victory was the outcome of years of lobbying that had led the activists across the entire globe. Organized around offices in Tangier, Paris, Cairo, and New York, the Moroccans successfully advocated for their country's independence.[8] Those executing this campaign, however, were not the leaders of the nationalist movement, known to us from the standard accounts of Maghribi historiography. Instead, a number of young activists relocated abroad to generate worldwide interest in the Moroccan question by assembling a global alliance demanding the abrogation of the colonial regimes. Moreover, after the North African kingdom had finally achieved independence in March 1956, all of them played important roles in the creation of the postcolonial state. Hitherto deemed to have been of minor relevance, these transnational activists made vital contributions to Moroccan history.

By the time the nationalists made their voices heard on the world stage, their country had been subject to colonial rule for more than three decades following the collapse of the Moroccan state in the early twentieth century.[9] Signed in March 1912 by then-sultan Abdelhafid, the Treaty of Fez had granted France the right and duty to "inaugurat[e] a regular regime in Morocco based upon internal order and general security, making it possible to introduce reforms and to insure the economic development of the country," with a resident general being "charged with the representation and protection of Moroccan subjects and interests abroad."[10] It also promised to "safeguard the religious status, the respect and traditional prestige of the Sultan."[11] Paris signed a separate agreement with Madrid eight months later, based on a clause in the Treaty of Fez that had promised an "understanding with the Spanish government regarding the interests, which this government has in virtue of its geographical position and territorial possessions on the Moroccan coast."[12] The deal designated a northern strip along the Mediterranean as the "Spanish zone of influence . . . governed by a caliph [*khalifa*] under the supervision of a Spanish high commissioner, which caliph shall be chosen by the sultan from two candidates proposed by the Spanish government."[13] The question of the port city of Tangier remained open until 1923, when France, Spain, and Great Britain agreed on a multinational administration led by a committee of control.[14]

Morocco's tripartite division led to the proliferation of anticolonial resistance movements—initially armed but later political—across much of the country.[15] By May 1930, the scions of the country's urban bourgeoisie challenged the protectorate authorities through mass protests against the so-called Berber *dahir* (edict), which replaced Islamic with customary law in many rural regions and thus aimed to fragment Moroccan society.[16] But the trajectories of the two zones diverged soon thereafter. The Spanish high commissioner in Tetouan granted legal recognition to *Hizb al-Islah al-Watani* (Party of National Reform, PNR) in December 1936 and encouraged its leaders' partial integration into the colonial apparatus. The French authorities, by contrast, temporarily exiled in November 1937 most of the activists from the territory under their control. Ultimately, the hardships caused by World War II proved pivotal for the transformation of Moroccan anticolonialism into a nationalist movement that openly called for an immediate abrogation of the protectorates. In December 1943 in Rabat, several dozen young men founded *Hizb al-Istiqlal* (Independence Party), which quickly grew into the country's largest political organization. Although separated by different colonial regimes, both parties coordinated their activities. This applied particularly to their campaign abroad.

The complex legal reality of the two protectorates forced the nationalists to structure their struggle for independence around two important facts.

First, Sultan Mohammed ben Youssef literally embodied the last vestiges of Moroccan sovereignty, since it was for his "protection" that the entire colonial edifice had been erected. Second, the Spanish protectorate existed solely as a French concession—if Paris ever nullified the Treaty of Fez, the government in Madrid would have to withdraw its officials as well. For these reasons, activists from both zones embraced Sidi Mohammed, as the monarch was also known, as the country's symbol of unity, fully capable of leading his people toward a prosperous future. Moreover, it meant that everyone—including the nationalists from Tetouan—directed their activities first and foremost against France. Doing so had become both easier and more difficult in the face of recent world events: whereas the UN provided an ideal platform for reaching out to world public opinion, the constraints of the emerging Cold War threatened to marginalize the interests of the decolonizing world. Nowhere did this become more apparent than in North Africa.

DECOLONIZATION AND THE COLD WAR

The end of World War II not only heralded the beginning of a new age on the European continent but also remade the relationships between the Western powers and the world's colonized peoples.[17] Having witnessed their empires contract during six years of total warfare, politicians in London, Paris, The Hague, and beyond sought to salvage their colonial possessions from the ruins of the global conflict. Yet that was easier said than done. France's Fourth Republic, for example, emerged materially devastated and morally tarnished by the legacy of the collaborationist Vichy regime. Many French citizens nonetheless expected the reconstruction of the colonies from Indochina to North Africa to secure their country's economic well-being and restore its shattered national pride. Even politicians that had risked their lives in the resistance against the Nazi occupation did not hesitate to order the brutal repression of anticolonial movements overseas.[18] But the defeat of the European armies by the German *Wehrmacht* had shattered their aura of invincibility in the eyes of the colonial subjects, who deemed a continuation of the status quo neither desirable nor inevitable. The two decades after 1945 thus saw the clash of two antagonistic currents: recolonization and decolonization.

Two events symbolized this contradictory transformation of global politics. Just three weeks after the Istiqlal Party had unilaterally declared Morocco's independence on 11 January 1944, the leaders of the Free French Forces gathered in Brazzaville, then capital of French Equatorial Africa, to plan the resurrection of a reformed empire following the end of the war (they emphatically rejected the "autonomy" and "self-government of the colonies even in the long term").[19] An even more emblematic incident occurred on 8 May 1945. While crowds from Los Angeles to Moscow celebrated Nazi Germany's surrender, the local population in Sétif commemorated VE Day by demanding an end to colonial rule. Instead of acknowledging the validity of their demands, though, the French authorities massacred thousands of Algerian Muslims.[20] European statesmen denied their colonial subjects the very same freedoms for which they had fought against Hitler and his allies. What seemed like a moment of liberation to some actually meant new forms of oppression for others.

Yet despite the colonial powers' feverish attempts to reassert their control, a tectonic shift in international relations had made such endeavors unfeasible: politicians in European capitals no longer decided the fate of the world, but their counterparts in Washington and Moscow seeking to recruit client states to their respective camps did.[21] The ultimate symbol of this dramatic transformation occurred during the Suez Crisis of November 1956, which came to an abrupt conclusion when US president Dwight D. Eisenhower and Soviet first secretary Nikita Khrushchev jointly forced Britain, France, and Israel to withdraw their invading armies from Egypt. Such moments of cooperation remained rare, however, since the wartime alliance between the United States and the Soviet Union had already given way to a new rivalry that soon enough encompassed all five continents.[22] As the promise of "a world free of want and fear" outlined by the Atlantic Charter in 1941 became an ever-more-distant dream, the hopes of many observers rested on a new intergovernmental organization designed to promote international cooperation.

The United Nations symbolized the nascent global order after its establishment in 1945; its two-tier structure consisting of the Security Council and the General Assembly emphasized the organization's hierarchical nature, and it initially did little to encourage anticolonial nationalism around the globe. It sought stability, not revolutionary change.[23] But notwithstanding its founders' conservative intentions, the UN soon came to embody the hopes of many Africans and Asians, who viewed it as a forum through which they could mobilize "world opinion" against the colonial powers.[24] After all, its founding charter had proclaimed "the principle of equal rights and self-determination of peoples" and thus appeared to fulfill the promises made by the Allies during the war years; three years later, the Universal Declaration of Human Rights outlined the "common standard of achievement for all peoples" that included the "dignity and . . . equal and inalienable rights of all members of the human family" and permitted "rebellion against tyranny" as a last resort.[25]

Although the colonial powers had done everything possible to prevent the gathered delegates from incorporating radically anticolonial language into the UN's founding documents, they left the conference fearful that the nascent intergovernmental organization would inevitably herald the end of their empires.[26] The flood of petitions inundating the UN demonstrated its appeal to women and men across the colonized world.[27] Transnational alliances of nongovernmental organizations such as the International Association of Democratic Lawyers and the International League of the Rights of Man helped African nationalists appeal to a global public as well as to the responsible UN committees.[28] And an itinerant clergyman established the Africa Bureau in New York to advocate for Namibian independence.[29] These activists also received support from influential grassroots movements such as the NAACP (National Association for the Advancement of Colored People), which used its contacts among US politicians to actively assist a wide range of anticolonial causes.[30] "Everything done to inform the world about the situation of the subject peoples slowly promotes their emancipation," French legal scholar André Mathiot noted in 1949 with regard to the organization's ability to "submit colonial policies to public opinion."[31]

The emergence of the UN as the center of international diplomacy thus both contributed to and paralleled the age of decolonization.[32] The Moroccan nationalists visiting New York sought to take advantage of trends that pointed to the decline of empire across the globe, only some of which can be attributed to the intergovernmental organization. The Philippines in 1946, India and Pakistan in 1947, Burma in 1948, Indonesia in 1949, Libya in 1951,

and Vietnam in 1954 all secured their independence within the decade following the end of World War II and inspired others to follow in their foot-
steps. Seeking to make the voices of Africa and Asia heard around the world,
twenty-nine non-Western nations met in Bandung in 1955 to take a stance
against imperialism and reestablish their peoples as independent historical
actors.[33] A different world suddenly seemed possible. Statesmen from across
the globe founded the Non-Aligned Movement in Belgrade six years later
to move beyond neutrality toward a much more assertive stance that would
exploit the tensions of the Cold War to their own benefit.[34] Unwilling to
maintain their subservient position vis-à-vis the former colonial powers, they
sought to transform the entire world;[35] the resulting rise of South-South relations created a new sphere of politics outside the confines of Western control.[36] Whereas the global conflict between the United States and the Soviet
Union had begun as a bilateral confrontation, it quickly became a multipolar
conversation.[37] And the Moroccans wanted to participate in it.

The potential of decolonization to bring about radical change was best
expressed by the term *Third World*, which many opponents of Western he-
gemony eagerly embraced.[38] Originally coined by the French geographer
Alfred Sauvy in 1952, it echoed the ideals of the French revolutionaries so
famously expressed by Abbé Sieyès in 1789. ("What is the Third Estate?
Everything. What has it been until now in the political order? Nothing.
What does it want to be? Something.")[39] But within the context of the Cold
War, the expression also advocated for the "positive neutrality" of the non-
Western world with regard to the binary geopolitical conflict. It reflected the
desire of the colonial peoples to assert themselves on the world stage as sovereign nations and galvanized the hopes of many—including some in Europe
and North America—at the height of the era of decolonization.[40]

Morocco was no exception in this regard. Even before the notion of a
Third World became an integral part of the global political vocabulary, the
country's nationalist press had advocated for the creation of "a third force of
small states at the UN maintaining a balance . . . [between] the two powerful states," thus indicating that it understood the local anticolonial struggle
as inherently intertwined with the Cold War.[41] At the same time, though,
the Moroccans rejected the term's more radical implications. Although they
wanted to free themselves from all vestiges of the colonial era, they did not

seek a fundamental rupture with either Europe or the United States. Their goal was acceptance as equals within a global system based on representative democracy and liberal capitalism. Aspiring to close relations with both Western and Afro-Asian capitals did not seem like a contradiction to them.

GLOBALIZING THE MOROCCAN QUESTION

The rapidly shifting international landscape of the post–World War II decade shaped the Moroccans' struggle for independence. From a global perspective, it was exactly the right moment to make their case abroad: the European empires displayed clear symptoms of decay, while two new superpowers outbid each other to gain the sympathies of the decolonizing peoples. The bipolar conflict thus provided nationalist movements with leverage to gain independence on their own terms despite the constraints it imposed on them.[42] It was now or never—the Moroccans had to seize this unique opportunity by appealing directly to the conscience of what came to be known as world public opinion. Thereby, they would exert international pressure that might force France and Spain to relinquish their respective protectorates.[43] The solution was the formation of an international network of supporters that allowed them to successfully advocate for Moroccan independence on the global stage.

But whereas this networked approach proved very useful throughout the liberation struggle, it became a liability after the end of the protectorates as the country descended into a power struggle that pitted the political elites against each other. Although they had closely cooperated during the years of the anticolonial campaign, the royal palace and the nationalists now vied to fill the vacuum created by the withdrawal of the colonial authorities. The country's monarch ultimately emerged victorious as he took control of the levers of power by co-opting the central nodes of the advocacy network, thus weakening the Istiqlal and turning it into an opposition party. Its informal nature, lack of a clearly defined membership, and failure to establish a coherent ideology had once constituted advantages but suddenly turned into liabilities; the skills, resources, and personal connections acquired by the nationalists during their campaign abroad strengthened the monarch's hand as soon as he had drawn the network's central participants to his side. Through a careful analysis of the liaisons of activists working on the global level, we can understand how the Istiqlalis managed to win the battle for independence but then abruptly lose the prize of political dominance over the post-colonial state. Instead, Sidi Mohammed laid the groundwork for the authoritarian monarchy that still rules the country today.

The Moroccan nationalists repeatedly referred to their own outreach activities as propaganda.[44] Of course, that term carries a negative, even derogatory, connotation today. At the time, however, they self-consciously embraced the importance of "confronting the world conscience through propaganda [*di'āya*] and dissemination of information [*tanshīr*] about the activities of the oppressors."[45] And the nationalist press regularly celebrated those traveling abroad "to conduct propaganda for the Moroccan case."[46] The term used in this way implied objectivity and truth, not bias and deceit. Even US media outlets such as the *New York Times* occasionally used the term approvingly ("Motion pictures . . . are . . . the best kind of propaganda for the American way of life" one article argued in the context of the early Cold War).[47] Considering the international media's general sympathy toward France's policies, the Moroccans knew that they had to craft their own narratives. To achieve this end, they needed to provide verifiable facts to validate their claims.

Publications such as *Morocco under the Protectorate: Forty Years of French Administration* promised a detailed "analysis of the facts and figures," all of which had been taken from French government reports.[48] In the United States, the nationalists' monthly periodical *Free Morocco*, which reached curious individuals across the entire country, informed its readers that "the Moroccan demands are not extreme" but merely called for the restoration of their compatriots' "rights and liberties."[49] The Moroccans saw their best chance of success in appealing to the liberal conscience of Western publics—at no point did they consider working with the Soviet Union or its allies. ("The foremost aim . . . is to establish a democratic government—a liberal constitutional monarchy and social democracy, where the Moroccan citizens can exercise all their rights as free citizens," a booklet published in New York in 1953 explained to the reader.)[50] This tactic proved extremely effective in gaining the sympathies of Western observers, whose increasing hostility toward the colonial regime in Morocco ultimately contributed to the demise of the two protectorates.

NETWORKS, BROKERS, AND SOCIAL CAPITAL

The global campaign conducted by the Moroccan nationalist movement constituted a transnational advocacy network that leveraged international support in order to influence domestic politics.[51] Such networks can span large distances to bring together diverse actors with regard to a specific purpose.[52] Yet they are not free-floating entities, as their individual members remain embedded within multiple sets of overlapping social relations, both within the network and beyond.[53] Methodologically, social-network analysis deals with the interplay of innumerable distinct actions, both complementary and contradictory, and the wider political landscape.[54] Since the Moroccan struggle for independence occurred within so many spheres simultaneously—French and Spanish imperialism, Cold War diplomacy, Afro-Asian anti-imperialism, intra-Arab politics, and North African nationalism—it offers a suitable approach for understanding the country's complicated decolonization process.[55]

Central to my argument is the concept of the broker, an individual bridging a structural hole between separate clusters of nodes within a larger network.[56] These strategically positioned actors are able to channel the flow of resources and thus benefit from their location within the network.[57] Brokers play crucial roles in consolidating the larger network structure even though they do not necessarily belong to the official leadership of a given social movement.[58] Their individual success thus cannot be reduced to personal abilities.[59] As members of transnational coalitions of activists, brokers often fulfill a wide range of important functions simultaneously: as translators, they diffuse knowledge; as coordinators, they distribute resources and information; as articulators, they can negotiate common positions; and, finally, at public events, they might serve as representatives.[60] Furthermore, they can strengthen the network by serving as bridges to the outside world. It usually is not participation within a dense web of social relations but rather weak ties to persons beyond the intimate circle of close associates that provide access to unique resources.[61] The Moroccan activists and their foreign allies fulfilled these functions in places as far apart as Baghdad and Rio de Janeiro.

This discussion of brokers as central figures within larger network structures is based on the concept of social capital, which is "embodied in relations among persons" rather than innate in individual actors.[62] By moving beyond a narrow focus on human capital, we can understand the roles played by specific individuals through analyses of their positions within networks of political activism.[63] A pivotal factor influencing the quality of social capital is a person's ability to actually access these resources when needed, which means that the quality of interpersonal relations—the strength of each individual link—is just as important as the quantity.[64] Although the acquisition of social capital might occur as an unintended consequence of someone's activities, this does not prevent actors from constantly seeking to gain structural autonomy by situating themselves in strategically important locations within the larger network.[65] Brokers can thus leverage their positions in order to obtain personal benefits to the detriment of their colleagues.[66] Moreover, their withdrawal has the potential of irreversibly damaging the social movement by drastically reducing the available social capital.

The best way to understand social networks is not as stable entities but as dynamic processes resulting from the constant remaking of interpersonal connections. The Moroccan anticolonial activists continuously recruited new supporters to their movement so as to broaden their coalition. At the same time, the members of the already existing network developed new ties among each other, a process called triadic closure.[67] The presence of shared acquaintances often brings together individuals that previously had no contact with each other, thereby increasing the network's density through a multiplication of ties among its nodes. No other organizational structure provides the same degree of flexibility necessary for political activists seeking to spread their message on the global stage. And this, in turn, shapes this book's analytical framework, which combines the domestic and the international stages into "dynamic interaction scales" to accurately capture the complexity of the Moroccan anticolonial struggle.[68]

The Moroccan advocacy network consisted of three types of participants: members of the two nationalist parties working to end the protectorate, the sultan who actively supported their efforts, and non-Moroccans who maintained strong connections to the core of activists over extended periods of time. Many of the Moroccans' foreign supporters formed subgroups that remained independent of each other and stood only in contact with a small number of nationalists—although numerous cases of triadic closure did occur. These clusters were divided along lines of geography (some lived in North America, others in Europe and the Middle East), religion and culture (Jews, Christians, and Muslims), and interest and motivations (Islamist activists and Western intelligence agents, British Orientalists and French socialists). Together they targeted journalists, diplomats, and politicians on four different continents with anticolonial propaganda in order to create international pressure on France and Spain that would ultimately force them to relinquish their respective protectorates.

Within this transnational advocacy network, numerous individuals—both nationalists and some of their foreign supporters—came to occupy central positions that increased their personal standing. They became invaluable assets for the global advocacy campaign by bridging structural holes between Morocco and the outside world. Unlike the official leaders of the Istiqlal and PNR who seemed nominally in charge, these brokers often remained marginal within the official party hierarchies but held positions of great importance within its informal network of contacts.[69] After the transnational alliance had achieved its goal, however—namely the end of colonial rule—the sudden disappearance of its sole purpose led to the quick unraveling of the entire network. The monarch also contributed to its demise by co-opting individual participants through promises and charisma; some began to work directly inside the palace as press liaison or royal adviser, while others were rewarded with ambassadorships that conveniently removed them from the domestic political stage. Many nationalists gladly left the Istiqlal to work for Sidi Mohammed when offered the prospect of a fulfilling professional career.

In each individual case, the decision seemed quite plausible—after all, had they themselves not constantly portrayed Mohammed ben Youssef as the embodiment of the Moroccan nation throughout the struggle for independence? Clearly, it was an honor to serve their beloved monarch directly. Few viewed this as a binary choice between party and palace, as it might appear to us today. But at the same time, the aggregate of these individual decisions proved fatal for the organized political opposition led by the Istiqlal, which suddenly lost many of its most talented members. The monarch focused his efforts on several brokers because he needed their social capital to legitimize his regime both domestically and internationally. Uniquely capable of seeing the network's fault lines, he skillfully exploited its inherent weaknesses. The very structure of the nationalists' advocacy network might have assured the Istiqlal's success in the short term, but it contributed to its defeat in the long term. Drawing a clear distinction between the colonial and postcolonial eras thus no longer seems appropriate, as the dynamics of the former clearly shaped the latter.

ANTIREVOLUTIONARY INTERNATIONALISM

It becomes clear when we move beyond domestic politics that the advocacy campaign conducted by the nationalists was also an important moment in international history. But the Moroccans' activities differed from those of much more radical anticolonial movements that entered the world stage after them. The members of the Algerian *Front de Libération Nationale* (FLN), for example, embarked on a "diplomatic revolution" while also conducting a military insurgency against the French colonial state.[70] Their emphasis on appealing to world public opinion certainly paralleled the strategy adopted by the Moroccans, who generously assisted their Algerian brothers when the latter arrived in New York in early 1955. But unlike the Moroccans, the FLN played off states on both sides of the Cold War divide to further its own cause. Support from several Afro-Asian states became particularly central to its liberation struggle; as a result, the Algerian capital developed into a "Mecca of revolution" after independence in 1962 and attracted anticolonial pilgrims from across the Third World.[71] Within less than a decade, the guerilla fighters of the Palestine Liberation Organization (PLO) also commenced a "global offensive" that ultimately reached from Hanoi and Beijing, via Algiers, to Havana.[72] And they, too, challenged the international order in hope of securing a liberated Palestinian homeland.

The Moroccans, by contrast, never developed a fundamental critique of the world within which they operated. Although fully aware of its flaws, they believed that the UN would ultimately support their quest for independence. They also idealized the United States as a potential ally even though consecutive administrations in Washington failed to provide any tangible support. Even France maintained a certain attraction among the nationalists. That the Moroccans' honest admiration of many aspects of Western culture never diminished can be traced back to the generous support provided by private citizens throughout the years of the liberation struggle. Moreover, their shared class background inoculated the leaders of the nationalist movement against any notion of radical change. As the scions of the country's old commercial and religious elites, they wanted to regain their rightful social status within Morocco and beyond; the skepticism inherent in socialism toward private property and religion did not appeal to them. Of course, they vigorously opposed colonial racism wherever it manifested itself, and the nationalist press covered liberation struggles from Palestine to Indonesia in great detail. Afro-Asian solidarity constituted an integral part of their identity. Still, the Moroccans rejected the much more extreme implications of Third Worldism and instead positioned themselves as "Wilsonian universalists" firmly planted within the Western camp.[73]

The history of the Moroccan struggle for independence thus offers new insights into the politics of the early Cold War. The role played by nonstate actors in the making of the post-1945 world order becomes particularly apparent. Their influence certainly did not match that of diplomats from Western capitals, who designed the global institutions to serve their own needs. But these activists carved out spaces for themselves within the international hierarchy. Rather than passively awaiting the eventual collapse of the European empires, they actively contributed to their demise. The Moroccan nationalists surpassed so many who had come before them—or would follow them—due to their ability to create a vibrant coalition of supporters who successfully advocated for their cause worldwide. The status of the North African kingdom had initially seemed like an issue of little importance in the eyes of most contemporary observers, but the nationalists successfully made their concerns global ones.

What follows, then, is a history of the globalization of the Moroccan question through transnational activism and the making of the postcolonial state. It begins during the last years of World War II and concludes after Mohammed ben Youssef's state visit to the United States in late 1957. This book does not talk about heroes or villains but focuses on the myriad individual actors that made Morocco's independence a reality. Most importantly, it analyzes the dynamics that shaped the era of decolonization—perhaps the single most important historical process of the twentieth century—not only in North Africa but across the entire world. Ultimately, it demonstrates the ability of social movements to successfully engage with international politics in order to effect local change.

CHAPTER ONE

TANGIER:
GATEWAY TO THE WORLD

A S THE SUN WAS SETTING over the old city of Tangier on 9 April 1951, an enthusiastic audience looked attentively at several men prominently seated in comfortable armchairs in the courtyard of a beautiful villa. Just hours before the gathering, the representatives of Morocco's four nationalist parties had finally formulated a "national pact" that would coordinate their efforts to "fight for the complete independence of Morocco."[1] They had "judged it necessary to form a united front" in order to "internationalize the Moroccan question and present it to the United Nations."[2] After signing the one-page document, each placed his right hand on the Quran and swore to respect the treaty.[3] As the ceremony concluded, a steadily growing throng of sympathizers filled the streets of the international city, shouting "Long live independence!" and "Down with colonialism!"[4] The local police force observed the spectacle for less than thirty minutes before it "intervened energetically" and dispersed the excited but peaceful crowd with the help of its wooden batons.[5] Despite its unfortunate finale, though, the nationalist press celebrated this "important historical day" and praised "the big demonstration by thousands of inhabitants marching through the streets to express their joy and delight about this event."[6]

To supervise the formation of the so-called National Front, a delegation consisting of five Egyptian journalists had traveled to Tangier to meet up with a representative of the Arab League, a regional organization consisting of seven nominally independent states.[7] The local population provided their guests with an enthusiastic welcome: "a huge crowd" greeted the Arab delegation to a city in which "all houses had been decorated in the Egyptian and Moroccan colors."[8] The event also received some media attention abroad as Radio Cairo broadcast the news to its listeners across the Middle East within hours of the signing ceremony.[9] Mahmud Abu al-Fath, the head of the delegation, explained that he and his colleagues had come to Tangier to "inform Egyptian public opinion about the current situation in Morocco."[10] Upon their return to Egypt, the delegates presented the signed pact to Foreign Minister Mohammed Salah al-Din and Abderrahman Azzam Pasha, the Arab League's secretary general.[11] In an article subsequently published in the widely read *al-Misri,* the representatives described their activities in Tangier as a "victory against the imperialist forces" and "a big nail . . . driven into the coffin of colonialism."[12] The French press offered a less sympathetic interpretation of the entire affair. In the words of *Le Figaro,* "The mask has fallen. The Istiqlal [Party] and its associates have commenced their anti-French game."[13]

The signing of the national pact was the culmination of a long process. In 1949, Sultan Mohammed ben Youssef had ordered all of his "loyal servants" to cooperate in the service of national unity, but to no avail.[14] The leadership of Morocco's largest anticolonial organization, *Hizb al-Istiqlal* (Independence Party), refused to treat the much smaller *Hizb al-Shura wa-l-Istiqlal* (Party of Democracy and Independence, PDI) and *Hizb al-Wahda al-Maghribiyya* (Moroccan Unity Party, MUP) like equal partners. By contrast, it did not hesitate to cooperate with *Hizb al-Islah al-Watani* (Party of National Reform, PNR), the country's other mass movement based in the Spanish zone. Since the end of World War II, the two major parties had ac-

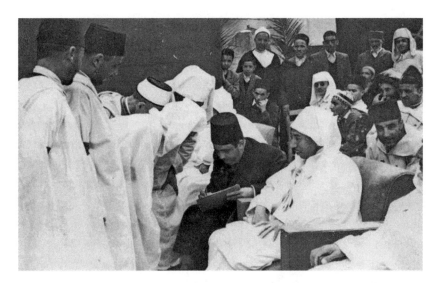

IMAGE 1. Abdelkhaleq Torres signing the National Pact, 1951. Seated to his left is Mekki Naciri. (Source: Aboubakr Bennouna. Reprinted with permission.)

tively pursued an international advocacy campaign to make the case for Moroccan independence on the global stage. Their leaders had recognized the importance of "absolute solidarity" as well as "the formation of a nationalist front" as pivotal from the very beginning.[15] But they had hesitated to legitimize their miniscule competitors.[16]

Ultimately, however, global politics played the decisive role. The end of World War II and the establishment of the United Nations and the Arab League in 1945 had heralded the dawn of a new age. Like so many other anticolonial activists around the world, the Moroccans sought to benefit from this historic moment. They did so by creating a network of supporters that would help them bring their demands to international attention. Soon thereafter, they were campaigning for Morocco's independence on four different continents. But in order to be taken seriously, they needed to present themselves as united in their rejection of the status quo. Therefore, they ultimately formed the National Front. According to a US diplomat stationed in Rabat, the Istiqlal had been "willing to sign [the document] although [it considers the] other parties insignificant," because the Arab states had offered to "raise [the] Moroccan question at [the] UN."[17] The desire to gain international recognition finally forced the nationalists to overcome their petty rivalries.

The city of Tangier played a vital role in the global campaign for Moroccan independence even though most of nationalists' day-to-day activities took place in the country's other urban centers—Rabat, Casablanca, Fez, and Tetouan. Due to its legal status as an international zone governed by a committee of control, it offered freedoms unavailable anywhere else in Morocco; activists from both the Spanish and French zones could congregate without fear of immediate arrest or deportation. This had made the city the logical choice for hosting the formation of the National Front. Moreover, it constituted an ideal location for recruiting some of the many foreigners who had been arriving in Morocco in recent years, ranging from former US military personnel to British journalists; even the American Federation of Labor eventually became a forceful advocate for Morocco's independence. Tangier thus developed into a hub connecting the interior and exterior as the war years were finally coming to an end in North Africa.

THE REEMERGENCE OF MOROCCAN NATIONALISM

The reemergence of Moroccan nationalism occurred in the wake of Operation Torch, the coordinated landings of Allied troops across North Africa on 8 November 1942.[18] Many Moroccans witnessed the quick collapse of the Vichy French forces with great satisfaction, since it exposed the evident military weakness of the colonial power. Another source of inspiration for the native population was the Atlantic Charter of 1941, the joint US-British declaration that had promised to "respect the right of all peoples to choose the form of government under which they will live." Although conceived as a broad outline of the goals of the anti-Nazi alliance, many Africans and Asians interpreted it as an anticolonial manifesto.[19] And the Moroccan nationalists shared this much more radical interpretation. A final impetus came from an unofficial meeting on the sidelines of the Anfa Conference in January 1943. During a private dinner with Mohammed ben Youssef, US president Franklin D. Roosevelt promised to support Morocco's independence once the war with Germany and Japan had ended.[20] After returning home, he sent a letter to the royal palace in which he encouraged the sultan to "count on the truly unselfish aid from the people of the United States" and invited him "to visit us in Washington just as soon as this dreadful war is over."[21] In the words of Tomás García Figueras, one of the most influential Spanish protectorate officials, "The landing of the Americans . . . constituted a new injection of optimism for the nationalists . . . [and] Roosevelt's conversation with the sultan increased [it] to a frenzy."[22]

News of these events quickly spread across the country and "shook Morocco so violently" that it "woke the sleeping and opened their eyes to the truth," as one nationalist described it.[23] Benefiting from the less restrictive atmosphere in the Spanish protectorate, the nation's so-called awakening began in the northern city of Tetouan, where the PNR had been gathering a substantial following since 1936. Together with the MUP's leader, Mekki Naciri, the party's president, Abdelkhaleq Torres, submitted an independence manifesto not only to the Spanish high commissioner and the khalifa but also to the American and British legations in Tangier on 14 February 1943.[24] The document called for "the fall of the so-called protectorate" and demanded "the independence and [complete] sovereignty of Morocco . . . under the patronage of the Alaoui royal family . . . in accordance with current international political developments."[25] It was the very first time that the nationalist movement openly insisted on the immediate dissolution of the colonial order.

Although the situation in the French zone differed quite substantially, local activists also seized the opportunity created by the US presence on Moroccan soil. They had not been openly organized since a wave of repression had forced most of their leaders into exile in November 1937. But recent events had changed everything. The nationalists founded Hizb al-Istiqlal under the leadership of the French-trained educator Ahmed Balafrej and published their own independence manifesto in Rabat on 11 January 1944.[26] Putting aside their previous calls for reform, they now demanded full independence from France "within the framework of a constitutional-democratic monarchy" with help of "the Allies . . . shedding their blood for the cause of liberty."[27] Global events had directly inspired this pivotal moment in Moroccan history. According to nationalist leader Allal al-Fassi, "Nobody can deny the impact of the War, the Atlantic Charter, the Allied landings in North Africa, and the declaration of independence of Syria and Lebanon . . . upon the nationalists."[28]

Parallel to these developments inside Morocco, a radical transformation of the international political structure occurred, epitomized by the United Nations, which had replaced the now-defunct League of Nations. With much of Europe still in ruins, the geopolitical center had shifted across the Atlantic as symbolized by the conferences in Bretton Woods and Dumbarton Oaks that would shape the postwar order; world politics were now made in Washington and New York. The nationalists considered this a great opportunity. Mohammed Lyazidi—on behalf of the Istiqlal's executive committee—sent letters to the delegates gathered in San Francisco to establish the UN in the spring of 1945, requesting them to "extend an invitation to the qualified representatives [of the Moroccan people] to participate in the international conference . . . in order to defend [their] cause and claim their rights."[29] Their enthusiasm did not diminish even though they never received the desired response. According to their own understanding, the UN Charter "outlined the duties of the [member] states . . . to preserve the basic rights of humans and peoples and work for justice."[30] Consequently, the Moroccans viewed the nascent intergovernmental organization as an important ally.

In order to increase their chances of success on the world stage, nationalists from both zones joined forces. This certainly did not come as a great surprise, given that many activists from Fez, Rabat, and Tetouan had developed close friendships while working together during the interwar period.[31] By publishing the monthly journal *Maghreb* in Paris and participating in the General Islamic Congress in Jerusalem in 1931, they had brought their grievances to the attention of foreign audiences with the hope of obtaining political support. The borders between the two protectorates had always been much more permeable than one might assume. Following an audience with Mohammed ben Youssef in October 1946, the leaders of the PNR and the Istiqlal convened a secret meeting in Rabat during which they agreed to coordinate the struggle on the exterior under the aegis of the sultan.[32] "We knew that we [had to] have foreign support if we were to succeed; therefore, we thought it proper to declare before the opinion of the world our grievances and our demands," one activist later recalled.[33]

The Moroccans nevertheless displayed an acute awareness of the shortcomings of the global order. Already in 1946, an article in the Istiqlal Party's

official daily, *al-'Alam*, dealing with the legacy of Roosevelt's famous Four
Freedoms criticized that "as soon as the [recent] war had ended, a new war
was announced against the dreams of mankind seeking deliverance from tyranny" since "the small nations did not obtain their freedom."[34] Three years
later, the same newspaper singled out the death of "the father of the UN
charter" as a turning point for the colonized peoples.[35] Contrary to popular
expectations across Africa and Asia, the "reactionism" of the world's leaders
had made "the [global] situation . . . worse than it was before the war. Years
have passed since . . . the establishment of the UN and still the peoples are
in the shackles of serfdom."[36] Yet the Moroccans maintained their hope that
the United States, or at least its citizens, would eventually embrace their liberation struggle. After all, "it is known that the progressive American people
are hostile to colonialism because they themselves have tasted the bitterness
of colonial rule."[37] The increased presence of US citizens on Moroccan soil
thus offered a unique networking opportunity.

THE ROOSEVELT CLUB

The US military maintained several installations in Morocco long after
World War II had ended, because the Mediterranean had become central to
the country's European defense strategy.[38] When postwar euphoria eventually gave way to a confrontation with the Soviet Union, Morocco's great strategic value became abundantly clear. The government in Paris granted the
United States several naval and air bases on the coastline that could serve as
relay points for potential military campaigns on three different continents.
It was thus in the American interest to maintain regional stability, a fact not
lost on the colonial authorities.[39] With France joining NATO (North Atlantic Treaty Organization) in 1949, it made even less sense to openly challenge the French empire in North Africa. As a consequence, the political
aspirations of the Moroccan people remained of secondary importance to
Washington.[40] A statement made by the US ambassador in Paris in 1947
proves this point. According to his French interlocutor, Jefferson Caffery explained that "the leanings of the United States [toward France] have never
been more favorable. . . . They have been completely reversed since the times
of Roosevelt."[41]

While such larger strategic considerations did not benefit the nationalist movement, the postinvasion US military buildup also brought some concrete advantages. One obvious consequence was an increasingly large number of soldiers stationed on Moroccan soil. Given the nationalists' desire to internationalize their independence struggle, they immediately decided to reach out to these servicemen. The effort was led by Abdellatif Sbihi, a passionate monarchist and a nationalist of the first hour who would eventually become Mekki Naciri's personal assistant. In the fall of 1944, Sbihi organized a tea party that brought together prominent Moroccans as well as US diplomats and army officers. According to US consul Maurice Pasquet, the event was held in an "atmosphere of friendship" with pictures of Roosevelt and the sultan prominently displayed on a tall stand against the background of a large American flag.[42]

Abdellatif Sbihi subsequently decided to institutionalize the meetings between Moroccans and Americans; in February 1946, he cofounded the "Roosevelt Club" to replace the hitherto informal gatherings.[43] In a letter to friends, Sbihi explained that by "creating our Moroccan circle to honor the memory of Roosevelt" the nationalists would inevitably "consolidate the links of friendship that unite the children of our country to the noble American people, which won't be without certain advantages."[44] He even contacted former First Lady Eleanor Roosevelt to obtain her blessing of the project.[45] This greatly angered Residency officials, who instructed US diplomats to advise Mrs. Roosevelt against recognizing the Roosevelt Club in order to avoid having her family's name "sullied" by a "good-for-nothing" like Sbihi.[46] No reply from Hyde Park ever came, and the protectorate authorities forbade the inaugural meeting of the Roosevelt Club just hours before it was to take place on the first anniversary of the late president's death.[47] But these setbacks did not discourage Sbihi, who relocated to the international zone in order to evade French control.

The Roosevelt Club finally held its first public meeting in Tangier on 12 April 1947. More than two hundred Moroccans as well as about fifty US diplomats attended the ceremony "during which . . . mint tea and cakes were served to the assembled multitude," according to an account provided by US consul general Paul Alling.[48] It was also "reliably reported" that the monarch had explicitly encouraged Sbihi's endeavor so as to "stimulate American interest in Morocco."[49] He even provided most of the financing.[50] The highlight of the evening occurred when Abdellatif Sbihi gave a lengthy speech in Arabic. "Frequent and loud applause greeted his praise of . . . the concern of the late President for the welfare of small nations and his well-known attachment to fundamental human rights and freedom," noted the head of the American Legation in Tangier. Nationalists from across the entire country attended, and PNR member Mehdi Bennouna from Tetouan "conveyed the sense of Sbihi's remarks in good English."[51] According to Alling, the entire event was "wholly beneficial to American prestige in Morocco."[52] The same might be said from the Moroccan point of view.

The first meeting of the Roosevelt Club turned into such a big success because it overlapped with the sultan's visit to Tangier. On 10 April 1947, Mohammed ben Youssef had delivered a historic speech in which he called for his country to "regain its rights and to endeavor toward progress that will place . . . Morocco as a whole among the league of countries and most civilized and refined nations."[53] Instead of praising the achievements of the European colonizers, he had extolled the recently founded Arab League. French officials were livid. Many in the audience had noticed the omission, since the speech's original text had been precirculated among the city's diplomatic corps.[54] Two days later, Sidi Mohammed caused another scandal during a luncheon with foreign diplomats: as he invited the guests to his table, he seated French resident general Eirik Labonne to his left and US consul general Paul Alling to his right, the seat of honor, which the American deemed a highly "embarrassing" breach of diplomatic protocol.[55] The British representative considered the sultan's move "hardly [a] factor calculated to please or reassure the French."[56] Upon his departure from Tangier two days later, the monarch gave an improvised press conference during which he repeated his desire to obtain Morocco's freedom and develop stronger links to the Arab world.[57]

Other events further underlined the importance of the sultan's trip to Tangier. Throngs of jubilant Moroccans had greeted the royal train as it passed through the Spanish zone on its way toward the Mediterranean city, whose inhabitants gave him an "extremely warm reception."[58] The nationalist movement had seized this unique opportunity to stage large-scale demonstrations in support of the Alaoui monarchy.[59] Already, during a luncheon in the coastal town of Asila, the sultan had sent for the correspondent of an

Egyptian newspaper and—in front of several European diplomats—praised the work of the Arab League.[60] Once in Tangier, Sidi Mohammed granted audiences to representatives of all anticolonial parties.[61] Details of the event spread like wildfire to remote rural areas hitherto outside the reach of the urban-based nationalist movement thanks to the most important technological invention of the age of decolonization—the cheap and portable transistor radio.[62] "The demonstrations of Tangier highlighted Morocco's deep-rooted unity, and its desire for complete liberation and independence under the progressive leadership of the energetic King," according to an interpretation provided by Allal al-Fassi a few months later.[63] Full of enthusiasm, *al-'Alam* declared, "The pen is incapable of describing this historic day in Tangier . . . about which [future] generations will talk . . . and of which they will be proud until the end of time."[64]

News of this assertive speech quickly traveled around the world. The *New York Times* concluded that the sultan had "emerged as a new and potentially powerful factor in France's troubled overseas scene," whereas *The Times* of London remarked that "this unprecedented warmth for the Arab League is interpreted in Paris as the fashioning of a new instrument of pressure on the colonizing Powers."[65] The French press also discussed the potential impact on French-Moroccan relations of this event, which, according to *Le Monde*, constituted "the spectacular outcome of a continuous and subtle policy of nationalist demands."[66] In the Middle East, Radio Cairo proclaimed that "the demands of the Moroccan people are now taking on an official character" and would thus inevitably attract the sympathies of the Arab League.[67] The correspondent of *al-Misri* saw Mohammed ben Youssef as "not only a king, but also a nationalist *za'im* (leader) raising aloft the flame of freedom."[68] What had originally been planned as an inconspicuous visit by the sultan to the northernmost part of his kingdom ultimately caused a huge publicity disaster for the colonizers. Sidi Mohammed's public embrace of the nationalist movement shattered the French illusion that he might remain an ally amid the upsurge of anticolonial sentiments among the local population.

This internationalization of the Moroccan question did not occur by chance, however. The nationalists had set up a press office in the elegant Hotel Minzah to provide logistical support to the foreign journalists covering the sultan's visit and disseminate information materials as well as video footage.[69] Meanwhile, Moroccans residing abroad publicized the anticolonial events in the Middle East. According to an article published in *al-'Alam*, "the visit of His Highness our King to Tangier had a great impact," not only because of "the awesome dispatches which the Egyptian journalist Ibrahim Moussa sent to the newspaper *al-Misri*" but also due to the relentless efforts by Moroccan activists in Cairo "spreading the news among all strata of the population."[70] Rather than remaining passive observers, the nationalists had actively shaped the image of a people united behind their beloved monarch. "Morocco obtained a great propaganda victory . . . because the people [of the Middle East] understood that the propaganda conducted by the Moroccans in Egypt had been truthful," the newspaper informed its readers.[71] Exactly one year later, Abdelkabir al-Fassi, who had organized the Istiqlal's media outreach in Tangier, explained that "the global buzz" surrounding the monarch's speech "had still not ended."[72]

The events taking place in Tangier in April 1947 demonstrated the international zone's role as a hub of the nationalists' global advocacy campaign. Because it lay outside the control of the colonial powers, they could engage in an impressive range of activities that brought their case to the attention of both domestic and foreign audiences. Furthermore, it became evident that the monarch and the nationalists cooperated closely in their fight against the protectorate regimes. The Roosevelt Club had grown out of this strategy, and so did the sophisticated media campaign organized by the nationalists during the sultan's visit. Yet such public events constituted only one aspect of the Moroccan struggle for independence. Even more important was the constant expansion of the nationalists' network of supporters, which soon included a number of Americans residing inside the North African kingdom.

THE LEGACY OF WORLD WAR II

The rise of US influence in North Africa had begun long before Operation Torch. In accordance with the Murphy-Weygand Accord of 1941, the US government allowed Vichy France to import food and manufactured goods to sustain its North African colonies in exchange for keeping these territories outside the control of Nazi Germany. Under the pretext of supervising these shipments, Washington dispatched a group of OSS (Office of Strategic Services) agents, military officers operating under the diplomatic cover of the American Legation in Tangier.[73] The so-called "twelve apostles" concerned themselves with providing intelligence about infrastructure and climate, but they also provided detailed summaries of existing natural resources, especially phosphates and cobalt.[74] Moreover, they assessed the local political situation, although their conclusions did not always accurately reflect the complex reality. A 1942 OSS dossier incorrectly dismissed the nationalists as "strongly pro-Axis"; its authors instead rested their hopes on the local Jewish community and the sultan, who allegedly would have been "delighted with an American Protectorate over Morocco."[75] One of the not-so-secret agents, Kenneth Pendar, later published a fascinating memoir detailing how he had spent "two years of adventure, spying, political maneuvering and international intrigue almost incredible to Yankee minds."[76]

Whereas most US diplomats frequented only official circles and therefore remained aloof from native society, the OSS officers quickly became acquainted with the Muslim population.[77] Having finished the manuscript of the college textbook *Principles of Anthropology* just days before his deployment, Carlton S. Coon soon found himself in secret meetings with Ahmed Balafrej and other nationalists as part of his reconnaissance operations. ("However worthy their ambitions and ideals, [they] were not men of action," he concluded condescendingly.)[78] Their superior James Rives Childs did not share the intelligence agents' interest in the opinions of ordinary Moroccans. In the eyes of the highest-ranking US diplomat in the country, fraternizing with individuals "debased by many hundred years of benighted rule prior to the establishment of the protectorate" seemed completely unacceptable. "I have come in contact with a great many native peoples, but I have never known any so lacking in the qualities necessary for self-government as the Moroccan," Childs informed his colleagues in Washington.[79] The head of the American Legation developed a special dislike for Kenneth Pendar, whom he would later describe as "an American Vice Consul who roamed about Morocco . . . at considerable detriment to American interests."[80] Apparently, the intelligence and diplomatic branches of the US government in Morocco developed a rather problematic rapport during World War II; their relations would not improve in subsequent years.

From the Moroccan perspective, the presence of the intelligence officers offered a unique opportunity to establish contacts with American citizens. One individual drawn into the orbit of the nationalist movement was
Gordon Browne, who had already developed a friendship with Allal al-Fassi
while residing in Morocco during the interwar years.[81] As an OSS officer,
Browne warned his superiors "that if the US shows no interest in the problem of Moroccan Moslems . . . if we choose to ignore their plight, to omit
them from the Four Freedoms and the Atlantic Charter, they will be anti-
American and look to Russia for political relief."[82] His advocacy on behalf of
Moroccan anticolonialism did not necessarily endear him to his colleagues.
In November 1943, a US diplomat described Browne as "distinctly anti-
French and as distinctly pro-Arab" because "his whole activity was without
question aimed at undermining French power and prestige in this area."[83]
Browne's contacts with the North African kingdom continued after his return to civilian life; in October 1945, he came back to Morocco on behalf of a
New York import-export company but never actually engaged in any type of
commercial activity.[84] Instead, he spent his time meeting with the leadership
of the Istiqlal Party as well as two suspected British intelligence agents.[85] Although what exactly brought him back remains unclear, Browne's undertakings demonstrated the Moroccans' ability to befriend American citizens.

The French authorities remained extremely sensitive regarding the presence of former US intelligence officers on Moroccan soil, as can be seen in
the case of the Arabic-speaking anthropologist Walter B. Cline. During the
war, French officials had repeatedly protested against his alleged "indiscreet
utterances" vis-à-vis various native interlocutors and had asked for his removal.[86] Whereas his superiors within the OSS praised Cline's "excellent reputation," the diplomatic agents in Rabat and Tangier supported the French
calls for his dismissal. He returned to his teaching duties at the University of
Minnesota by spring 1945.[87] Two years later, Cline published an article in the
very first issue of the *Middle East Journal* titled "Nationalism in Morocco,"
in which he cautiously opined that "the Nationalist movement, under the
cautious leadership of the Sultan, may yet begin to demonstrate a political
maturity which it has lacked in the past."[88] The Residency became extremely
suspicious when Cline suddenly resurfaced in Morocco in the presence of a
leading Istiqlali in April 1949.[89] But after a brief investigation, the State De-

partment informed the French authorities that Cline had no connection to the CIA and was simply conducting archeological fieldwork.[90]

These two cases concerning former OSS agents revealed the fear of the protectorate authorities regarding contacts between Americans and the Muslim population. Although French sensitivities on this issue might initially seem to have been the outcome of extreme paranoia, they certainly were not without merit. Several former spies remained in close contact with the leaders of the nationalist movement and provided them with help even after their return to civilian life. Seated at the intersection of the private sector, academia, and the military, well-connected individuals such as Cline and Browne became valuable allies for the Moroccan nationalists, not only allowing them to present their case before the American public but also providing direct links to the US intelligence community. Much more important than these infrequent visitors, though, was another group of American veterans, who had established private businesses in the country after leaving the military and would become central nodes in the nationalists' global network of supporters.

ROBERT E. RODES AND
THE AMERICAN TRADE ASSOCIATION

Following the end of hostilities in September 1945, Morocco experienced an economic boom that attracted numerous American entrepreneurs.[91] *Harper's Magazine* explained that "as a result of the war . . . Morocco had awakened," with numerous veterans taking advantage of the "low-tax paradise" and turning the "young country vital with rich resources" into "a ready market for almost everything America will export."[92] Whereas some of them invested in mining and industrial production, others became involved in import-export trade due to a legal loophole that put them in a privileged position vis-à-vis their French competitors.[93] Unlike all other Western nations that had done so following the Treaty of Fez in 1912, the United States never renounced its nineteenth-century capitulations that conferred extraterritorial jurisdiction over its citizens residing in Morocco. Americans were thus not subject to the commercial regulations of the protectorate authorities and used this privilege to circumvent the strict limits on currency exports and

IMAGE 2. Robert E. Rodes (left) and Senator Bourke Hickenlooper (right). (Source: Rodes family. Reprinted with permission.)

import licenses.[94] They usually teamed up with native merchants, many of whom were members of the Istiqlal, who provided the necessary local contacts for their enterprises.

The Residency began applying the existing regulations to all foreign residents by the end of 1948. This greatly infuriated the members of the American Trade Association (ATA) in Casablanca, and the organization's president Robert E. Rodes subsequently traveled to Washington to lobby the federal government to intervene on their behalf.[95] During a testimony before a House Appropriations subcommittee, the former lieutenant colonel complained about the "strong anti-American clique" in charge of the protectorate that "employed high-handed, illegal methods in an attempt to run all American business out of Morocco."[96] But he reserved the brunt of his criticism for the State Department, which seemed "determined to destroy all independent American trade in Morocco."[97] Indeed, US diplomats remained extremely reluctant to support such small-scale economic endeavors against the explicit will of the French authorities.[98] Confronted by the resident general on this issue, an American diplomat denounced Rodes's "questionable practices" and complained that "these so-called merchants" continuously "threaten to invoke the help of the American Legion and their congressmen . . . to oust their 'ineffective' consular representatives."[99]

Robert E. Rodes's campaign in Washington eventually bore fruit. In August 1950, Congress passed the Hickenlooper Amendment, which threatened to halt Marshall Plan aid to countries that violated treaties to which the United States was a partner.[100] According to a State Department memo, "Mr. Rodes had been very active in Congress and has succeeded in persuading one of the Senate committees to add to the ECA [Economic Cooperation Administration] Appropriation Bill a very strong amendment."[101] The OSS veteran had demonstrated how perseverance and personal connections could lead to tangible results in Washington. America's diplomats felt that if they were forced to choose between "treaty rights in Morocco and the security of the United States, as expressed in NATO, the latter would appear to be the logical choice."[102] But the country's elected officials had ignored their concerns. The protectorate authorities also remained very worried about Rodes's activities, viewing them as "rapprochements with both the sultan and the nationalists in order to put pressure on us at every opportunity."[103] French ambassador Henri Bonnet was convinced that the ATA was linked to the CIA, since this seemed the only logical explanation for Rodes's influence on Capitol Hill.[104]

The French government ultimately presented the issue to the International Court of Justice (ICJ) with the hope of putting an end to this scheme. On 27 August 1952, the judges in The Hague confirmed American "consular jurisdiction in all cases, civil or criminal, brought against citizens or protégés of the United States" but rejected the assertion that "the application to citizens of the United States of all laws and regulations in the French Zone of Morocco requires the assent of the Government of the United States."[105] This Solomonic judgment satisfied neither of the involved parties. An editorial published in the *New York Times* condemned the US government's role in "protecting the privileges of a small group of American businessmen" and instead called for "a friendly agreement with the French authorities."[106] Robert E. Rodes, by contrast, put on a brave face and lauded this "very good" de-

cision, which—according to a statement published in the nationalist press—
"allows free projects of the American type to blossom in Morocco."[107]

The Moroccan nationalists had been directly involved in the legal case.
Obviously, they approved of Rodes's anti-French campaign, and *al-'Alam*
regularly covered the activities of the "American merchants . . . protesting
in Washington" who sought to "return to the previous free trade regime."[108]
The entire issue had significant legal implications from the viewpoint of the
Istiqlal; as a US diplomat recalled after meeting Ahmed Balafrej in October 1949, the party's secretary general had complained "that any acceptance
by us of the French restrictions . . . was a violation of treaties with Morocco
and as such tended to weaken the remaining vestiges of Moroccan sovereignty."[109] Sultan Mohammed ben Youssef also paid close attention to the
dispute. A few weeks after the French had curtailed the American import-
export privileges, he informed the consulate in Rabat of his desire that the
United States "retain [its] capitulatory rights until Morocco recovered its independence."[110] A US diplomat characterized the sultan as "strongly pro-
Rodes" since he supported the veteran's campaign against both the French
government and the State Department.[111]

The Istiqlal—on behalf of the National Front—sent a delegation to The
Hague in the summer of 1952 in order to disseminate a detailed legal brief
among the presiding judges and gathered journalists.[112] Meanwhile, further east, Allal al-Fassi explained the importance of the case to Arab politicians. "The position of the Moroccan nationalist movement and His Highness the Sultan is that France must not monopolize the Moroccan market
. . . because it is an aggression against Moroccan sovereignty," he clarified
in a letter to the Egyptian foreign minister.[113] The ICJ's verdict thus thrilled
the Moroccans. Whereas the American businessmen saw the judicial case
mainly through an economic lens, the nationalists realized that the United
States had successfully challenged the legal foundations of the protectorate
regime.[114] According to an editorial in *al-'Alam*, the judgment was "entirely
beneficial" because it "confirmed the international treaties signed by Morocco," whose "sovereignty emerged strengthened from the trial."[115] Due to
its legal implication for debates on the Moroccan question at the UN General Assembly, "the verdict . . . pertains not only to France's future in Morocco, but in all North African countries."[116]

Robert E. Rodes himself did not benefit from the verdict, because it still subjected his business to French regulations. To make matters even worse, just weeks later a group of businessmen "known for their francophile feelings" took over the ATA and sidelined him.[117] A dissatisfied Rodes returned to the United States, where he continued his anti-French activities. In November 1953, an aide to President Dwight D. Eisenhower complained, "There is a man called Rhodes [*sic*] . . . who has been deluging me with literature and telephone calls on the subject of Moroccan independence."[118] The head of the American Legation in Tangier remarked, "Rodes has carried on one of the most effective one-man lobbies known to Washington and has considerable influence in Congress."[119] Having moved beyond purely economic issues, he began "identifying himself with the nationalists and [was] often posing as their champion. . . . He [began] living in New York and [was] seen from time to time at the United Nations."[120] Rodes became the perfect ally for the Moroccan nationalists seeking to make their case before the American public. But he did not remain the only OSS veteran aiding their campaign for independence.

KENNETH PENDAR AND COCA-COLA

While Rodes occupied himself with—in the words of Assistant Secretary of State Henry A. Byroade—a "one-man crusade to impose his views on the Department [of State]," one of his past military subordinates enjoyed much greater economic success in Morocco.[121] A former Harvard librarian and mosaic conservator at the Hagia Sophia in Istanbul, Kenneth Pendar had arguably been the most outspoken US vice-consul during World War II. Who could forget the intelligence agent whose reports the acerbic James Rives Childs had once called "as worthy of credence as a Japanese war communiqué"?[122] His marriage to the daughter of an illustrious Argentinian diplomat even made it onto the pages of the *New York Times*.[123] After his discharge from the OSS, Pendar returned to Casablanca, where he quickly established a flourishing business enterprise; in 1947, together with his friend James Hall, he cofounded the *Compagnie des Boissons Hygiéniques*, which bottled Coca-Cola for the local market. Of course, such a colorful individual seemed a natural ally for the nationalist movement.

Building on the local contacts he had made during his years of service, Pendar and his partner quickly began to network among the Moroccan elites, many of whom subsequently invested in their business. The company's board included four well-known nationalists, and members of the royal family became major shareholders.[124] Coca-Cola also began to advertise in *al-'Alam* within months of the bottling plant's establishment, thereby underlining its close links to the Istiqlal.[125] Ranging from sketches of blonde and blue-eyed children to Orientalist drawings of joyfully dancing veiled women or hypermodern depictions of electric-powered trains and transcontinental airplanes, the ads associated the soft drink with both traditional Moroccan society and seemingly endless examples of Western-style modernity. Coca-Cola combined the country's past, present, and future—readily available by the bottle for only fifteen francs. The company not only executed a sophisticated advertisement campaign but also sponsored nationalist literary festivals and athletic competitions, which led to its reputation as "the drink of the Moroccan patriot," as an unsympathetic French journalist angrily noted.[126]

The French authorities quickly noticed this suspiciously close liaison between the American businessmen and the nationalist movement. In December 1949, they protested to Mohammed ben Youssef that Coca-Cola had used the symbol of the Alaoui royal family in some of its advertisements, thus insinuating the sultan's approval to consume this foreign beverage.[127] Furthermore, posters distributed in Casablanca announcing the annual celebration of the Feast of the Throne included a clearly visible "Drink Coca-Cola" graphic. Sidi Mohammed showed himself "indifferent to any criticism" and defended the entire affair as a harmless form of corporate sponsoring.[128] The royal family continued to publicly demonstrate its support for the company; when Pendar and Hall inaugurated a new plant in Casablanca in January 1951, Crown Prince Hassan honored the opening ceremony with his presence.[129]

The American entrepreneurs also stood in close contact with the nationalist movement in the Spanish zone by way of their second facility in Tangier.[130] In February 1952, they sponsored the welcome party for the PNR leaders Abdelkhaleq Torres and Mehdi Bennouna as they finally returned to Tetouan after four years of forced exile in the international city. According to a Spanish informant, "The Americans had donated 1,250 bottles of

Coca-Cola as publicity for this very popular soda producer."[131] But the support provided by the former OSS agent went much further than that. In a letter to the secretary general of the Arab League written during his time in exile, Abdelkhaleq Torres praised Pendar's "great efforts in the service of our cause."[132] According to the nationalist's testimony, "He is the link between the Istiqlal party on the interior, us here [in Tangier], and our delegates in Paris and London. . . . He travels between the fronts carrying letters and documents . . . because all means of communication are censored by the French and Spanish."[133] Pendar had become an active member of the Moroccans' anticolonial network while pursuing his own business interest.

Apart from conquering the local market, the Atlanta-based soft-drink manufacturer's presence in Morocco also secured its unrestricted access to the metropole. The French government had restricted Coca-Cola's efforts to gain a foothold in France after World War II due to economic and cultural considerations. In 1949, the company retaliated by shipping a central ingredient from Casablanca to its plant in Marseille, which was completely legal since "Moroccan" products could always be imported without a license.[134] Soon, though, a French judge closed the loophole.[135] Coca-Cola was in a unique position, however, to exert substantial pressure on the French government due to its excellent contacts to influential politicians in Washington. Just as Robert E. Rodes did on behalf of the ATA, the company persistently lobbied the American government to punish the French government for its economic policies.[136] The powerful French "sugar cartel" especially aroused Pendar's ire, not only because refined sucrose was "one of the mainstays of [the Moroccans'] diet" but also because it hurt his business. As he explained to US senator William Benton, "To bottle about 17,000,000 bottles of Coca-Cola a year one uses a great deal of [it]."[137] These activities obviously overlapped with the interests of the nationalists, who sought to expose Morocco's status in the United States.

The two American businessmen faced another challenge when several local newspapers claimed that Egyptian scientists had discovered residues of pork in Coca-Cola in September 1951.[138] Shocked by these rumors, the Muslim population immediately stopped consuming the American soft drink, thus threatening the very survival of the hitherto booming business. Luckily, though, Pendar could count on his Moroccan friends: Mekki Naciri publicly declared the rumors to be false, and *al-ʿAlam* explained that "Coca-Cola is halal . . . and counts among the drinks sometimes offered during festivities at the royal palace."[139] The newspaper repeatedly published pictures of pilgrims "drinking Coca-Cola at the gates of the Holy City of Mecca" in order to provide visual evidence for this assertion.[140] On one occasion, its front page contained a large photo of the royal guards waiting outside a mosque while the monarch was performing his Friday prayers, and conveniently enough for the thirsty faithful, a Coca-Cola vendor was hawking his refreshing product right next to the entrance of the house of worship.[141] Several members of the royal family also consumed bottles of Coca-Cola in public.[142] The company quickly regained its market share following such demonstrations of royal approval.[143]

The French authorities obviously tried everything possible to undermine this—at least in their eyes—unsavory alliance between the nationalists and "the active sympathizer of the nationalist cause."[144] In retaliation for Coca-Cola's close links to the anticolonial movement, French security forces repeatedly inspected the bottling plant "to count the ice-picks on hand" lest they be "distributed clandestinely to the nationalists as weapons."[145] Although the Residency did not have the same authority in Tangier, it could harass the American businessmen in countless other ways: when James Hall tried to leave the French Zone to return to his office in the international city in September 1954, soldiers of the Foreign Legion stopped his car and subjected him to a full-body search under the pretext of looking for illegal items.[146] Although meant to demonstrate vigilance, such actions rather showcased the French authorities' impotence in face of the brazen collusion between the nationalist movement and US citizens residing in Morocco.

Pronationalist businessmen such as Kenneth Pendar posed a fundamental threat to the integrity of the protectorate from the viewpoint of the Residency. "The representatives of Coca-Cola are often propaganda agents . . . who encourage with all means, including publicity gifts and remittances, the most hot-headed nationalists," according to an internal French report.[147] The colonial press also picked up the story of "this strange businessman, who lives in a beautiful Hispano-Moorish villa in Rabat, [and] entertains on a royal scale those young people in colorful *djellabas*, who have sworn to liberate Morocco from the French oppressor."[148] In a letter to the US consul in

Rabat in April 1952, Resident General Augustin Guillaume described Pendar's undertakings as evidence that "the American authorities . . . are determined to remain the friends of the Moroccans who are the enemies of France."[149] His undertakings thus put the American diplomats in Morocco in an extremely awkward position. Of course, they disapproved of his activities, which undermined the official foreign policy of the US government and infuriated the French authorities. Yet they had no means at their disposal to put an end to them.

Kenneth Pendar also directly supported the nationalist movement's advocacy campaign. In a letter sent to the US ambassador in Paris in October 1951, Pendar sought to convince the diplomat that "the Istiqlal party . . . is the mouthpiece of the vast majority of the Moroccan people" and urged him to ensure that "our Government at the UN . . . lend a sympathetic ear to their cause."[150] Rumors in Paris had it that Pendar was a high-ranking US intelligence agent serving as an undercover liaison with the Istiqlal.[151] A Spanish report also classified him as "a North American informant."[152] Confronted with this hypothesis in the winter of 2012, a former nationalist admitted that everybody knew of Pendar's connections to the US government. He not only regularly conveyed insider information from Washington and Paris but also established contacts between Moroccans and high-ranking American officials.[153] This put great pressure on the US diplomats stationed inside the protectorate, who repeatedly sought to assure their French counterparts that Pendar "was acting only on his own initiative and without any support whatsoever from the State Department."[154] While certainly true, such statements did not rule out that he sometimes coordinated his activities with other branches of the US government.

But what might have caused the intelligence community to counteract the official policies of the State Department? One way to understand this rift is by looking at the trajectories of many former intelligence officers, who during their deployment in North Africa had come to appreciate the local Muslim population. Although the majority of them eventually returned to civilian life, others joined the successor organization of the OSS. Together with agents that had served in other parts of the Arab world, they brought their anticolonial inclinations to bear on the nascent CIA. Even though it might seem difficult to imagine today, a somewhat subversive spirit characterized the agency throughout the first years of its existence—at least until the overthrow of the democratically elected prime minister of Iran, Mohammed Mossadeq, in August 1953.[155] A variety of motives had led the intelligence agency to get involved in the Moroccan struggle for liberation: to remove the French from a region now vital to US interests; to ensure that "global communism" would not gain a foothold in North Africa; and to establish a close working relationship with the elites of a future independent Morocco. Unlike many others in Washington, the CIA's analysts viewed the end of the European empires as inevitable and recommended securing the friendship and raw materials of the world's decolonizing peoples.[156]

It obviously remains impossible to ascertain whether Kenneth Pendar worked for the CIA. But his story nonetheless demonstrates that veterans of the OSS agents maintained at the very least informal contacts with their former colleagues. Individuals such as Pendar and Rodes stood at the intersection of civilian life and the intelligence community, seeking to both promote their personal economic affairs and serve their country's perceived national interests. A clear distinction between these two sectors evidently did not exist. Moreover, the biographies of some former officers indicate that they chose a path that we might call serial enrichment: after loyally serving their nation, they retired in order to pursue lucrative business ventures based on personal contacts and local knowledge acquired during their years of service. The fluidity of the post-1945 era made such endeavors relatively easy to execute, even if they ran counter to the official agenda pursued by the State Department.

The activities of the former intelligence officers not only allow us to gain insights into the bifurcated nature of US policy toward Morocco but also provide us with a better understanding of the nationalists' anticolonial propaganda campaign.[157] One illuminating case was the dispute on import regulations that ultimately landed before the ICJ. Although the trial itself obviously drew international media coverage to the legal status of the protectorate, the Istiqlal had also sent a delegation to The Hague to present the nationalist viewpoint on this issue. Interestingly enough, the legal brief distributed by the party's representatives among the gathered press corps found its way into the hands of American diplomats in Morocco—weeks before its publication and by way of the nationalists' foreign supporters. The US consul in Rabat deemed it "more than a mere coincidence that both Mr. Pendar and Mr. Rodes have advance copies of it."[158]

The Moroccans actively recruited Americans in order to gain international support for their struggle against the protectorate regimes. At a time when the Istiqlal and the PNR had already begun expanding their activities to places as far away as Cairo and New York, they did not remain oblivious to the resources that foreigners residing in Morocco might provide. US citizens could move freely across borders and thereby maintain the links between the nationalist parties inside the North African kingdom and their representatives abroad. That these non-Moroccans also had ulterior motives to support the struggle for independence did not decrease their value as allies. All participants, whether Moroccan or American, benefited from this relationship. The two businessmen were not the only foreigners aiding the nationalist movement, however; US labor activists had also joined the anticolonial cause at a time when the mobilization of the Moroccan working class became a central aspect of the Istiqlal's overall strategy.

THE AMERICAN FEDERATION OF LABOR

Just months after the US army had "liberated" Morocco from the control of the Vichy regime, French workers revived the local labor movement; in December 1946, they unified their efforts by founding the *Union générale des syndicats confédérés du Maroc* (UGSCM), which instantly allied itself with the far-left *Confédération générale du travail* (CGT).[159] Fearful of politicizing the native population, the Residency prohibited Muslims from joining the union.[160] Yet this ban proved unenforceable. Although initially hesitant to associate with French communists, the Istiqlal eventually allowed its members to infiltrate the UGSCM in order to "unite the political and the social struggles . . . [against] reactionism and exploitation."[161] The union's progressive "Moroccanization" led to the election of two Muslims, Tayeb Bouazza and Mahjoub Ben Seddiq, to its central bureau in June 1950.[162] Acknowledging that "their unionization . . . has always been tolerated and, today, the UGSCM is led by a Moroccan member of the Istiqlal," the Residency finally legalized the process two months later.[163] Sidi Mohammed ben Youssef had publicly supported this development all along. At an audience on the eve of

Labor Day in 1949, the sultan told a delegation of Moroccan workers, "We are in no way opposed to the granting of union rights to our subjects. . . . We are sparing no effort to this end and, with the help of God, we shall soon attain the goal we seek."[164]

This seemingly obscure development held great significance from the American viewpoint.[165] Fully aware of Washington's foreign-policy priorities during the Cold War, representatives of the Istiqlal regularly warned US diplomats of the allegedly increasing communist influence in Morocco.[166] An American observer who usually depicted the anticolonial movement solely as a threat to regional stability concurred with this assessment. In November 1948, he theorized that the founding of a truly independent labor union "might be able indirectly to restore some of our lost prestige among the Moroccans and, by freeing the Nationalist leaders from Communist pressures, to encourage them to continue a moderate course."[167] With regard to this goal, the Moroccans could count on the American Federation of Labor (AFL), which emerged as an influential global player during the Cold War.[168] Seeking to combat the pro-Soviet World Federation of Trade Unions (WFTU), Irving Brown, the AFL's Paris-based representative, cooperated with labor activists from around the globe, including those in Asian and African colonies. In 1949, he organized a congress in London that established the International Confederation of Free Trade Unions (ICFTU), which would serve as an umbrella organization for noncommunist syndicates.

One of the first global allies pursued by the AFL was the *Union générale tunisienne du travail* (UGTT), which maintained a symbiotic relationship with the nationalist Neo-Destour Party led by Habib Bourguiba. Founded in January 1946 by the charismatic activist Farhat Hached, it was the only independent North African union. From Irving Brown's perspective, this made the UGTT an ideal partner. Together with the US consul general in Tunis, he successfully persuaded the Tunisian labor leadership to break away from the WFTU and join the ICFTU in the spring of 1951.[169] As a reward, he invited both Hached and Bourguiba to the AFL's annual conference in San Francisco a few months later; the gathered attendees adopted a resolution calling for Tunisia's independence in honor of their Maghribi guests.[170] The partnership between the two organizations thus proved beneficial for both sides: Brown ensured that the Tunisian labor movement sided with his anticommunist agenda, and the native nationalist movement gained an influential international partner.

The ICFTU also developed a vivid interest in Morocco's nascent labor movement.[171] After sending a delegation to meet with Bouazza and Ben Seddiq in November 1950, the organization lobbied the French government to permit the creation of a "free and democratic" union open to all Moroccans.[172] Irving Brown regularly conferred with Abderrahim Bouabid, the Istiqlal's labor organizer, throughout this period.[173] Yet despite his best efforts, the situation only worsened—following the outbreak of impassioned protests in Casablanca in December 1952, the Residency arrested the UGSCM's leaders. This did not end the relationship with the international labor movement, however. In a thirty-three-page memo secretly written in his prison cell, Ben Seddiq praised "the support . . . [the Moroccans] find amongst the workers' organizations of the free world, . . . in particular the representatives of the ICFTU."[174] Meanwhile, the directors of the labor confederation vowed "to continue their struggle against colonial oppression."[175] And eventually they succeeded. Following a meeting with French prime minister Pierre Mendès-France on 3 August 1954, the protectorate authorities released the imprisoned labor activists.[176]

Suddenly everything happened quickly. The Moroccans submitted "a fraternal appeal . . . to the ICFTU to give the new organization their collective support."[177] Encouraged by this development, the trade confederation sent a delegation to Morocco to secure the consent of the Residency.[178] Finally, on 20 March 1955, Moroccan workers under the leadership of Ben Seddiq and Bouazza founded *al-Ittihad al-Maghribi li-l-Shughl* (*Union Marocain du Travail*, UMT), which—unsurprisingly—immediately joined the ICFTU. Although primarily a Moroccan undertaking based on years of grassroots organizing, Irving Brown and his colleagues had provided pivotal financial and logistical support.[179] The local activists subsequently thanked Brown for "the friendship of the American trade unionists towards the workers of Morocco, who won't be able to forget the efficient support that you have provided."[180] Their former French comrades at the CGT did not share this enthusiasm and condemned the establishment of the UMT as "a prefabricated maneuver . . . prepared by financial exchanges with Irving Brown in Paris, who is known to be an American agent in charge of dividing labor unions."[181]

What were the reasons behind the AFL's anticolonial campaign in French North Africa? Most importantly, its overseas initiatives closely paralleled Washington's strategic interests during the Cold War.[182] According to numerous studies, funds diverted from the Marshall Plan as well as the CIA financed Irving Brown's activities in order to turn the future independent states into bulwarks against Soviet influence.[183] The leaders of the American labor movement shared their government's anticommunist zeal, but they also believed that unionization would lead to higher wages around the world and thus reduce the probability of US businesses relocating abroad. The colonial authorities remained acutely aware of the labor organization's subversive activities.[184] Whereas the American media celebrated Brown for his role in the global anticommunist struggle, the Governor General of Algeria, Robert Lacoste, called him "the master corrupting force in North Africa" during a speech before the French National Assembly.[185] A Spanish diplomat described Brown as an "extremely aggressive anti-colonial individual."[186]

The ICFTU emerged an effective advocate for the anticolonial movements in North Africa due to its global standing. According to an American observer, its "supporting messages" proved pivotal to maintaining the morale of the Istiqlal's leadership.[187] Which other organization had enough clout for its secretary-general to be granted an audience with France's prime minister in order to criticize the country's colonial policies? Of course, the nationalist press regularly praised the Brussels-based organization for its "strong support of the emancipation of the colonized peoples."[188] Even newspapers in the Spanish zone acknowledged the important role played by foreign labor activists. When the delegates at the AFL's annual congress in 1953 called on the French government to grant "democratic rights to the peoples of Tunisia and Morocco and release all imprisoned labor activists and members of the nationalist parties," *al-Umma* proclaimed that all Moroccans "must thank the American Federation of Labor" for its unrelenting struggle against "France's violent policies."[189]

The growing network of outspoken foreign supporters benefited the nationalist movement's campaign for independence by bringing their demands to the attention of an international audience. Whether the supporter was Robert E. Rodes, Kenneth Pendar, or the AFL leadership did not matter—all of them held considerable sway on Capitol Hill, which they used to draw attention to the Moroccan question. Although they failed to change the policies of the US government, they exposed the French authorities to increased international scrutiny and thereby put them on the defensive. Their efforts directly served the interests of the nationalist movement. But that was not enough. The Moroccans would have to present their case themselves in order to have a real impact in the United States and beyond. And they needed the help of media-savvy individuals capable of assisting them in this regard. Once again, they got lucky. Parallel to their collaboration with the Americans, they successfully recruited three British citizens as they passed through the international city.

THREE BRITISH JOURNALISTS

In the summer of 1946, a BBC broadcaster commenced a close relationship with the North African kingdom that would eventually include dinners with Ahmed Balafrej and secret meetings with Prince Hassan.[190] Nina Epton had a global reputation—an Australian newspaper once celebrated the "attractive" journalist as "Britain's most glamorous explorer, author and radio commentator," whose countless travels brought her worldwide audiences into contact with faraway cultures.[191] Her local guide in Tangier introduced her to several nationalists who quickly convinced her of their cause; by the time she left the country a few weeks later, Epton had already become a member of their anticolonial network. "Tell people abroad the truth. That is all that is necessary," Allal al-Fassi instructed the British journalist before her departure.[192] After her return to London, Nina Epton wrote several articles critical of French colonial policies, thereby handing the nationalists a great publicity victory.[193] She was the first mainstream Western journalist to provide entirely sympathetic accounts of the Moroccan nationalist movement.

Nina Epton also published a book, which she dedicated to "the nationalists . . . [who] work and fight to live as free people."[194] Her work recounted dinners with Resident General Eirik Labonne as well as meetings with nationalist leaders, who "quoted freely from the Atlantic Charter" and communicated their firm belief in the ability of world public opinion to bring about Moroccan independence.[195] Epton concluded *Journey under the Crescent Moon* by expressing her hope that "the question of North Africa's independence is brought up before the United Nations" and that "the Americans may decide that it will be to their ultimate interest to espouse the North African cause."[196] *Al-'Alam* praised it as the first book "that depicts the real Morocco as the Moroccans themselves see it."[197]

Thanks to the reputable Nina Epton, the Moroccans could finally legitimize their struggle before a global audience. One of them underlined "the importance of contacting these foreign journalists who come to our country, in order to inform them about our various concerns, because they usually contact [only] one side and therefore report about us and our lives in a harmful manner."[198] The nationalist press in the Spanish zone offered a similar assessment. An article published just a few months after Epton's first visit to Morocco in 1946 expressed "the Moroccans' deep love and great esteem . . . towards the free woman who . . . has dedicated herself to conducting propaganda for Morocco and defending it before world public opinion."[199] Epton had become the perfect conduit for disseminating the anticolonial message abroad.

Whereas the nationalists appreciated their prominent supporter, the colonial authorities began to regard Nina Epton as a serious threat. In August 1947, as she was about to cross from the French into the Spanish zone, security forces arrested the journalist and interrogated her about her suspicious activities. The reporting officer later described Epton as "a very active agent of the [British] Intelligence Service . . . beautiful, seductive, cunning, educated, and very intelligent."[200] A different French counterintelligence official concluded somewhat more accurately that "the principal danger, which Miss Epton presents, is making the nationalist leaders gradually believe that they will find the support of Anglo-Saxon public opinion."[201] This concern was definitely not unfounded, but the French authorities lacked a counterstrategy. To make matters even worse, another British woman soon added to their worries regarding the internationalization of the Moroccan question.

As a Middle East correspondent for numerous English newspapers, Margaret Pope had initially caught the attention of the French authorities while organizing a press conference for Moroccan nationalists residing in Cairo in November 1946.[202] Residency officials thus became very anxious when Pope relocated to Tangier four years later. And their worries were justified. Almost immediately following her arrival in the international city, she assisted the

Moroccan delegates preparing to attend the sixth session of the UN General Assembly in Paris by translating their propaganda material into English.[203] Pope also maintained the links between Cairo and Tangier by sending important mail via the British post office in Gibraltar, thus bypassing the vigilant postal censors.[204] Her relationship to the Moroccans grew so close that she even received an invitation to the wedding of Ahmed Ben al-Bashir, the right-hand man of the khalifa and a fervent support of the nationalist movement.[205] Pope "attends all nationalist meetings" and "edits all publications and letters sent to Anglo-Saxon countries," according to a French surveillance report.[206]

In order to put an end to this "sinister comedy"—as *L'Echo du Maroc* described Margaret Pope's activities—the French authorities worked tirelessly to have her expelled from Tangier.[207] Yet despite the fact that their British counterparts concurred that she was indeed a "tiresome and unreliable person," they could not simply ban one of their own citizens.[208] The Foreign Office knew that anticolonial members of Parliament such as Fenner Brockway would not tolerate such a drastic measure, even though Pope had "certainly done more harm to Anglo-French relations in North Africa than any other single person."[209] US diplomats seemed rather amused by the entire affair regarding "Moroccan nationalism's British Joan of Arc" and noted with relief that "Great Britain has replaced the United States . . . as a whipping-boy on whom all Moroccan disturbances are blamed."[210] The head of the American Legation in Tangier noted that "Miss Pope has long been a thorn in the side of the French because of her nationalist sympathies."[211] She had become a central node in the Moroccans' transnational network of supporters. But the contributions of a third British citizen would soon eclipse her efforts.

Rom Landau arrived in Morocco the summer of 1949 in order to write a travel book. It was not his first visit to the Muslim world. Before the outbreak of the war, he had toured the Middle East to meet with Hajj Amin al-Hussayni, the mufti of Jerusalem, and Abdelaziz Ibn Saud, the ruler of Saudi Arabia, in an effort to convince them to join Sir Francis Younghusband's World Congress of Faiths.[212] Landau was an affable extrovert who easily made new friends. His flamboyant demeanor, undisguised homosexuality, and ability to draw attention to himself in virtually every situation always left lasting impressions on his interlocutors. Given his original birth name of Romuald Zbiniew Landau and his Polish heritage, many observers thought he was of Jewish origin, but he always insisted on his Roman Catholic background. Landau's eclectic interests ranged from plastic arts to spirituality; *Pilsudski: Hero of Poland* (1930), *God Is My Adventure* (1935), and *Sex, Life and Faith* (1946) were his best-known oeuvres. He regularly socialized with prominent European intellectuals like T. S. Elliot, Aldous Huxley, George Bernard Shaw, and John Maynard Keynes. The British writer seemed like the perfect ally to bring the Moroccan case to global attention.

As soon as Rom Landau disembarked in Tangier, the sultan's local representative introduced him to the Istiqlalis residing in the city. It was the beginning of a friendship that would last for the rest of his life. When Landau passed through Rabat, his nationalist acquaintances presented him to Crown Prince Hassan, who arranged an audience with his father that same afternoon. A cordial atmosphere characterized the meeting, and the sultan seemed "visibly touched" by Landau's lavish "praise of the Moroccan people" and "its sovereign," as one French observer remarked.[213] The royal encounter convinced Landau to support the nationalists' anticolonial campaign. Upon his return to England, he "threw [him]self wholeheartedly into [his] self-appointed task, and within a year or so there were few among the leading British journals in which [he] had not published articles on Morocco."[214] Landau also generously distributed copies of his newest book among the British elites; Anthony Eden, Winston Churchill, Arnold Toynbee, and many others acknowledged receiving copies, and even King George VI conveyed "his sincere thanks . . . for sending him a copy of . . . *Invitation to Morocco*, which he [was] much pleased to accept."[215]

Rom Landau remained in close contact with his new friends after his departure. "The coming publication of your book will greatly impact and delight the Moroccans," Allal al-Fassi assured him in January 1950.[216] He also informed Landau that the Istiqlal had begun circulating Arabic translations of some of his writings throughout the country.[217] Before publishing *Invitation to Morocco*, Landau sent a few pages of the manuscript to al-Fassi to ensure that it accurately reflected the opinions of the nationalists.[218] A few months later, the za'im politely expressed his reservations concerning an article Landau had published in a British magazine in which he had described the nationalist movement as consisting primarily of the country's elites. "In reality, our movement does not only include intellectuals, but all [social] classes," al-Fassi argued, and he pointed out the workers' demonstrations organized by the party on May Day.[219] The British writer clearly enjoyed his close connection to the Istiqlal's leadership. "You may also wish to know that so far every article I have written on Morocco has been reprinted in the Moroccan press," he informed his literary agent.[220]

The protectorate authorities still hoped to recruit Rom Landau despite his increasingly close relationship to the nationalist movement. They organized an official tour of southern Morocco in October 1950, and both sides courted him when he arrived in Rabat a few weeks later. Landau made several appearances on the French-language *Radio Maroc*, while *al-ʿAlam* celebrated the presence of the "famous English writer" with an article and a large photo on its front page. Dressed in a Bedouin garment reminiscent of Lawrence of Arabia, he looked like an awkward adventurer rather than a serious scholar.[221] But that did not bother him. Instead, he enjoyed the attention he received ("I have never had one tenth of such publicity").[222] Landau presented *Invitation to Morocco* to Sidi Mohammed and Prince Hassan during a private audience, and the two showed their appreciation by inviting the British traveler to the official Throne Day celebration at the royal palace. Just prior to his departure, the Moroccans asked him to write "a little booklet on the Sultan . . . for sending it to selected people in Great Britain and the USA."[223] He had officially become a propagandist for Moroccan independence.

Rom Landau's rationale for joining the nationalists' network cannot be reduced to a strong sense of justice; it was also influenced by a desire to preserve the "authentic" Morocco from the pressures of a westernizing colonialism. As a true Orientalist, he had romantic ideas about an East filled with exotic natives whose simple and friendly natures were a welcome alternative to the cold rationality of the West. In an article for the *New York Times*, he expressed his admiration for "the Moslem . . . [who] like a child . . . throws caution to the winds and seeks all the luxuries" while "a degree of complacency makes him an easy prey of the rapacity of greedy pashas and effendis."[224] Undisguised homoeroticism also filled many pages of his writings; Landau repeatedly referred to the handsome crown prince and praised the sexual prowess of Moroccan men in general. When a local journalist later asked Landau why he had remained a bachelor all of his life, the British writer explained, "I had chosen Morocco as a wife, and I cannot marry two wives—I am happy with my spouse, because she delights me."[225] Landau was a truly idiosyncratic character, and his contributions to the nationalists' global advocacy campaign would be numerous and of great importance.

CONCLUSION

The internationalization of the Moroccan question began at home but was inspired by recent developments in world politics. A report submitted to the Spanish high commissioner in April 1947 concluded that "the English and Americans, especially the latter, are motivating . . . the nationalists, who . . . express their achievements in the ideology put forth . . . in the Atlantic Charter."[226] Benefiting from the rapidly increasing number of non-French foreigners in the country as a long-term consequence of World War II, the nationalist movement recruited numerous individuals to their network of supporters. Especially astonishing was the incredible diversity of their activities. Whether they lobbied on Capitol Hill, smuggled mail, broadcast on BBC radio, or wrote travel books, each one made substantive contributions to the anticolonial campaign. That both Nina Epton and Margaret Pope were women constituted an additional advantage, because it provided a necessary corrective to the stereotype of North African society as chauvinistic and "backward"; Landau's flamboyant character contributed additional luster to their movement. Previously familiar with only France and the Middle East, the Moroccans could utilize their British supporters as bridges to the Anglophone world.

The assistance provided by several American citizens was of equal importance. Thanks to their excellent connections in Washington, individuals such as Robert E. Rodes and Kenneth Pendar served as brokers between the nationalists and high-ranking US officials. As acclaimed war veterans and entrepreneurs, they used their social status to draw attention to the Moroccan case. Representing a different sector of American civil society, Irving Brown threw the full weight of the US labor movement behind the Moroccan struggle for independence. The AFL held considerable sway over politicians dependent on working-class voters due to its large membership. Although it might surprise us to find businessmen and labor activists on the same side of a political dispute, their interests converged with regard to ending French colonial rule and defeating communism in North Africa. The constraints of the Cold War did not always prove detrimental to the interests of Third World nationalists but instead sometimes provided opportunities for leveraging their anticolonial agendas on the global stage.

The activities of their American supporters also shed light on the inner workings of the nationalist movement's network of supporters, which often experienced cases of triadic closure. For example, Rodes worked hand in hand with the AFL during his anti-French campaign in Washington. While preparing for another hearing before a US Senate committee in December 1953, he informed an influential labor advocate that "it would be important for [the] AFL to testify."[227] On a different occasion, the American businessman requested that AFL president George Meany intervene directly with President Eisenhower.[228] Similar forms of cooperation took place inside Morocco. A State Department official visiting the US consulate in Rabat accepted a dinner invitation from Kenneth Pendar but was subsequently "a little surprised to find on his arrival that the only other dinner guest, besides himself and his wife, was Mr. Rodes."[229] Rather than working parallel to each other, the nationalists' supporters coordinated their anticolonial activities. Brought into contact by their shared efforts on behalf of Moroccan independence, they established new links among each other that furthered the anticolonial cause.

Yet the Moroccans' foreign supporters did not always see eye to eye. Rather than collaborating with his countrywomen, Rom Landau jealously defended his privileged position as the nationalists' Anglophone mentor against all perceived rivals. When Nina Epton published *Journey Under the Crescent Moon* in 1949, he wrote to Allal al-Fassi to criticize the book's content. The za'im thanked Landau for his "good intentions towards Morocco, which—do not doubt it—knows how to cultivate its gratitude towards those who are willing to take interest in its fate." With regard to Epton, however, al-Fassi explained that the Moroccan cause could only gain from a "diversity" of foreign writers and topics and that the nationalists "do not have the right to direct these authors."[230] Despite numerous examples of network closure, not all of their supporters seemed eager to cooperate. Overall, though, the countless relationships formed by the Moroccans complemented each other well and advanced the nationalist agenda abroad. Moreover, they highlighted the malleable nature of their advocacy network, which continued to expand its reach and form new links among existing nodes.

Tangier became the nodal point that brought together all these activities. A Spanish report described it as "the ideal city for all kinds of intrigues and secret meetings" between activists "from our zone . . . and the French zone," adding that they "were frequently visited by adventurers . . . whose mission it was to keep the nationalist flame alive."[231] Although the nationalists recruited their American supporters mainly inside French Morocco, the international city became the gateway between the organizers on the interior and the propagandists on the exterior. It also served as a haven for those banned from entering the protectorates because of its legal status. Only after the leaders of all four parties had spent several years together in exile in Tangier did they finally thrash out their differences and come to an agreement. The founding of the National Front in April 1951 thus highlighted the city's importance for the global anticolonial campaign. Another beneficial aspect was the availability of a British mail service, which allowed the Moroccans to bypass the colonial censor (although only the postal office in Gibraltar provided an absolute guarantee that confidential letters would not be read by French intelligence agents). Even the Coca-Cola managers opened an office there, more than three hundred kilometers away from their bottling plant in Casablanca. Finally, Tangier hosted the American Legation, the most important diplomatic representation operated by the United States in Morocco prior to 1956.

The ultimate targets of the Moroccan advocacy campaign, however, resided abroad. So far, little had changed in the realm of international politics increasingly dominated by the binary logic of the Cold War. As late as September 1950, an internal State Department memo confirmed as its "primary objective . . . the maintenance of peaceful and stable conditions under a regime which is friendly to the United States," with France being "the nation best equipped to exercise international responsibility for the area."[232] Nothing indicated that Washington might rethink its attitude anytime soon. Yet it remained pivotal to gain the support of the United Nations in order to exert pressure on the colonizers. To achieve this goal, the Moroccan nationalists had already begun lobbying the Arab League, whose seven member-states would inevitably prove central to winning the support of the intergovernmental organization. The Moroccans might be able to gather a majority of votes at the General Assembly with their help. And the campaign to obtain Arab diplomatic support had already commenced parallel to the nationalists' recruitment efforts inside Morocco. Beginning with the first official delegation to the Arab League's cultural committee in February 1946, the Moroccan nationalists established a permanent presence in Cairo that would serve as the basis for anticolonial propaganda across the entire Middle East.

CHAPTER TWO

CAIRO: THE SEARCH
FOR ARAB SOLIDARITY

O N 7 F E B R U A R Y 1 9 4 6 , a large crowd of politicians, journalists, and members of the local Maghribi
community gathered in Port Said, Egypt, to welcome three passengers as
they disembarked from their ship.[1] The foreign travelers were nationalists
who had come to represent Spanish Morocco at the Arab League. Within
days of their arrival in Egypt, King Faruq granted them a private audience;
one month later, they returned to the royal palace to celebrate the first anniversary of the Arab League together with numerous Middle Eastern diplomats.[2] At the subsequent meeting of the League's cultural committee,
M'hammad b. Ahmed Benaboud, the head of the delegation, declared that
"Morocco has great hope . . . in solving its [colonial] problems and it relies
upon itself and the Arab League [regarding this]."[3] The local press celebrated
the North African nationalists, public figures spoke out on their behalf, and
the governments of Egypt and Iraq expressed their willingness to present the

case of Morocco before the United Nations. Behind the scenes, the anticolonial activists worked on a report Arab diplomats could use to defend the
Moroccan case on the international stage. As Benaboud wrote in a letter to
his colleagues in Tetouan, "The Arab officials assign great importance to our
cause, which makes us very optimistic."[4]

The small delegation formed the vanguard sent by the nationalist movement to establish a bridgehead in the Middle East. If the Moroccans truly
wanted to create international pressure on the colonizers, they needed the
support of the Arab League, whose members formed an important voting
bloc in the UN General Assembly. More so, the League's diplomats would
then rally other non-Western nations to the Moroccan cause. The nationalists decided to bring their struggle to the attention of the wider Arab world
in order to benefit from the wave of anticolonial fervor that had been sweep-
ing across the region since 1945. Cairo seemed like the perfect place to do
so. As a publication by the PNR explained to its members, "The Egyptian
press has great influence upon public opinion in the Middle East."[5] For this
reason, the nationalists turned the Egyptian metropolis into another hub of
their transnational advocacy network, which would quickly expand to other
Arab capitals such as Beirut and Baghdad. By recruiting countless supporters
ranging from anti-imperialist Islamists to liberal nationalists, the Moroccans
sought to rally regional public opinion behind their cause and ultimately
gain Arab diplomatic support at the UN.

This chapter examines Cairo as the second center of the global Moroccan
campaign for independence.[6] Following the founding of *Maktab al-Maghrib
al-ʿArabi* (the Office of the Arab Maghrib) in February 1947, the nationalists conducted an impressive advocacy campaign that established their anticolonial struggle in the Middle East. Although initially quite successful in
recruiting numerous influential figures, their success was short-lived: following the coup d'état that brought the Free Officers to power in July 1952, the
Moroccans' local network of supporters quickly unraveled and thereby par-
alyzed their activities in the Arab world. The 23 July revolution thus proved
detrimental to the goals of the nationalist movement, contrary to the heroic
image of Gamal Abdel Nasser that would remain commonplace in Morocco
even decades later. Whereas the nationalists had received considerable levels
of political encouragement under the Egyptian monarchy, the new republi-

IMAGE 3. M'hammad Benaboud (left of center with white scarf) is being received by Egyptian king Faruq (seated with sunglasses), 1946. Abderrahman Azzam Pasha is standing between them. (Source: Aboubakr Bennouna. Reprinted with permission.)

can regime actively undermined their diplomatic campaign. The Moroccans eventually shifted most of their resources from Cairo to more promising endeavors in Paris and New York in reaction to this disappointing development. In order to understand this turn of events, though, we must first look back at the emergence of intra-Arab politics toward the end of World War II.

AT THE ARAB LEAGUE

At the same time as the United States began establishing its foothold in North Africa, an event of equal importance was taking place in the Middle East. On 22 March 1945, six states founded the Arab League, which consisted of a loose association with the ambiguous goal of drawing "closer the relations between member States and co-ordinat[ing] their political activities" in order to "safeguard their independence and sovereignty."[7] Its members chose Abderrahman Azzam Pasha as the League's first secretary general, and the Egyptian diplomat publicly dedicated himself to the liberation of the non-independent Arab territories.[8] At his insistence, the gathered representatives expanded the organization's foundational document to contain a section promising that it would "deal with questions affecting the entire Arab world," including "the Arab countries not currently members of the council," in order to work for their "aspirations" and "future."[9] The League immediately became an important point of reference for anticolonial activists across the Maghrib, especially in Morocco, due to these ambitious yet vague pledges.[10]

The elites of the North African kingdom had always maintained close links to the Middle East despite their geographical remoteness. During the interwar years, several leaders of the nationalist movement had studied in the Egyptian capital, where they had immersed themselves in the region's vibrant political scene by participating in the General Islamic Congress in Jerusalem in 1931 as well as the Arabic-Islamic Parliamentary Conference for the Defense of Palestine in Cairo in 1938. A group of students even founded the Committee for the Liberation of Morocco in the Middle East to educate the general public about North African affairs. Writing to his brother in Tetouan in 1944, Mehdi Bennouna explained that he had begun to work as a journalist after concluding his studies in order "to fill the [Egyptian] press with propaganda for the beloved homeland."[11] Back home in Morocco, the general interest in events taking place in the wider Islamic world also did not abate during World War II. According to a secret French report written a few weeks after VE Day, "The Moroccan nationalists have attached themselves to repeating the most anti-French commentaries of foreign radio stations, particularly those . . . from Ankara, Cairo, and Delhi."[12]

Within weeks of its founding, Azzam Pasha called on High Commissioner José Enrique Varela to send a delegation representing Spanish Morocco before the cultural committee of the Arab League. The protectorate authorities initially hesitated to accept this offer but eventually decided to seize this "opportunity" to "improve our standing in the Islamic world."[13] Varela ultimately allowed the khalifa to nominate two Moroccans for this task: M'hammad b. Ahmed Benaboud and Mohammed al-Fassi al-Halfaoui, both of whom had studied in Cairo.[14] The colonial authorities then expanded the delegation to include M'hammad b. Abdelsalam Benaboud, an education inspector known for his personal loyalty to the high commissioner.[15] In February 1946, the three men embarked on their diplomatic mission to Cairo. This decision to accept the Arab League's invitation, which took place at a time when the French protectorate authorities continued to deny the legitimacy of the nationalist movement, can be understood only within the logic of post-war Spanish foreign relations.

Spain's military dictator Francisco Franco had sought to strengthen his country's links to the Arab world ever since commencing his military rebellion against the Second Spanish Republic in 1936. After World War II, this issue became even more urgent, because his Fascist regime remained a pariah on the global stage and could not join the newly founded United Nations. This diplomatic quarantine subsequently shaped the country's foreign policies, especially with regard to the Middle East.[16] The US Department of State understood "the pro-Arab policy of General Franco" as originating from "the isolated position of Spain."[17] For example, Spain did not recognize the state of Israel until 1986, one decade after Franco's death. Madrid also pursued a cultural diplomacy that culminated in a number of bilateral agreements with Arab states facilitating the exchange of scholars and artists.[18] The decision to send a Moroccan delegation to the Arab League was part of this larger project. Eventually, these policies yielded the desired results despite a UN resolution calling on all member states to isolate the Francoist regime.[19] Egypt permitted Spain to upgrade its diplomatic mission in Cairo to the status of embassy in 1949, and three other members of the Arab League followed suit four years later.[20]

An equally important driving force behind Madrid's attitude toward the Moroccan nationalist movement can be found in the colonial discourse of *hermandad hispano-árabe* (Spanish-Arab brotherhood), which had developed during the second half of the nineteenth century.[21] The notion of fraternal links between Iberians and North Africans as the legacy of a mythical al-Andalus transformed the self-understanding of a nation recovering from the collapse of its empire in Latin America by reorienting its colonial gaze toward the south.[22] Due to these shared historical bonds, many Spaniards saw themselves as uniquely capable of uplifting the "backwards" Moroccans not as foreign invaders but as relatives.[23] The idea of brotherhood also had the very concrete advantage of allowing the resource-poor Spanish state to focus on the metaphysical rather than the material aspects of the colonial regime.[24] In the words of Tomás García Figueras, "Spain is not a colonial nation, [because] it does not have imperialist . . . but [only] spiritual ambitions" that would ultimately lead to "its protectorate being valued and recognized by the Moroccan people."[25]

Another reason for the Spanish attempts to accommodate the Moroccans can be found in the history of the civil war. The Fascist "crusade" against the Second Spanish Republic began in North Africa and relied on tens of thousands of Moroccan soldiers who distinguished themselves in numerous battles.[26] To portray himself as a friend of the Islamic world, Franco subsequently organized a pilgrimage to Mecca by converting a navy ship into a "floating mosque."[27] Established in 1938, the General Franco Institute for Hispano-Arab Research published Moroccan scholarship that both celebrated the colonial regime and advocated for Pan-Islam.[28] Many Spanish officials remembered the contributions made by the Moroccans long after the war had ended. But they never regarded them as peers. Even García Figueras described the Moroccans as "a people that is far away from having come of age," thus echoing the pervasive notion that non-Westerners were immature and in need of colonial tutelage.[29] Paternalism, not equality, characterized the relationship between Spaniards and the local population.

The protectorate authorities had sought to establish a good rapport with both the nascent nationalist movement and the wider Arab world ever since opening the *Casa de Marruecos*, or *Bayt al-Maghrib*, in Cairo in 1938.[30] Though initially conceptualized as a student residence and cultural mission that would strengthen trans-Mediterranean relations, a group of young nationalists soon took over the center and turned it into a hotbed of radical anticolonial activism. (An exacerbated Spanish diplomat concluded in 1943 that "the only fruit of these [student] missions is to spur on Moroccan nationalism.")[31] But despite this disastrous outcome, the Spanish government had not yet given up the hope of recruiting new allies in the Arab world. Therefore, the protectorate authorities decided to take their chances and dispatch a delegation to the Arab League. And the nationalists in Tetouan were once again well positioned to take advantage of this opportunity and spearhead the advocacy campaign in the Middle East.

In March 1946, the three Moroccan representatives attended the meeting of the cultural committee in Cairo, but the affair did not work out in accordance with the Spanish plan. While M'hammad b. Abdelsalam Benaboud praised the colonial regime, M'hammad b. Ahmed Benaboud publicly denounced his companion as a traitor, and al-Halfaoui proclaimed with lofty rhetoric that "if Morocco were a truly independent state, the [subsequent] strengthening of Arab unity would be the key in the hands of the Arabs to the gate of the Western Mediterranean."[32] Furious about the two delegates' perceived betrayal, Varela ordered their immediate return to Morocco, but to no avail: M'hammad b. Ahmed Benaboud and Mohammed al-Fassi al-Halfaoui announced that they would remain in Cairo to continue publicizing the Moroccan demands for independence.[33] M'hammad b. Abdelsalam Benaboud, meanwhile, "had lost all of his prestige" and was "shunned" by his neighbors upon returning to Morocco—even his own brother publicly denounced him as a Spanish "propagandist."[34] News from Cairo traveled fast and found an eager reception among the inhabitants of Tetouan.

In coordination with other nationalists from Tunisia and Algeria already present in the Egyptian capital, the two nationalists lobbied the Arab League to condemn the colonization of North Africa and to present their respective cases before the United Nations.[35] "The propaganda abroad develops quickly and is propelling our case . . . onto the international stage. . . . Azzam Pasha has become completely convinced that the northern zone must . . . obtain its independence," the enthusiastic delegates wrote to their colleagues back home.[36] "Our situation could not be better," explained Benaboud in a private letter to his family. "We have met with many ministers, pashas, ambassadors, religious scholars. The Egyptian newspapers have been very interested in us."[37] The PNR distributed a pamphlet inside the Spanish protectorate in which it informed its members that "our Moroccan delegation to the Arab League continues . . . to propagate the Moroccan case in Arab political circles [where] it has encountered great sympathy."[38] Proud of these achievements, the Tetouanis sent a letter to the royal palace in Rabat, informing the monarch that their two colleagues were "presenting the Moroccan case to Arab kings and presidents . . . and requesting them to authorize their delegations to present the issue at the United Nations."[39]

It suddenly dawned on the Spanish authorities that their latest plan to charm Arab public opinion had backfired. Spanish ambassador Carlos de Miranda informed Varela that two of the three representatives had commenced an anticolonial campaign supported by their compatriots from the

French zone with "the obvious compliance of the extremist nationalists [of Egypt]."[40] The embarrassed high commissioner tried to assure his colleagues in Madrid and Cairo that he had been unaware of the delegation's nationalist leanings.[41] Blinded by the bizarre belief that colonizer and colonized could somehow become partners, or maybe even friends, the Spanish authorities had failed to take the nationalist movement seriously. Tomás García Figueras, looking back at a range of events that had occurred in 1946, bemoaned that the Moroccans had taken advantage of "Spain's difficult international position" because the country had been weakened by "a violent international conspiracy."[42] The French press, meanwhile, enjoyed the failure of the Spanish plan but also expressed concern about the impact the anticolonial campaign in Egypt might have on their own protectorate.[43] Encouraged by the warm reception they had received in Cairo, the nationalists took their campaign to the next level.

THE OFFICE OF THE ARAB MAGHRIB

On 15 February 1947, activists from across Morocco as well as from Algeria and Tunisia organized a weeklong "Conference of the Arab Maghrib."[44] The participants declared the French protectorates in Morocco and Tunisia "void" and the colonization of Algeria "illegal," and they asked the Arab League to "present the North African case before the international organizations and do everything possible to help the Maghrib obtain its complete independence."[45] Azzam Pasha gave a keynote address in which he reminded his audience that the Arab League served the interests not only of its seven member states but also of all Arab peoples living under the yoke of colonialism.[46] The main reason for the conference, however, was to announce the opening of Maktab al-Maghrib al-ʿArabi, which came to serve as the Cairo headquarters for nationalist movements from across the region.[47] The name chosen for this new institution offers some interesting insights into the ideology of the anticolonial activists. By referring to North Africa as "the Arab Maghrib," they submerged the region's considerable Amazigh (Berber) and Jewish minorities under their own definition of the region as exclusively characterized by an Arab-Islamic civilization.[48] This misleading description allowed them to associate their struggle directly with the popular ideology of Pan-Arabism and thereby appeal to Middle Eastern public opinion.

The bureau's Moroccan staff consisted of nationalists from both the Spanish and the French zones; Abdelmajid Benjelloun, Ahmed Ben al-Melih, Abdelkarim Ghallab, Abdelkarim Ben Thabet, and several others had stayed in Cairo after completing their studies in order to serve as local representatives of the Istiqlal Party. They occupied themselves with organizing a library covering the region's history, politics, and society. Moreover, they held press conferences whenever the need arose and distributed bulletins about current events in North Africa among journalists.[49] To introduce the Maghrib to the Egyptian public, the Moroccans wrote a detailed critique of French colonialism with the telling title *Widyan al-Damm* (Rivers of Blood) as well as thematic booklets such as *Huquq al-Dawla al-Marrakushiyya* (The Rights of the Moroccan State) and *'Arsh Marrakush* (The Throne of Morocco).[50] These publications—usually consisting of thirty to forty pages of text—dealt with the situation inside the North African kingdom and contained photos depicting the royal family or the life of the native population under colonial rule. After receiving a copy of a lengthy book entitled *Hadha Marrakush* (This Is Morocco), Azzam Pasha praised it as "offering the reader a clear picture of [the] country by presenting its geography, history, and its [institutions] . . . and everything else that is needed to . . . participate in the struggle to reclaim its rights."[51] Well written and based on meticulous research, these publications were excellent exposés of the colonial order and thus proved invaluable assets in the struggle to inform Arabic public opinion about Morocco.[52]

Of even greater importance were the personal contacts created by the members of Maktab al-Maghrib. The Moroccans organized receptions on a regular basis in order to attract the attention of the media. Whether it was the annual celebration of Mohammed ben Youssef's ascension to the throne or the anniversary of the Arab League, the activists always found a reason to invite important individuals to a party. Prominent guests such as Syrian prime minister Jamil Mardam Bey and Lebanese prime minister Riyad al-Sulh Bey as well as intellectuals such as the literary critic Ahmed Amin and the (future) Islamic theorist Sayyid Qutb attended these meetings, thus adding their luster to the proceedings.[53] Traveling regularly between Tangier and Cairo, the English journalist Margaret Pope helped the Moroccans reach out to Westerners passing through the Egyptian capital. An extremely unsympathetic American observer later recalled the "sharp-nosed, thin-lipped, toothy Englishwoman . . . [whose] apartment served as the Maghreb Office; her

telephone number was its telephone number."[54] Evidently successful in propagating their cases in Egypt, the North Africans' activities did not go unnoticed; the French embassy showed itself alarmed by "the intensive press campaign, which the Maghribis work hard to maintain against us."[55] A French
journalist concluded that "the Office of the Arab Maghrib is the true center
of North African nationalism in the world today" because the nationalists
"are like fish in the water in Cairo."[56]

The staff of Maktab al-Maghrib needed all the help it could get to advocate for Morocco's independence throughout the region. Therefore, Abdelkhaleq Torres and Allal al-Fassi joined the efforts in the Middle East in
the spring of 1947. Their appearance immediately drew additional attention
to the anticolonial campaign since both were well-known across the Arab
world. They gave speeches and interviews, published newspaper articles, and
met politicians; thanks to financial support provided by the Arab League, al-
Fassi also wrote his seminal *Al-Harakat al-Istiqlaliyya fi al-Maghrib al-ʿArabi*
(The Independence Movements in the Arab Maghrib), which continues to
be one of the most important sources on the history of Moroccan nationalism.[57] Overall, their very presence proved beneficial at a time when most
Egyptians paid little attention to French North Africa. Al-Fassi confirmed
this in a letter to the executive committee of the Istiqlal in Rabat. "Upon my
arrival in Egypt," he wrote, "I realized that the climate was not favorable for
great propaganda for our case—the questions of Palestine and Egypt dominated all others."[58] It clearly required more time and effort for the nationalists' demands to become an integral part of Arab political discourse. To
achieve this end, they recruited a wide range of prominent public figures to
join their advocacy network.

One of the organizations openly embracing the two Moroccan nationalist leaders was the Muslim Brotherhood. Upon Torres's arrival at Port Said
on 16 May 1947, a huge crowd welcomed him with cries of "We will give our
lives for the Maghrib!" and "Long live Arabism!" At a tea reception given in
his honor, he received a pin with the organization's insignia and gave a long
interview to its newspaper.[59] When the charismatic Islamic scholar Allal al-
Fassi reached Cairo one week later, the Muslim Brothers provided him with
an equally enthusiastic welcome.[60] The organization's publications sometimes featured articles about or written by al-Fassi, thus exposing its signif-

icant membership to the situation in Morocco.[61] General Guide Hassan al-Banna regularly attended events organized by Maktab al-Maghrib, such as the annual celebrations of Throne Day.[62] On 24 July 1947, the anniversary of the 1830 occupation of Algeria by France, the Muslim Brothers organized a rally during which al-Banna and Torres called for a boycott of French products.[63] A French intelligence officer reported that the organization supported the Maghribis both logistically and financially because Allal al-Fassi had become a "friend" of its leader.[64] The Brotherhood's radical anti-imperialist stance in combination with its influential media apparatus was an ideal relay for spreading their message across the Middle East, and the Moroccans actively cultivated this important link. Moreover, it provided their movement with additional legitimacy, at least until the temporary banning of the organization in December 1948 and the assassination of al-Banna on 12 February 1949.

Another important supporter of the Moroccan nationalist movement was the former grand mufti of Jerusalem, Hajj Amin al-Hussayni, who had become president of the exiled All-Palestine Government following the Arab-Israeli War of 1948. He attended most receptions held at Maktab al-Maghrib.[65] The nationalists took pride in their friendship with such a prominent public figure, and al-'Alam occasionally printed articles about the mufti to demonstrate to its readers that this famous Arab leader supported their anticolonial struggle.[66] Although he belonged to the old Palestinian leadership that lost much of its standing after the state of Israel dispossessed the local population in 1948, he still maintained a strong rapport with numerous Arab politicians. Remembered today mostly for his unsavory alliance with Nazi Germany, the mufti enjoyed great prestige in the Middle East during the postwar decade. According to Allal al-Fassi, "The mufti of Palestine helps us to be accepted in official circles."[67]

Besides recruiting outspoken Islamists to their network, the Moroccans also gained supporters among Egypt's liberal elites. One of them was Senator Mahmud Abu al-Fath, a prominent member of the liberal Wafd Party whose newspaper al-Misri had always been a strong advocate for North African independence. In April 1951, he headed the Arab League's delegation to Tangier that supervised the formation of the National Front. Moreover, he ensured that his journalists kept in close contact with the members of Maktab

al-Maghrib and regularly covered stories pertaining to the region.[68] The Moroccan nationalists repeatedly expressed "their thankfulness and gratitude
for his efforts" on behalf of the independence struggle.[69] In his position as a
politician from a UN member state, Abu al-Fath repeatedly submitted complaints to the international organization about human rights violations committed by the colonial authorities.[70] The French ambassador in Cairo noted
bitterly that Abu al-Fath "seems passionate about his new role as the defender
of North African independence."[71] The Egyptian senator epitomized like
few others the networked nature of the Moroccan struggle for independence.

Another individual supporting the Moroccans was the Francophone
journalist—and Egyptian delegate to the UN—Mahmud Azmi, whose contacts with the nationalists convinced him to travel to Morocco in December
1946.[72] Greeted by enthusiastic crowds wherever he went, Azmi gave a couple
of lectures mildly critical of the colonial regime when he returned to Cairo.[73]
After numerous additional encounters with Moroccans, he again toured the
North African kingdom in the spring of 1951 and was even granted a personal audience by Sultan Mohammed ben Youssef. This time, though, he not
only briefed Egypt's foreign minister Mohammed Salah al-Din about "the
true events in Morocco" upon his return but also published a series of commentaries in the newspaper *al-Ahram* that made a strong case for the country's independence.[74] Though less radical in his critique of colonialism than
Abu al-Fath, the nationalists praised Azmi for his "long articles explaining the Moroccan case before Arab and world public opinion."[75] Another
Egyptian visitor later confirmed Azmi's enduring "veneration" in Morocco.
Speaking on Radio Cairo in 1955, the traveler reported that Moroccans "often have tears in their eyes when they think of [the man] who raised his voice
at the [UN] to demand the emancipation of Morocco."[76]

It was this networked approach that made the Moroccans' struggle for
independence so powerful. They themselves not only actively reached out to
the general public but also integrated a diverse group of individuals into their
anticolonial advocacy network, making these people central nodes that facilitated the flow of information to remote locations they otherwise would have
been unable to reach directly. Influential institutions of Egyptian civil society such as *Jama'iyyat al-Shubban al-Muslimin* (the Young Men's Muslim Association) used their large membership to pressure politicians to speak out

against colonialism in North Africa;[77] the famous legal scholar Abderrazzaq al-Sanhuri penned a detailed legal report that explained how to best present the Moroccan case before the United Nations;[78] and Margaret Pope edited a number of publications in English and smuggled the nationalists' mail to Tangier via a personal friend residing in Gibraltar.[79] All of this furthered the anticolonial cause. Whether radical Islamists or Francophile diplomats, liberal nationalists or Western journalists, their supporters' often contradictory political affiliations proved beneficial to their campaign for independence. But besides such meticulous work, unpredictable events could also propel the Moroccan case to the forefront of international attention.

THE ESCAPE OF ABDELKARIM

The members of Maktab al-Maghrib celebrated their biggest achievement just a few months after the founding of their organization: the escape of Mohammed b. Abdelkarim al-Khattabi, known as Abdelkarim, the legendary Berber warrior who had led a large-scale revolt against the colonial armies in the Rif Mountains of northern Morocco from 1920 until 1926 and was subsequently exiled to the island of Réunion after his capture by the French authorities. Since the end of World War II, Moroccan nationalists had repeatedly petitioned for the liberation of the amir, as everyone respectfully called the former resistance fighter.[80] Abdelkarim's heroic struggle against the colonizers during the 1920s had stayed very much alive in national public memory, and the Moroccans viewed it as an obligation to free their revered compatriot. Even the Middle Eastern press had repeatedly demanded the "immediate liberation of this Arab leader" and called on all Muslims "to do whatever they can to get the Moroccan hero out of his painful banishment."[81] Suddenly, however, his case took an unexpected turn.

On 27 May 1947, the prominent Cairo-based Palestinian journalist Mohammed Ali al-Tahir informed his Moroccan friends that the French authorities had decided to relocate Abdelkarim and that he was currently embarking on a ship in the Yemeni port of Aden that would take him through the Suez Canal to the metropole.[82] This seemed like a golden opportunity. During an urgently convened meeting, the members of Maktab al-Maghrib agreed to send Ahmed Ben al-Melih and M'hammad Benaboud to welcome

IMAGE 4. The members of Maktab al-Maghrib al-ʿArabi celebrating the escape of
Mohammed b. Abdelkarim al-Khattabi (left of center in dark-gray garment), 1947.
(Source: Aboubakr Bennouna. Reprinted with permission.)

Abdelkarim to Egypt and convince him to stay. The two nationalists drove
to the city of Suez, where they boarded the ship by hiding themselves among
other visitors when it briefly anchored at the southern entrance to the canal.[83] After many hours of persuasion, Abdelkarim and his family disembarked in the early hours of 31 May, unnoticed by their French keepers, and
then traveled to the Egyptian capital.[84]

The arrival of Abdelkarim in Cairo was a stunning publicity success for
the Moroccan nationalist movement. According to the *New York Times*, he
was given a "hero's welcome" and interviewing him proved impossible since
"he was interrupted so frequently by Arabs rushing in to shake his hand and
congratulate him."[85] King Faruq welcomed the amir and his family as official guests of the Egyptian state, and the country's entire political class,
including Prime Minister Mahmud Fahmi al-Nuqrashi, came to visit the
former Moroccan warrior in order to associate with him before the public
eye. Hundreds of prominent citizens contacted Maktab al-Maghrib to submit their regards, while congratulatory telegrams from around the Islamic
world poured into the Istiqlal headquarters in Rabat.[86] The amir's arrival

in the Egyptian capital once again brought international media attention to the Moroccan case less than two months after the sultan's influential speech in Tangier. Seeking to benefit from the Abdelkarim's global reputation, the North Africans in Cairo eventually announced the formation of *Lajnat Tahrir al-Maghrib al-'Arabi* (Committee for the Liberation of North Africa) under his nominal leadership—in reality M'hammad Benaboud, the Tunisian Habib Bourguiba, and the Algerian representatives ran the organization.[87] The nationalists back home in Morocco received this news "with great joy" and "hoisted flags to celebrate [it]."[88]

Not everyone shared the Moroccans' enthusiasm about this event, which many French observers viewed as a conspiracy concocted by the Arab League. *Le Monde* argued that "the Arabs" apparently took French lenience as a sign of "weakness" and therefore "redoubled their campaign of anti-French excitements . . . at every new manifestation of our fair play."[89] Spanish sources noted that the increased media coverage of the Moroccan delegation in Cairo in the aftermath of the escape posed a serious problem, because "the Egyptian press . . . [has] great influence on Middle Eastern public opinion."[90] According to a French diplomat, "The arrival in Cairo . . . of several Moroccan leaders, followed after a few days by . . . the escape of Abdelkarim, have brusquely placed the North African question at the first level of world events."[91] The Moroccans shared this assessment. His "liberation . . . permitted our movement to draw upon his glory, his experience, and his world-wide reputation," noted Allal al-Fassi.[92] The nationalists' international campaign for independence seemed to be working.

CAIRO, A CENTRAL NETWORK NODE

Maktab al-Maghrib was important mainly because of its role as a hub for transnational activism across the entire Middle East. In 1947, Abdelkarim Ghallab and M'hammad Benaboud attended the Arab League's annual cultural conference in Beirut to conduct "extensive propaganda among the biggest gathering of Arab intellectuals" and thereby ensure that "the new generation in the Arab world will know the Maghrib just like the Mashriq."[93] Meanwhile, the Tunisian nationalist Youssef Roussi opened a local branch of Maktab al-Maghrib in Damascus.[94] Four years later, in preparation for an upcoming discussion of French North Africa at the UN General Assembly, Allal al-Fassi toured various Arab capitals in the company of Ahmed Ben al-Melih. In Beirut, the enthusiastic members of the Association for the Liberation of the Arab Maghrib in Syria and Lebanon organized a reception for the za'im;[95] the Iraqi press reported in detail about the talks between al-Fassi and the government in Baghdad;[96] and Jordanian King Talal granted a private audience to the Moroccan representative.[97] During a lecture in Damascus, Si Allal showed himself content that the Arab states had "finally decided, after listening closely to the representatives of Morocco, to present our case to the UN during its coming session . . . [because] the world is ready to take notice of our complaints."[98]

Besides using Cairo as the gateway for such transnational outreach, the Moroccan activists abroad also aimed at a domestic audience; the nationalist press provided detailed coverage of the Arab League and other events taking place in the Middle East and beyond throughout the years of the liberation struggle. To demonstrate the effectiveness of their campaign in the heart of the Arab world, the activists in Cairo regularly sent their most recent publications—both books and monthly newsletters—so that the PNR and the Istiqlal could distribute them among their members.[99] In an op-ed published in *al-'Alam*, Abdelkarim Ben Thabet emphasized Egypt's role as "the leader . . . and vanguard directing the ship of the Arabs in the midst of the colonial storms and independence calls."[100] Moreover, the two nationalist parties commemorated the founding of the Arab League each year with ceremonies across Morocco.[101] A US diplomat in Rabat reported in the spring of 1947 that the most recent festivities on the anniversary of the Arab League had taken place in a "dignified manner" and had been attended by several thousand persons. The event was celebrated in and around the Istiqlal headquarters.[102]

The strong emotional attachment of many Moroccans toward the land along the Nile became evident in March 1950, when an Egyptian theatre troupe visited the North African kingdom to participate in a cultural festival in Casablanca. Sultan Mohammed ben Youssef granted the artists an audience followed by a tea reception hosted by the crown prince, thereby underlining the monarchy's connection to the wider Arab world.[103] Deeply moved by the throngs of people that greeted him and his colleagues wherever they appeared in public, the famous actor Youssef Wahby Bey exclaimed, "I am in a dream," and then he assured his hosts that "the Egyptian people are ready to spill their blood for the sake of their Moroccan brothers."[104] Al-'Alam dedicated an entire special issue to the visitors and explained that this trip was "another clear sign for the links between the Arab East and Morocco."[105] Cairo had taken up a prominent place in the Moroccan national imaginary despite its geographical remoteness.

Seven months after the arrival of the actors, several influential Egyptian journalists visited Morocco under the leadership of Mahmud Abu al-Fath's brother Hussayn, the editor of al-Misri. The Istiqlal seized this opportunity and rallied a large crowd that provided "the apostles of brotherhood between dear Egypt and the Arab Maghrib" with an equally enthusiastic welcome on their arrival at Casablanca airport.[106] Although the journalists had been invited by a French media association seeking to paint a positive picture of the situation inside Morocco, the Istiqlal skillfully subverted the protectorate authorities' efforts through private dinners and public displays of solidarity. When the delegation visited the great mosque in Fez, the faithful welcomed them so passionately that "the pillars of the Qarawiyyin shook under cries of 'Long Live the Arabs, Egypt, Morocco, Faruq and His Majesty the Sultan.'"[107] The nationalists inside Morocco supported the activities of Maktab al-Maghrib to attract the attention of the Arab world to their situation under colonial rule.

Yet the Moroccan campaign in Cairo soon faced a serious crisis. On 12 December 1949, M'hammad Benaboud, the Tunisian Habib Thamir, and the Algerian Ali al-Harnami died in a tragic accident in Pakistan. The three North Africans had been on their way to attend the Islamic Congress when their plane crashed near Karachi and killed all passengers aboard, thus decapitating the nationalist campaign in Egypt and putting the very existence of Maktab al-Maghrib into question.[108] Thousands of people came to receive Benaboud's coffin when it arrived in Tangier, and Allal al-Fassi wrote a moving obituary in honor of the three "martyrs . . . who died while fulfilling a great Arab duty."[109] The funeral ceremony itself demonstrated the successful internationalization of the Moroccan struggle for independence. According to the nationalist press, "Benaboud's body was transported in a car decorated with the flags of Morocco, the Arab states, Indonesia, and Pakistan," and the forty-day memorial service included the reading of eulogies sent by Azzam Pasha and other prominent figures from across the Islamic world.[110]

High Commissioner Varela still had not forgotten Benaboud's "betrayal" almost four years earlier and therefore prohibited the funeral procession from entering the Spanish Zone. M'hammad Benaboud thus had to be buried in Tangier.[111] When the Ministry of Foreign Affairs in Madrid considered sending a new representative from Spanish Morocco to the cultural committee of the Arab League a few months later, it immediately received a negative response from Tetouan. "It is not considered convenient," argued the high commissioner before reminding his colleagues that "the ministry is already familiar with the counterproductive outcome of the previous appointment, which was detrimental to our interests."[112] The country's foreign policy evidently did not enjoy unanimous support among Spanish officials. Whereas the central government was still hoping for an alliance with the Arab world, colonial officials in Morocco had become unwilling to play their parts since all previous attempts to cooperate with the nationalist movement on the international stage had failed. The embarrassment caused by the nationalists abroad had not been forgotten in Tetouan.

The tragic accident only added to the difficulties faced by the staff of Maktab al-Maghrib. Almost since the very beginning, the bureau had suffered from chronic financial problems, despite the fact that the Arab League, the Egyptian king, and the khalifa subsidized its activities.[113] A frustrated Benaboud complained one year before his death, "If the Arab League provided us with the same political efforts and money as the Palestinians, the Maghrib could perform miracles."[114] The tragic plane crash in December 1949 further aggravated the situation as Maktab al-Maghrib lost its most capable organizers. The interest of the Egyptian media in the activities of the North African nationalists in Cairo decreased steadily.[115] Alarmed by the desperate state of Maghribi propaganda in Cairo, Azzam Pasha recommended a total reorganization of a campaign described by French observers as "struck by paralysis."[116] In October 1952, the secretary general of the PNR, Tayeb Bennouna, traveled to Cairo to request more financial and political support from the League "so that the Arab nations are not humiliated before the universe."[117] Still, his passionate appeal did not yield any tangible results.

Another issue that hampered the anticolonial campaign in Cairo was the continuous infighting among the various North Africans in Cairo. This bickering absorbed much of their energy, to the detriment of their lobbying duties.[118] Especially serious was the rift between Abdelkarim and virtually everybody else; within months after his arrival in Egypt, it became clear that he did not think too highly of his supposed colleagues and therefore withdrew to his elegant villa.[119] In a letter to his nephew in the Rif, he explained that Allal al-Fassi and Abdelkhaleq Torres had turned out to be "playful children" rather than mighty warriors.[120] The situation had deteriorated even further by the summer of 1952. In interview with *Le Monde*, the amir claimed that "opportunism has ruined our national cause," because the members of Maktab al-Maghrib were spending "the money of the nationalist movement . . . on a struggle that is limited to the city of Cairo and the printing of luxurious publications."[121] The purpose of political outreach that did not at least parallel military actions seemed lost on the battle-hardened guerrilla fighter. Such public statements of discontent undermined the Moroccans' desire to present a united national front before the Arab public.

Despite the obstacles they faced, the members of Maktab al-Maghrib always maintained their eyes on the ultimate prize: having the Arab governments present the Moroccan case before the UN. Azzam Pasha remained their most outspoken supporter.[122] In a private letter addressing the Arab League's attitude toward the North African territories, he confirmed that everyone "works for their freedom and independence, because the League is against all forms of colonialism in any Arab territory."[123] A message sent by al-Melih to the Istiqlal leadership in Rabat in 1951 acknowledged Azzam Pasha's relentless efforts; during a recent visit to the United States, "He missed no opportunity to talk about the Arab Maghrib."[124] His repeated contacts with the Moroccans further cemented his pan-Arab views.[125] The secretary general's embrace of Maghribi nationalism also served the Arab League itself. "Although member countries do not all agree on certain Near Eastern questions, they can agree unreservedly on the North African question, and thus foster League unity," the US Department of State noted in an internal document.[126]

The second passionate champion of Moroccan independence was Mohammed Fadil al-Jamali, who served as both foreign and prime minister of Iraq following World War II. He supported Azzam Pasha's efforts and even spoke before the UN General Assembly in order to denounce the on-going colonization of the Maghrib. According to a journalist reporting from the UN in 1952, "The efforts of the Iraqi delegate . . . to get the Moroccan question put on the agenda . . . were most impressive."[127] A French official described the Iraqi politician as "our fiercest enemy" due to his relentless work on behalf of the Moroccan nationalist movement.[128] A CIA report confirmed that "Iraq, together with Egypt, has led the attack on France's activities and policies in Morocco."[129] In close cooperation with the secretary general, al-Jamali played a major role in pushing the Arab League member states to actively pursue the independence of France's North African colonies. Thanks to their support, the Moroccan case had indeed become part of the official discourse of Arab diplomacy. Suddenly, though, an unexpected turn of events jeopardized the Moroccans' accomplishments in Cairo.

REVOLUTIONARY EGYPT

On 23 July 1952, the Free Officers overthrew King Faruq and subsequently transformed Egypt into a republic governed by a Revolutionary Command Council (RCC). The new leaders constituted a close-knit brotherhood under the leadership of Colonel Gamal Abdel Nasser, the "first among equals."[130] Their primary objective was to rejuvenate their country by dismantling the corrupt political order and reducing British influence. Although initially focused on domestic politics, Nasser soon became famous for his passionate anti-imperialist stance.[131] The new regime also embraced Pan-Arabism from its very inception.[132] Already in 1953, Nasser emphasized the intertwined relationship between Egypt and the wider Arab world. ("Our history has been mixed with it and . . . its interests are linked with ours.")[133] In order to spread his message and consolidate Egypt's regional preeminence, he sought to gain control of the Arab League, and on 4 July 1953, the RCC inaugurated *Sawt al-'Arab* (Voice of the Arabs), a new program on Radio Cairo that broadcast pan-Arab propaganda across the region.[134] Cairo now emerged as a center of radical anticolonialism, and the Moroccan nationalists expected to benefit from this dramatic transformation.

Throughout the fall of 1952, the members of Maktab al-Maghrib remained confident that the new regime intended to strengthen the Arab

League's resolve to support the peoples of the Maghrib. Abdelkarim Ben Thabet predicted that "the Arab League will follow the new prevailing spirit in
Egypt;"[135] Abdelmajid Benjelloun expressed his hope that the revolutionary
government would "renew the foundations of the Arab League . . . so that it
fulfills the hopes of the Arabs once again;"[136] and Ahmed Ben al-Melih concluded that "the coup in Egypt will strengthen [the country's] pride in Arabness and Islam as well as its interest in those that are helpless like us," thereby
inevitably causing the Arab League to "double its resolve to defend the Arab
Maghrib."[137] Yet these optimistic assessments turned out to be inaccurate.
Rather than increasing its support for the diplomatic campaign conducted by
the Moroccan nationalists, the new regime actually undermined their efforts
on the global stage—both intentionally and inadvertently.[138]

The most devastating blow to the Moroccan advocacy campaign occurred when the new Egyptian government removed the country's old elites
and replaced them with its own people. Azzam Pasha immediately lost his
position as chief Arab diplomat to Abdelkhaleq Hassouna; French observers celebrated the arrival of the new secretary general who seemed willing to
"spare [them] many difficulties" since he lacked his predecessor's "inoppor-
tune zeal."[139] After a brief honeymoon, the new regime dissolved the Muslim Brotherhood in January 1954; it had already forbidden all other political parties one year earlier.[140] Islamists such as Sayyid Qutb disappeared in
prison. Legal scholar Abderrazzaq al-Sanhuri left the country after the new
rulers had forced him into retirement. Meanwhile, a court sentenced media mogul Mahmud Abu al-Fath to ten years' incarceration in absentia for
allegedly having disseminated antigovernment misinformation in *al-Misri;*
the new regime had brought the entire Egyptian press under state control
by May 1955.[141] Hajj Amin al-Hussayni's standing also eroded following the
Free Officers' coup, and he eventually moved to Lebanon after refusing to
join the PLO when it was founded—with the active support of Nasser—in
1964.[142] The nationalists' network of supporters, which they had so diligently
crafted for several years, disintegrated within months.

The situation became quite difficult for the Moroccans as well. Egypt's
elites had received them with broad sympathy prior to July 1952, but the atmosphere deteriorated steadily following the ascendance of the RCC. When
Allal al-Fassi returned to Cairo in January 1953, he quickly realized that the

local media and politicians displayed no interest in his activities. A major problem was his close personal connection to the Muslim Brotherhood; that tarnished his image in the eyes of the new ruling class. The Egyptian authorities even began "harassing" those North Africans they suspected of having close contacts to the organization.[143] A French observer gloated that "al-Fassi's position in Cairo seems to worsen. . . . He is under constant surveillance and . . . it is possible that the government will ask him to leave Egyptian territory."[144] Another French diplomat noted that "the Maghribi nationalists are now totally discredited in Egyptian political circles."[145] The Moroccans' initial enthusiasm about the regime change had evaporated rather quickly.

Amid this increasingly challenging climate, the remaining members of Maktab al-Maghrib continued their activities until the eve of Moroccan independence, although on a modest scale. "The situation in Egypt is not encouraging for our cause—for that reason, our brothers are busy watching TV series and do not want to do anything else at the moment," Allal al-Fassi complained in a letter written in May 1953.[146] "The Arab League is weak . . . and the press disinterested, which is why you do not witness the desired campaign," he informed the leadership of the Istiqlal back home.[147] Nonetheless, the Moroccans also profited somewhat from the city's emergence as a center of global anti-imperialism: they met with Yugoslavian, Iranian, and Indonesian diplomats, and even the secretary general of the Asian Socialist Conference visited Maktab al-Maghrib to become acquainted with the situation in North Africa.[148] The activists tried to benefit at least indirectly from the new foreign policies pursued by the revolutionary regime. Moreover, they participated in cultural events such as the Cairo exposition and continued to travel to other countries across the Arab world.

The ambiguity of Egyptian support became abundantly clear in the aftermath of Mohammed ben Youssef's dethronement on 20 August 1953. Following years of tensions between the Residency and the sultan regarding his outspoken support for Moroccan independence, French security forces surrounded the palace with tanks and deported the monarch and his relatives; the royal family would ultimately spend almost two years in exile on Madagascar.[149] But instead of solving the problem, the French authorities had only added fuel to the fire: within days, armed resistance groups mushroomed across the country and the Moroccan question became an issue of global concern. The PNR requested the UN to "send an investigative committee to examine the situation inside the country" and "compel France to return our beloved King Sidi Mohammed ben Youssef to the throne."[150] A CIA report predicted that "the removal will create strong resentment in the Arab and Muslim world, with agitation for UN action certain. The prestige of the US will probably suffer . . . because it will be assumed that the US supports French policy."[151] Now more than ever, much depended on the stance of the Arab League.

To bolster its reputation as the leading advocate for Arab anti-imperialism, the Egyptian government granted the Moroccans access to Radio Cairo.[152] Allal al-Fassi made his first appearance on *Sawt al-'Arab* just hours after the resident general had deposed Mohammed ben Youssef, calling for violent resistance and inciting his countrymen to "continue the struggle for [their] existence."[153] Radio Cairo became the voice of the nationalist movement abroad from that moment on, broadcasting messages to the inhabitants of Morocco on an almost weekly basis. In a speech disseminated on the first anniversary of the sultan's forced exile, Abdelmajid Benjelloun supported the "armed struggle" and declared that "the triumph of Mohammed ben Youssef . . . [is] the triumph of the people who will only accept complete independence."[154] A combination of news, political statements, appeals to the resistance fighters, and nationalist music completed the regular broadcasts organized by the few Moroccans that remained in Cairo.

The entire Maghrib followed *Sawt al-'Arab* closely on the abundantly available transistor radios, and even the sultan was rumored to have said that he "felt like living in Egypt among my Egyptian brothers" while listening to Radio Cairo during his exile.[155] At the height of the Franco-Moroccan crisis, a high-ranking Istiqlali declared, "There is only one voice remaining which the Moroccans receive . . . and that is the Voice of the Arabs from Radio Cairo."[156] The *New York Times* also commented on the "effectiveness" of the "this new voice," which was inciting "the peoples of the Middle East and Africa . . . to cast off the yoke of imperialism and colonialism."[157] Contrary to the dire reality encountered by the Moroccan activists in Cairo, the radio station's North African listeners came to imagine Nasser as an outspoken benefactor of their campaign for independence.

Arms and military training constituted the RCC's other means of support for the North African liberation struggles. In March 1953, the regime established a training center for Maghribi commando units to instruct them in guerilla tactics.[158] On 3 April 1954, Nasser organized a meeting of all North African nationalist parties: in return for the promise of weapons and money, the gathered delegates signed a treaty that established a liaison office in Cairo that would consolidate their respective military efforts with the goal of "the complete independence of the three territories."[159] The Egyptian support proved pivotal to the creation of the Moroccan Liberation Army, a small but well-organized force that sought the return of the sultan as well as immediate independence. Whereas Maktab al-Maghrib received an annual allowance of EGP 15,000 from the Arab League, the Egyptian government had spent more than EGP 100,000 on military equipment and training of North African commandos by early 1956.[160] The new Egyptian regime clearly prioritized armed resistance over diplomatic engagement. And although the Istiqlal tried to bring the Liberation Army under its control, the resistance fighters refused to submit to the political leadership in exile and thus challenged the supposed unity of the nationalist movement.[161]

The outbreak of the armed resistance in French Morocco brought to light the simmering rivalry between the two colonial powers. Franco had granted Abdelkhaleq Torres a private audience in February 1953 and refused to accept Sidi Mohammed's dethronement seven months later.[162] His regime also permitted the small student community in Madrid to host a reception for Arab and Asian diplomats, and the Moroccans seized this opportunity to give "speeches harshly criticizing France's actions in Morocco and its oppression of the people."[163] Meanwhile, the nationalist movement sent Abdelkabir al-Fassi to the Spanish capital to facilitate the smuggling of arms to the resistance fighters across Morocco.[164] US diplomats took note of "the Spanish . . . desire to annoy the French to the outmost over the Moroccan question.[165] The French consul in Tetouan explained this "illogical" policy as the result of "the emotional . . . Spanish temperament" as well as the "Francophobia" prevalent among "many Spaniards, especially the military officers in Morocco."[166] But he also admitted that recent public celebrations of "Hispano-Moroccan understanding" and "friendship between the two peoples" had "increased Spain's prestige in Morocco and the Arab world" and led to "perfect calmness in their zone."[167] The bifurcated nature of the colonial regime thus continued to benefit the nationalist movement.

Of course, the French authorities repeatedly protested to the Egyptian government against both the military aid and Egypt's decision to grant the Moroccan "extremists" a platform on Radio Cairo. But overall they remained surprisingly unconcerned about these two forms of support.[168] "What does the aid of Cairo to the revolt in the Maghrib consist of right now?—Altogether, not very much," noted the French ambassador in Cairo in the fall of 1955, one year after the outbreak of the Algerian revolution, adding that he saw no reason to discontinue French military cooperation with Egypt.[169] France could apparently live with the limited level of support granted by Egypt to the anticolonial movements across North Africa. Having once put their hopes on the diplomatic aid they might receive from the Arab League in general and from the Egyptian government in particular, the Moroccan nationalists now realized the futility of their efforts. Back home in Rabat, the residency remarked on the Istiqlalis' "bitterness towards Egypt" because of the inadequate levels of support provided by Nasser's regime.[170] And a Spanish report noted "the great dissatisfaction with . . . Abdel Nasser and his government for having ordered the Voice of the Arabs to abstain from attacks against France for the violence perpetrated in North Africa."[171]

But what had caused this transformation of Egyptian foreign policy following the coup d'état of 1952? Why did the Moroccan nationalist movement not benefit from the ascendance of a regime that increasingly portrayed itself as the vanguard of the global struggle against colonialism? The shift in Egypt's foreign policy—away from the cautious yet steady diplomatic campaign under the monarchy toward a more radical rhetoric, more arms supplies, and more radio propaganda but less political support—was more consequential than it might have appeared at first. The reasons for this change can be found in the backgrounds of the Free Officers. Influenced by their training as soldiers as well as by the evident failure of the multiparty system under King Faruq, the members of the RCC were men of action rather than words. Gamal Abdel Nasser advocated for a global revolutionary struggle to free the colonized peoples of the Third World and remained deeply distrustful of political parties in general.[172] Moreover, their links to the Muslim Brotherhood discredited the Moroccans at a time when the secular-minded Egyptian government engaged in a ruthless power struggle with the Islamist organization.[173] Nasser also preferred supporting anticolonial movements more in line with his ideals of armed struggle and socialism, such as the FLN. Unsurprisingly, the aged warrior Abdelkarim fared relatively well during his remaining years in Cairo, as the Egyptian government held him in high-esteem.[174]

Another reason for the RCC's critical stance toward the Moroccans can be found in the nationalists' close relationship with the Egyptian monarchy as well as in their strong attachment to Sultan Mohammed ben Youssef. Having overthrown King Faruq, the Egyptian leaders had little sympathy for what they perceived as the neofeudal regimes of Iraq and Saudi Arabia—or the Alaoui dynasty in Morocco.[175] When the Residency in Rabat deported Sidi Mohammed in August 1953, the Moroccan nationalists asked the Egyptian government to intervene on his behalf, but President Mohammed Naguib hesitated to submit a formal protest to the French government.[176] Although *Sawt al-'Arab* condemned the exiling of the monarch, the Egyptian government did nothing concrete to express its opposition.[177] This policy evidently pleased French officials, who correctly concluded that "the North African problems seemed of secondary importance in the eyes of Egypt."[178]

The regime change in Cairo weakened the position of the Moroccan nationalists in the sphere of international diplomacy as well; only Iraq still aided their coreligionists under French colonial rule. At a press conference in January 1954, Mohammed Fadil al-Jamali emphasized, "The Iraqi government supports the Moroccan people and will not hesitate to help them morally and materially."[179] The US embassy in Baghdad remarked that the prime minister had become a major supporter of the Moroccan struggle for independence and seemed "always interested in North African problems."[180] Within the Arab League, however, Egypt regularly thwarted Iraq's calls for a cultural or economic boycott of France, advocating instead for a more moderate approach to the entire affair.[181] French officials regularly lamented al-Jamali's "zeal" and "aggressiveness" regarding North Africa, and they contrasted it negatively with the careful attitude displayed by the Egyptian government.[182] A French report analyzing Cairo's efforts on behalf of the North African nationalists since the ascent of the RCC concluded, "Egypt, despite being the instigator behind the Arab League, does not always lead this offensive that is often surpassed in violence by other Arab states, in particular Iraq."[183]

The new Egyptian secretary general of the Arab League also failed to distinguish himself as a fervent supporter of the Moroccan case, and he regularly tried to persuade al-Jamali to drop the issue as well.[184] In October 1954, the delegates of the Arab League organized an informal meeting in New York in order to find a solution to their diverging attitudes concerning French North Africa. The Istiqlal Party's secretary general, Ahmed Balafrej, who was in attendance, certainly did not enjoy the irreconcilable differences he witnessed. Despite a Pakistani attempt to settle the dispute, Egypt continued to reject Iraq's aggressive anti-French stance and even accused al-Jamali of putting personal motivations before the interests of the Arab League in general.[185] The Moroccan question repeatedly had to take a back seat in the General Assembly due to the lack of a coherent Arab diplomatic front.[186]

The French delegation had long been aware of this schism within the Arab-Asian bloc and tried to benefit from it. The diplomats in New York differentiated between countries "tending towards moderation," such as Egypt, Lebanon, and Syria, and those "tending towards extremism," such as Iraq and Pakistan.[187] An internal memo by the US State Department confirmed this assessment in October 1954. During a private discussion with American diplomats, Abdelkhaleq Hassouna had signaled that he was willing to "defer" any discussion on the status of Morocco at the UN as long as the French government showed itself ready "to expedite the negotiations" on the issue. But al-Jamali subsequently "expressed a somewhat dissenting opinion" and claimed that "the Arabs . . . were prepared to make a particularly strong case on Morocco" on the floor of the General Assembly.[188] Amid this cacophony of voices, the Moroccans knew they could not expect much support from the Arab League.

In order to properly understand al-Jamali's embrace of the North African nationalist movements, we must consider Iraqi domestic politics as well as the geopolitical rivalry between Cairo and Baghdad that characterized the Middle East during the 1950s.[189] Pan-Arabism had become the dominant political ideology in the country after World War II, because it united large sections of the population of the ethnically and socially fragmented country.[190] Nonetheless, the Iraqi state pursued a pro-Western foreign policy that culminated in the signing of the Baghdad Pact under US-British patronage in 1955.[191] Recurring popular protests against Iraq's close relationship with Britain provided an incentive for the country's political elites to demonstrate their anticolonial credentials.[192] Moreover, Gamal Abdel Nasser had become very popular among ordinary citizens, many of whom followed the broadcasts on Radio Cairo closely.[193] From the Iraqi point of view, standing up for the nations of the Maghrib thus served the dual purpose of undermining Egypt's claim to regional leadership and appeasing a domestic audience angry about the continuing influence of European imperialism in the Arab world.

The revolutionary Egyptian government, though, focused on issues it deemed of greater importance than Morocco's independence. Above all, it needed to consolidate its rule both at home and abroad without expending time and energy on a diplomatic row with France. Its ongoing struggle against Great Britain's continuing role in the region made it seem particularly inappropriate to simultaneously pick a fight with another powerful European country. Egyptian deputy foreign minister Khayrat Said informed his French counterpart in 1955 that his government came to the defense of North Africa only to keep Baghdad from becoming the region's sole champion of anti-imperialism and Pan-Arabism.[194] The struggle for Moroccan independence no longer rallied the members of the Arab League around a common cause. Instead, it had become a peripheral issue that made a mockery of public calls for Arab unity.

The complicated regional dynamics regarding the Moroccan quest for independence became apparent during the legendary Bandung Conference in April 1955. For the first time in history, representatives from twenty-nine recently decolonized states convened in order to discuss "means by which their people could achieve fuller economic, cultural and political co-operation."[195] The Moroccans had been waiting for such an opportunity for more than a decade, because they anticipated that the conference participants "will study . . . French colonialism and decide that [they] must aid the Maghribi countries fighting" for their independence.[196] Due to their relative proximity to the Indonesian city as well as the contacts they had established among Asian diplomats stationed in Cairo, Allal al-Fassi and Abdelmajid Benjelloun accompanied their colleagues from Algeria and Tunisia to the first truly global anticolonial meeting.[197] The two Moroccans were able to participate as members of the Yemeni delegation since the convention admitted representatives only from sovereign states.[198]

The Bandung Conference attracted substantial attention back home, and numerous articles in the nationalist press explained how this world historical event pertained to the Moroccan liberation struggle. In a detailed analysis published on the conference's opening day, *al-Umma* addressed those readers "doubtful of the value of the [propaganda] conducted abroad."[199] Pointing out the invitation to Bandung as a "tangible result, which Morocco obtained by defending its just cause on the international stage," the author of the article reiterated the importance of the nationalist movement's campaign to "incite world public opinion against French colonialism."[200] According to the newspaper, "There is no doubt that all the states on the Asian and African continents support Morocco's independence without reservation."[201] The Bandung Conference provided a unique platform "to present the crimes of French colonialism in the Arab Maghrib before world public opinion."[202] Morocco's quest for independence would undoubtedly benefit from this historical event.

Yet even the conference that symbolized the emergence of the Afro-Asian states failed to overcome the divisions among Arab leaders. Mohammed Fadil al-Jamali once again positioned himself as the most outspoken defender of "our Arab brothers that suffer under the French yoke in North Africa."[203] One month earlier, the Egyptian government had also proclaimed its desire to support the Maghribis. (According to an article in *al-Ahram,* "The question of North Africa will be the most important colonial problem examined by the congress.")[204] But beyond paying lip service to pan-Arab solidarity, Nasser provided only a modicum of assistance to the Moroccan cause in Bandung. The conference's final resolution "declared its support of the rights of the people of Algeria, Morocco and Tunisia to self-determination and independence" and called on France "to bring about a peaceful settlement of the issue without delay."[205] French diplomats noted with relief, however, that Egypt and India had purged the final communiqué of a much more violent critique proposed by the Iraqi delegation.[206]

A final joint declaration by the North Africans indirectly addressed the tensions between rhetoric and action that characterized the Bandung Conference. Although they explicitly praised the gathered states for "having played a vital role in the liberation of the peoples of Tunisia, Algeria, and Morocco," the activists also urged them "to conduct a diplomatic campaign" and "continue to provide aid" to their respective movements.[207] News of the event also resonated back home. According to a Spanish official, "The nationalists in Tangier are talking very favorably about the debates at the conference in Bandung," which they ascribed to the great work done by the Moroccan delegation.[208] The meeting in Indonesia thus epitomized the contradictory experiences of the Moroccans throughout the anticolonial campaign in Egypt and beyond: while seemingly a success that rewarded them for years of networked activism, it certainly did not fulfill the hopes that they had initially had in the leaders of the Arab world.

CONCLUSION

How should we thus evaluate the Moroccan campaign in Cairo? As a success or failure? And what ramifications did it have for the broader struggle for independence? Most importantly, it revealed both the opportunities and dangers inherent in organizing the anticolonial struggle abroad as a network. Their reliance on interpersonal relationships had allowed the Moroccans to successfully bring their demands to the attention of the Arab world generally and the Egyptian public specifically. Thanks to their friends in parliaments and royal courts, at universities and community centers, and in newsrooms and mosques, they had successfully pushed their demands to the forefront of regional public debate. As anybody who witnessed the crowds attending the annual celebrations of Throne Day in Cairo or welcoming the Moroccan nationalists at Baghdad airport could attest, the members of Maktab al-Maghrib had indeed aroused a great deal of public interest. This in turn convinced several diplomats to draw on the resources of the Arab League to inscribe the issue on the agenda of the UN General Assembly. All of these must be seen as impressive achievements by the Moroccan nationalists.

Still, the rapid collapse of their campaign in Egypt following the revolution of July 1952 underlined the dangers inherent in the Moroccans' networked activism. What initially seemed like a golden opportunity for their anticolonial struggle soon turned into a nightmare as many of their supporters lost their prominent positions in Egyptian society. This occurred not so much because Nasser and his colleagues did not desire Morocco's independence but because they opposed the nationalists' methods, ideological moderation, and monarchism. They chose to fund the Liberation Army instead of supporting the Istiqlal's diplomatic campaign. And the untimely death of M'hammad Benaboud a few years prior had already weakened the network's fragile structure. Deprived of their personal contacts, the members of Maktab al-Maghrib eventually had no supporters left willing to defend their cause, which gradually disappeared from public awareness. In other words, the very strength of their approach, namely, relying on extremely flexible informal alliances, contributed to the quick unraveling of their network in the Egyptian capital.

The developments in Cairo also transformed the hierarchies within the nationalist parties. Although the members of Maktab al-Maghrib had initially situated themselves as important nodes that facilitated the flow of information from the Istiqlal and the PNR to the elites of the Arab world, the disappearance of many of their interlocutors suddenly weakened their respective positions. Instead of establishing themselves as important bridges between Morocco and the Middle East, they quickly lost much of their status in an increasingly hostile environment. Whereas activists such as Abdelkarim Ghallab and Abdelmajid Benjelloun would ultimately build successful professional careers due to their acquired human capital—specifically, their knowledge of the modern mass media and familiarity with Arab and Asian diplomats—they lacked the social capital of their colleagues in Paris or New York. The logic of networked activism relegated them to the second tier within the Moroccan nationalist movement.

Yet the erroneous image of unwavering pan-Arab solidarity at the height of the anticolonial struggle still persists. The nationalists themselves contributed to the longevity of this inaccurate historical narrative. One example can be found in Allal al-Fassi's memoires about his time in Cairo in which he explicitly praised "the help which [he] received from . . . Gamal Abdel Nasser and various [other] Arab governments."[209] But this testimony had less to do with historical reality and more with the za'im's desire to emphasize his contributions to the national cause during his many years in exile. Instead, a more nuanced image of both cooperation and conflict seems more appropriate, because of the RCC's preference for radical forms of decolonization as opposed to the moderate approach of the Moroccan nationalists. Already in 1953, French historian Charles-André Julien concluded correctly that "Arab solidarity has revealed itself much more verbally than through action . . . [because] the calls for unity did not conceal the internal disagreements of the League, the ambiguity of its attitudes, and its almost complete impotence."[210] The Moroccan campaign in the Middle East had exposed the limits of Arab anticolonial solidarity.

The consequences of these developments were twofold. In the short term, the nationalist movement began to shift its resources—both human and financial—away from Cairo to more promising ventures. Although these decisions were also based on factors that had nothing to do with the latest developments inside Egypt, the increasingly difficult atmosphere caused by the revolutionary regime accelerated the trend to concentrate on the campaigns in Paris and New York. Maktab al-Maghrib remained an active center of Moroccan propaganda until shortly before independence, but the nationalist press's rapidly dwindling coverage of events in Egypt indicated that the movement's focus had shifted elsewhere. The long-term consequences came to be felt only after the end of colonial rule in March 1956. Still disappointed by their experiences in Nasser's Cairo, Morocco's new political elites maintained a skeptical distance from the Egyptian regime. Quite tellingly, it would take the North African kingdom until October 1958 to finally join the Arab League as a full member.

CHAPTER THREE

PARIS: CONQUERING THE METROPOLE

TERRIBLE NEWS SPREAD across North Africa on 5 December 1952: French right-wing extremists had assassinated the popular Tunisian labor leader Farhat Hached, a staunch nationalist whom many Moroccans greatly admired. The Istiqlal immediately called for a general strike, and the working masses of Casablanca flooded the streets to protest against France's colonial policies. On 6 December, unable to control an angry crowd in the slum *Carrières centrales*, French troops opened fire on the unarmed demonstrators and killed hundreds of them. Resident General Augustin Guillaume subsequently declared that "the true persons at fault were those who, through a criminal propaganda of excitation, had sent a misled and fanaticized mass out into the street."[1] The protectorate authorities then banned the Istiqlal, shut down its two newspapers, and put several nationalist leaders on trial for having allegedly incited the riots. Facing this unprecedented wave of repression, the Moroccan nationalists decided to reach out to a group of sympathetic intellectuals in Paris with the aim of bringing the brutal actions of the colonial police to the attention of the French public. Their efforts immediately bore fruit.

On 17 January 1953, the newly minted Nobel laureate François Mauriac used his weekly column in the conservative daily *Le Figaro* to denounce the conduct of the security forces during the so-called Casablanca riots.[2] An eye-witness account by a group of nuns living in the Carrières centrales provided the basis for his article, which questioned the moral legitimacy of French colonialism in Morocco and called on "all Christians . . . of the French Union and the metropole, to force themselves to confront this racism born out of acquisitiveness and fear, which gives birth to collective crimes."[3] An austere man deeply devoted to his Christian faith, Mauriac counted among the best-known French intellectuals of his time, and the bold stance taken by such an outspoken conservative immediately caught the attention of his compatriots. His status as a prominent Catholic gave his statements additional weight that anticolonial critics from the political left lacked. Mauriac's articles, soon to be followed by several more, awakened the French public, which began to debate the future of the protectorate for the first time.

What might have seemed like an emotional outburst by an outraged individual actually resulted from many years of Moroccan nationalist activism that had begun in the wake of the liberation of Paris in August 1944. The leaders of the Istiqlal dedicated a substantial amount of the party's resources to the campaign in the metropole, inspired by their own anticolonial activities in the French capital as young students during the interwar period. The nationalists effectively brought their demands to the attention of the elites of the Fourth Republic with help from the steadily growing local Moroccan community. Their impressive skills at creating personal relationships with prominent public figures proved pivotal to their success once again, as they adroitly expanded their network of supporters among journalists, intellectuals, and politicians. Critical discussions of Morocco's colonial status proliferated in the French media by 1953 as ever more French citizens questioned the protectorate's future. The colonial lobby's grip on public opinion suddenly began to unravel. By the fall of 1955, the National Assembly voted overwhelmingly in support of negotiations with a newly formed Moroccan government under the auspices of Sultan Mohammed ben Youssef.

Central to the Moroccan advocacy campaign inside the metropole was the *Bureau de documentation et information du Parti de l'Istiqlal*, which the nationalists founded in March 1947. It quickly emerged as a pivotal center of nationalist activism, despite the difficult political and economic situation in postwar France. The members—predominantly university students—of the nationalist movement's second office abroad stood in constant contact with their colleagues in both Morocco and Egypt, thereby underlining the transnational character of the Moroccan struggle for independence. Moreover, they reached out to the international diplomats attending the annual sessions of the UN General Assembly, which took place in Paris in 1948 and 1951. Despite their best efforts, colonial officials failed to halt the Moroccans' subversive activities. While the members of Maktab al-Maghrib al-'Arabi in Cairo struggled to make their case heard in the Arab world, the success of the Istiqlalis in the French capital underlined the tremendous possibilities inherent in their networked approach to anticolonial activism.

THE FOURTH REPUBLIC

In order to situate the history of the Moroccan campaign in Paris within its proper context, we first need to look at the political situation inside the metropole. A new generation of politicians had replaced the discredited elites of the collaborationist Vichy regime following the end of the German occupation in the fall of 1944.[4] But the Fourth Republic displayed the same symptoms of instability that had contributed to its precursor's collapse. (It witnessed no less than twenty-one different heads of government in only twelve years.) The political establishment was torn between the socialist *Section Française de l'Internationale Ouvrière* (SFIO), the Christian Democratic *Mouvement Républicain Populaire* (MRP), and the conservative *Rassemblement du Peuple Français* (RPF). It was only the shared fear of the Stalinist *Parti Communiste Français* (PCF) that united these parties.[5]

France's relationship with its colonies remained one of the most pressing issues occupying all postwar governments. The stability of the French empire faced numerous challenges, such as the beginning of the Indochina War in 1946 and the nationalist uprising in Madagascar in 1947; the outbreak of the Algerian Revolution in 1954 would eventually bring the colonial problem to the doorstep of the metropole.[6] The constitution of 1946 sought to contain this global upsurge of anticolonialism and thus established the French Union, which replaced the empire's administrative framework with an association of "supposedly equal peoples."[7] But the document, rather than signifying, as its supporters claimed, a "revolutionary change in French colonial policy" or "the crown of the history of France whose qualities of humanity and universality have been the source of her greatness" was a thinly disguised attempt to preserve the country's overseas possessions in the face of the increasing restlessness among the subject populations.[8] Although Morocco could not be forced into the French Union due to its legal status as a nominally independent state under French "protection," the government in Paris nonetheless pressured Sultan Mohammed ben Youssef to join it.

Paris quickly reemerged as a world center of thought and debate during this tumultuous period as numerous politically committed intellectuals entered the public stage.[9] Jean-Paul Sartre, Simone de Beauvoir, Albert Camus, and others held discussion circles in the university district *Quartier latin*. The French press also experienced a revival after years of censorship under the Vichy regime—*Le Monde* became the vanguard of a new type of newspaper dedicated to high journalistic standards independent of parochial political interests; the emerging Catholic Left published *Esprit* and *Témoignage Chrétien*; and Claude Bourdet founded the weekly *L'Observateur* in 1950, which constituted a forum for intellectuals critical of French colonialism.[10] Moreover, magazines like *Étudiants Anticolonialistes* or *Présence Africaine* provided venues for non-European intellectuals such as Samir Amin or Aimé Cesaire to actively participate in the political debates taking place in the French capital.[11] The vibrant intellectual scene and media landscape in France thus provided a unique opportunity for the Moroccans to extend their efforts to the metropole. The presence of a large number of their compatriots also helped.

THE MOROCCAN COMMUNITY IN PARIS

France had become home to a significant Moroccan community following the arrival of the first workers during World War I; French officials estimated the total number of Moroccans residing in the larger Paris region to range between five thousand and ten thousand by 1946. This group consisted predominantly of industrial workers living as a lumpenproletariat under miserable conditions.[12] Many of them had joined the *Confédération générale du travail* (CGT), since the left-wing labor union was the only organization actively fighting for their economic interests.[13] The Moroccan laborers regularly held public meetings to discuss politics, although a condescending French observer doubted that many of them truly understood the meaning of "the Atlantic Charter," the "aspirations of the Arab countries," and other abstract terms under discussion.[14] A miniscule cohort of less than two dozen students still resided in Paris as well. Moreover, a group of businessmen had arrived since the 1930s, some of whom accumulated huge fortunes under the German occupation. According to a meticulously researched sociological study by French army officer Roger Maneville, "The North African merchants constitute the bourgeoisie of the Muslim community . . . and their influence among [their] coreligionists is . . . considerable."[15]

The leadership of the Istiqlal quickly became aware of the potential resources that the Moroccan community in Paris could provide to the national cause. The students constituted the nationalist vanguard in the metropole since many of them had already become politicized through their memberships in the *Association des étudiants musulmans nord-africains* (AEMNA), which had served as a clearinghouse for anticolonial ideas in the French capital since 1927.[16] Now they joined the Independence Party and soon became so absorbed in politics that Captain Maneville wondered whether "classifying newspapers clippings . . . and holding . . . secret meetings . . . did not absorb most of their energy to the detriment of their exams."[17] The sultan as well as the Istiqlal provided many of them with generous stipends in order to benefit from their youthful zeal; in return the students converted the local Moroccan working class to the nationalist cause, created contacts among French journalists, and distributed nationalist pamphlets.[18] The party leaders appreciated their contributions to the advocacy campaign, but they also hoped that the students would eventually form a vanguard of native technocrats, willing to put their skills at the disposal of the party upon their return to Morocco.

Several of the students stand out for their commitment to the nationalist cause. One of them was Mehdi Ben Aboud from Salé, who had come to France in 1941 to study medicine on a scholarship administered by the

French authorities. Having previously lived in Montpellier, Tours, and Lille, he was well connected at universities across France. He also served as the president of the AEMNA for a while and helped organize Moroccan students in the Paris region on behalf of the Istiqlal. He ultimately returned to Morocco after completing his studies in the spring of 1950 to work as a physician and join the leadership circle of the party.[19] His replacement was Abderrahman Youssoufi, who quickly became "one of the most effective activists of the Istiqlal" in France before opening a law office in Tangier in 1952.[20] The third leading activist was Abderrahim Bouabid, who—despite his young age—had been a cosigner of the independence manifesto and had subsequently spent more than twelve months in prison. He dedicated himself to labor issues during his years as a law student, and upon his return to Morocco in 1949, he became responsible for organizing the working class of Casablanca.[21] He also served as the editor in chief of the new Francophone weekly *al-Istiqlal* when it first appeared in October 1951. One of his French acquaintances would later recall how Bouabid "conducted . . . propaganda in French political and intellectual circles with this poise and charm reputedly reserved for aristocrats."[22]

The most prolific organizer for the Istiqlal Party, however, was Ahmed Alaoui, who remained in Paris until late 1955. Born in Fez and remotely related to the royal family, he had come to France in 1940 to study medicine but failed to complete his degree. He joined the Istiqlal in January 1944 and soon became one of the most efficient networkers in the French capital. Alaoui remained a highly controversial figure inside the Moroccan community— some of his colleagues described him as self-aggrandizing and unreliable, and the leadership of the Istiqlal repeatedly scolded him for violating party discipline. Yet despite his undeniable shortcomings, Alaoui was an eloquent and elegant young man, who skillfully used his charm to make an impressive array of contacts among the elites of French society. For this reason, he would continue to play a prominent role in Paris until Morocco's independence.[23]

The Istiqlalis also benefited from a small number of successful Moroccan businessmen who bankrolled their campaign in France. The most prominent financer was Hajj al-Hadi Diouri, a merchant from Fez who had made a small fortune selling Moroccan artisanal goods and was rumored to have collaborated extensively with the Nazis during the occupation.[24] A French observer described him as "devilishly clever, . . . a puritan, the *éminence grisé* of the Paris Mosque," whose regular contributions to numerous charitable causes had given him an "indisputable prestige among the Moroccan community of the capital."[25] When Sidi Mohammed ben Youssef came to France to be awarded the *Croix de la Libération* by Charles de Gaulle in the summer of 1946, Diouri accompanied the monarch to all official receptions. A "fervent nationalist," his main job for the Istiqlal consisted of collecting donations and organizing the finances of the party.[26] His unofficial role as a leader of the Moroccan community in Paris as well as his personal dedication to the Moroccan cause made Hajj Diouri a pivotal player in the Istiqlal's advocacy campaign.

The nationalist activism in the French capital became extraordinarily effective due to the well-established local Moroccan community, and the zealous students proved especially vital to the efforts inside the metropole. Although the Istiqlalis organized their efforts in France without the help of the PNR, news of their activities always found an enthusiastic audience inside the Spanish zone. As early as October 1946, a newspaper published in Tetouan announced the existence of "an amazing group of North African activists in Paris who are in permanent contact with French parties, the press and the numerous international delegations attending the [Paris] Peace Conference."[27] As the article reminded its readers, "One of the most important goals of the nationalist [movement] is to internationalize the Moroccan question."[28] No location seemed more suitable in this regard than the French capital, even though the city was still suffering under the legacy of World War II.

ORGANIZING THE ISTIQLAL IN PARIS

The first major step toward the political organization of the Moroccan community occurred in the spring of 1946, when a group of students and merchants founded the *Association marocaine de bienfaisance* (Moroccan Welfare Association, AMB). Mohammed ben Youssef attended its official inauguration during his visit to Paris three months later, and the organization thus came to be known as *Dar al-Sultan*. Located in the working-class suburb of Gennevilliers, it offered a range of services to the Moroccan community:

stage plays and a radio provided entertainment, an imam from the Paris
mosque taught Arabic classes for children, medical students delivered basic
health-care services, and volunteers assisted new arrivals looking for housing
and work.[29] The association was a barely disguised attempt to draw the la-
boring masses into the orbit of the nationalist movement.[30] Students under
the leadership of Bouabid spent many hours of their spare time at the association; fundraisers for patriotic causes—like striking dockworkers in Casablanca—generated not only additional income but also new members for the
Istiqlal.[31]

From the viewpoint of the nationalist press, the AMB epitomized the
almost sacred character of the anticolonial campaign inside the metropole.
"This association was the starting point for increasing the contacts between
us and the workers," *al-'Alam* explained to its readers.[32] The volunteers also
engaged in direct political indoctrination. According to another article in
the nationalist daily, "Some of the students . . . hold educational lessons and
cultural lectures among the workers residing in the Paris area in order to instruct them about their duties towards themselves and their nation."[33] The
Istiqlal sought to establish itself as a truly mass-based political organization
by spreading the nationalist message among a social class hitherto largely untouched by modern political ideologies. The welfare association's reach even
extended beyond France's borders. "It is like the heart of the body, because
we have additional branches in all parts of Paris and its suburbs, in the most
important French industrial cities as well as in Belgium, Switzerland and
even Germany," one young activist pointed out.[34]

The Residency in Rabat followed the AMB's activities with great concern and eventually persuaded the Ministry of the Interior to shut it down
in July 1951.[35] The police demanded that "no politics should take place" at
the association[36]—"the member[s] of the Istiqlal Party or the students" especially were no longer to direct its activities.[37] Several nationalists ultimately
agreed to resign from its board following lengthy negotiations with the authorities. Renamed *Oeuvre marocaine de bienfaisance* (OMB), it reopened its
doors one year later and continued to serve as the center of Moroccan communal life in the Paris region. But apparently the attempts to depoliticize the
association had not really succeeded. A report compiled by the *Sureté nationale* in 1955 claimed that the OMB "had not ceased to demonstrate its anti-

French character through propaganda, collections to aid terrorism in Morocco, and the ultra-nationalist activities of its principal leaders."[38] Although perhaps surprising at first, the decision to tolerate the organization did make sense from the standpoint of the local authorities: the religious conservatism preached by the Istiqlal seemed perfectly suitable to immunize Moroccan workers against the specter of subversive communist indoctrination, even if it unnerved colonial officials.

Operating a welfare association on the outskirts of the French capital certainly did not suffice to conduct an effective anticolonial campaign inside the metropole. At first, the Istiqlalis rented a room in the center of the city as a provisional office. But thanks to a generous donation by Hajj Diouri, they soon relocated their *Bureau de documentation et d'information du Parti de l'Istiqlal* (BDIPI) to the Avenue Kleiber—situated between the Eiffel Tower and the Champs-Élysées—in March 1947.[39] This permanent representation in the affluent sixteenth arrondissement increased the party's prestige, and its location provided geographic proximity to the Palais de Chaillot that hosted the General Assembly two times before the inauguration of the UN's permanent headquarters in New York in 1952. The staff of the BDIPI immediately began to print brochures in order to enlighten the French public about the demands of the nationalist movement. Written in a dry academic French, these publications provided details about topics such as the "French administration," "public liberties," and "public education" in Morocco, and they usually finished with a reminder that "the only solution to the problem . . . of Morocco . . . is its independence."[40]

In the fall of 1947, the Istiqlal also opened the *Foyer des étudiants marocains*, which provided room and board to needy students. A large portrait of Sidi Mohammed in the common hall reminded all visitors that the monarch had made a significant financial contribution to its establishment.[41] Conveniently located in the Rue Serpente in the heart of the Quartier Latin and less than seven hundred meters away from Jean-Paul Sartre's favorite coffeehouse, it exposed the young Moroccans to the lively intellectual scene of postwar Paris.[42] The inhabitants of the Foyer des étudiants regularly organized rallies to mobilize the local Moroccan community.[43] During a reception arranged for a group of recent high school graduates visiting Paris, one of the student leaders declared, "It always pleases us to welcome Moroccan visitors to . . . the club of the students of the Istiqlal Party, especially if they are young activists like you who will soon be responsible for their country."[44] The Foyer des étudiants was one of three centers of anticolonial activism in the French capital.

The most important event bringing together the Moroccan community of the larger Paris metropolitan region was the annual celebration of Throne Day. In 1946, the Istiqlalis organized the first commemoration of this event, which not only "thousands of businessmen, workers, and students" attended but also Arab diplomats and French government officials.[45] Even a former resident general of Tunisia, Armand Guillon, joined the festivities.[46] After an inspiring live performance of classical Andalusian music, the attendees listened attentively as the renowned Orientalist scholar Louis Massignon gave a short speech in Arabic and poet Jean Amrouche read a letter by the famous writer Albert Camus in which the future Nobel laureate reminded the audience that "Moroccans and Frenchmen . . . conduct the same struggle . . . to live in a world of peace."[47] One of the student leaders had the honor of delivering the text of the sultan's official speech, which the royal palace had transmitted from Rabat prior to the event. With a Moroccan flag and a French tricolor prominently displayed side by side, the festivities underlined the nationalists' desire to project an image of trans-Mediterranean friendship. In order to substantiate this message, the Istiqlal repeatedly sent party representatives from Morocco to reach out directly to the French public.

MOROCCAN VISITORS

The nationalists' anticolonial campaign in the metropole had already begun on VE Day, when the Istiqlal congratulated "the brave Allied armies" on their victory over "the spirit of intolerance and oppression."[48] In an open letter to "the people of France" published eight months later, they listed the sacrifices made by the Moroccan population during World War II on behalf of the metropole and announced the sending of a "delegation . . . to enter into contact with the people of France" regarding the "emancipation of the Moroccan people."[49] With the help of Ahmed Alaoui and Mehdi Ben Aboud, the Istiqlalis distributed their appeal among the elites of the Fourth Republic—a left-wing newspaper even printed its complete text.[50] Yet the overall echo remained feeble. Although French officials seemed relieved that the nationalists had published their petition only in an insignificant publication "unknown to the majority of Frenchmen," they also worried about the long-term impact on French-Moroccan relations of this "rather violent" attack against the protectorate.[51]

In the fall of 1946, the Istiqlal dispatched its first official delegation to Paris; Omar Benabdeljalil, Abdelkarim Benjelloun, and Ahmed al-Hamiani sought to present their demands to the French government.[52] The local Moroccan community provided them with an enthusiastic reception, and the nationalist businessmen organized a banquet to celebrate their arrival.[53] The delegates also spent considerable time with the students to plan future campaigns. Anticolonial activities had occurred rather haphazardly so far, but that was about to change. This increasing professionalization included a couple of publications outlining the history of the nationalist movement and its demands for Moroccan independence. Encompassing about twenty pages each, they contained all the necessary information anyone interested would need to understand the delegation's aims.[54] "Its principal mission consists of attracting the attention of the French public to the urgency of the Moroccan question [and to] refute the biased remarks of those who hold strong opinions of a sometimes-unconcealed malevolence against the Istiqlal," one brochure awkwardly explained to the reader.[55]

The Moroccan delegates met with influential French politicians during their stay in Paris. Omar Benabdeljalil's brother Friar Jean, a convert to Catholicism, introduced them to members of the MRP, who displayed an honest interest in the demands of their Moroccan interlocutors. The leader of the PCF also received the Moroccan delegation to discuss the situation in North Africa. The Istiqlalis even managed to meet two members of the French government as well as high-ranking officials at the Ministry of Foreign Affairs.[56] Finally, they held a press conference, which more than fifty French journalists attended. In a declaration read out to the gathered press corps, they proclaimed that the nationalist movement did not oppose "the legitimate interests of the French" but that it wanted to replace the protectorate with a "voluntary treaty of alliance, which would turn the French . . . into true friends and genuine advisers."[57] Responding to questions posed by the journalists, the Istiqlalis provided details about their plans for a future "modern

and democratic" Morocco under the guidance of its "wise" sultan, "the symbol of its unity."[58] An officer at the US embassy in Paris noted that the Moroccan delegates had "furnished some interesting details regarding the program
of their party."[59] News of the delegation's visit traveled fast and eventually
found its way onto the pages of the Belgian press, although French newspapers still showed limited interest in the Moroccan liberation struggle.[60] A
few months later, though, another Moroccan visitor from Tangier received
substantially more attention.

Allal al-Fassi arrived in Paris in April 1947 "to defend the Moroccan
case."[61] As an important proponent of Islamic reformism, French officials
had always portrayed him as a "xenophobic" religious extremist unwilling
to adapt to the modern character of Western civilization. It thus became extremely important for the nationalists to present their prominent leader as
a voice of moderation. Like others before him, he tried to be received by
Georges Bidault, but the foreign minister displayed no inclination to meet
al-Fassi. Instead, the za'im appealed directly to French civil society. During a speech before former members of the *résistance*, he praised his hosts for
"having preserved the principles of freedom, equality, and fraternity . . . by
standing up to the cancer of Nazism." For this reason, he told the audience,
"You alone, Ladies and Gentlemen, can appreciate the spirit which makes us
fight for freedom . . . and the independence of our country."[62] With even the
leader of the party's Islamic-conservative wing capable of charming a French
audience, the Istiqlal's advocacy campaign in the metropole clearly seemed
poised for success.

Allal al-Fassi also sought to consolidate the local efforts in consultations with the nationalist students. Moreover, he met with Arab diplomats and spoke to the members of the AEMNA.[63] Accompanied by Mehdi
Ben Aboud and Abderrahim Bouabid, al-Fassi even undertook a brief ex-
cursion to Lyon to organize a nationalist cell in France's second most important city.[64] But the highlight of his stay was a huge rally at the AMB
that introduced the za'im to the local Moroccan community. On 27 April
1947, a crowd of over four thousand North Africans—including the Tunisian
Habib Bourguiba and the Algerian Messali Hajj—offered him an enthusiastic welcome in a hall decorated with the flags of all three Maghribi territories. After a short introduction by Ahmed Alaoui, al-Fassi recited the open-

ing verse of the Qur'an, praised the sultan's recent speech in Tangier, and spoke "calmly" about his own vision for an independent "Arab Maghrib."[65] The meeting ended with the singing of nationalist songs and the distribution of brochures.[66] A few years later, in an internal report summarizing years of nationalist activism in the French capital, a police official grudgingly admitted that "the Istiqlal has numerous supporters among the Moroccan immigrants in the Paris region."[67]

By looking at the flurry of activities surrounding the visits of the Istiqlal's initial delegation and of Allal al-Fassi, we can obtain insights into the party's strategy on the exterior. The Moroccan nationalists repeatedly presented their case directly to the general public in order to gain its acceptance. But more importantly, they made an array of personal contacts among leading members of French society in order to turn them into brokers for their cause. A profound understanding of French society as well as a considerable dose of pragmatism informed their activities in France—they did not hesitate to work with individuals from across the political spectrum if they deemed it beneficial to the larger cause. Their decision to structure their campaign as a social network laid the groundwork for their ultimate successes, although that would take a few more years to become apparent.

Central to these efforts was the conciliatory tone used by the nationalists to appeal to their French interlocutors. In a memorandum presented in January 1947, Ahmed Balafrej called on the French government to abolish "a regime of tutelage incompatible with its dignity [and] history" and to grant independence to the Moroccan people who had "generously spilled [their] blood on the battlefields" of World War II.[68] The Istiqlalis repeatedly declared that they did not resent France but only its oppressive colonial policies in North Africa. Even Resident General Eirik Labonne had to admit that "nobody can be insensitive to this part of the argumentation by the nationalists, who evoke the spirit of the résistance, the principles of 1789, the human dignity, the (universal) conscience, the Charter of the UN, and the constitution of the new Republic" before declaring it his "goal" to "reconcile these principles and the Moroccan reality and to adapt them progressively there."[69] The Moroccans' understanding of French culture and their quite honest admiration of it were major advantages in their attempts to win over their hosts' hearts and minds. By flattering their colonial masters, they came to be seen as a grateful subject people steeped in the republican tradition and potentially worthy of self-rule.

Another pivotal aspect of the nationalists' anticolonial discourse was the figure of the sultan as both the incarnation of the Moroccan nation and the wise leader of his people. During a speech at the Throne Day celebration in 1946, Omar Benabdeljalil portrayed the monarch as "the symbol of national unity" while calling for an end to the colonial regime in order to transform "the French [into] our true friends and advisors."[70] Such public associations with the monarchy allowed the nationalists to legitimize their movement, since Sidi Mohammed quite literally embodied the last remnants of Moroccan sovereignty. Moreover, the idealized image of a sagacious Arab ruler leading "the reform of Moroccan society" and "the struggle against ignorance" was highly suitable for capturing the attention of Western audiences. In the short term, this alliance with the sultan proved beneficial to their campaign, although it would eventually also contribute to the defeat of the Istiqlal following independence in 1956.

It should thus not surprise us that trips to France by members of the royal family became events of extraordinary importance to the anticolonial campaign. When Crown Prince Hassan came to Paris in August 1949, he visited both the AMB and the AEMNA. According to al-ʿAlam, "The Moroccan community spared no efforts to present its sympathies to the prince . . . and the Arab brothers joined to demonstrate Arab unity during festivities at the Paris Mosque."[71] At a large gathering held at a private event hall, Hassan singled out the students in the audience, reminded them of the importance of their "embassy" in the metropole, and then read a short greeting he had brought from his father. (At a different event one year later, the prince would describe the students as the "representatives of [the] nation, in this capital and other cities of France.")[72] The royal praise excited the attendees, who responded to his remarks "with cheers coming from the bottom of their hearts."[73]

When Sidi Mohammed visited France in October 1950 to discuss plans by the French government to reform the protectorate regime, great excitement gripped the Moroccan community. Besides conducting his official business, the sultan hosted a tea reception for the members of the Bureau du Parti de l'Istiqlal before inspecting the facilities of the AMB.[74] He awarded Hajj Diouri the *Ouissam Alaouite,* the highest honor of the state, thus demonstrating his appreciation of the business community's efforts on behalf of the patriotic cause.[75] Abderrahman Youssoufi eloquently expressed the emotions felt by many of his compatriots during a huge rally held in the monarch's honor. "Our hearts overflow with sincere thanks . . . and pride before our Arab and Muslim brothers and our French friends . . . at this appearance of the father of the Moroccan renaissance, the democratic king, the symbol of Moroccan unity," the student activist proclaimed before the gathered crowd.[76] Many in Paris took notice of this event. Even the US ambassador in France remarked on "the delirious enthusiasm of the Moroccan people for their returning sovereign."[77] The nationalist movement had established the French capital as the third center of its transnational anticolonial activism despite the fact that the general public still remained largely oblivious to its demands.

PARIS AS A HUB

The nationalists also used the city as a hub for anticolonial activism across Europe and North Africa. Members of the Bureau du Parti de l'Istiqlal regularly shared their most recent publications with their colleagues in Morocco; in return, they received the latest copies of the nationalist press, which they disseminated in Paris.[78] Moroccans in cities such as Marseilles stayed in contact with the cell in Paris and organized public celebrations of holidays— both religious and secular—that brought together the local Maghribi community; students from Sri Lanka, Indochina, and even France attended the 1951 Throne Day festivities in Toulouse.[79] When the sultan and his entourage passed through Bordeaux on their way to Paris in the fall of 1950, the enthusiastic welcome organized by the local nationalists angered the police enough to arrest two students for having allegedly disturbed the peace.[80] According to the Residency's representation in the French capital, the *Office du Maroc,* even the indoctrination of the Moroccan working class served a transnational purpose: upon their return home, many laborers "carried the message of the party to all the tribes of the Sous and the Anti-Atlas," rural regions hitherto largely untouched by the spread of nationalist ideology.[81]

The activists in Paris also traveled to other countries; Ahmed Alaoui, especially, became an itinerant spokesperson for the nationalist cause at events such as the Arab Student Congress in The Hague and an anti-imperialist convention in Zagreb.[82] When the members of the UN Human Rights Committee in Geneva returned to their seats after a short break one afternoon in May 1950, they discovered an official statement by the Istiqlal on their tables—Alaoui had entered the building and distributed the propaganda material with the help of an Arab diplomat while the delegates were enjoying their coffee.[83] He also attended a meeting of the Congress of Peoples against Imperialism in London in February 1951.[84] Besides providing opportunities for meetings with local journalists and officials at the Foreign Office, the trip served as the perfect chance to network with anticolonial activists from across the British Empire.[85] London's centrality in transcolonial circuits of migration made it an ideal location for disseminating the Moroccan nationalist message beyond the borders of Europe. Commenting on Alaoui's attempts to internationalize the Moroccan problem, a French official acknowledged that the impact of his activities "can be perceived . . . in all the Arab countries and even the East Indies."[86]

Colonial officials in Rabat had grown so worried about this flurry of activities undertaken by the Istiqlal in Paris and beyond that they decided to undermine the nationalist campaign through counterpropaganda. For this task they chose Mohammed b. Mokhtar Temsamani, who had worked for the BBC and the Free French Forces in London during the war years.[87] Fluent in five different languages and imbued with unlimited self-confidence, he seemed like an ideal spokesman for the French cause. Beginning in May 1951, Temsamani sought to combat the activities of the members of the BDIPI.[88] The growing sympathy among French politicians toward the nationalists especially worried him.[89] After learning that the MRP had invited the Moroccans to attend its party congress, the French counterpropagandist met with his old friend Maurice Schumann, the party's former president, to inform him about the "extremist" nature of the independence activists. He also warned the renowned diplomat and outspoken Zionist René Cassin about the threat that the nationalist movement allegedly posed to Morocco's Jewry.[90]

Temsamani then traveled to Great Britain, where he drew on his media contacts to defend French rule in North Africa. He reached out directly to the British elites during a talk before the distinguished members of the influential think tank Chatham House. Nina Epton—an important participant in the nationalists' advocacy network—attended the presentation but apparently refrained from asking any tough questions.[91] Inspired by Temsamani's speech, former government minister Sir Ivan Thomas traveled to Morocco and subsequently published a "very favorable" series of articles in the *New Chronicle*.[92] The French ambassador in London himself praised Temsamani's efforts and emphasized that "the contacts he . . . made . . . in London during the War . . . give him access to circles susceptible to the propaganda of the Istiqlal and not much inclined to be affected by arguments made by the French."[93] But even Temsamani ultimately proved incapable of derailing the Moroccans' highly sophisticated campaign. As he admitted in a report to his superiors in Rabat, "The agents of the Istiqlal have established numerous contacts with the English press and [those] dealing with Arab questions. . . . The voice of the Istiqlal is widely disseminated."[94] Apparently, nothing could stop the anticolonial activists abroad.

LOBBYING THE UNITED NATIONS

The nationalists' activities in Paris aimed not only at the local Moroccan community but also at the delegates attending the UN General Assembly, which convened two times in the Palais de Chaillot—located opposite the Eiffel Tower—before permanently settling in New York.[95] In order to support the members of its Paris office in 1948, the Istiqlal dispatched Mehdi Ben Barka, whose role as the party's chief organizer had made the young mathematician an influential figure. With the help of a sympathetic diplomatic delegation, he managed to obtain a press card that granted him access to the UN premises.[96] Meanwhile, in Cairo, Allal al-Fassi informed Abderrahman Azzam Pasha that "the Arab representatives could obtain all the necessary statistics [about the situation in Morocco] by contacting the Bureau de documentation et d'information du Parti de l'Istiqlal."[97] Together with their colleagues from Tunisia and Algeria, the Istiqlalis submitted a letter to Secretary General Trygve Lie in which they sought to "respectfully attract the attention of the UN to the gravity of the situation in North Africa created by the imperialist policies of France and Spain."[98] For the moment, however, their appeal fell on deaf ears. The Moroccans could not yet realistically expect any diplomatic support as long as the Arab League remained preoccupied with the Arab-Israeli War. But when the UN returned to the French capital three years later, the situation had changed dramatically.

As the General Assembly was reconvening in Paris in the fall of 1951, the Moroccans were ready for a diplomatic fight.[99] Allal al-Fassi had visited numerous Middle Eastern capitals before the Arab delegations traveled to the French capital; explaining the reason behind his journey during a press conference in Beirut, the za'im declared that the Istiqlalis needed the assistance of the Arab states, because they "had decided to submit the Moroccan question to the UN during its session next month in Paris."[100] In a letter to Azzam Pasha, he confirmed that "all parties are cooperating in conformity with the Tangier pact" and went on to explain that "this matter is urgent and the Arab states must get the votes . . . at the UN meeting in Paris."[101] The staff of Maktab al-Maghrib tirelessly lobbied the Arab League to finally present the Moroccan case before the General Assembly. Eventually they succeeded. Pressured by its secretary general, the member states did indeed send a telegram to Trygve Lie in support of "the Moroccans' right to independence."[102] Other Muslim nations soon joined their demands.[103]

The nationalist press praised the League's "very important decision," because it underlined Morocco's status as part of the Arab world.[104] Victory nonetheless remained uncertain. "It is not said that the battle between truth and falsehood at the UN will end with a victory of truth right away," al-'Alam cautioned its readers, "but either way it is a great episode in the history of our national struggle during which the world will listen closely to our voice."[105] Another editorial celebrated the fact that "the case of Morocco . . . has been presented on the international stage" as an important "phase in the country's struggle against colonialism."[106] The General Assembly's willingness to discuss the issue was an incredible victory independent of the final outcome. Apparently, the French government shared this assessment. During a debate on the topic in the Trusteeship Council, the infuriated French diplomats left the room under loud protests against what they claimed was an outside interference in an internal affair.[107] An annoyed US diplomat noted that "French sensitivity regarding Morocco has nearly reached a psychopathic stage."[108]

The members of the BDIPI organized an especially lavish celebration of Throne Day to showcase the widespread support for independence among their compatriots; diplomats from as far away as Mexico, Denmark, Czechoslovakia, and Siam gathered in the presence of thousands of Moroccans and their French supporters to listen to patriotic speeches. Printed English-language summaries were available to those not fluent in Arabic or French.[109] The third session of the General Assembly also created great excitement back home as dozens of civic associations sent telegrams to the UN delegations in Paris to demand their country's independence.[110] With Arab politicians such as Mohammed Fadil al-Jamali calling for an end to the protectorate by emphasizing the countless sacrifices made by North African soldiers during World War II, the French government had to defend its record in Morocco before an international audience for the first time.[111]

One question lingered in everyone's minds as the debates on the Moroccan question went on behind closed doors: would the United States continue to back France in the dispute over its North African colonies? Confronted by a Moroccan journalist, the head of the US delegation avoided giving a direct answer ("I do not know") before talking about his country's friendship with the Arab world in general terms.[112] But in internal memos, the Department of State admitted that it prioritized "maintain[ing] stability in Morocco so that [it] can make the maximum contribution to Western security."[113] Because of the American air and naval bases in the country, "the threat of political instability in Morocco has increased almost in direct ratio to the increase in our strategic interest."[114] The only solution seemed to be a "middle-of-the-road policy toward that area," which included "redoubl[ing] our efforts to get the French to adopt a program of political reforms in Morocco which will meet the legitimate demands of the Moroccans."[115] At that moment, though, "the Moroccans [were] not prepared to assume the responsibilities which would result from immediate independence."[116] With the world's most important country still backing the colonizer, the outcome of the diplomatic debates in Paris seemed obvious.

The General Assembly ultimately voted to postpone the debate on the status of Morocco for another year. Although not entirely surprised, the nationalists could hardly hide their frustration; in a telegram to Trygve Lie, Allal al-Fassi showed himself "astonished" about the result since "the Moroccan people . . . expect the UN to listen to their voice and acknowledge their demands."[117] But they soon realized that they had nonetheless gained a "moral victory" and therefore interpreted the proceedings as a sign of "solidarity between the Islamic, Arabic, Asian, and African states in their struggle against colonialism." Twenty countries had voted in favor of the Arab League's resolution ("representing a total of one-third of the human population"), whereas twenty-three had opposed it, and no fewer than sixteen delegates had given speeches on behalf of the rights of the Moroccan people on the assembly floor.[118] For the first time, the "French colonial mind [had to] stand in the prisoner's dock while being interrogated by an international organization."[119] Even al-Fassi eventually acknowledged the debate's "[positive] impact on our propaganda . . . as the pillars of the General Assembly trembled under the speeches of the Arabs and Orientals."[120] The very process was a great success for the nationalist movement despite having fallen short of the desired outcome. Yet it also meant that the Moroccans needed to intensify their anticolonial campaign if they wanted to ultimately succeed.

THE FRENCH SUPPORTERS

The Istiqlalis sought the help of well-respected public figures to speak out on their behalf in order to spread their message before the French public. One of these brokers was Pierre Parent, who had settled on a small farm in Morocco in 1916 after losing his left arm on the battlefields of World War I. He had served as the French envoy negotiating the surrender of Abdelkarim in 1926 and as president of the influential veterans group *Inter-fédération nord-africaine des Victimes de la guerre*; due to his support for the French résistance during World War II, he even got elected to the constituent assembly of the Fourth Republic in the fall of 1946.[121] Parent's experience as one of the first French pioneers in Morocco, his position as a center-left advocate for the rights of the working class, and his status as a disabled veteran made him one of the most respected Frenchmen inside the protectorate. His anticommunist stance also endeared him to American observers, who described Parent as "irreproachable from every moral point of view."[122] Parent symbolized the ideal citizen for a country seeking to reconstitute itself after four years of devastating warfare and collaboration with Nazi Germany.

Pierre Parent had taken a lively interest in native society since his arrival in Morocco; as early as 1933, he published an essay entitled *Les Marocains et nous* in which he urged his countrymen to improve their relations with the local population.[123] After World War II, Parent also wrote a series of small brochures in order to expose the Residency's "dictatorial" policies.[124] He regularly sent copies of his publications to the Bureau du Parti de l'Istiqlal, whose members distributed them widely as propaganda material.[125] Even many Englishmen had read the anticolonial settler's writings and used them to attack French rule in North Africa, as Mohammed Temsamani realized during his trip to London.[126] Pierre Parent's activities provided significant legitimacy to the claims of the Moroccan nationalist movement in the metropole. After hearing him speak to a large group of students in the city of Lille, a French official noted, "Parent seems to me . . . much more dangerous . . . [because] he speaks well and attracts the sympathy of his audience."[127] Parent eventually became a columnist for the Francophone weekly *al-Istiqlal*, thus lending additional moral support to the vindications of the nationalists, whose "right . . . and duty" to fight for independence he wholeheartedly supported.[128]

The eminent historian Charles-André Julien, an influential member of the Socialist Party, became another important ally.[129] In January 1946, he met with two other prominent scholars—Jean Dresch and Jean Sauvaget—to help Abderrahim Bouabid draft a protest letter to the French government. The document explained that the protectorate "no longer responds to the profound wishes of the Moroccan people, who aspire to their political emancipation in accordance with the principles proclaimed by the United Nations."[130] The authors submitted it to the Ministry of Foreign Affairs after collecting the signatures of eleven other academics. In the spring of 1952, Julien and the MRP politician André de Peretti traveled to Morocco on a semiofficial mission to convince Mohammed ben Youssef to join the French Union. Upon their return, they submitted a detailed report to French president Vincent Auriol that called for drastic reforms to end the institutionalized discrimination of native Moroccans.[131] A book published by Julien one year later claimed that the protectorates in Morocco and Tunisia had "become outdated" and should be replaced by a "new treaty" based on equality.[132]

Numerous individuals from across the political spectrum also began to assist the Moroccan nationalists. These ranged from the editor of *Témoignage Chrétien*, Robert Barrat, to the Trotskyite journalist Jean Rous, a leading member of the Congress of Peoples against Imperialism.[133] Having already mentored the first generation of nationalist students in the French capital during the 1930s, the socialist lawyer Robert Longuet now founded the *Ligue de Défense du Maroc Libre* to bring together French voices opposed to colonialism. Even the highly decorated general Georges Catroux openly criticized the French protectorate regime; in November 1950, the former governor general of Algeria published an article in *Le Figaro* that called for the gradual emancipation of the North African kingdom.[134] Meanwhile, Louis Massignon and André de Peretti founded the *Comité chrétien d'entente France-Islam* as a Catholic association skeptical of colonialism.[135] Thanks to the efforts of the Istiqlal, the MRP soon invited representatives of the group to attend its annual party congress.[136] A surprised US official remarked on the Moroccan question regarding the "number of important French politicians in key positions . . . engaged in missionary work within their organizations."[137] The members of the Bureau du Parti de l'Istiqlal had laid the groundwork for their anticolonial campaign by recruiting a network of supporters among the elites of French society, but they still needed to make their case before the general public.

THE COMITÉ FRANCE-MAGHREB

The majority of Frenchmen had remained oblivious to the situation inside Morocco, but this abruptly changed with the massacre in Casablanca on 6 December 1952. The Residency reacted quickly by banning the Istiqlal Party and deporting pronationalist settlers like Pierre Parent. The French press initially limited its coverage to the reproduction of official accounts, which blamed Muslim "fanatics" for the bloodbath. But on 18 December, a group of high school teachers from Casablanca published an open letter that questioned the authorities' version of events and demanded an impartial investigation.[138] Now the nationalists' supporters inside the metropole jumped into action; within two days, Robert Barrat met François Mauriac, who had just returned from his Nobel Prize award ceremony in Stockholm.

The journalist had so far failed to recruit the prominent writer to his group of anticolonial Catholics.[139] This time was different, though. After reading an eyewitness account by a group of nuns living near the site of the massacre, Mauriac decided to speak out against the atrocities.[140]

François Mauriac published his weekly column in *Le Figaro* under the title "The Mission of the Christians in the French Union" six weeks after the so-called riots in the Moroccan port city. The novelist demanded "a clear understanding of the bloody events" and refused to accept "that we return to business as usual."[141] Encouraged by the massive media echo to his article—both positive and negative—Mauriac continued to write in various newspapers about the situation in North Africa. In one of a series of articles on Morocco, Mauriac asked his readers to "no longer think of certain young men of the Istiqlal as the enemies of France . . . but as interlocutors."[142] When Robert Barrat published a special issue of *Témoignage Chrétien* dealing with the same topic, Mauriac's contribution called on his readers to "speak out" in the face of "the crimes of history."[143] The novelist had moved from cautious criticism of the colonial authorities to a direct assault on the protectorate's legitimacy in less than two months. This development shocked many of his readers.[144] That someone with Mauriac's stature "could evoke 'crimes' and speak of 'racism' . . . regarding Morocco . . . which the good French conscience thought to be the masterpiece of colonialism . . . astounded the good, pious, and wealthy clientele of *Le Figaro*," according to his biographer.[145]

The new outspokenness of its lead columnist inspired the editorial board of *Le Figaro* to dispatch the prominent journalist Jean-Marie Garraud to find out what exactly had happened in Casablanca. Upon his return in March 1953, the newspaper published a six-part series on the general situation in Morocco, which included a long interview with Sultan Mohammed ben Youssef. The articles cautiously blamed the French side for the bloody events, concluding that the "psychosis of fear that had reigned in certain European circles" had created an "atmosphere favorable" for the "repression" that occurred in December 1952.[146] In other words, the dread of an uprising by the Muslim population had become so powerful among the settler population that it triggered the brutal overreaction by the security forces at the slightest sign of native unrest. The situation in Morocco had finally become a topic of national debate.[147]

François Mauriac's critical articles sent shock waves across the protector-ate, and many settlers responded with angry letters. The high-ranking pro-tectorate official Robert Baudouy scolded the novelist for having "written without prudence and justice," and the Casablanca-based journalist Mau-rice Eonnet reminded the Nobel laureate that the true perpetrators had been a "gang fanaticized by the troublemakers of the Istiqlal."[148] A woman from Rabat advised Mauriac to start working for a communist newspaper, because "*Le Figaro* is the most widely-read French daily in Morocco," and its recent articles had been like a "betrayal by a loved one, a perfidious friend."[149] An-other reader complained that his writings would further encourage the in-dependence struggle, because "your articles, your campaign, have primarily given unexpected support to the sultan."[150] The French press on both sides of the Mediterranean also did not hide its anger. *Paris* expressed its incredu-lity about his "monstrous statements"; *La Vigie Marocaine* found it "difficult to take François Mauriac seriously"; and the reactionary *Aspects de la France* decried "the champion of the Istiqlal," declaring that "the sultan and the Is-tiqlal are no longer placing their hope on the UN or open rebellion, but on the thousands of Mauriacs" willing to disparage their own country.[151]

But not all responses were negative. One Frenchman living in Casablanca lauded "this act of human integrity," although he asked to remain anony-mous to avoid problems with his neighbors;[152] a Catholic friar in Algeria showed himself "profoundly moved" by Mauriac's "clear understanding" of the situation in North Africa;[153] and a professor at the University of Paris thanked him for his "courage" and "perspicacity" in "challenging the official account . . . of the events in North Africa."[154] Mauriac received a number of letters from Muslims that must have been especially pleasing: a "humble Mo-roccan" from Rabat praised the writer's "noble heart," and a young national-ist from Fez informed Mauriac that his "article [had] been translated into Ar-abic in order to be well-understood by all classes of Moroccans."[155] Others expressed their "infinite thankfulness" for his "support" and confirmed that his "favorable intervention" had a "great impact among Moroccans" since it proved that they "had not been totally abandoned."[156] Even Mohammed ben Youssef sent a signed photograph to "the friend of the Muslims" to thank him for "following his generous conscience in order to preserve the Franco-Moroccan friendship."[157]

This outpouring of support convinced Mauriac to continue his campaign against France's colonial policies.[158] As the nationalist movement's British mentor Rom Landau would later remark, "Public conscience had been awakened in France."[159] A Tetouani nationalist informed his colleagues in New York that the "article published by the famous writer François Mauriac in *Le Figaro* had great repercussions here."[160] Even foreign observers commented on the public echo of his writings. According to a US diplomat in Rabat, "The series of articles . . . appearing in *Figaro* of Paris, together with the articles by François Mauriac, have stirred up a hornet's nest in the Moroccan-French press—comments have been lengthy and bitter."[161] News of his anticolonial critique also traveled to the Middle East. In order to inform Mauriac about his global impact, the members of Maktab al-Maghrib sent him a copy of a Jordanian newspaper that had praised "the greatest French writer" for "enlightening world public opinion about the damning truth."[162] The long-established colonial narrative portraying France as a benevolent benefactor seeking to uplift the native population no longer seemed tenable amid this international uproar.

What had begun with an inconspicuous column in a conservative newspaper soon enough metamorphosed into a passionate public debate.[163] On 26 January 1953, Robert Barrat organized a conference in Paris to discuss the situation in Morocco, convening scholars such as Charles-André Julien and Louis Massignon; the ever outspoken General Catroux; the famous lawyer Georges Izard; politicians, including François Mitterand and André de Peretti; and the politically engaged couple Eve and Roger Paret (a journalist for *L'Observateur* and a librarian, respectively).[164] Their condemnation of French colonial policies united them despite their diverging political and religious viewpoints. At a press conference after the meeting, the attendees announced the formation of the *Comité France-Maghreb* (CFM), which aimed to improve relations between the French and the North Africans. Moreover, they demanded an independent investigation into the bloody events in Casablanca as well as an end to the harassment of Sultan Mohammed ben Youssef by protectorate officials.

The CFM sought to "use all legal means so that the human rights principles . . . are applied, without distinction, in North Africa."[165] Its members organized public events such as a silent memorial in front of the Paris mosque on the first anniversary of Farhat Hached's assassination and a peace vigil at Notre Dame Cathedral in June 1954 in order to bring their point of view to the attention of the French public.[166] The CFM also published a news bulletin to denounce "the indifference of public opinion . . . about the situation in North Africa," but a lack of subscribers led to its discontinuation after only four issues.[167] Although sharp divergences of opinion over the outbreak of the Algerian Revolution in November 1954 caused the dissolution of the CFM soon thereafter, the association played an invaluable role by exposing the French elites to prominent voices critical of colonialism.[168] According to a CIA report from January 1954, "The Comité France-Maghreb, egged on by General Catroux and François Mauriac, is bringing pressure to bear on the Quai d'Orsay," as the French Ministry of Foreign Affairs was also known.[169] Julien later recalled that the CFM "did not have any financial means, but its members knew how to use their connections; Mauriac, for example, had a great prestige that permitted him to have contacts on the highest level."[170]

The activities of the CFM had a concrete impact on the political discourse inside the metropole by bringing the question of the Moroccan protectorate to the forefront of public attention. Robert Barrat repeatedly traveled to Morocco, where he met with colonial officials, nationalists, and the sultan.[171] Following an extended stay during the summer of 1953, Barrat published a high-profile book titled *Justice pour le Maroc*, which he dedicated to his "imprisoned Moroccan friends."[172] Even public figures not necessarily opposed to colonialism per se criticized specific French policies. In March 1953, the magazine *La Nef* published a special issue dealing with Morocco and Tunisia, which contained articles by politicians such as former government ministers Robert Schuman and Edgar Faure as well as by leading scholars such as Robert Montagne. The issue covered a wide range of opinions, but most authors called for improving the French colonial system through administrative reforms based on a combination of "benevolence" and "firmness."[173] The publication even included a brief declaration by the Moroccan nationalist movement. None of the authors deemed independence a viable solution, however.

The rise of critical voices did not confine itself to the metropole. It also included a small portion of the European settler population in Morocco. Inspired by the rapidly deteriorating situation following the deposition of Sidi Mohammed ben Youssef in September 1953, a group of French settlers decided to speak out against the ongoing oppression of the Muslim population. On 8 May 1954, they submitted the *Lettre des 75* to President René Coty, expressing their "anxiety" and "worry" about the situation and demanding political reforms. Moreover, they founded the organization *Conscience française* with the goal of "setting off a change of opinion, in Morocco as well as in France, in favor of the return of the [Moroccan] sovereign . . . and to bring the promise of hope to the Moroccans."[174] Other groups of critical settlers— such as *Amitiés marocaines* and *Groupe d'études et de réalisations économiques et sociales*—also tried to engage in a dialogue with the Muslim population.[175] Even the influential Catholic newspaper *Maroc-Presse* appealed for French-Moroccan reconciliation. Nonetheless, these outspoken settlers failed to change the general mood among the European population, and one of its leaders had to flee to France following an assassination attempt by a right-wing terrorist group.[176]

The members of the CMF maintained close relationships with the representatives of the Istiqlal in Paris. Many of them had known the Moroccan nationalists since the 1940s, but their contacts intensified dramatically in the wake of the Casablanca massacre as they synchronized their efforts.[177] Alaoui had eaten dinner with a group of Catholic intellectuals just days before Mauriac's first article. And from his new home in Tangier, Abderrahman Youssoufi regularly provided the Nobel laureate with materials for his articles.[178] Pierre Parent also "played an important role in this matter, because he contacted Mauriac and told him the truth about the situation," as a nationalist in Spanish Morocco remarked.[179] A French intelligence report noted that the opinion of *Le Figaro* on the Moroccan question "evolved" throughout 1953 due to Ahmed Alaoui's "unremitting interventions" with its editorial staff, "which he visits frequently like all Paris newsrooms."[180] From his bureau in Madrid, Abdelkabir al-Fassi stood in regular contact with Roger Parent, providing him with information that his wife Eve could use for her work at *L'Observateur*. "We have to enlighten French and foreign public opinion patiently about the real aspirations of the Moroccan people and the atrocities committed by the French colonialists on a daily basis," he explained to his French friends.[181]

The mechanisms of the nationalists' network of contacts can be studied by looking at the transnational cooperation surrounding the death count of the Casablanca events. Fully aware that the official estimate of just of a few dozen victims was much too low, Mauriac and his colleagues happily received a note from the Istiqlal that stated that the French police had killed "approximately" 1,044 natives.[182] The CFM subsequently adopted the number uncritically but eventually had to backtrack after procolonial circles demanded proof for this extremely high body count. In response, the Istiqlal compiled a detailed list of every single individual who had been reported dead or gone missing following the demonstrations, including their addresses and other personal details.[183] Thereafter, the staff of the BDIPI submitted the document to the CFM, whose members used it as evidence when talking about the massacre committed by the French security forces. Robert Barrat embraced the nationalists' new number of 315 victims in *Justice pour le Maroc*, but he also repeated the CFM's earlier call for a neutral investigation into the bloody events.[184] A powerful symbiosis had developed between the nationalists providing detailed reports and their French brokers bringing this information to public attention. This collaboration allowed the anticolonial campaign in Paris to function efficiently.

The Moroccans continued their anticolonial activities in France until the beginning of the bilateral independence negotiations in Aix-en-Bains in September 1955. The country's political class had begun discussing the future of the North African kingdom thanks to their supporters' efforts. Secretary General Ahmed Balafrej, who was living in exile in Geneva at that time, stood "in permanent contact with the members of the party office in Paris . . . who work[ed] day and night to convince a number of French parliamentarians of the viewpoint of the Moroccan people."[185] One major victory occurred in the summer of 1954, when the Socialist Party's annual congress adopted a resolution calling on "France to recognize Moroccan sovereignty and the right of Morocco to independence after a limited period."[186] Pressured by Charles-André Julien and Jean Rous, the country's oldest political party had realized the futility of holding on to the protectorate. André de Peretti and other internal critics eventually convinced the members of the MRP to embrace the idea of ending the colonial regime as well.[187] These developments received great attention inside Morocco. In December 1954, a

Spanish report noted that "the vast majority of Muslims in Tangier are commenting on the debates about the Moroccan question that have begun to take place in the National Assembly."[188] The nationalists' Paris-based anti-colonial campaign had finally obtained the desired results following years of hard work.

THE REACTION OF THE FRENCH AUTHORITIES

An excellent assessment of the Moroccan advocacy campaign in the metropole can be found in a report filed by the French security authorities in June 1955. According to its authors, "The metropolitan representation of the Istiqlal is an active political organization . . . predominantly constituted of young persons of a quite high intellectual level, [who] display a rather shrewd sense of politics."[189] Financed by businessmen and supported by the working class, the campaign was conducted by "the students . . . [who are] the best trained, most active and most dangerous members of the nationalist community in France."[190] The party managed to achieve "an almost complete unity among the Moroccan community in France"—the AMB ("allegedly a philanthropical association, but in reality a propaganda and recruitment office") played an especially "pivotal role" in this regard.[191] The nationalists in Paris could not only "self-finance" their activities but also transfer their surplus to Cairo in support of Maktab al-Maghrib, because rich and poor sympathizers alike regularly donated "considerable amounts."[192]

Most interestingly, though, was the fact that the nationalists structured their campaign around a network of supporters who presented their message to the French public. "It does not seem that a hierarchy among the members of the delegation exists, but rather a sort of specialization," argued the same report.[193] This stood in clear contrast to the otherwise top-down structure of the Istiqlal Party. "The propaganda is conducted verbally by way of [personal] contacts . . . to politicians, writers, journalists, and academics" rather than through regular publications.[194] As a result, "some of the most influential and distinguished Frenchmen" have come to believe that the problems in Morocco are entirely due to the "misguided actions of our compatriots . . . and the Republic's successive governments."[195] The conclusion seemed obvious: "by obtaining vital support in different circles and among influential persons," the BDIPI "must be considered a significant instrument for the realization of the Istiqlal's primary objective, the independence of Morocco."[196] Even the nationalists' adversaries had come to acknowledge the success of the Moroccan advocacy efforts in France.

On reading this report, however, one question immediately comes to mind: why did the French authorities allow the Moroccans to unfold their anticolonial campaign inside the metropole for an entire decade? After all, the Office du Maroc had repeatedly sought to halt the Istiqlal's activities. Moreover, the country's security agencies spent an incredible amount of resources surveilling the Moroccans' movements on both sides of the Mediterranean. But apart from a brief shutdown of the AMB, the nationalists faced no major hurdles in their attempts to delegitimize the protectorate. One answer can be found in their friendships with important French politicians. When the Office du Maroc requested the deportation of Abderrahman Youssoufi in the winter of 1951, a wave of protests inundated the Paris police prefecture. Even former prime minister Robert Schuman insisted that the young nationalist be allowed to conclude his studies in Paris, thus underlining the reach of the Moroccans' network of supporters among the elites of the Fourth Republic.[197]

But there was an additional reason behind their freedom to maneuver inside the metropole: several Moroccans had become police informants. In the summer of 1951, while attending the Congress of Peoples against Imperialism in Zagreb, Alaoui informed a French intelligence agent about conversations taking place during the convention.[198] Even Hajj Diouri "sometimes provided services" to security officials.[199] It seems that the Moroccans used their contacts among working-class immigrants to provide details about communist efforts in the larger Paris region in return for a tacit acceptance of their own activities. The French authorities failed to adopt a uniform policy toward the Moroccan activists, thus highlighting the parochialism of public institutions during the Fourth Republic. The frustrated head of the Office du Maroc informed his colleagues in Rabat that it had proven impossible to expel Ahmed Alaoui, because he "enjoys official protections in Paris."[200] He explained to the resident general on a different occasion that "we are powerless to fight against the Istiqlal . . . which has supporters as powerful and varied as the SFIO, the Préfecture de Police, the MRP, and the Foreign Ministry."[201]

CONCLUSION

Uninhibited by the French authorities and instilled with a youthful zeal, the Moroccan nationalists in France made a significant contribution to the expansion of the nationalists' global advocacy network. What had begun with a small group of students adopting the demands of the recently founded Istiqlal Party quickly developed into a sophisticated campaign that eventually reached the highest echelons of the Fourth Republic. The activists established a solid social basis for the liberation struggle within the metropole by uniting the previously fragmented Moroccan community. They focused their efforts on the country's elites rather than seeking to convince the general public. A trio of nationalist institutions—the Foyer des étudiants marocains, the Association marocaine de bienfaisance, and the Bureau de documentation et d'information du Parti de l'Istiqlal—were the pillars on which the nationalist campaign rested. Yet the campaign extended beyond the capital as cities across France as well as in the neighboring European countries became battlegrounds in the global struggle for Morocco's independence.

The most important reason for the Moroccans' success can be found in their network of supporters. Just as they had done in Tangier and Cairo, the anticolonial activists established personal relationships with important figures of French public life, who then became spokespersons for their cause. It is especially noteworthy that they managed to recruit allies from across the political spectrum, thereby increasing both the reach and depth of their campaign in the metropole. The nationalists' demands entered public discourse when highly respected individuals such as General Catroux and François Mauriac publicly spoke out on their behalf. Beginning in 1951, the influential *Le Monde* abandoned its uncritical support of French colonialism in North Africa and began to advocate for conciliation with the nationalist movement; *Le Figaro* and other important mainstream newspapers followed suit by 1953.[202] It became increasingly acceptable for France's political leadership to work out a diplomatic solution to the Moroccan crisis as misinformation and fear gave way to understanding and appreciation. On 8 October 1955, when the vast majority of delegates of the National Assembly expressed their support for the "formation of a Moroccan government" capable of engaging in negotiations, a decade of anticolonial activism had finally born fruit.[203]

Although initially intended to be mere recipients of instructions from the party leadership back home, the student activists in Paris quickly became central figures within the Istiqlal. Alaoui, Bouabid, Youssoufi, and their colleagues not only acquired invaluable skills in media affairs and political organization but also established countless personal contacts spanning French society. The Istiqlal's campaign in France quickly came to depend on their expertise, which gave them a privileged position despite their nominally low rank within the party hierarchy. Even more importantly, these activists had become central nodes within the party's international advocacy network; by bridging the structural hole between the leadership inside Morocco and politicians and journalists in the metropole, they developed into increasingly powerful brokers. Already of great importance during their years of the liberation struggle, the social capital that these student activists acquired would eventually enable them to secure influential positions in postindependence Morocco.

Yet not everyone contacted by the Moroccans chose to support their struggle for independence. Robert Montagne was a famous procolonial sociologist and expert of the Moroccan Amazigh tribes who had provided much of the scientific information necessary for the French expansion into rural areas during the 1920s, and he declined Mauriac's invitation to join the CFM.[204] His colleague Jacques Berque decided to leave his position as *contrôleur civil* in Morocco in 1953 in order to work for UNESCO in Egypt, thus fleeing the deteriorating situation in North Africa instead of taking a stance on the issue of independence.[205] Both criticized the Residency's increasingly repressive policies but still believed in the value of the protectorate in general.[206] Their actions demonstrated the complexities of networking among individuals whom one cannot simply categorize as either opponents of colonialism or uncritical apologists of the French authorities.

Even some of those actively supporting the Istiqlal had not yet openly embraced the idea of complete Moroccan independence by 1953. Many liberals and socialists believed in the deeply flawed French Union as a new forum for cooperation between Moroccans and the French on the basis of equality.[207] Influenced by the so-called republican values and Enlightenment-based notions of progress, they thought that French tutelage—despite its evident imperfections—could theoretically benefit the native population amid the new "threats" posed by American capitalism or Pan-Arabism.[208] For most French citizens, it would take until the end of the Algerian revolution in 1962 to view decolonization as a logical stage in the inevitable progress of history.[209] The fact that even individuals sharply critical of France's actions in North Africa appeared incapable of rejecting all aspects of colonialism demonstrates the difficulties faced by the Moroccans in France. Despite the success of the nationalists in bringing their case to the forefront of public debate, the French elites did not reach a consensus on the necessity of granting Morocco's independence until 1955.

The Moroccan campaign in Paris went beyond targeting the legislative and executive branches of the French state; it also aimed at the international delegates attending the two sessions of the UN General Assembly held in Paris during the postwar years. Building on the work done by the members of Maktab al-Maghrib in Cairo, the activists in the French capital energetically lobbied the member states of the Arab League to present their case before the international organization in 1951. But the moment was not yet right. After heated discussions, the gathered delegates decided to postpone any official debate of the status of Morocco, which meant that the diplomatic battle would continue in New York one year later. Therefore, the fourth part of the international campaign for independence unfolded across the Atlantic. Having sent their first representative to the United States in 1947, the nationalists finally opened the Moroccan Office of Information and Documentation in Manhattan just in time for the inauguration of the UN's new headquarters in 1952. The anticolonial campaign in North America built on the activities taking place in Tangier, Cairo, and Paris and brought together activists from both the Spanish and French zones. And it would eventually surpass all previous efforts in both scope and sophistication.

CHAPTER FOUR

NEW YORK:
CAPITAL OF DIPLOMACY

O N   T H E   E V E N I N G   O F   14 July 1947, Mehdi Bennouna sat down at the desk of his small apartment in
Manhattan and reflected on the profound differences between North Africans and North Americans. While visiting a cinema with several Arab
friends, he had noticed how "the American[s] were often forced to laugh
when [my friends and I] found no reason to do so, frowned when we were
smiling, and disapproved of things that we deemed normal—and the other
way around."[1] Bennouna then immediately transitioned to the true reason
for his stay in New York. "We cannot reach the hearts and minds of the
Americans unless we understand how to present things in a way they deem
acceptable," he noted in his letter.[2] Anticolonial activism in the United States
could potentially bring great benefit to Morocco's struggle for independence
despite being "more difficult than [activism] in the Middle East."[3] As Bennouna pointed out to his readers, "The US government is nothing but the

mirror of the people, following its will and pressure; we must thus begin our offensive with regard to the people as the government will then follow suit."[4] The nationalist also offered practical advice to his colleagues back home. "We need the help of Americans capable of addressing the general public" in order to overcome the considerable cultural barrier.[5]

These astute observations, written down just weeks after Bennouna's journey across the Atlantic Ocean, underlined the increasing sophistication of the Moroccans' advocacy campaign. In addition to conducting their campaigns in Tangier, Cairo, and Paris, the nationalists kept their eyes on the most precious prize: New York, the emerging capital of international diplomacy. Beginning with the General Assembly's second annual session in 1947, the largest American city captivated the imagination of anticolonial activists everywhere, who sought to make their voices heard before the organization claiming to represent world public opinion. Nobody could doubt that the center of gravity of international politics had shifted from Europe to North America after the end of World War II. The Moroccans had already found that out in the wake of the arrival of Allied troops across the region in November 1942; those landings had allowed them to establish contacts with US citizens residing inside the North African kingdom. But the ultimate goal had always been to leverage these relationships in order to persuade the government in Washington to rethink its support for French colonialism. With the UN now also being established on US territory, it became of paramount importance for the nationalist movement to expand its efforts to the Western Hemisphere.

But the Moroccans lacked the linguistic skills and cultural knowledge that allowed them to conduct successful campaigns in Egypt and France. Whom were they going to send to North America? How could they successfully make their case in this faraway, alien place? Who might be willing to support their demands for an end to the protectorate regimes? The leaders of the Istiqlal Party and the PNR decided to cooperate closely with regard to their activities in the United States in the face of these daunting challenges. Their first delegate to the UN in 1947 came from Tetouan, but subsequently, activists from the French zone took charge and opened the Moroccan Office of Information and Documentation in Manhattan in 1952. Just as they did everywhere they went, the Moroccans quickly established a network of supports that penetrated local civil society; many influential US citizens eventually advocated publicly for Morocco's independence, including a former First Lady and a Supreme Court justice. A series of publicity victories put the French authorities under great pressure despite the fact that both the Truman and Eisenhower administrations remained skeptical of the nationalists' demands.

THE FIRST MOROCCAN DELEGATE

During the weeks following the founding of the UN in the spring of 1945, the Istiqlal's acting secretary general had sent a letter urging the international organization to listen to the Moroccan demands. No reply ever came, but the nationalists eventually decided to send their own delegate to New York. They had one colleague qualified to execute this difficult mission. Mehdi Bennouna, a son of the legendary "father of Moroccan nationalism," Hajj Abdelsalam, had become a student leader during his years in Egypt; he counted among the few Anglophone Moroccans of his time and had completed coursework at the American University of Cairo.[6] He had also worked as a freelance journalist before returning to the Spanish zone in 1945, where he edited the PNR's official newspaper.[7] Always smartly dressed in a fashionable suit with round glasses and neatly combed hair, Bennouna had the appearance of a modern professional and could thus easily blend into a crowd of international diplomats. His nationalist credentials and familiarity with the workings of the mass media made him the ideal choice for the task at hand.

By the spring of 1947, the moment had finally come to expand the anticolonial campaign beyond Tangier, Cairo, and Paris. Following lengthy deliberations with the nationalists in Tetouan, the khalifa wrote a letter to Mohammed ben Youssef to request the sultan's blessing of this endeavor.[8] The US authorities provided Mehdi Bennouna with an affidavit in lieu of a passport and granted him a visa for the United States, because the Spanish authorities refused to issue him the papers necessary for travel abroad. [9] How exactly he managed to obtain these valuable documents remains unclear, but it seems that he had been working for the US legation in Tangier as a media consultant ever since his return from Cairo.[10] Of course, the protectorate authorities reacted angrily as soon as they heard the news, but their protests

failed to change the situation.[11] A small group of friends bid Bennouna fare-
well at the port of Tangier as he embarked on his journey to New York on
6 June 1947—just hours after the former rebel leader Abdelkarim al-Khattabi
had escaped from French captivity 4,500 kilometers further east.

Much preparation had gone into this trip. Abdelkhaleq Torres had sent
a note from Cairo to suggest obtaining a letter from the leaders of Tetouan's
Jewish community to their "brothers" in New York, because "the Zionists
have a lot of influence in the United States."[12] The president of the PNR clarified, saying, "We do not have to cooperate with the Zionists, but we need
[to ensure] that they do not obstruct our case and that they become convinced that solving our case is good for the Jews in Morocco." Written at the
height of violence in Palestine, it demonstrated the nationalists' astonishing
pragmatism while anti-Jewish feelings were engulfing large parts of the Muslim world. Moreover, Bennouna's colleagues furnished him with a letter of
introduction to the various Middle Eastern representatives already present in
the United States, asking them to support his efforts to "inform public opinion about the situation in Morocco . . . and contact diplomats and political organizations . . . in order to defend our nation."[13] The Moroccans knew
the importance of having personal contacts in place when arriving in a completely foreign country and therefore prepared their representative to the best
of their abilities.

As soon as he arrived in New York, Bennouna began to reach out to
Arab activists working on behalf of the Palestinian cause.[14] The members of
the Arab Office embraced the Moroccan nationalist and arranged a meeting with a US diplomatic official.[15] Its director Cecil Hourani also offered
him a working space, but Bennouna politely declined this proposal so as to
"avoid the animosity of the Zionists."[16] This was a very wise decision given
that the Arab Office began to wind down its activities by the end of 1947
under the pressure of pro-Israeli lobby groups.[17] Another local mentor was
Ahmed Husayn, the leader of Egypt's fascist party, *Misr al-Fatat* (Young
Egypt), who recommended that Bennouna highlight both the economic
benefits the United States might reap from Morocco's independence and the
communist danger threatening North Africa.[18] Finally, Bennouna recruited
Abed Bouhafa, a Tunisian nationalist whose falling out with leadership of
the Neo-Destour Party had left him penniless.[19] After negotiations with his

colleagues in Cairo, Bennouna appointed him as spokesman for the newly established Committee for the Liberation of North Africa. It was a brilliant move, because Bouhafa would continue to energetically represent Maghribi nationalism in North America long after Bennouna's return to Tetouan.[20]

Undoubtedly the single most important ally Bennouna encountered in New York was Abderrahman Azzam Pasha, the Moroccan nationalists' perennial friend, who had contributed more than anyone else to the establishment of Maktab al-Maghrib al-'Arabi in Cairo. The Arab League's secretary general provided invaluable advice on the functioning of international diplomacy during their regular meetings, and he even promised Bennouna a generous share of the $5,000 that a Middle Eastern businessman had donated to promote Arab causes at the UN.[21] Moreover, the Egyptian used his stature as the foremost Arab diplomat to personally introduce him to other delegates gathered in New York. The liaison between the Egyptian and the Moroccan did not go unnoticed. According to a French intelligence report, "Bennouna attends all receptions organized by . . . members of the Arab League—he seems to be on particularly good terms with Azzam Pasha."[22] The two men quickly developed a close friendship; when Azzam Pasha left the United States a few weeks later, only Bennouna and Bouhafa came to the harbor to bid him farewell.[23]

High-ranking diplomats were not the only ones to embrace Bennouna's activities at the UN. Having already organized what must have been the first public celebration of Throne Day in the Western Hemisphere one year earlier, New York's community of Moroccans from the southern Sous region provided their countryman with a warm welcome upon his arrival.[24] Following a communal couscous dinner, Bennouna noted in his diary that he had "talked to them for a long time about the situation inside the country and [that] most of them know everything and are overzealous about the nationalist movement."[25] The Moroccan Amazighs also collected the considerable amount of $570 and offered it as their humble contribution to their nation's struggle for independence.[26] Although this act was certainly not comparable to the help the activists in Paris received from the much larger local Moroccan community, it highlights how widely disseminated the anticolonial message had become. Many of their compatriots supported the nationalists' advocacy campaign enthusiastically.

To protect the image of the Moroccan nationalist movement, Bennouna carefully eschewed prospective supporters whose friendship had the potential to hurt his reputation in the United States. This specifically meant avoiding communists at a time when the second Red Scare had begun to poison the political discourse. Although Bennouna developed a friendship with the Polish delegate, he feared associating his movement with the Eastern Bloc; when offered help in the corridors of the UN building, Bennouna discreetly "thanked him for his sympathies" but prudently decided to "not become involved with him on any issue."[27] He also shunned Benjamin H. Freedman, who had been working with the Arab Office on the question of Palestine; Bennouna explained his decision to avoid the company of the outspoken anti-Zionist activist by saying that "his reputation here is not good."[28] The Moroccan representative showed himself astutely aware of the need to project an appearance of respectability and thus treaded carefully so as to not jeopardize his standing in the public eye.

As a former journalist, Bennouna paid close attention to the workings of the US media; the significant influence wielded by news agencies such as United Press International especially fascinated him and would ultimately shape his personal career after independence. During his regular meetings with reporters for the *New York Times* and the *New York Herald Tribune*, he meticulously studied the way American journalists processed information.[29] Speed was the most important aspect—nobody showed any interest in facts about events that had taken place in North Africa weeks ago. Bennouna subsequently sent comprehensive instructions back home: all news had to be cabled directly from Morocco to the Bureau de documentation et information du Parti de l'Istiqlal in Paris, whose members should immediately relay the information via telephone to foreign correspondents based in the French capital.[30] Having already demonstrated their ability to engage with the international media during the sultan's recent visit to Tangier in April 1947, the Moroccan nationalists continued to adapt their anticolonial outreach to the global context in which they operated.

MEHDI BENNOUNA'S NETWORK IN NEW YORK

Bennouna also established close contacts with Arab media representatives in New York. His most important ally became Mahmud Abu al-Fath, who had been a vocal supporter of Matkab al-Maghrib since its establishment.[31] Now the media mogul ensured that his popular daily *al-Misri* presented news about the Moroccan campaign in New York to its readership in the Middle East. The relationship between the two men rested on mutual appreciation.[32] Impressed by Bennouna's intellect, Abu al-Fath sought to recruit him as his new UN correspondent, but the Moroccan nationalist declined this offer as incompatible with his already stressful life as an anticolonial lobbyist. He instead convinced the Egyptian newspaper owner to hire Abed Bouhafa.[33] This move killed two birds with one stone: it secured him the gratitude of both Abu al-Fath and Bouhafa while ensuring that *al-Misri* would continue to report on the North African cases before the UN for years to come.[34] Bennouna had established himself as an influential broker among the Arabs in New York within less than three months of his arrival.

Two anecdotes highlight how successfully Mehdi Bennouna networked in the United States. At the end of July 1947, Mahmud Fahmi al-Nuqrashi came to New York to support the Arab diplomats at the United Nations. One day before his arrival, the Egyptian delegates asked Bennouna to urge his press contacts to cover the visit of their prime minister; al-Nuqrashi's stay in New York ultimately received substantial media exposure as the direct result of the Moroccan's efforts.[35] Three months later, the Fortnightly Club for Women in Queens invited Bennouna to speak on the topic of French colonialism in North Africa. According to the official announcement distributed to the association's members, "Bennouna is known at the UN for his wide acquaintance with delegates and advisors—whenever someone cannot be found the saying is that one need only consult Mr. Bennouna to discover his whereabouts."[36] As his network of personal contacts across New York grew, so did his reputation.

The impact of the nationalist one-man campaign in New York quickly became apparent. Less than one month after his arrival, the *New York Times* notified its readers that Bennouna had come to the United States to conduct "an intensified drive to enlist the sympathies of this country in Moroccan and French North African independence" representing parties of "both Left and Right political thought but excepted the Communists."[37] The American media continued to show interest in his campaign. When Bennouna submitted a report to the UN secretary general, numerous media outlets reported that the Moroccan nationalist movement had asked for the coun-

IMAGE 5. Mehdi Bennouna (right of center with glasses) in the company of Vijaya Lakshmi Pandit, head of the Indian UN delegation, 1947. (Source: Aboubakr Bennouna. Reprinted with permission.)

try's independence in the name of "a universal sense of justice."[38] The French press quickly picked up on his activities as well, and *Le Monde* asked rhetorically whether the "North African nationalists enjoy the favor of the State Department?"[39] A satisfied Bennouna noted that whereas some Middle Eastern governments were spending thousands of dollars on newspaper advertisements to advocate for their respective cases, he remained the only Arab regularly receiving high-profile press coverage free of charge.[40] By way of his personal contacts, he had successful pushed the Moroccan case onto the pages of America's leading newspapers.

News about the Moroccan anticolonial campaign alarmed officials at the State Department, who notified the French foreign ministry that the current "situation [in North Africa] demands action urgently."[41] The continuation of American diplomatic support for France would depend entirely on the enactment of reforms setting Morocco on the path to self-government.[42]

Meanwhile, French diplomats "complained bitterly" that the nationalists had recently distributed a leaflet in Tangier that claimed that important US officials had received Bennouna "with sympathy and encouragement."[43] Worried Residency officials in Rabat considered recruiting procolonial Moroccan propagandists who could "cause a favorable impression and lessen the impact of the campaigns . . . directed against our colonial oeuvre."[44] Judging by such frantic reactions in Washington and Paris, the impact of Bennouna's activities had clearly surpassed all expectations.

AT THE UNITED NATIONS

His close relationship with numerous Middle Eastern representatives allowed Bennouna to familiarize himself with the mechanisms of international diplomacy despite lacking any official credentials. He regularly joined Arab delegates driving from their hotels in Manhattan to the UN's temporary headquarters at Lake Success. Soon enough, though, he realized that the diplomatic row over the future of Palestine overshadowed all other issues. During a meeting with the Syrian Farid Zayn al-Din, Bennouna complained, "The Arabs here are the only ones who get angry about my undertakings."[45] Hoping to persuade France as well as Spain's Latin American allies to vote against the partition of the Holy Land, the Arab League's member states decided against debating the case of Morocco on the floor of the General Assembly. Bennouna considered this strategy foolish, but his protests fell on deaf ears. When the UN member states ultimately recommended the division of Palestine into a Jewish and an Arab state on 29 November 1947, Bennouna experienced mixed emotions—while grieving over the Zionist victory, he showed himself relieved that no one could blame him for this diplomatic disaster.[46]

Yet Bennouna's presence at Lake Success had not been in vain, as he had learned a great deal about the inner workings of the UN, much of which did not inspire great confidence. Disturbed by the universal horse trading he had witnessed behind closed doors, the Moroccan wrote in his diary:

They all exchange promises. This one says to that one: vote for the delegate of Cuba and we will vote you into committee so-and-so. That one goes to the same person and says: do not vote for the delegate of Cuba and we will vote for you as the presi-

dent of so-and-so. . . . Then the man compares between the two offers and chooses
the one better for himself!! Everything is a lie and . . . the press does not mention
any of this. . . . It contains the basis for calamity, because he who haggles about an
election also haggles with the destiny of nations.[47]

The international organization evidently did not live up to the lofty ideals of the Moroccan nationalists; it rather seemed like a continuation of the
same backroom diplomacy that had paved the way for the colonization of
North Africa in the first place. The overwhelming influence exercised by the
United States was another problem. A few days before the vote on the future
of Palestine, Bennouna noted, "The American pressure on the small countries [to support the partition] increases every day."[48] Unofficial hierarchies,
parochial interests, and a general indifference toward the priorities of the
Arab world dominated at Lake Success. Maybe Bennouna had been too na-
ive about the nature of the UN. But at least his eye-opening experiences constituted "a very valuable lesson" for future Moroccan delegates.[49]

Bennouna could be proud of his achievements as he returned home despite the fact that the UN had not taken up the Moroccan question. Instead
of heading straight back to Tangier, though, he spent two weeks in London, where he held a press conference that resulted in a number of favorable newspaper articles and culminated in an interview broadcast via BBC
radio.[50] Unsurprisingly, the Spanish authorities did not appreciate his activities abroad and consequently prevented him from reentering the northern zone upon his arrival in January 1948. Together with his fellow nationalists Abdelkhaleq Torres and M'hammad b. Ahmed Benaboud, who had
both recently come back from Cairo, he remained stranded in Tangier. Although the PNR sent telegrams to the United Nations and Arab League demanding an international intervention to "stop the assault of Fascist Spain
against the Moroccans," Bennouna would be unable to return home for another four years.[51]

Although certainly cruel on a personal level, his time in forced exile allowed Mehdi Bennouna to write a book on the history of European colonialism in Morocco. He published *Our Morocco—The True Story of a Just Cause*
in November 1951 in the hope that it would "awaken world public opinion,
which alone can influence the United Nations—and France and Spain—to
. . . give the Moroccan people the right of self-determination."[52] The nation-

alist press proudly printed excerpts from "the first book written by a Moroccan writer in English about the just cause of Morocco" and announced that it would be "widely distributed in all Asian, African, European, and American countries and at the UN."[53] Illustrating in detail the nationalists' grievances against the protectorate regimes and explaining their demands for an independent and sovereign state, it immediately became an integral part of the Moroccan propaganda efforts. That several North American university libraries still possess copies of the book underlines the continuing legacy of the nationalists' North America campaign.

Mehdi Bennouna's remarkable finesse allowed him to function as a one-man diplomatic corps for the nationalist movement in a totally foreign country. His talent for organization enabled him to successfully execute the demanding tasks he faced on a daily basis, and his affable personality permitted him to befriend individuals from all walks of life. He always worked until late at night and designated only Sundays for rest and leisure. Every evening, Bennouna wrote down his latest activities in a diary, which he shared with his fellow nationalists by sending copies to Tetouan on a weekly basis; his extremely clear handwriting reveals a man of great patience. Even the French diplomats surveilling him noted these personality traits. According to UN ambassador Alexandre Parodi, Bennouna did "not seem like a powerful speaker and a manipulator of masses, but much rather like an intellectual with a fine mind and a cold and determined character."[54] Such qualities obviously made him the ideal networker-in-chief for the nationalist movement.

The Moroccans' initial campaign in the United States must be considered a great success because it brought their case to global attention once again. Bennouna's colleagues definitely saw it that way. In a newsletter distributed in Tetouan, the PNR thanked its representative for "winning the first battle by creating a positive climate and propagating the [national] cause." Bennouna had "established contacts to the heads of the international delegations" at the UN, but also, due to his efforts "the world's biggest newspapers had talked about the Moroccan question" and thereby enabled it "to reach the majority of states and world leaders."[55] On a more personal level, the social capital he had acquired during his trip to the United States made him an invaluable member of the nationalist movement's apparatus; the former newspaper editor had become a diplomat who was its only lifeline to North

America. He bridged the gap between the core activists inside Morocco and influential supporters in New York. But despite Bennouna's unquestionable accomplishments, the nationalist movement would not dispatch a permanent delegation to New York until 1951.

ROM LANDAU: MENTOR AND BROKER

Mehdi Bennouna's six-month stay had laid the groundwork for future campaigns in North America, but a long road still laid ahead. As Abdelkhaleq Torres noted in November 1947, "We have not yet done enough preparations to combat colonialism before the tribunal of the world conscience."[56] American support seemed especially pivotal in this regard ("they have sympathy for us and we have to make them help us").[57] Therefore, the Moroccans needed to engage in "powerful and efficient propaganda . . . at the UN" that was "well-documented with reports and statistics," with the goal of creating "a favorable atmosphere across the entire world, particularly in the United States."[58] In order to do so, the Moroccans needed a native English speaker who could teach them how to make their case to the American public. Of course, their network of supporters already included two female Anglophone journalists, each of whom would render numerous services to the movement. But with regard to their planned expansion across the Atlantic, their choice fell on a different Briton, who had first arrived in Morocco in the summer of 1949.

Rom Landau returned to Tangier once again in the fall of 1951, after making two earlier trips and having written countless publications about the North African kingdom. This time, however, both French and Spanish officials declared him persona non grata and refused to let him reenter their respective protectorates.[59] Stuck in the international city, the British writer helped his nationalist friends by creating a leaflet that greeted the sailors of several berthed US navy ships in the name of "the Moroccan people" and reminded both groups of their shared "free, enlightened, and democratic way of life."[60] He also helped Mehdi Bennouna by editing the English-language version of *Our Morocco*.[61] Eventually, the nationalists asked him to travel to the United States in order to "enlighten certain authorities as to the true situation in Morocco."[62] Landau had never been across the Atlantic and had to

borrow money to make the trip, yet he agreed to his friends' request and decided to depart for North America as soon as possible. As he informed his
publisher, "My friends want me to [do] a number of things for them in the
USA, and as the American Legation has proved most helpful, I have decided
to go for a brief time to New York and Washington."[63]

The US diplomats in Tangier understood why the nationalists had asked
Rom Landau "to bring the American people up-to-date on developments in
Morocco."[64] He certainly seemed like the ideal advocate for the kingdom's
independence. "In person, Landau is attractive and vital [and] . . . has genuine popular appeal," while his "books are easily read, interesting and informative," according to a report sent to the State Department in December 1951.[65] Neither "anti-French" nor "anti-American," he appeared uniquely
capable of appealing to Western audiences "whether through interviews, articles or a lecture tour" due to his reputation "as a British 'expert' on this
area."[66] For these reasons, he could serve as a broker between the nationalist movement and the American public and solve the problem identified by
Mehdi Bennouna more than four years earlier.

When Landau finally boarded a ship to the United States, he was accompanied by the businessman Mohammed Laghzaoui and his family. A
highly successful industrialist from Fez married to a Moroccan woman with
British citizenship, Laghzaoui had made a fortune in real estate, in choco-
late production, and with his bus company, the *Société marocaine des trans-
ports Laghzaoui*, which still exists today. He had long been at odds with the
protectorate authorities due to his role as one of the Istiqlal's chief financiers
and his very close relationship to the sultan, and so he sought to evade his
impending arrest by the French authorities.[67] Moreover, Laghzaoui wanted
his soon-to-be-born son to become a US citizen. This way, the Moroccan
businessman would be able to register all of his companies under his off-
spring's name and thus protect the family's assets from potential confisca-
tion.[68] Laghzaoui began setting up a commercial enterprise as soon as he arrived in the United States, while biding his time until the end of the five-year
waiting period required for obtaining citizenship for himself and the rest of
his family.[69]

Landau, in the meantime, met with Secretary of State Dean Acheson,
Texas senator Tom Connally—the chairman of the Senate Foreign Rela-

tions Committee—and many other key politicians on Capitol Hill.[70] He lec-
tured at Princeton and Columbia, talked to members of the Council on Foreign Relations, wrote articles for influential outlets such as the *New York
Times* and *The Nation*, gave TV and radio interviews, and briefed personnel at the State Department and the CIA.[71] He even made a contribution
to the Carnegie Foundation's renowned International Conciliation series in
which he explained that "in a world in which all international politics have
become global politics . . . the outcome of the Moroccan crisis may possibly
stem from events in Tunis, Cairo, or Moscow."[72] French officials became extremely worried about this publication, which they considered "a striking
victory for our enemies."[73] The Residency retaliated by banning all book-
stores in Morocco from selling Landau's works.[74] Nonetheless, his nationalist friends expressed their confidence "that his new book will encounter a
[warm] welcome among the Americans, who are familiar with . . . the author's noble sympathies towards the just Moroccan cause."[75] Excited about
Landau's achievements in the United States, the nationalists decided to finally establish a permanent presence in New York.

THE MOROCCAN OFFICE OF
INFORMATION AND DOCUMENTATION

The Istiqlal had already sent Mehdi Ben Aboud to the United States in November 1951 to lay the foundation for a more structured campaign. The prac-
ticing physician had worked as a nationalist organizer during his student
years in Paris, and that experience had provided him with the necessary experience to lead the expansion of the anticolonial advocacy campaign across
the Atlantic. He later worked for the Voice of America radio service in Tangier, where he met US officials and learned English; it also seems likely that
his familiarity with the diplomats at the American Legation helped him
procure a visa for the United States. When he finally arrived in New York,
Moroccan businessman Mohammed Elmanjra helped him get settled; Elmanjra's oldest son, Mehdi—a freshman at Cornell University at the time—
became Ben Aboud's personal assistant. The Istiqlali could also count on the
support of Abed Bouhafa, who had been working for the Committee for the
Liberation of North Africa ever since Mehdi Bennouna had installed him

as the official representative of the Maghribi nationalist parties in the fall of 1947.

The Moroccan nationalists attached great hopes to their campaign in New York, although it had taken them much longer to initiate their activities in North America than in Europe or the Middle East. In an article on "the power of public opinion in democratic countries," *al-ʿAlam* argued that the colonized peoples needed "to make their cases understood," because "the world conscience might be able to support the liberation movements."[76] The continuous support provided by American citizens residing in Morocco had certainly contributed to this optimistic outlook toward the United States. The UN had especially captured the nationalists' imagination. During a speech at the University of Virginia, Ben Aboud described the international organization as "Morocco's only refuge" while expressing his hope that "it will doubtlessly do its outmost to make the French administration behave in accordance with the principles of human rights."[77]

But the Moroccans did not embrace the UN uncritically, as can be learned from numerous articles published in the nationalist press. The organization's informal division into "a bloc allied with the United States opposed to the communist bloc gathered around Soviet Russia" was particularly problematic, because it meant that "the goals of the majority of countries composing the General Assembly" continued to be "ignored."[78] Moreover, the Security Council's undemocratic nature posed "a threat to world peace by consistently putting the interests of the Western countries above those of the decolonizing world.[79] Although its establishment in the aftermath of the "war against Fascism" had made the UN "the object of the hopes of the peoples not yet free and sovereign," its record—especially in the case of Palestine—had not always been positive. But not all hope was lost. As an article commemorating the organization's five-year anniversary explained, "Despite these obstacles that block the path of the UN, the peoples still trust in it, because they are confident about the fairness of the international conscience."[80] This realistic yet cautiously optimistic assessment motivated the nationalists advocating for Morocco's independence in the United States.

Soon after of their arrival, Mohammed Laghzaoui and Mehdi Ben Aboud held speeches at private clubs, churches, and universities to raise public awareness for the Moroccan cause.[81] With the help of the prominent scholar Carlton S. Coon, they even gave talks on American radio and TV stations; a former OSS agent and future head of the American Association of Physical Anthropologists, Coon was another link between the group of US wartime spies and the nationalist movement.[82] The results of the Moroccans' initial efforts became apparent within just a few weeks as the *New York Times* published a detailed article explaining the demands of the Istiqlal Party.[83] From Capitol Hill to the conference rooms of the Council on Foreign Relations, many influential Americans displayed a great interest in the situation in Morocco. Even some officials at the State Department privately expressed their sympathies for the demands of the nationalists. "The work was nice and easy," Ben Aboud later recalled, because "the overwhelming impression was . . . that the Office of Information and Documentation had already succeeded . . . before being opened."[84] News of their activities traveled fast. In a letter to Paris, Resident General Augustin Guillaume vented his anger about the activities of the nationalists, who "do not hesitate to put forward counter-truths that might seem useless to us due to their enormity, but which are in fact susceptible to touch American public opinion."[85]

The Moroccan activists also established working relations with the Arab and Asian representatives in New York. Following a cordial meeting with Ben Aboud, the Indonesian ambassador "took the telephone and fixed appointments . . . with almost all of the delegations at the United Nations."[86] Meanwhile, Arab diplomats organized a press conference to introduce the Moroccan activists to the journalists covering UN affairs. In October 1952, Laghzaoui rented an apartment on Manhattan's East Side just a few blocks away from the new, permanent UN headquarters, which became the home base for the nationalist campaign.[87] A few weeks later, Ben Aboud registered the Moroccan Office of Information and Documentation (MOID) under the Foreign Agents Registration Act, with its main office in New York and a satellite bureau in Washington DC. Now the nationalists could finally present their case in a more organized manner.

By the time the Arab League announced that it would put the Moroccan question on the agenda of the seventh session of the General Assembly in December 1952, the Moroccans had already decided that it was time to present their case on the "public platform where the world's opinion on international affairs would be formed."[88] They asked Landau to act as their "chief

IMAGE 6. Mehdi Bennouna (left) and Rom Landau (center) in conversation with an Iraqi diplomat, 1952. (Source: Aboubakr Bennouna. Reprinted with permission.)

adviser"—an offer he could not refuse—and the British writer immediately made plans to return to the United States.[89] Several activists from both French and Spanish Morocco traveled across the Atlantic in the meantime. With his previous experience and talent for organization, Mehdi Bennouna managed the activities of the MOID and assigned each member to one specific task: Abderrahman Abdelali lobbied the General Assembly, Mehdi Ben Aboud maintained contact with the Special Political Committee, and Bennouna himself served as press liaison.[90] A few weeks later, the Istiqlal's secretary general Ahmed Balafrej also arrived in New York to serve as the nationalist movement's chief diplomatic representative.

The MOID enabled the anticolonial activists to embark on an extensive lobbying campaign, which included the writing of countless letters to the editors of leading newspapers, informing them that "for the Moroccans there is only one way to freedom and progress—independence."[91] Moreover, the nationalists published pamphlets on topics such as Morocco's economic and social development, a history of the protectorate, and a brief biography of Sul-

tan Mohammed ben Youssef.[92] They also distributed the works of historian
Charles-André Julien as well as French settler Pierre Parent, whose writings
condemned the colonial regimes with the authority of the European eye-
witness.[93] In a detailed account about their efforts in New York, Bennouna
called on his countrymen to be proud of the MOID, "which is financed by
workers, peasants, merchants, civil servants, and other citizens" and permitted "Morocco to raise up its head, because it does a magnificent job unlike
any office belonging to a member state of the UN."[94]

Rom Landau's duties ranged from holding public lectures to penning pronationalist publications. French consul general Louis de Guiring attended
one of Landau's talks at the Commonwealth Club in San Francisco, not-
ing that it "constituted . . . the most dangerous and skillful attack against
our policies I have ever heard" and that it had been extremely well received
by a large audience consisting of very important people.[95] Al-'Alam praised
such efforts by the British author "known for the extent of his sympathy . . .
towards the Moroccan case."[96] As a self-confessed Roman Catholic, Landau also became a regular contributor to the Jesuit weekly America. His lu-
cid writing style made him the ideal candidate for introducing the Moroccan
question to his American readership, whether he dealt with "the lobby that
runs North Africa" or lamented the region's "gradual decline into Communism" due to the failures of French colonialism.[97] "Today the nationalism of
suppressed peoples has become so powerful a force . . . that no threat of bay-
onets can stifle it," Landau argued before adding that "the examples of India,
Pakistan, Burma, and Indonesia should be warning enough."[98] The nationalist press printed translations of these articles "to show its readers how some
independent writers and unbiased magazines defend the truth."[99]

The British writer also supervised the production of two periodicals, the
Moroccan News Bulletin and Free Morocco, which consisted, respectively, of
press clippings covering current affairs in the North Africa kingdom and
longer background articles about the history of French colonialism. The nationalists captivated their readership by describing Morocco as home to an
"ancient civilization" and a "people aspiring to freedom" who were willing
to protect "American strategic interests."[100] Moreover, they appealed to "the
conscience of the world," evoked "the USA [as] the land of freedom and hu-
manitarianism," and went out of their way to disown "the pernicious doc-

trines of Communism" as a threat to world peace and completely incompatible with Islam.[101] To legitimize the Moroccan demands for independence,
the two publications regularly reproduced statements by well-known US citizens such as Congressman Lawrence Smith and Supreme Court justice William O. Douglas, who viewed the nationalist movement favorably.[102]

Printed on high-quality paper and well written, the MOID's official
newsletters became an instant success; *Free Morocco* had a monthly circulation of 50,000, and the nationalists issued more than 100,000 copies of the
pamphlet "Morocco Under the Protectorate," according to both French and
Moroccan accounts.[103] These numbers were extremely impressive. The official newsletter of the French embassy, by comparison, had a circulation of
only 3,500.[104] A sympathetic American journalist informed the anticolonial
activists that "the comments upon *Free Morocco* (and you cannot imagine
how quickly everyone is reading this pamphlet) have all been in high praise
of your new work. . . . Most of the people who have reported their comments
to us, asked: 'When is there going to be another?'"[105] Overwhelmed by the
work of producing and distributing their publications, the members of the
MOID decided to buy an electronic printing press, because the old manual
one could no longer "carry out [the] work with the required speed."[106]

The nationalists in New York synchronized these activities with those of
their colleagues in Morocco and beyond. During his visit to the kingdom in
1950, Sidi Mohammed had asked Rom Landau to write his biography and offered him all the necessary documentation to do so. The fruit of Landau's labor was an illustrated hagiography rather than a serious piece of scholarship,
putting emphasis on the monarch's "sagacity, diplomatic skill and . . . talent for moderation."[107] It played with Orientalist stereotypes by painting an
image of an exotic country inhabited by a freedom-loving people seeking to
reconcile tradition and modernity. Meanwhile, at Maktab al-Maghrib, Abdelmajid Benjelloun translated the book by "one of the world's leading experts on the affairs of [Morocco]" into Arabic so that it could be disseminated as propaganda material across the Middle East.[108] In the Anglophone
world, virtually every person of importance—including all members of the
House of Commons in London—received free copies of *The Sultan of Morocco* via mail.[109] The book was written as "source material for the delegates
during the debates on Morocco [at] the United Nations," and its trajec-

tory demonstrated how the anticolonial struggle relied on continuous cross-border cooperation between the royal palace, the nationalists, and their foreign supporters.[110]

Rom Landau bridged the structural hole between the Moroccans and the American public. Many North Americans curious about global affairs appreciated what they saw as his impartial expertise; his undeniable charisma made him an especially effective advocate for the Moroccan cause. "We were very fortunate in having such an authority as yourself" give an "interesting and informative talk on French Morocco," the organizers of a lecture in Vancouver informed him after the event;[111] and an announcement for a speech he gave in Connecticut described him as "one of the world's outstanding authorities on North Africa."[112] Rom Landau's outreach proved especially effective at drawing attention to Morocco amid an abundance of global conflicts. The president of a women's club in Los Angeles thanked him for his "very informative and factual talk on Morocco, . . . a vital and strategic but little known land," because it had allowed the audience to "understand many things in the present world picture a great deal better;"[113] his audience in Portland made "many comments, . . . all most complimentary," because "people are so emotionally involved with the Arab-Israeli problem that they often forget all of the other important developments taking place in the Arab World";[114] and even the inmates of a California state prison expressed their "appreciation" of his stimulating lectures.[115] Rom Landau had come to embody the networked character of the Moroccan anticolonial struggle like few others, and the acquired social capital would ultimately secure him a prominent position in the North African kingdom long after independence.

In procolonial French circles, by contrast, few felt like congratulating the man who "despite his [Jewish] race had been welcomed with open arms by the palace and the Istiqlal."[116] France's hysterical tabloids shared this assessment: *Aspects de la France* had "no doubts . . . that the Jew Rom Landau is an enemy of France . . . who defends the Istiqlal [like François] Mauriac and the members of the Comité France-Maghreb," and *Paris* speculated that he might be a "covert Soviet agent" who had kept his name "from his time in the Polish ghetto."[117] Even the famous ethnographer Robert Montagne complained about "the Jew of East European origin in the service of the [Istiqlal] Party."[118] The Moroccan's anticolonial campaign abroad had clearly

hit a nerve at home; no insult seemed too outrageous, no anti-Semitic stereotype too vile when it came to those who challenged French colonial rule on
the global stage.

DEBATING THE MOROCCAN QUESTION

In anticipation of the General Assembly's discussion of the status of French
North Africa, the Istiqlal sent Allal al-Fassi and his assistant Abderrahman
Anegay on a tour across Scandinavia and Latin America to "conduct propaganda for the Moroccan cause" and secure the necessary votes.[119] During a
stay in Stockholm in July 1952, al-Fassi met an influential diplomat as well as
the personal secretary of the foreign minister, which caused great excitement
at home.[120] Journalists from all major Swedish newspapers attended a press
conference during which they bombarded the za'im with questions regarding the situation in North Africa; the popular *Aftonbladet* even published
an interview in which al-Fassi expressed the hope that his hosts would "help
us bring the Moroccan question before the UN," because "the Scandina-
vians hold human rights in high regard."[121] His brief stay in Norway proved
equally successful. As al-Fassi informed his colleagues in Morocco, Prime
Minister Oscar Torp had sat down with him for "forty-five minutes during
which we talked about everything necessary and he expressed his sympathy
towards us and our case."[122] Satisfied with the results of their trip to northern Europe, al-Fassi and Anegay—after brief visits to the Netherlands and
Spain—traveled across the Atlantic to continue their outreach campaign.

On 26 September 1952, al-Fassi gave a press conference in Brazil to kick
off his month-long tour of Latin America, during which he met numerous
politicians, such as the governor of Rio de Janeiro and a Uruguayan senator. The Moroccan nationalist explained that "if we obtain the assistance of
the twenty Latin American nations and . . . the three Scandinavian countries" in addition to those of the "solid Asian-African bloc," the Moroccan
case before the UN would become "invincible."[123] One month later, in Santiago, Chile, al-Fassi reaffirmed that he sought to "establish contacts with
the governments and publics of each Latin American country . . . so that the
case of Morocco will be included on the agenda of the current session of the
General Assembly."[124] Members of the influential Syrian-Lebanese commu-

nity organized a meeting with President-elect Carlos Ibáñez del Campo, who promptly pledged his "unconditional support for a debate of the [Moroccan] case."[125]

Allal al-Fassi's public appearances received considerable press coverage. The Uruguayan newspaper *El Debate* announced that he had come to Latin American "to inform about the situation in his country and search for the support of the peoples and governments of this continent"; the Brasilian *Última Hora* called him "the Moroccan Bolivar"; and the Chilean *El Diario Ilustrado* published al-Fassi's appeal to "aid us in achieving our legitimate aspirations."[126] The nationalist press back home enthusiastically celebrated the "splendid work done by the leader of the Istiqlal party . . . which will have a most positive impact on . . . the case of Morocco at the UN."[127] French diplomats showed themselves impressed by al-Fassi's campaign across the continent but cautioned against overstating the encounter between the Chilean leader and the Moroccan nationalist. (According to their interpretation, Ibáñez simply owed a favor to "the magnates of the Chilean textile industry, the Yarur, who supported [him] during his election campaign.")[128] Nonetheless, it demonstrated the support Arab communities across the world were willing to lend to the Moroccan cause. Satisfied with the outcome of their diplomatic outreach campaign, al-Fassi and Anegay traveled to "the land of freedom" to help their colleagues "explain the Moroccan question before the UN."[129]

The members of the MOID had done everything possible to adequately prepare for the debate in the General Assembly by November 1952. To demonstrate that they truly spoke for the entire country, they were joined by a delegation representing all members of the National Front, including Mohammed Hassan al-Ouazzani, Mohammed Cherkaoui, and Ahmed Ben Souda for the PDI and Mekki Naciri for the MUP. Lacking official credentials, the activists had to gate-crash the UN building, but eventually the representatives of various Islamic countries provided each of them with a diplomatic passport or press accreditation.[130] The recent verdict by the ICJ especially provided a much-needed boost to the Moroccan efforts. The case had profound implications for the upcoming debate in the General Assembly, even though the judges had dealt only with the import restrictions imposed by the Residency on US citizens conducting business inside the French protectorate. "From the legal standpoint, the decision of the court in The Hague acknowledges the jurisdiction of the UN with regard to the Moroccan problem," the Paris-based activist Ahmed Alaoui commented in *al-'Alam*.[131]

The Moroccans also organized a huge party to celebrate Throne Day on 18 November, a publicity strategy that had proven very effective in Paris and Cairo in previous years. Dressed in traditional Moroccan caftans, the four daughters of the Elmanjra family served drinks and snacks to the invited guests gathered in a hall decorated with Moroccan and American flags. Pakistan's foreign minister Mohammed Zafrullah Khan praised the efforts of the MOID and wished "all success to His Majesty, his people, his country, and to all those who desire the liberation of Morocco."[132] The nationalists also distributed works by Rom Landau and Pierre Parent to the attendees.[133] By the end of the night, they had done everything in their power to charm the numerous diplomats in attendance. Everybody worked hard to "enlighten the opinion of the members of the United Nations and to furnish them with documentation about the Moroccan problem," Ahmed Balafrej later recalled.[134]

The Arab and Asian representatives met repeatedly to devise a common strategy for gathering the votes necessary to pass an anti-French resolution. After congregating in the office of the Syrian delegation, diplomats from Pakistan, India, and Indonesia helped the members of the MOID draft a detailed report about the Moroccan question, which they subsequently submitted to UN secretary general Trygve Lie.[135] Since the new Egyptian regime had grown increasingly indifferent toward North African nationalism following the revolution that had taken place just a few months prior, the government of Iraq led the diplomatic offensive in New York.[136] Foreign Minister Mohammed Fadil al-Jamali personally informed the Moroccans that his country would "spare no effort" on their behalf.[137] And for the first time, these promises of support led to concrete actions as Zafrullah Khan gave a stirring speech on behalf of Moroccan independence on the floor of the General Assembly while New York's Amazigh community staged a demonstration outside the building to attract media attention.[138]

Little could be gained at the UN, however, without approval from the United States, as the Moroccans had learned in Paris one year earlier. In an interview with *al-Misri*, Allal al-Fassi expressed his hope "that the US gov-

IMAGE 7. Members of the Moroccan Office of Information and Documentation at the UN, 1952. The photo includes Ahmed Balafrej (seated on the far right), Abderrahman Abdelali (standing on the far right), Mehdi Bennouna (standing, second from the right), and Abderrahman Anegay (standing, fifth from the left). Their associate Levon Keshishian is standing on the far left. (Source: Aboubakr Bennouna. Reprinted with permission.)

ernment changes its position . . . because its past attitude on the Moroccan question is incompatible with . . . the principles [of the Atlantic charter]."[139] An article in the nationalist press optimistically claimed that "the propaganda conducted by the independence movement" had led to an "awakening of American public opinion" that would inevitably "influence the stance of the US government."[140] In reality, though, the attitudes of many US diplomats had not fundamentally changed; some of them urged the outgoing Truman administration to support France "to the greatest extent possible" rather than embrace "the extreme nationalist demands for immediate independence."[141] A memo submitted to the State Department's "working group on colonial problems" likewise emphasized "the need for a moderate middle-of-the-map policy which will neither permanently alienate the good will of the North Africans . . . nor drive the French to emotional acts of desperation."[142] After all, "the power of the West, if wisely used, will induce the

Moslem world to accept *gradual* progress towards independence" and could thus combine "long term traditional interest leads . . . [with] shorter range policy."[143]

The proceedings of the seventh annual session of the General Assembly nonetheless created great excitement inside the North African kingdom. "Although the UN had . . . postponed the Moroccan case last year," the nationalists still viewed the international organization as an "object of hope for securing security, peace, and freedom."[144] It seemed reasonable to remain optimistic since the activists had "spread propaganda for Morocco all over the world . . . through immense activities . . . in states whose votes count a lot at the UN."[145] The intensified cooperation between all members of the National Front had especially "given the Moroccan case a boost on the international stage," which the nationalists thought could lead to "a much more successful outcome than in the preceding year."[146] In a series of letters from Tetouan, Tayeb Bennouna informed his brother Mehdi that "the people's interest in the case is at its peak and their joy over your success is indescribable."[147] The nationalists in Tangier resurrected the Roosevelt Club to welcome US naval personnel visiting the international city. ("All of Tangier seemed decorated with Moroccan and American flags. . . . The French are very upset.")[148] The popular excitement even reached the royal palace, as Sultan Mohammed ben Youssef "expressed his delight" about the activities of the MOID and "heaped lavish praise" on its members.[149] It almost seemed as though the entire country was looking across the Atlantic with great anticipation.

When the UN General Assembly finally adopted a resolution regarding "the question of Morocco" on 19 December 1952, the nationalists experienced contradictory emotions. Several Central American states had bowed to US pressure and backed away from the critical language of the Arab-Asian bloc, instead proposing a cautiously worded compromise. The Moroccans did not hide their frustration that it merely called for "negotiations on an urgent basis towards developing the free political institutions of the people of Morocco . . . in an atmosphere of goodwill, mutual confidence and respect."[150] They had hoped for a UN special commission to investigate the situation in North Africa, especially in the wake of the Casablanca massacre that had taken place less than two weeks before. Mehdi Bennouna wrote a letter to the US ambassador one day before the vote to express his "shock" that his country seemed to be undermining the resolution on the status of Morocco.[151] Back home, "the decision of the UN struck everyone like a thunder and nobody [was] content."[152]

But after the immediate feeling of disappointment had dissipated, the members of the MOID took pride in their achievements. One outcome was an increasing number of articles on the topic in US newspapers. "When our people speak out before the UN, the world will at last know the true state of affairs in Morocco," the *Washington Post* quoted a nationalist from Rabat saying in a long article on the Moroccan liberation struggle.[153] Although certainly not a forceful condemnation of French colonial rule in North Africa, the General Assembly's resolution had brought their case to the attention of world public opinion and thus dealt a serious blow to the colonizers. According to Rom Landau, the resolution, though "unsatisfactory," represented a "modest victory for Morocco and a moral defeat for France."[154] Not only had "none of the pro-French delegates made any effort to praise French achievements in Morocco" but the General Assembly had also deemed itself competent to intervene in what France considered an internal affair.[155] Moreover, Washington had partly broken with Paris concerning the status of North Africa and thus demonstrated that it would no longer offer unconditional support.

The developments in New York therefore caused a rude awakening for the French government. It was not so much the content of the resolution that seemed troubling but rather the increasing international legitimization of the struggle for Moroccan independence. Ultimately, this would force Paris to engage with the nationalists.[156] For the moment, though, revenge seemed like the most appropriate answer: as the members of the National Front headed to LaGuardia Airport to board their return flights, they learned that Tangier's Committee of Control had banned them from reentering the international zone.[157] Expelled from their home base, Allal al-Fassi and his associates had to relocate to Cairo. This was a major setback for the Moroccans' transnational advocacy campaign since the neutral city served as one of the four central hubs for coordinating their global efforts. But this harsh reaction also seemed like a badge of honor because it demonstrated the protectorate authorities' increasing frustration in the face of the Moroccans' transnational anticolonial activities.

NETWORKING ACROSS THE UNITED STATES

The work of the MOID really began only after the seventh session of the General Assembly had ended. Facing financial difficulties following the increased repression in the wake of the Casablanca bloodbath in December 1952, the Moroccans relocated their office from Manhattan to a more modest residence in Queens.[158] Mehdi Ben Aboud and Ahmed Balafrej traveled to Washington on several occasions to meet with midlevel officials at the State Department with the goal of obtaining the diplomatic support of the US government.[159] And their colleagues in Morocco sent telegrams to the White House asking for American intervention to stop France's oppressive policies.[160] US officials courteously listened to nationalists' complaints on each of these occasions but did nothing to meet their demands, as the newly elected Eisenhower administration remained unwilling to provoke France. But this did not diminish their zeal. "The comrades have been working day and night . . . and [their] efforts are worthy of admiration. They are in contact with all delegations, the press, and [those activists working] abroad," remarked a Moroccan after passing through New York in September 1953.[161]

The nationalists also continued to expand their network of supporters on the East Coast.[162] Public lectures on college campuses on the status of North Africa were especially important and convinced a few young activists to join their movement.[163] One such supporter was student leader Gilbert Jonas of the National Student Association (NSA). He had once heard Rom Landau speak at Columbia University and subsequently decided to volunteer as an unpaid staffer at the MOID.[164] Jonas later became a public relations advisor to the Algerian revolutionaries and other African independence movements during the 1950s and went on to serve as the NAACP's chief fund-raiser for three decades.[165] In 1967, *Ramparts* magazine revealed that the CIA had infiltrated the NSA and used its international program as a conduit for funding overseas anticommunist operations. Its credibility destroyed, the NSA dissolved itself a few years after this revelation. Nonetheless, the MOID had proven itself a nodal point for US citizens eager to support both foreign and domestic anticolonial movements.[166]

Even more important for the Moroccans was their cooperation with Benjamin Rivlin, a political scientist at Brooklyn College who had served as an OSS officer in North Africa during World War II. As a consultant to the World Bank, the UN, and the State Department, Rivlin could offer both useful information and connections; his numerous sympathetic publications legitimized the Moroccan nationalist movement in the eyes of his American readership.[167] During a conference in May 1953, Rivlin emphasized that "East and West are competing with each other for the bodies and souls of the colonial peoples" and warned that "if the United States does not heed . . . it will come out with the short end of the stick."[168] He also joined Mehdi Ben Aboud and the press attaché of the Egyptian delegation as they debated three procolonial speakers during a public symposium.[169] A French observer later recalled Rivlin to have been "the most harmful one, strongly supporting the theories of the nationalists."[170] The US academic even traveled to Morocco for a few weeks with the help of the Istiqlal in order to study the situation inside the protectorate.[171]

Rivlin also arranged a meeting between the Istiqlalis and representatives of the American Jewish Committee (AJC) in October 1954. Worried about the rise of nationalism inside Morocco and how it might affect their coreligionists, the American activists expressed their "interest and concern in the problem . . . of the Jewish community."[172] Of course, the nationalists proved extremely accommodating and promised to issue a communiqué reiterating their belief in complete religious equality. The AJC demanded some revisions after reviewing the first draft, and the Moroccans gladly accommodated their request. Just a few weeks prior to the General Assembly's ninth session in 1954, Ahmed Balafrej issued a statement promising Jews the "same rights and privileges as their Muslim compatriots" in postindependence Morocco.[173] Two years earlier, the *Moroccan News Bulletin* had included an article titled "The Problem of the Jews in Morocco" that "explained the situation" and contained excerpts from "a letter sent by the sultan to René Cassin, the leader of the Jewish community in France, in 1949."[174] The members of the MOID repeatedly sought "contacts with Jewish organizations . . . to present the case of the Moroccan Arabs," according to a French observer.[175] And they ultimately secured the support—or at least acquiescence—of an influential sector of US civil society through such brilliant tactical maneuvers.

The Istiqlalis also became aware of the existence of an outspoken liberal elite whose support they needed in order to sway public opinion in their favor. Rom Landau visited Eleanor Roosevelt at her rural retreat in upstate New York on Christmas Day 1952 to discuss the Moroccan problem. After a long conversation, the former First Lady asked him, "What do you want me to do?"[176] Clearly convinced by his account of the suffering of the native population under French colonialism, Roosevelt subsequently used her influential syndicated column *My Day* to urge her readers to "get as much enlightenment as possible on this situation."[177] While admitting that "Korea is perhaps the most difficult question before the United Nations at the present time," she argued that "the question that concerns Morocco is a very serious one, too."[178] This was, of course, exactly what the Moroccans had been arguing all along. When Landau visited Los Angeles a few months later, two of Roosevelt's children, Anna and Elliott, invited him to a family dinner. Landau continued sending Eleanor Roosevelt his latest publications, and the former First Lady politely thanked him every time.[179]

Eleanor Roosevelt's anticolonial beliefs were widely known, and her opinion carried much weight in public debates. She had served as acting chairwoman of the US delegation to the United Nations and remained in regular contact with high-ranking politicians, including the president himself. Mrs. Roosevelt had already personally intervened with the US authorities on behalf of several Moroccans in the fall of 1952 to ensure that they could obtain the necessary visas to travel to New York.[180] A few months earlier, she had even called Secretary of State Dean Acheson and "urged [him] very strongly" to allow the discussion of the Moroccan question in the UN Security Council so that "more stability in that vital area would be created."[181] As one of the most esteemed public figures of her time, Roosevelt's support opened doors both in Washington and New York.

The members of the MOID also stood in contact with Supreme Court justice William O. Douglas, who eventually became a passionate advocate for Moroccan independence. After reading numerous nationalist publications—including *The Sultan of Morocco*, several issues of *Free Morocco*, and a collection of François Mauriac's articles—he agreed to receive Rom Landau and Mehdi Ben Aboud in his office.[182] The meeting apparently went as planned, because Douglas traveled to Morocco in the summer of 1954 to get a firsthand impression of the situation inside the protectorate (the French authorities, however, rejected his request to visit a group of jailed national-ists). "It's a wonderful nation—wide and handsome. I hope it soon gets its freedom," the judge informed Ben Aboud following his return.[183] Most im-portant, though, was the illustrated piece Douglas published in the highly popular *LOOK* magazine; the article lambasted the "racism" of the French "police state" and concluded that "all colonialism must come to an end. All colonies must be liquidated."[184] The secretary general of the Arab League mentioned the article during a meeting with US diplomats a few days later as an "accurate portrayal" of the situation.[185] It was an astonishing public af-fairs success for the Moroccans, whose case had been brought to the atten-tion of a mass audience once again.

A colorful and media-savvy individual whose numerous marriages and extravagant lifestyle had turned him into a well-known celebrity, Douglas also became an experienced globetrotter paid to report on his foreign ad-ventures. As "an independent-minded libertarian," he opposed all forms of imperialism.[186] All of this made him an excellent conduit for getting the Moroccans' message out to the American public. The French Embassy ap-parently shared this assessment and published a twenty-seven-page "answer" to his article in *LOOK* magazine, proclaiming that "democratic freedoms are guaranteed to all Moroccans" while blaming "the extremist party al-Istiqlal" for the volatile situation inside the protectorate.[187] This heated re-sponse demonstrated how worried colonial officials had become about the activities of the MOID. A French diplomat correctly noted that the Moroc-cans' "goal seems to be . . . to get the endorsement of highly-qualified or im-partial individuals for [their] claims in order to impact public opinion."[188] It became increasingly apparent that the nationalists had successfully used their contacts to spread their message, whereas the colonial power lacked an effective counterstrategy.

Another person assisting the Moroccans was Levon Keshishian, an opaque character working for the Egyptian *al-Ahram* and other international newspapers who later cofounded the predecessor of the *al-Jazeera* television network. Keshishian had obtained a considerable reputation in the corridors of the UN building through his work as an omnipresent freelance journalist. The Istiqlal hired him as a "special correspondent" for *al-Istiqlal* and *al-'Alam* in September 1952.[189] He not only wrote articles but also used his vast network of personal connections to promote the Moroccan case in private talks with diplomats, politicians, and other members of the press corps.[190] According to State Department officials who had met him in the summer of 1954, Keshishian explained that the Moroccans were becoming "increasingly restive and disappointed with the United States" and advocated for "independent North African allies" as the best regional protection against "Soviet imperialism."[191] Although such interventions did not immediately convince American officials to abandon their stance, it made them realize that large parts of the non-Western world had become sympathetic to the demands of the Istiqlal. The cautious attitude of the US government with regard to French North Africa seemed increasingly anachronistic.

One major forum for contacts between the Moroccans and local civil society was the American Friends of the Middle East (AFME), an association cofounded by the famous journalist Dorothy Thompson and other important US citizens. It regularly organized high-profile public events to explain current affairs in the Muslim world, thanks to generous contributions from both the oil industry and the CIA.[192] In an article reprinted in *al-Istiqlal*, the AFME's codirector Reverend Garland Evans Hopkins complained that "despite considerable pressure by labor organizations and the press, the United States still has not . . . joined the Arab-Asian nations . . . in their efforts at the UN."[193] Of course, the nationalists missed no opportunity to personally inform their members about the latest developments in Morocco.[194] And the nationalist press praised the AFME, whose goal it was "to increase the interest of US public opinion in the peoples of the Middle East."[195] French observers obviously offered a less positive assessment of the association, which they deemed "a disguised pan-Arab organization formed by intellectual and political pressure groups."[196] Its "close collaboration with North African nationalists and support for their demands in American circles" especially worried them.[197] For the members of the MOID, though, the AFME offered another path to bring their message to the attention of a wider audience.

BROKERS IN ACTION

The flurry of activities undertaken by the members of the MOID highlighted not just the Moroccans' ingenuity when making their case in foreign cultural settings but also the benefits of structuring their campaign around a transnational network of supporters. The AFL, especially, provided considerable aid that went far beyond assisting the nascent labor movement inside Morocco. Using their influence in Washington, American union leaders repeatedly brought the issue of Morocco to the attention of Secretary of State John Foster Dulles.[198] When the United States government voted against a UN resolution condemning the dethronement of Sidi Mohammed in August 1953, the AFL denounced this "ostrich diplomacy" in the face of "this outrageous crime of French imperialism" as a sign of "utter contempt of the anticolonialist traditions of our country."[199] The delegates at its annual convention adopted a resolution calling on the "State Department [to] espouse the national independence of Tunisia and Morocco and support their case before the UN."[200] French diplomats considered the labor union "one of the most influential groups in the United States associating with the representatives of the Istiqlal."[201]

Seeking to benefit from this alliance with a pillar of American civil society, *Free Morocco* often contained quotes—and sometimes entire articles— by prominent labor activists. The AFL's influential foreign policy adviser, Jay Lovestone, constantly sought to convince the US ambassador to the United Nations, Henry Cabot Lodge Jr., to support the aspirations of the North African peoples. In a memo summarizing a wiretap of a conversation between the two men in August 1954, an FBI agent noted, "The AFL policy has long supported freedom from colonialism for North Africa. . . . Lodge is apparently agreeable to listening to the AFL position."[202] The labor union would continue to pressure the American government to distance itself from France's colonial policies for years to come. And it became a leading advocate for Algeria's independence following Morocco's liberation from French rule.

The leadership of the AFL also cooperated with Robert E. Rodes by making financial contributions to his travels between the United States and North Africa; in return, the businessman submitted detailed reports on the Moroccan question and wrote articles for the *International Free Trade*

Union News.[203] Moreover, Rodes asked the AFL leadership to testify before the Senate Appropriations Committee about France's continued treaty violations in Morocco and urged Jay Lovestone to warn the secretary of state about France's intention to incorporate Morocco into the French Union.[204] The OSS veteran also visited the MOID on a regular basis. In 1955, *Free Morocco* published a lengthy article by Rodes that condemned France for "contraven[ing] our national foreign policies . . . and American private investments abroad."[205] His wife, Marjorie, also penned two booklets in coordination with the MOID, which were subsequently printed and disseminated by the AFL.[206]

When it came to their activities in North America, the Moroccans' most important supporter was Kenneth Pendar. As the scion of a prominent New England family, the former intelligence agent frequented the highest circles of American society; the Roosevelts especially always enjoyed Pendar's company due to the wartime experiences he shared with both the late president and his son Elliott. He also used his prominence as a veteran and businessman to support the nationalists publicly during his regular visits to the United States. In March 1952, when Robert Montagne gave a speech at Georgetown University, Pendar severely criticized the distinguished procolonial scholar directly while his two Moroccan companions exchanged pleasantries with the French diplomats attending the event.[207] Because of his ability to circumvent the strict currency-exchange regulations imposed by the Residency, he also transferred the nationalists' money to New York in order to finance their international activities.[208]

Kenneth Pendar not only provided logistical support to the MOID but also welcomed Americans visiting Morocco. For example, he received Benjamin Rivlin at the airport when the latter returned to Morocco to conduct research for a study on French colonialism.[209] But Pendar's most prominent tour guest was none other than William O. Douglas; in July 1954, he organized the judge's trip across the North African kingdom with himself as "guide" and an "Arab[ic] speaking Moor as chauffeur."[210] The two men developed a close friendship during the weeklong journey and subsequently exchanged countless letters on the Moroccan question; before finishing his famous piece in LOOK, Douglas incorporated a number of corrections suggested by Pendar, whom he considered his "brain-trust on the Morocco article."[211] Following its publication, the Coca-Cola manager informed him that the Moroccans "are more than pleased by your article."[212] The relationship between them only grew closer in subsequent years. By December 1955, with Morocco's independence finally within reach, Douglas asked Pendar to admonish "my friend Balafrej and others" to ensure a "fair and honorable treatment" of the country's Jewish minority; "that will go far towards solving many of their problems in terms of world attitudes and opinion," the judge explained.[213]

Such anecdotes reveal the fascinating inner life of the nationalists' advocacy network, which facilitated the continuous creation of new contacts among the movement's supporters. Interestingly enough, it was Eleanor Roosevelt who had introduced Pendar and Douglas to each other. Thanking the former First Lady for her efforts on behalf of Moroccan independence, Pendar pointed out, "Those of us who live here and want so desperately for things to take another course are doing all we can on the spot, but we need allies and encouragement."[214] The judge's visit had been an excellent opportunity to show the Moroccans that "the outstanding liberal minded, courageous people of this world are interested enough in their problem."[215] Yet it was not only individuals but also information that circulated across borders. As soon as the nationalists in Rabat had read the final draft of Douglas's article, they sent a French translation to their office in Paris in order to have it published in the influential *L'Express* ("a weekly . . . read by everyone really interested in politics," as Pendar noted).[216] The Moroccan campaign for independence had reached an astonishing level of sophistication.

FRENCH COUNTERPROPAGANDA

Because the Moroccans continued to score publicity victories in the United States, the French authorities decided to step up their efforts to undermine the nationalists' advocacy campaign. That task fell to Mohammed Temsamani once again. In the summer of 1952, the Residency's communication and information counselor made his first of many trips across the Atlantic to defend French rule in Morocco.[217] According to the procolonial propagandist, France's biggest problem was not the Eisenhower administration, which continued to accommodate the government in Paris with regard to the situation in North Africa. He instead singled out private organizations such as the Carnegie Foundation and Aramco (the Arabian American Oil Company) as the top supporters of the nationalist movement.[218] Arab and Asian students at universities across the United States were another factor contributing to the success of anticolonial activism; the Istiqlal "used" them to harass pro-French speakers on their campuses.[219]

Mohammed Temsamani sought to enlighten the American public about the "real situation in Morocco" by revealing that the Istiqlal was a "fascist and totalitarian party . . . torturing the population of the country" while promoting the interests of the Cominform.[220] He used a press conference to warn the gathered journalists, "The Istiqlal has already collaborated with the Communists and is willing to . . . make out of Morocco what Mossadeq wanted to make out of Iran."[221] Such statements—while neither correct nor particularly coherent—were an intelligent approach to reaching the US public amid the hysteria of McCarthyism that had gripped the country. But they also revealed the desperation of the colonial officials, who felt overwhelmed by the sophisticated campaign being conducted by the anticolonial activists on the global stage.

Temsamani displayed a grudging admiration for the activities of the nationalists despite his deeply felt aversion to them. Almost immediately upon his arrival, he confirmed that the publications issued by the MOID were "very well written and produced."[222] To make matters worse, "their works [and] their documents are spread out across the country—even in the libraries of small towns one finds the publications of the Istiqlal and books by Rom Landau and Charles-André Julien."[223] The British spokesman of the Istiqlal especially attracted his ire—whenever Landau was invited to speak somewhere, Temsamani sought an invitation too; when Landau appeared on radio or television, he demanded airtime as well; and when Landau published another lengthy article in *America*, his Moroccan opponent asked its editors to print his reply in the next edition.[224] The nationalists "repeatedly hold conferences across the United States [and] speak on radio," Temsamani informed his superiors, adding that "too many Americans identify the Istiqlal with Morocco."[225] During a conference at the Middle East Institute in Washington in January 1954, the Residency's procolonial propagandist did not hesitate to call Landau a "double traitor" for having changed his Polish nationality and denying his Jewish religion.[226] Temsamani became increasingly irritated by his inability to undermine the nationalists' vast campaign in North America and soon experienced the same frustration as many other French officials—from New York to Cairo—had before him.

THE LEGACY OF THE MOID

The Moroccan nationalists' campaign in North America had certainly been successful, a fact that even their most zealous opponents had come to acknowledge. This achievement must be considered truly remarkable given the global political constellation of the early Cold War. Most importantly, the developing conflict between the Western and Eastern Blocs cast a shadow over all aspects of world politics; the situation in the Maghrib seemed relatively stable and thus less urgent in comparison to armed confrontations such as the Korean War or the civil wars in China and Greece. Although the outbreak of an armed uprising in the wake of Sidi Mohammed's dethronement in the fall of 1953 brought increasing international attention to the North African kingdom, it did not immediately change the attitudes of Western politicians regarding France's presence in the region. The stability of NATO remained the top priority for the United States; upsetting an important ally over a seemingly minor issue such as the status of Morocco seemed unreasonable.[227] Another problem was the composition of the United Nations. With most of Africa still under colonial rule, the Western nations and their junior partners exercised a disproportionate influence within the international organization. The decolonizing world, by contrast, remained largely absent from the most important debates taking place in New York.

It would nonetheless be an exaggeration to declare the nationalists' campaign in the United States a complete success given the Eisenhower administration's hesitation to embrace their demands for Morocco's immediate independence. In the fall of 1953, Secretary of State John Foster Dulles emphasized that his government needed to "assist our French friends and allies in [the] UN—even though we hardly consider Franco-Moroccan relations satisfactory"; his assistant Henry A. Byroade publicly confirmed the importance of maintaining "a middle-of-the-road policy," since it was not in the country's "interest to 'choose sides' for the sake of choosing sides."[228] Such statements symbolized the "considerable progress made by the American administration in understanding the colonial problems"—at least in the minds of French observers.[229] Washington's attitude never really changed until the return of Sultan Mohammed ben Youssef in November 1955 and the country's independence four months later.

Another reason for the UN's inaction can be found in the Arab League's increasingly reluctant attitude toward the Moroccan nationalists. Less than one month prior to the outbreak of the Algerian revolution, Secretary General Abdelkhaleq Hassouna assured the government in Washington of his willingness to "defer" any discussion of the situation in North Africa as long as the French government would "expedite the negotiations with the Tunisians and Moroccans."[230] Only Mohammed Fadil al-Jamali "expressed a somewhat dissenting opinion" and demanded immediate UN intervention.[231] French diplomats showed themselves unsurprised that "the attitude of Baghdad regarding our affairs in North Africa remains as aggressive as it has been in the past." Iraq allegedly used the situation in the Maghrib to "affirm its Arabness" both at home and abroad at a time when it had become "isolated in the Arab world suspicious of its egoistic foreign policies."[232] Yet the Arab League's other members did not display a similar zeal. Because the Egyptian regime under Gamal Abdel Nasser continued to remain largely indifferent to the situation in Morocco, the lack of diplomatic pressure from the Arab world allowed the US government to maintain its moderately procolonial stance as well.

Many Moroccans eventually showed signs of frustration over their apparent inability to secure their country's independence via diplomatic means. Writing from a hotel room in Washington in November 1954, Ahmed Balafrej informed his friend Rom Landau in blunt language, "As you know, our case has been put at the end of the [General Assembly's] agenda. The United States will support France. The result is thus the same as before."[233] In an article published in al-Umma just two months later, Abderrahman Anegay explained that "there is no one in Morocco who believes that the victory of independence is possible by way of the UN alone" given that the international organization "had not made a decision last year and . . . postponed an investigation of the issue at the current moment."[234] Such statements should not be surprising, because the General Assembly had concluded its ninth session by merely "expressing confidence that a satisfactory solution will be achieved" without offering any concrete steps to actually solve the Franco-Moroccan crisis.[235] The plan of decolonizing Morocco with the help of the UN faced seemingly insurmountable obstacles.

Yet despite these setbacks, the anticolonial campaign in New York did prove very important for the Moroccan liberation struggle. The UN's actions became central to the anticolonial movement, although the intergovernmental organization never spoke out directly against the French protectorate. According to Benjamin Rivlin, the "United Nations Charter . . . provided the nationalists with important, internationally accepted principles and an ancillary arena in support of the primary struggle taking place inside Morocco itself to regain their freedom."[236] Moreover, the General Assembly resolution in 1952 legitimized the Moroccan campaign for independence on the world stage despite its vague language. It also led to an upsurge in global media attention and substantially increased the diplomatic pressure on France. Such were the tangible effects of the anticolonial campaign executed by the members of the MOID. But the nationalists' efforts also left their mark in less noticeable ways.

Although the Moroccans failed to sway the US government to publicly support their demands, they managed to convince some American officials of the importance of their cause. The US delegation to the United Nations strongly supported a moderate resolution on the Moroccan question in order to avoid "damaging . . . our relations with the Arab-Asian states" and "disappoint[ing the] Latin Americans," as John Foster Dulles acknowledged in an internal memo in the fall of 1953.[237] One year later, in a conversation with a French diplomat, Henry Cabot Lodge Jr. clearly communicated his strong disapproval of the procolonial votes that his government had instructed him to cast.[238] Such anecdotes indicate that the anticolonial front created by the Moroccan nationalists and their allies in New York did have a noticeable effect. Whether through personal meetings with members of the MOID, private conversations with African and Asian diplomats, or phone calls with Jay Lovestone, the American diplomats at the UN developed a very different understanding of the situation in North Africa than did their colleagues based in Washington.

It was for these reasons that the nationalists continued to view the internationalization of the Moroccan question as pivotal to their liberation struggle and consequently maintained a dynamic presence in the United States until the eve of independence. A French diplomat noted in September 1955 that the members of the MOID were still "very active, increasing contacts and meetings, and distributing propaganda materials."[239] Other observers confirmed this assessment. "The newspapers are full of details . . . about the situation in Morocco," an American supporter wrote in a letter to Tetouan.[240] Another acquaintance noted that "much is written about Morocco in the newspapers, especially in the *New York Times*" before adding that "there is much sympathy for Morocco."[241] The anticolonial campaign in New York did not decrease in either intensity or scope despite the UN's failure to live up to the Moroccans' expectations.

At the same time, the Algerian nationalists had just begun to establish their own permanent delegation in New York. Of course, the members of the MOID welcomed their colleagues with open arms and put the resources of their bureau at the *Front de Libération Nationale*'s (FLN) disposal; the state-of-the-art printing press served the Algerians especially well during the weeks following their arrival.[242] A decade of North African anticolonial solidarity in Paris, Cairo, and beyond thus transferred across the Atlantic. And the Algerians could obviously learn a great deal from the Moroccans, who had successfully internationalized their case during the previous years. After having received adequate training by the members of the MOID, the FLN representatives would eventually open the Algerian Office in Manhattan and commence their own outreach campaign. Anti-French activism thus continued in the United States long after Morocco obtained its independence in March 1956.

CONCLUSION

The Moroccan nationalist movement's advocacy campaign must be considered a success since it put substantial international pressure on the colonizers; the frantic reactions by French officials and the procolonial propaganda tour by Mohammed Temsamani affirm this point. But what else does this story tell us? How do the anticolonial efforts in the United States allow us to reassess the history of Morocco's decolonization? Most importantly, they highlight the efficacy of the nationalists' networked approach, which allowed them to carry their message to places as diverse as Ivy League campuses and civic associations, churches and think tanks, Capitol Hill and the Supreme Court. Using the same tactics that had proven effective in Paris and—at least temporarily—in Cairo, they formed countless friendships with influential individuals from across civil society who subsequently spoke out on behalf of Moroccan independence. Both regional radio stations and national newspapers regularly invited the members of the MOID to comment on the latest developments in North Africa. Within a decade of the publication of Morocco's two independence manifestos, a previously largely unknown geopolitical issue had entered the public discourse.

The activities in New York also brought several activists to the forefront of the nationalist movement who had gained pivotal skills while serving as the MOID's permanent members. Mehdi Ben Aboud became the Istiqlal's primary authority on American politics; Mehdi Bennouna emerged as the PNR's leading media expert; and Abderrahman Abdelali had learned the ins and outs of international diplomacy. Due to their unique positions in the transnational anticolonial network, they closed the structural hole between the nationalist movement and the American public, thus occupying privileged positions with regard to "broker[ing] the flow of information between people, and control[ling] the projects that bring together people from opposite sides of the hole."[243] Their acquired social capital made them precious assets to the nationalist movement, and the leaders of the Istiqlal and the PNR continuously praised them for their activities on the exterior. Together they continued to serve the anticolonial movement loyally until independence, when all of them began to work directly for the royal palace following independence. When using the nationalist movement's social network as our unit of analysis, these activists no longer seem like marginal figures but instead appear as central players in a web of personal contacts that reached from North Africa across the entire United States via New York.

The social network approach also highlights the contributions that a diverse group of non-Moroccans made to the anticolonial struggle. One fascinating personality was the multilingual soldier of fortune Levon Keshishian, who leveraged his unique access to the corridors of power in New York and Washington to lobby on behalf of various Middle Eastern governments. Over the years, Keshishian managed to acquire "five passports . . . for services rendered to assorted regimes of varying degrees of unsavoriness," according to a remote acquaintance.[244] Whereas regular citizens such as Benjamin Rivlin and Gilbert Jonas played important roles in supporting the MOID's activities, prominent individuals such as Eleanor Roosevelt and William O. Douglas brought the topic of Moroccan independence to the attention of the general public. Equally fascinating was the cooperation among organizations with otherwise contradictory interests—even the labor movement and the business community worked hand in hand on this issue. Moreover, the support provided by individuals associated with the US intelligence community demonstrated that at least some officials in Washington sympathized with the goals of the Moroccan nationalist movement as well. Unlike many elected representatives and career diplomats, the (former) intelligence agents displayed a shrewd understanding of their country's long-term interests in North Africa and acted accordingly.

Yet the Moroccans most important supporter was none other than their mentor Rom Landau, a truly fascinating character. His outsized role in the liberation struggle did not go unnoticed. In a book review published in 1963, Ernest Gellner emphasized the "importance of Mr. Landau as . . . propagandist of the Moroccan cause during the struggle for independence." The eminent British anthropologist even grasped Landau's structural role within the larger anticolonial network, describing him as "a bridge or channel of information between the oppressed nation and the wider world."[245] Landau also benefited personally from his activities as the spokesman of the nationalist movement, because they led to an entirely new career. He became a professor of Islamic and North African studies at the American Academy in San Francisco in 1954 and, from 1956 on, at the University of the Pacific in Stockton, despite the fact that he had never completed an academic degree. Landau had finally found fulfillment in his double role as an esteemed scholar and the unofficial spokesman for the Moroccan nationalist movement after two decades of constantly switching jobs. Of course, he continued to advise his Moroccan friends and write articles for *Free Morocco* even after relocating to California, and his close relationship with the North African kingdom would endure long after its independence.[246]

The campaign in the United States was the last—and most important— phase of the Moroccan struggle for independence on the global stage. When the negotiations between the representatives of the sultan and the French diplomats commenced in Aix-en-Bains in November 1955, the end of the protectorates became just a matter of time. The office in New York had served its purpose, and its members consequently seized the opportunity to return to their homeland. But their journey was far from over. Equipped with unique skills and personal contacts, they secured for themselves prominent positions in postcolonial Morocco in the direct service of Sultan Mohammed ben Youssef. Loyalty to the royal palace suddenly trumped party membership and a commitment to a democratic constitutional monarchy. The legacy of the MOID thus lived on through myriad individual trajectories that bridged the transition from the colonial period to the era of independence.

CHAPTER FIVE

RABAT: THE HOMECOMING

A WAVE OF ENTHUSIASM SWEPT across Morocco when a plane carrying Sultan Mohammed ben Youssef and his entire family landed just outside Rabat on 16 November 1955. His impassioned reception demonstrated that the monarch had come to embody his country's liberation struggle during his more than two years in forced exile. The slow procession to the royal palace turned into a victory march as hundreds of thousands celebrated not only the return of their beloved sovereign but also the quickly approaching end of the protectorate regimes. According to the *New York Times*, "As [the sultan] went in an open limousine, Moroccans on foot and horseback greeted him with shouts of loyalty and devotion" to celebrate their "day of victory."[1] The *Los Angeles Times* reported that "tens of thousands of Moslems screamed out their happiness" and that "his frenzied welcome was in dramatic contrast with the grim hour" of his exile.[2] Enthusiastic comments filled the pages of the nationalist press—*al-ʿAlam* claimed that the Moroccan people had just witnessed the "turning of a page filled with hopes and tears . . . sacrifice and heroism," because "these historical events" foreshadowed "a new age filled with freedom and progress."[3]

Sidi Mohammed's triumphant return marked the beginning of the end of the colonial era. Numerous factors had led to this historic juncture. An armed insurgency inside Morocco had destabilized the colonial regime to a degree not seen since Mohammed b. Abdelkarim al-Khattabi's revolt during the 1920s. Simultaneously, the steadily growing anticolonial sentiments among its own population had changed France's attitude toward its North African protectorate; thanks to the tireless efforts of the nationalist activists in Paris, a majority of French politicians no longer supported the oppressive policies pursued by the Residency. Moreover, the government needed to focus its resources on defeating the Algerian Revolution, which had engulfed its most precious overseas possession for more than a year.[4] Following several months of tough negotiations, France finally surrendered control over Morocco on 22 March 1956; Francisco Franco agreed to end the Spanish protectorate two weeks later. The national liberation struggle had come to a successful conclusion after more than four decades of colonial rule.

Besides domestic and regional factors, it was the international political constellation that had ultimately convinced the French government to relinquish its protectorate. During a speech before the UN General Assembly on 29 September 1955, Foreign Minister Antoine Pinay had used the word "independence" for the first time while expressing his government's willingness to "form a Moroccan government" in order to "turn Morocco into a modern, democratic and sovereign state."[5] Although he still envisioned a relationship of "freely consented interdependence" between the metropole and the North African kingdom, Pinay's statement indicated a sea change in official French policy.[6] That the conservative politician had given the speech in New York underlined the global character of Morocco's decolonization: it had been the mounting worldwide hostility toward French colonialism—expressed mainly at the UN—that provided the final impetus.[7] The anticolonial propaganda campaign on the exterior especially had contributed to the demise of the colonial regimes by putting international pressure on the governments in Paris and Madrid to surrender their North African possessions.

The Moroccan Office of Information and Documentation, the Bureau de documentation et information du Parti de l'Istiqlal, and Maktab al-Maghrib al-'Arabi came to a standstill during the fall of 1955 as their members returned home to enjoy the rewards of their victory. Rabat now replaced New York, Paris, Cairo, and Tangier as the epicenter of Moroccan politics. The nationalists had been working toward this outcome for a long time. Yet the transition process quickly turned into a power struggle that pitted the monarchy against the country's independent political parties. Soon enough, the royal palace dominated the domestic political arena. The vacuum created by the withdrawal of the colonial powers led to a ruthless free-for-all in which the country's elites battled over the spoils offered by the modern state apparatus, ultimately culminating in the adoption of the first constitution in December 1962, which cemented the rule of the Alaoui royal family.

Having achieved its original purpose, namely, the end of the colonial occupation of Morocco, the nationalists' propaganda network suddenly underwent a dramatic transformation. This happened not solely due to an inevitable structural logic but because Mohammed ben Youssef decided to strengthen his own position to the detriment of the nationalist movement. He skillfully co-opted the network's brokers, thereby weakening the Istiqlal and transforming it into an opposition party. This brilliant move secured him pivotal social and human capital. Having lost competent personnel and important international contacts, the Istiqlal no longer had the resources necessary to successfully compete with the monarch. Sidi Mohammed, meanwhile, consolidated the rule of the Alaoui dynasty; by the time of his state visit to Washington in November 1957, he had established himself as his nation's sole legitimate representative.

REESTABLISHING THE ALAOUI DYNASTY

Sidi Mohammed had not traveled directly home from his exile in Madagascar but instead had gone to Paris first in order to personally negotiate the conditions of his pending return. On 6 November, after several days of deliberations with Antoine Pinay, the two statesmen published a joint declaration in which they announced Mohammed ben Youssef's reinstatement as the rightful sultan. The new provisional government, under the leadership of his confidant Mbarek Bekkai, was in existence by the end of the month and subsequently negotiated the abrogation of the Treaty of Fez.[8] The monarch had thus actively participated in the diplomatic row over the end of the protectorate, thereby ensuring his influence over the transition process to full independence. From the perspective of the government in Paris, Sidi Mohammed suddenly appeared to be the perfect ally in those tumultuous times, as his success would ensure an orderly decolonization that might serve France's long-term interests.[9]

Many Moroccan nationalists hoped at this time to remake their nation as a constitutional monarchy, combining in harmony its ancient royal family with a freely elected parliament. Both the Istiqlal and the sultan had repeatedly stated the case for this kind of political system throughout the struggle for independence. Upon his arrival in Rabat, Sidi Mohammed had also publicly reaffirmed his "desire to be the constitutional king of a strong, modern, free, democratic, and independent country."[10] Soon enough, though, the contradictions between rhetoric and reality became apparent as the Istiqlal and the monarchy commenced a fight best described as a zero-sum game for control of the state apparatus.[11] The sultan displayed little inclination to share any political power with the nationalist parties. He also sought to avoid the fate of the Egyptian king Faruq, whom the Free Officers had overthrown in July 1952 in order to establish a republic. Together with his son Hassan, the Moroccan monarch thus devised a sophisticated divide-and-conquer strategy that would eventually enable him to gain a quasi monopoly over politics in independent Morocco.

Sidi Mohammed's position had actually been strengthened by his time in exile.[12] In a society prone to saint veneration, he had turned into an inviolate figure who stood on direct speaking terms with the divine and whose blessing guaranteed the well-being of his subjects. Of course, the leaders of the nationalist movement also retained widespread popularity. The inhabitants of Tangier passionately welcomed the Istiqlal's delegates upon their return from Paris; coming from Cairo via Madrid, Allal al-Fassi encountered enthusiastic crowds when his plane touched down in Tetouan.[13] But despite their unquestionable stature, the nationalist leaders could not compete with the attention Sidi Mohammed received wherever he went. Even the nationalist press celebrated the fact that "almost 400,000 tongues greeted the sovereign of Morocco and independence in Casablanca" following his first visit to the kingdom's largest city.[14] When the sultan returned from the final negotiations with Francisco Franco in April 1956, hundreds of thousands gathered in Tetouan "to honor the leader of rebirth, renewal and reform, Mohammed ben Youssef, who broke the shackles of colonialism."[15] He had become the "great liberator" who had brought about "the beginning of a new age fulfilling the noble dreams of the Moroccan people."[16] According to an article that expressed both admiration and resignation, "All that remains is for us to wish good luck to His Majesty."[17]

Yet Mohammed ben Youssef's success did not rely solely on his widespread popularity; he also benefited from the fact that the French government viewed him as a regional ally and therefore strengthened his position. As the protectorate authorities organized their withdrawal from the country, they handed over large parts of the highly efficient state apparatus directly to his control.[18] The most striking example was the founding ceremony of the national army in May 1956. Following a speech by Sidi Mohammed, the gathered officers swore "loyalty to God and [their] King . . . to serve [their] fatherland . . . and execute the order of [their] supreme commander, His Majesty the King."[19] Then they lined up before the monarch to kiss his hand in the ultimate gesture of complete submission.[20] A few days later, he appointed his son Hassan as the head of the appropriately named Royal Armed Forces—the crown prince subsequently rarely appeared in public without his uniform. Consisting of both former anticolonial guerilla fighters and veterans of the French colonial army, Morocco's newly formed military became a staunchly monarchist force at the disposal of the Alaoui family.

The monarch also worked hard to be seen as the sole representative of the Moroccan nation, both at home and abroad. The projection of legitimacy became central to his rule, especially since no national legislative elections took place until May 1963. One event highlighting this process occurred on 23 July 1956, when the Security Council voted to admit Morocco as a new member to the UN. Sidi Mohammed immediately seized this unique opportunity to reaffirm his standing in the eyes of his subjects; he informed them via radio that "this historical event confirms our independence and makes us stand . . . on equal footing with other free nations."[21] The monarch took another important step to cement his image as a modern ruler in Au-

gust 1957 when he dropped his old title and instead became King Mohammed V. This act symbolized his transformation from a traditional feudal lord
to a "progressive" and "enlightened" head of state.[22] Sidi Mohammed positioned himself as the leader of the nation by way of such public performances
of authority.

Yet Mohammed ben Youssef also intervened directly in the political process. Most importantly, he breathed new life into Mohammed Hassan al-
Ouazzani's PDI as an alternative opposition party and created successive
governments staffed with loyalists such as Mbarek Bekkai. He also formed
an alliance with the conservative rural nobility, which would remain a central pillar of his power for years to come. This allowed him to counterbalance
the urban-based nationalist movement.[23] Furthermore, the monarch encouraged the establishment of royalist parties such as *Al-Haraka al-Sha'biyya* (the
Mouvement populaire), which had its base among the conservative Amazigh
tribes of the rural hinterlands and rejected the leadership claim of the Istiqlal.
The palace continued the centuries-old tradition of securing its power by dividing and controlling the elites of the country, with the important differ-
ence that it suddenly had its own superior power base that consisted of a
modern army and an efficient administration.[24]

Another reason for the defeat of the nationalist movement was the increasing fragmentation of the Istiqlal itself. It initially consolidated its strength by
merging with the PNR on 16 May 1956, a move that was the logical outcome
of more than a decade of close nationalist cooperation on the exterior.[25] But
the party also experienced a generational split between conservatives such as
Allal al-Fassi and the younger cohort of nationalists, many of whom had been
exposed to more radical political ideas during their time in France.[26] On
6 November 1959, several high-ranking members left the Istiqlal and founded
al-Ittihad al-Watani li-l-Quwwat al-Sha'biyya (*Union nationale des forces populaires*, UNFP), which called for agrarian reforms, complete economic liberation, and a truly democratic government. Led by Abderrahim Bouabid, Abderrahman Youssoufi, and Mehdi Ben Barka, the UNFP became a left-wing
competitor intent on challenging the former colleagues as well as the royal
palace. This was a major setback for the Istiqlal, especially since the renegades
had filled extremely important roles within the party prior to their defec-
tion: Bouabid had organized the working masses of Casablanca and partici-

pated in the founding of the *Union Marocain du Travail* (UMT), Youssoufi counted among only a handful of Moroccan lawyers, and Ben Barka had become the "true boss of the party" during the 1950s due to his impressive organizational skills.[27]

Sidi Mohammed's increasing dominance of postindependence Morocco also rested on structural factors, however. Because the nationalist movement had organized its global propaganda activities around a flexible network of supporters, it had been able to create a wide array of contacts around the world. These foreign associates had helped the Istiqlal and the PNR spread their message abroad. But although it had proven extremely useful throughout the years of the anticolonial struggle, this mode of organization suddenly became a liability during the postindependence era. The monarch now co-opted the key nodes of the nationalists' network, thus securing for himself invaluable social capital while significantly weakening the political opposition. Those activists that had staffed the MOID became his primary targets.

CO-OPTING THE NATIONALISTS

Mohammed Laghzaoui had been one of the central nodes of the nationalist movement's network on the exterior, not only because of his position as the Istiqlal's main financier but also due to the numerous contacts he had created during his residence in the United States. The monarch thus regarded the staunch royalist as a logical ally. Within a few weeks after Morocco's independence, Sidi Mohammed asked his old friend to return home to serve in an official position. Laghzaoui heeded the monarch's call and left his self-imposed exile in such haste that he forgot to clear out his account at Chase Bank in Manhattan.[28] Mohammed ben Youssef ordered him to build up the kingdom's national police force, a position of incredible importance given the still-volatile security situation inside the country.[29] It did not matter that the businessman lacked any experience that might have justified this choice. Laghzaoui's personal loyalty to the monarch seemed much more important. "From today on . . . national security, which is the guarantee of our sovereignty and stability, . . . has come under the complete control of His Majesty," Laghzaoui declared following his appointment in April 1956.[30]

Laghzaoui fulfilled his role as the first security chief with great efficiency until 1960, when he handed over the staunchly royalist police force to the regime's most ruthless henchman, Colonel Mohammed Oufkir. The security apparatus remains today one of the central pillars underpinning Morocco's monarch.[31] As a reward for his services, the king appointed Laghzaoui as director of the *Office Chérifien des Phosphates*, the country's most important industry, before asking him to head the Ministry of Commerce.[32] Known as "Monsieur 51%" for his practice of demanding majority stakes in private companies in exchange for political protection, he became one of the most influential figures at the intersection of the royal palace and the business sector.[33] He also maintained the contacts established during his residence in North America throughout this period; in August 1962, Laghzaoui met with an AFL activist who had been paid by the CIA to discuss Algeria's independence with him.[34] The first Moroccan head of national security embodied Sidi Mohammed's desire to capture the state apparatus while benefiting from the social capital acquired by former nationalists during their years abroad.

Another individual rewarded for his activism outside Morocco and his personal loyalty to the monarch was Mehdi Bennouna, whose media skills made him an invaluable asset to the palace. He had played a pivotal role in the establishment of the MOID before returning to Tetouan in November 1953 and serving as the editor of the PNR's newspaper *al-Umma*. After independence, Sidi Mohammed made him the press secretary of the royal cabinet to benefit from the unique professional experiences that he had acquired in New York. During Bennouna's tenure, the palace brought the Ministry of Information under its control, and the radio—hitherto the voice of the nationalists in exile—became the most important tool for disseminating royal propaganda among the general population.[35] On 31 May 1959, Mehdi Bennouna founded the *Maghreb Agence Presse* (MAP), which he led for sixteen years with the main goal of replacing the dominance of the local media market by French outlets. The news agency openly embraced its founder's royalist sentiments and became the monarchy's semiofficial mouthpiece. The Moroccan state eventually nationalized the MAP in 1973, and it continues to reside in an office building located directly next to the palace grounds in Rabat.

IMAGE 8. Mohammed V inspecting the recently established *Maroc Agence Press*, 1959. He is accompanied by Prince Hassan (back left) and Mehdi Bennouna (left with glasses). (Source: Aboubakr Bennouna. Reprinted with permission.)

Sidi Mohammed also co-opted Mehdi Ben Aboud, who had cofounded the MOID and spearheaded the nationalist propaganda campaign in North America. Seeking to benefit from his expertise in diplomacy, the sultan awarded him the Ouissam Alaouite, the highest honor of the state, and ordered him to establish the first Moroccan embassy in the United States.[36] On 5 September 1956, Mehdi Ben Aboud presented his credentials to President Dwight D. Eisenhower and thereby inaugurated a new phase in the history of US-Moroccan relations. His friend William O. Douglas showed himself very content with the appointment. The Supreme Court justice immediately sent Ben Aboud a letter to welcome him back and express his desire for a private meeting "to receive the current news of the birth of a new and independent Morocco."[37] Due to his many years of service in New York and Washington, Ben Aboud was uniquely qualified to represent the North African monarchy in the United States.

The royal palace also made good use of other nationalists who had promoted the Moroccan case before the UN. Abderrahman Abdelali, also a former member of the MOID, returned to Morocco after independence to begin a career in the Ministry of Foreign Affairs, where he took charge of establishing relations with other recently decolonized states. In November 1956, he joined the new Moroccan embassy in London; two years later, he celebrated his engagement to Aicha Laghzaoui, whom he had met while working with her father in New York. The official reception attracted substantial media coverage, not least because Sidi Mohammed himself attended as the guest of honor. Abdelali subsequently served as both minister of agriculture and minister of public works and accompanied the monarch on his first journey across the Middle East in January 1960.[38] His promising career soon came to a tragic end, however: after a short but painful battle with pancreatic cancer, he died in a hospital in Boston on 10 March 1964.[39]

Abderrahman Anegay also returned to Morocco during the final months prior to independence. He had served as Allal al-Fassi's personal assistant in places as far-flung as the Middle East, Scandinavia, and the Americas. In order to secure his experience, the monarch made him chief of the royal cabinet, the very center of Moroccan political power.[40] Sadly, though, Anegay died in a car crash on 29 January 1959. Although his sudden demise was a painful loss for the monarch, Sidi Mohammed once again demonstrated his ability to make the best out of any situation. Just a few months after the funeral, he appointed Anegay's young widow as cultural attaché to the embassy in Washington, thus representing himself as the emancipator of Morocco's women. This move quickly yielded the desired result. According to the *New York Times*, the "pretty" Halima Anegay "had scored in unofficial polls—conducted in the lounges and meeting rooms—as the most attractive delegate to attend a General Assembly session in many years."[41]

The monarchy's co-optation campaign did not limit itself to lesser-known figures of the anticolonial struggle—even Ahmed Balafrej ultimately joined the sultan's patronage circle. The Istiqlal's secretary general initially held brief assignments as foreign minister and prime minister in governments appointed by Mohammed ben Youssef, but he eventually left party politics for a career in the direct service of the monarch. As the "personal representative of His Majesty," he advised Sidi Mohammed on foreign policy and maintained contacts to the nationalist movement's former foreign supporters.[42] Balafrej had always been a dedicated monarchist and thus enjoyed the privilege of serving the royal palace directly.[43] He also drew on his time in New York to lead several Moroccan delegations to the UN. His new assignments symbolized the growing power of Sidi Mohammed, who managed to co-opt the leader of the country's largest party and thereby highlight the fragility of the political opposition.

Mohammed ben Youssef's campaign of co-optation also targeted those nationalists previously active in France. Ahmed Alaoui had served as a leading member of the Bureau du Parti de l'Istiqlal in Paris and correspondent for *al-ʿAlam*; his countless contacts among the French press corps made him a central node in the Istiqlal's global network. Given his close relationship to the royal family, it proved quite easy for the palace to recruit him. Alaoui came back to Morocco aboard Sidi Mohammed's plane during his triumphant return from exile and was immediately appointed chief of the royal press services.[44] He later went on to climb the ladder of public service as a member of several different governments and even served as minister of information in 1960.[45] Still, Alaoui did not dedicate himself only to politics—he also played a leading role in the establishment of the first national television channel in 1961 and founded the two influential Francophone newspapers *Le Matin* and *Maroc Soir*, all of which faithfully reproduced the opinions of the monarchy on a wide range of issues.[46]

A major reason behind Ahmed Alaoui's successful career seems to have been his centrality in the nationalist propaganda network. Despite having spent more than a decade in France, Alaoui had failed to complete his studies in medicine, which had angered the Istiqlal leadership eager to witness the rise of a new class of modern professionals. Instead he had learned the ins and outs of the French media through his friendships with countless journalists in Paris. Nobody else seemed more qualified to establish a pro-monarchy propaganda apparatus. Not everybody held Alaoui in high regard, however. Many foreign observers showed themselves unenthusiastic about a man once described "as an energetic and disorganized person, who is sometimes amusing but often exasperating."[47] Alaoui's "reputation is generally low among foreign newsmen who are apt to regard him more of an obstruction than a help in obtaining news from the Palace," noted a US diplomat in 1957.[48] But despite such disparaging remarks, Sidi Mohammed knew how to appreciate the unique skills offered by Ahmed Alaoui to the royal family.

Those nationalists formerly networking in Cairo also enjoyed illustrious careers in independent Morocco. Abdelmajid Benjelloun had served as the director of Maktab al-Maghrib and attended the Bandung conference in 1955; after independence he helped the Ministry of Foreign Affairs establish diplomatic relations between Morocco and the postcolonial states of Asia and Africa.[49] His companion Abdelkarim Ghallab occupied a leadership position in the Ministry of Foreign Affairs as well.[50] But after four years in the direct service of the state, he returned to journalism and served as al-'Alam's editor in chief until passing away four decades later. Ghallab also became one of the country's most influential novelists, publishing a number of widely acclaimed books and serving as the head of the state-subsidized Union of Moroccan Writers (*Ittihad Kuttab al-Maghrib* or *Union des écrivains du Maroc*) during the 1970s. Through their countless contributions to the making of postcolonial Morocco—both as state functionaries and active members of civil society—Benjelloun and Ghallab directly served the interests of the royal palace.

Mohammed ben Youssef not only recruited many former anticolonial activists but also "ambassadorized" the country's political elite. Within just a few years after independence, many high-ranking members of the Istiqlal had begun serving as Morocco's diplomatic representatives abroad: Abdelkabir al-Fassi in Iran and Jordan; Tayeb Bennouna in Spain; Abderrahim Bouabid in France; Abdelkhaleq Torres in Spain and Egypt; Ahmed Ben al-Melih across the Arab world as well as in Iran and Turkey; Abdellatif Sbihi in various Latin American and Scandinavian states; and Abdelkarim Ben Thabet as cultural attaché in Tunisia before his premature death in 1961.[51] Even ex-khalifa Hassan ben al-Mehdi served as his country's first postcolonial ambassador in Great Britain.[52] The monarch's decisions ostensibly acknowledged the indisputable qualifications of these men while also rewarding each for his efforts during the liberation struggle. But their appointments also resulted from a shrewd political calculation. After all, by removing these well-connected individuals from the domestic political stage, the monarch directly weakened the political opposition. With many of its most influential members spread out across the globe, the Istiqlal had even fewer resources at its disposal to counterbalance the increasing power of the royal palace.

Sidi Mohammed's campaign of co-optation reveals a clear pattern. Evidently, he had developed a profound understanding of the nationalist move-

ment's organizational structure and therefore focused his efforts on those activists occupying central positions within its global anticolonial network.
Their absences inevitably weakened the Istiqlal. Nationalists such as Ben
Aboud, Bennouna, Balafrej, and Alaoui had bridged structural holes between the party and influential supporters abroad. Now they had become
royal assets. In addition to gaining social capital, the monarchy also obtained
invaluable human resources, namely, a corps of technocrats fluent in foreign
languages and trained in diplomacy and media relations. Those remained
rare sets of skills given the abysmal failure of the colonizers to establish a
modern education system (only 640 Muslims had obtained high school di-
plomas during forty-four years of French rule).[53] Moreover, since Laghzaoui
had been the chief donor of the Istiqlal, his loss was also a painful blow to
the party's finances. Taken together, these individual moves reveal a larger
strategy that ultimately secured the hegemony of the royal palace in postindependence Morocco.

CO-OPTING THE FOREIGN SUPPORTERS

Sidi Mohammed's drive to co-opt the members of the nationalists' network
also took aim at their foreign supporters. He began his campaign during
his short stay in Paris in November 1955. The monarch organized a dinner
party to which he invited several of the Istiqlal's most important local allies;
Georges Izard, Charles-André Julien, General Georges Catroux, and François Mauriac all joined him at the elegant *Pavillon Henri IV* just outside
the French capital.[54] A cordial atmosphere characterized the gathering as the
monarch thanked each one of his guests for his efforts on behalf of Morocco's independence. His eldest son, Hassan, seized the occasion for a gesture
of triumph. Following the end of the meal, a visibly satisfied crown prince
showed the guests "a huge mountain of telegrams, many from the sultan's
enemies, congratulating him on his return."[55] The Moroccan royals maintained many of these contacts long after independence; in 1957, for example,
they invited Mauriac to attend the thirtieth anniversary of the monarch's
coronation as a guest of honor.[56]

   One of the first targets of the monarch's international co-optation campaign was Pierre Parent, whom he granted the opportunity to return to his be-

loved Morocco more than three years after the Residency had expelled him. As one of the nationalists' most outspoken French supporters, his numerous publications on the situation in Morocco had once played a central role in their global anticolonial propaganda campaign. Now the royal palace hired Parent as a host for the Francophone *Radio Maroc* in order to benefit from his reputation.[57] The disabled veteran passed away just one year later, however.[58] In an obituary dedicated to its former columnist, *al-Istiqlal* celebrated the "just man" and "fellow traveler of the Moroccan patriots," whose "memory will remain with the many that knew him or could appreciate his positions during the [liberation struggle's] most critical hours."[59] At least one fellow French settler shared this sentiment. "Pierre Parent did not only bring honor to his fatherland, but to mankind," he wrote in a letter to the editors of the newspaper.[60]

An even more important supporter of the nationalist movement was Robert E. Rodes, who restarted his commercial endeavors in Morocco following years of anticolonial activism in the United States. Based in both New York and Casablanca, he began to export items ranging from canned tomatoes to artisanal products to North America.[61] Rodes continued to draw on his contacts on Capitol Hill to further his business interests. In a letter to the House Committee on Agriculture written in 1967, he urged the congressmen to ease the import of Moroccan cotton in order to reward "a country which has consistently been friendly to us."[62] Although it remains unclear what kind of relationship—if any—he maintained with the royal palace, Rodes definitely cooperated with the authorities of the young state.[63] His activities must have appeared highly desirable from the viewpoint of the monarchy, because they contributed to the diversification of the Moroccan economy and thus lessened the country's dependence on the French market. Rodes's contributions to the struggle for national liberation had thus ultimately benefited him economically.

But the most important ally of the nationalists had undoubtedly been Rom Landau, whose contributions to the anticolonial campaign in the United States can hardly be overemphasized. Morocco's independence in March 1956 thus felt like a great personal victory. Ahmed Balafrej immediately invited his old friend to Rabat ("the happy outcome of [recent] events . . . should provide you with great satisfaction").[64] Finally Landau could return to the country from which he had been banned for almost five years.

He gave speeches at the Istiqlal headquarters, toured the countryside to participate in discussions with local party members, and gave a series of radio talks on the history of Morocco's struggle for independence.[65] The nationalist press lauded the "great British writer who dedicated his life to the defense of the Moroccan cause and whose name is connected to the struggle . . . for Moroccan independence."[66] Landau noticeably enjoyed the attention he received as he toured the country in the company of his Moroccan friends.

Mohammed ben Youssef had always been well aware of Rom Landau's importance—after all, he had authored the monarch's semiofficial biography, *The Sultan of Morocco*, which had served as propaganda material worldwide. With independence finally achieved, the monarch drew Landau ever closer into the royal orbit by making him commander of the Order of Ouissam Alaouite and inviting him to an official visit to the former Spanish zone. His alliance with the Alaoui dynasty continued even after Sidi Mohammed's death. Hassan was coronated in February 1961, and Landau finished his official biography just in time for the new king's state visit to the United States two years later. He presented the manuscript to the monarch at a private audience before accompanying him on a trip to Tangier.[67] The Moroccans also agreed to his offer to join their entourage in Washington.[68]

Rom Landau played a crucial role in the establishment of strong cultural ties between independent Morocco and the United States. He regularly gave lectures at the American cultural institute in Rabat at the request of the US embassy. He also developed a summer studies program that would allow North American students to learn about Moroccan culture at the newly established Mohammed V University, the country's first modern institution of higher education, inaugurated in December 1957.[69] Back in the United States, Landau continued to enlighten the general public about the North African kingdom by way of regular radio broadcasts and workshops for high school teachers. He even became an advisor to the newly established Peace Corps and organized training camps for volunteers about to embark on their mission to Morocco.[70] The former member of the nationalist movement's anticolonial network continued to serve as a broker between the North African kingdom and the Anglophone world long after independence. Ahmed Balafrej thanked him personally for "the great activity, which you do not cease to deploy in order to make Morocco better known."[71]

Although his writings consisted predominantly of highly entertaining personal anecdotes and certainly did not fulfill the basic requirements for serious academic scholarship, Rom Landau became a renowned expert on Moroccan affairs; his books remained among the few available on the subject at university libraries in the United States throughout the 1970s. His reputation even reached as far as Washington, DC. Following John F. Kennedy's famous July 1957 speech on the Senate floor calling for Algeria's independence, he submitted a copy to Rom Landau and explained, "I should very much appreciate having your comments on this address and I would be happy to send you further copies, if you would care to distribute them . . . in Morocco."[72] Landau sent the senator his latest book, *Moroccan Drama,* which Kennedy lauded as "a very fine piece of work."[73] Rom Landau's participation in the campaign for Moroccan independence had made him, according to Kennedy, "one of the leading authorities in America on the problems of North Africa."[74]

As the nationalist movement's semiofficial mentor, Rom Landau had bridged the structural hole between Morocco and the United States. After independence, though, he quickly turned from a spokesman for the Istiqlal into what one American observer disparagingly called a "court historian."[75] Landau relocated permanently to Marrakesh in 1968, where he lived in a beautiful villa given to him by the monarch until his death eight years later. The numerous contacts he had acquired during the struggle for independence increased the social capital at the disposal of the royal palace. And thanks to his reputation as an acclaimed North Africa expert, he could justify Sidi Mohammed's rule to those abroad. At the same time, the monarch legitimized himself domestically by demonstrating his close friendship with a reputable Westerner who had contributed significantly to Moroccan independence. The British writer continues to enjoy a stellar reputation in Morocco, where contemporary schoolbooks cite him as an authority on the kingdom's history.[76]

Charles-André Julien was another influential supporter drawn into the orbit of the royal palace. Sidi Mohammed asked the French historian to assist with the establishment of Mohammed V University. Julien gladly accepted this task and spent the next few years commuting between his apartment in Paris and his second home in the Moroccan capital. To underline the connection between the newly independent state and the legacy of the anticolonial struggle, he suggested dedicating the university's central auditorium to Louis Massignon, the famous Orientalist who had done more than most to legitimize the anticolonial activists in Paris after World War II.[77] Moreover, Julien regularly provided advice on the training of engineers, doctors, agronomists, and other modern professionals who could help Morocco became a truly sovereign nation independent of French expertise.[78] Throughout this period, he stayed in constant contact with individuals close to the monarch, including Prime Minister Mbarek Bekkai and Ahmed Bennani, the director of protocol at the royal palace.[79]

Unlike Rom Landau, however, Charles-André Julien did not become an uncritical supporter of the Moroccan monarchy. In November 1961, he resigned from his position as dean of the faculty of letters due to a disagreement with the political direction of the university leadership. Nonetheless, Julien did not break off all contact with the Alaoui family. He even traveled to Morocco for a final time in 1978 to present his latest book, *Le Maroc face aux impérialismes*, to King Hassan II during a private audience.[80] At the same time, Julien, the outspoken socialist, balanced his relationship with the Moroccan royals through friendships with the left-wing opposition leaders Abderrahim Bouabid and Mehdi Ben Barka. His British counterpart, by contrast, lacked any critical distance vis-à-vis the palace. Julien therefore regarded Rom Landau as an "apologist" of the monarchy rather than as a serious scholar.[81] But whether or not they had intended to do so, each of these Western academics had helped Sidi Mohammed in his own way by serving him during the important years of power consolidation after 1956.

Mohammed ben Youssef also established links to some of the most prominent American supporters of the liberation struggle, including Irving Brown. After independence, the labor activist stayed in close contact with the leadership of the UMT, whom he invited to the annual conference of the AFL-CIO's executive council in January 1957.[82] Both Mahjoub Ben Seddiq and Tayeb Bouazza claimed that the invitation would "strengthen the bonds of solidarity that unite our syndicalist movement as well as the friendship uniting our countries."[83] They also invited the American representative to the Labor Day parade held in Casablanca under the personal auspices of Sidi Mohammed.[84] US diplomats stationed in Rabat tried to use his influence to protect local American interests. As the UMT emerged as a left-wing critic of the Moroccan regime, Ambassador Charles Yost urged Irving Brown to persuade its leaders to refrain from any "steps which will harm both Morocco and the West."[85] The palace also acted and eventually deposed of Tayeb Bouazza by making him ambassador to Yugoslavia in 1959.[86]

Workers' issues had been of great importance to Mohammed ben Youssef since the days of the liberation struggle. Therefore, he granted an audience to the labor activists immediately upon his return from exile, and Crown Prince Hassan visited the UMT headquarters soon thereafter.[87] During his visit to Paris in 1955, Sidi Mohammed had called on a large gathering of Moroccan laborers "to unite in order to build a new Morocco . . . in which the working class . . . will obtain its freedoms, rights, and well-being."[88] The monarch specifically sought to benefit from the AFL-CIO's anticommunism in order to build a nonradical workers' movement. And the labor leaders, in turn, assured him of their commitment to order and stability.[89] Following the split between the Istiqlal and the UNFP in 1959, the UMT associated itself with the new socialist party. The Istiqlal consequently founded a new labor organization loyal to the party, *al-Ittihad al-'Amm li-l-Shaghalin bi-l-Maghrib* (the *Union générale des travailleurs du Maroc*, UGTM), on 20 March 1960. The US government called on the International Confederation of Free Trade Unions (ICFTU) to provide the new union with organizational support.[90] In addition to continuing his cooperation with both branches of the Moroccan labor movement, Irving Brown maintained a cordial relationship with the royal palace well into the 1970s.[91] His activism in Morocco aligned with the interests of the royal palace even though he neither unconditionally supported the monarchy nor opposed the Istiqlal.

Mohammed ben Youssef also established a lasting relationship with Kenneth Pendar, who accompanied the monarch on his journey to the United States in 1957.[92] The prominent entrepreneur and OSS veteran maintained good contacts with the US intelligence community; his personal career thus mirrored the trajectory of US-Moroccan relations in general. Although he continued to send "greetings from Coca-Cola to the King and the Moroccan people" via advertisements in *al-'Alam*, he also facilitated relations between US officials and the royal palace.[93] We should definitely consider him a principal architect of the increasingly close alliance between Washington and Rabat. Pendar continued to reside in Morocco and southern France until he

passed away in the city of Tangier in 1972.[94] The Coca-Cola bottling plant
in Casablanca is today one of the company's most important "forward operating base[s]" in the world and thus serves as a lasting testimony to his business acumen.[95]

Most American capitalists had supported the Istiqlal's struggle for independence due to economic considerations. They viewed Sidi Mohammed as
a pillar of stability in an increasingly volatile region. And the monarch had
good use for their capital and know-how as he tried to assert himself in a
poor nation that lacked an efficient industrial base. The role played by pro-
American businessman Mohammed Laghzaoui in postindependence Morocco also benefited the United States. By putting him in charge of phosphate mining, the sultan opened to American interests a key industry that
had attracted the covetous eye of the United States ever since the arrival of
the "twelve Apostles" during World War II. The amount of natural miner-
als exported to the United States unsurprisingly doubled between 1956 and
1962 even though overall production slightly fell.[96] The United States had
begun to replace France both militarily and economically, just as the protectorate authorities had feared since the landing of the Allied forces in November 1942.

Beyond such practical alliances, Sidi Mohammed also sought the symbolic benefits he could gain from associating himself with Eleanor Roosevelt.
The family name had taken on an almost magical aura in Morocco ever since
President Franklin D. Roosevelt had promised to facilitate the country's independence during the Anfa Conference in January 1943. Furthermore, nobody had forgotten how the former First Lady had publicly embraced the
members of the MOID; many Moroccans viewed her actions as a continuation of the support provided by her late husband. In the spring of 1956,
a black limousine pulled up at the Roosevelt residence in Hyde Park, New
York, and several Moroccans emerged from the vehicle. The head of the delegation placed a huge bouquet of flowers on FDR's grave and subsequently
conveyed to Mrs. Roosevelt an invitation to visit the sultan in Rabat. Upon
her arrival one year later, Kenneth Pendar led the welcome committee at
the Casablanca airport.[97] Sidi Mohammed received Eleanor Roosevelt in the
royal palace a few days later and personally expressed his gratefulness for her
contributions to Morocco's independence.[98]

Eleanor Roosevelt was not the only First Lady courted by the Moroccan royals. Just a few weeks before her husband's assassination in 1963, Jacqueline Kennedy accepted an invitation from Hassan II for a family vacation in Morocco. The prominent Americans visited many tourist sites, including a local market where a group of Moroccan women greeted them with a "strange, bird-like sound" by ululating in their honor.[99] In the time-proven Alaoui tradition of giving houses as gestures of appreciation, the monarch handed Mrs. Kennedy the keys to an ancient villa in the old city of Marrakesh. The First Lady "accepted gratefully [and] was deeply touched" by the noble gesture, according to royal spokesman Mehdi Bennouna.[100] Three years later, the Moroccan state named one of Casablanca's great boulevards after the late president; his brother, Senator Edward Kennedy, attended its inauguration as the family representative.[101] The Alaoui monarchs skillfully drew parallels between the American dynasties and their own royal lineage, thus increasing their reputation both at home and abroad.

The international arena offered numerous opportunities for Sidi Mohammed's co-optation campaign. Renowned scholars such as Rom Landau and Charles-André Julien helped create a national narrative centered around his persona. They legitimized the Moroccan regime whether through the writing of uncritical biographies or the establishment of a university located directly next to the palace grounds. At the same time, the monarch's good relationship with Irving Brown and Kenneth Pendar provided direct links to the United States. And by embracing Sidi Mohammed publicly, prominent individuals such as Eleanor Roosevelt and François Mauriac indicated that they viewed him as the rightful successor of the nationalist movement. Observers around the globe took notice of the monarch's circle of well-respected friends, whose amity identified him as a moderate pro-Western actor. His Moroccan subjects, meanwhile, saw that the international community had accepted him as their country's true representative. The only thing missing to solidify the king's image as the head of his nation was a state visit to Washington, the most powerful city in the world.

VISITING THE UNITED STATES

Mohammed V had expressed his desire to visit the United States on numerous occasions since his meeting with President Roosevelt in 1943.[102] Just a few

months after his country's independence, he again brought up the issue during a meeting with the newly appointed US ambassador.[103] And Cavendish
Cannon subsequently urged his colleagues in Washington to extend an invitation as soon as possible. Several other Arab leaders had visited the United
States in recent months, and the Moroccans—in the ambassador's words—
"being Orientals . . . tend to examine down to the last detail the attentions
paid to this or that monarch during their Washington visits."[104] His appeal
had the desired effect. In March 1957, Vice President Richard Nixon visited Morocco in order to assure his hosts of the US government's friendship
with their newly independent nation and extend the much-anticipated invitation.[105] Accompanied by his interpreter Abderrahman Anegay, Nixon even
plunged into a crowd of "cheering Moroccans," charming his hosts through
the time-proven tradition of "political handshaking and baby-admiring."[106]

The Eisenhower administration had decided to seize this opportunity to
promote its own strategic interests. First, it planned to secure guarantees for
the military bases, which France had leased to the United States in 1950.
Second, it wanted to expand the operations of its propaganda radio station
Voice of America, which transmitted "free" news from Tangier to the peoples of Europe and the Arab world. Third, it sought to promote regional stability as the Algerian Revolution threatened to spread chaos across North
Africa. Morocco's monarch seemed like an ideal Cold War ally. The State
Department considered "the primary objective for the royal visit to be added
stature for the King and his government, at home and abroad, in a context of
US-Moroccan amity."[107] It specifically sought "to strengthen the King, foster continued collaboration between the Palace and the moderate wing of
[the] Istiqlal, and encourage Morocco to seek closer ties to the US."[108] Mohammed V embodied the ideal counterpoint to Gamal Abdel Nasser's foreign policy of "positive neutrality" at a time when so-called radical Arab nationalism threatened America's regional interests.[109]

Much effort went into preparing for the state visit. Ambassador Mehdi
Ben Aboud suggested the production of a short film that would introduce
Mohammed V to the American public. The royal cabinet immediately approved this proposal and contacted David Schoenbrunn, who had already
made a CBS documentary about the monarch in 1952 in anticipation of the
debate on the Moroccan question at the UN General Assembly. Upon his arrival in Rabat, Foreign Minister Balafrej greeted Schoenbrunn and promised

full cooperation. In a highly unusual move that violated the rigid protocol, Mohammed V welcomed the American journalist in person at the palace gates to convey his personal interest in the project. The goal was to show a film on CBS containing highlights of the monarch's private life about a week before his planned arrival in Washington. This project provided "an excellent means of informing the American public on the King's present status, past record, and future prospects," commented the US embassy in Rabat.[110]

The king also granted an audience to Otto Fuerbringer, the assistant managing editor of *Time* magazine. His publication had recently featured a portrait of the monarch on its cover, and Mohammed V wanted to thank the journalist in person for his interest in Morocco. "The Moroccan ruler evidently realized that in the *Time* official he has a means of getting his views across to an important segment of American public opinion," noted a US diplomat.[111] Meanwhile, Mehdi Bennouna traveled to Washington in order to support the staff of the Moroccan embassy. The former anticolonial activist informed his old journalist acquaintances about the forthcoming visit and hired a public relations company to provide additional assistance.[112] The monarch's advisers also needed written materials to be distributed during the state visit. Therefore, they contacted Rom Landau, who immediately produced a new book titled *Mohammed V, King of Morocco*. The Moroccan press celebrated this latest publication by the man "known for his attachment to our country" as a "passionate biography" that accurately described "the profound communion between the king and his people . . . with great objectivity."[113]

One of those helping the Moroccans prepare for the trip was Lieutenant Commander Leon Blair, who had become a close confidant of Prince Hassan while being stationed in Morocco in 1954. He had initially served as the military liaison officer between the French and the US Navy and became a technical advisor to the newly established Royal Armed Forces after independence.[114] In the fall of 1957, Blair met with Abderrahman Anegay, the chief of the royal cabinet, to help him polish the English-language translations of the speeches the king intended to give throughout his visit.[115] He also assisted the Moroccans with regard to Rom Landau's new biography. Because the printers had completed the book only a few days prior to the scheduled trip, Blair arranged for the US Navy to transport one thousand copies on a military plane to ensure their timely distribution.[116]

The State Department did everything in its power to promote the royal journey. It ordered the United States Information Service (USIS)—its public diplomacy branch—to provide film and photo coverage of the trip, because it feared that the *Agence France Presse*, with its quasi monopoly on foreign news in Morocco, might underplay the visit.[117] Moreover, it decided to fly a dozen Moroccan journalists across the Atlantic to "influence [a] flow of news stories favorable to the United States."[118] The State Department even provided air transportation for Mohammed V and his entourage, which was extremely well received by the palace since it avoided the embarrassing situation of the king having to travel on a French plane.[119] Evidently, both sides—the Moroccans as well as the Americans—had a vital interest in turning the state visit into a success and therefore committed considerable resources to this endeavor.

After months of preparation, the big moment finally arrived. "All along the way from the castle to the airport . . . tens of thousands of citizens greeted the king and expressed their devotion to him" as his limousine passed them.[120] In the eyes of the king's countrymen, nothing symbolized Morocco's sovereignty more than their monarch's impending visit to the most powerful nation in the world. Sidi Mohammed then participated in an elaborate departure ceremony at the airport, which further asserted his independence from Paris and Madrid. He first took leave from the foreign diplomats gathered on the airfield before asking Cavendish Cannon to follow him aboard for a separate final salutation. Left behind on the tarmac while their American colleague was ascending into the plane, the ambassadors of France and Spain understood the meaning of this gesture.[121] The Moroccan sovereign had literally turned his back on the former colonial powers as he embarked into the future with the United States by his side.

One day later, on 25 November 1957, the White House held a state dinner for King Mohammed V, a rare honor reserved for a select few foreign dignitaries each year. President Dwight D. Eisenhower could not attend the reception in person, because he had caught a serious cold that morning while receiving his Moroccan guest at the airport.[122] But the event was nonetheless a complete success. Secretary of State John Foster Dulles organized a white-tie dinner the next day, bringing together a number of illustrious guests to welcome the Moroccan monarch over a repast of spinach cream soup, roasted beef filet, and strawberry mousse.[123] In addition to all members of the cabinet and the bipartisan leadership from Capitol Hill, a number of influential private US citizens attended these two events; William E. Robinson (president of Coca-Cola), Frank Stanton (president of CBS), and Henry R. Luce (founder of *Time* magazine) featured among the august selection of invitees suggested by the State Department.[124] At the explicit request of the Moroccan delegation, the White House also invited George Meany (president of the AFL-CIO labor union) and William O. Douglas (justice of the Supreme Court) to attend the dinner given in honor of the foreign visitor.[125] This prominent lineup not only confirmed the American interest in Mohammed V but also highlighted the multiple bonds—both visible and concealed—that had tied numerous US citizens to the North African kingdom since the late colonial era.

A major objective of Mohammed V's trip was to demonstrate Morocco's status as a sovereign nation. Upon his arrival at Andrews Air Force Base, he briefly spoke about his historic meeting with "the late President Franklin Roosevelt at a time when our armies boldly embarked side by side in the battle for freedom . . . based on mutual respect and appreciation."[126] Nothing could have indicated his desire for strong relations with the United States better than a reference to the venerated American leader, who had once promised to support Morocco's independence. The king also sought to distance himself from the former colonizers and thus insisted that only Arabic and English be spoken at all public events (although he did not mind conversing in French when shielded from the public eye).[127] French diplomats tried to show their respect for the visiting monarch on several occasions throughout his visit, but the Moroccan delegation rejected all such requests. Sidi Mohammed had become the leader of an independent state and did not care for their company while traveling across North America.

The details of Mohammed V's itinerary during his two weeks in the United States also highlighted the demise of the nationalist movement's global network of supporters. For example, the king demonstrated his friendship with the American military personnel stationed in Morocco by ensuring that most stopovers of the royal entourage took place "in communities from which a Naval Air Reserve squadron had visited Morocco during the preceding six months."[128] Although the American officials did not entirely comprehend this pattern, they duly noticed that "His Majesty is interested in the Naval Air Reserve Squadrons as some such squadrons have visited Port Lyautey [Kenitra]."[129] The king also seized the opportunity to visit the AFL-CIO headquarters in Washington to thank George Meany for the assistance his organization had provided during the liberation struggle.[130] Finally, he met William O. Douglas to express his appreciation of the judge's anticolonial publications. The Americans noted that it had always been extremely important for the Moroccans to visit the Supreme Court, since "Douglas [is] well-liked by [the] King" due to the article he had published in *Look* magazine in October, 1954.[131]

Arguably the most symbolic moment of Mohammed V's trip occurred in California, where he insisted on visiting the College of the Pacific in San Francisco. Although the State Department's chief of protocol did not understand why a head of state would want to attend such an obscure institution of higher learning, he dutifully made the necessary arrangements.[132] The reason behind the visit was, of course, the king's desire to thank his old friend Rom Landau in person for his untiring efforts on behalf of Morocco's independence. The British academic had an entire room decorated in the Moroccan style and personally served Mohammed V mint tea and dates upon the arrival of the royal entourage. Foreign Minister Ahmed Balafrej and several other prominent Moroccans used this opportunity to meet their old companion. In a brief speech held at the official reception, Mohammed V praised his "good friend Rom Landau" while emphasizing that the Moroccan people "will always be grateful to him for what he has done . . . standing by our side in our most difficult days."[133]

Mohammed V also used the trip to charm the American public. He wore a cowboy hat while visiting a ranch in Texas and ate fried chicken at a banquet given in his honor by the city of Los Angeles.[134] The monarch even enjoyed a private tour of Disneyland, where "he listened to the explanations of Walt Disney regarding the magic village built for children."[135] Once he arrived in New York, the king not only attended a performance of Puccini's *La Bohème* at the Metropolitan Opera but also went to the Bronx Zoo. Both events attracted massive media attention.[136] The *New York Times* published a picture the next day of the monarch petting a potto (a half monkey of the lemurine family) and reported that he had refused to touch a python presented to him by the zoo director.[137] His daughters Aisha, Nuzha, and Malika gave

IMAGE 9. Rom Landau (right) serving dates to Mohammed V (left) during his visit to the College of the Pacific in San Francisco, 1957. (Source: Rom Landau Papers, Special Collections Research Center, Syracuse University Libraries. Reprinted with permission.)

a press conference to talk about their own experiences in the United States. The gathered journalists fell head over heels for the "modern" and "emancipated" princesses, and the *Los Angeles Times* cheerfully announced that "Aisha has refused to hide her dark beauty behind the Muslim veil or her lively personality behind the traditional silence of Muslim women."[138] The American public had become fascinated by the idea that the members of the Alaoui family were just regular folks open to the Western lifestyle despite their royal status.

The king also visited the UN. In a speech before the General Assembly, he called for "a solution [to the war in Algeria] in accordance with the Charter of the United Nations" by appealing to "comprehension and cooperation, love and fraternity between the big and small nations."[139] He then held a reception at the Waldorf-Astoria Hotel, which more than one thousand diplomats, city officials, and members of the local Moroccan community attended.[140] As a sign of her close relationship with the royal family, Eleanor Roosevelt sat with his three daughters in the auditorium during the king's speech; afterward she praised him as a great leader who "can form a bridge between the West and the Near East."[141] Mohammed V had also planned to visit Mrs. Roosevelt at her private estate, but his full schedule forced him to cancel the meeting at the last minute. The Moroccan press enthusiastically celebrated their sovereign's diplomatic accomplishments. "Nobody can imagine a better crowning moment of His Majesty's triumphant voyage to the United States than the great speech, which international observers have described as wise . . . and of very high quality," *al-Istiqlal* informed its readers.[142]

The monarch's journey across the United States proved quite successful with regard to improving the bilateral relations between Washington and Rabat. Most importantly, the Moroccan head of state had presented himself as a potential ally amid the global tensions of the Cold War. US ambassador Cannon considered the state visit "a crucial event in consolidating Morocco's ties with the West" and explained that "it would be hard to imagine a better [investment] at this time for American interests in Morocco than the welcome accorded to Mohammed V by the American government and . . . people."[143] Even the *New York Times* cheered that Morocco "is an island these days, . . . being isolated from the stormy world current, . . . represent[ing] a force friendly to the West and hence a most desirable counterbalance to President Nasser of Egypt."[144] Yet from the Moroccan perspective, the urgent issue of the US military installations in their country had not been resolved. Sidi Mohammed failed to reach an agreement with Secretary of State John Foster Dulles on this issue. But at least they agreed to continue the negotiations in the near future.

The public response to the state visit surpassed all expectations as the American media found only lauding words for Mohammed V. The *New York Times* hailed him as "a hero of Moroccan nationalism, a friend of Franklin D. Roosevelt, a man who likes to drive his own car and enjoys bowling with his French cook, an apostle and champion of constitutional monarchy, democratic elections and the political emancipation of women, . . . [and] a dynamic leader of the twentieth century Arab world";[145] the *Washington Post* simply praised the monarch's "wisdom and forbearance."[146] The positive press coverage did not remain limited to the United States. The *New York Times* had sent a special correspondent to Rabat to write an article on Prince Hassan, the "dashing Moroccan heir . . . who points the way towards emancipation."[147] Nobody asked any inconvenient questions about the lack of a democratic political process in Morocco. The numerous public relations efforts by the Moroccan delegation had evidently led to the desired results.

The monarch's activities across the Atlantic prompted an equally positive echo back home in Morocco. Even the Istiqlal's newspapers called the state visit "a resounding success" and quoted a royal adviser who had explained that "Morocco, thanks to the prestige of His Majesty the King, plays its role . . . in the search for solutions to the big problems."[148] Moreover, it printed a series of photos detailing the "warm welcome" Mohammed V had received in the United States, thus portraying him as the personification of the nation.[149] His ability to open negotiations about the status of the US bases especially encountered widespread approval ("this is a new page added by Mohammed V to his registry of great deeds").[150] According to *al-'Alam*, "the success of the consultations in Washington is evidence of His Majesty's ability to reconcile the interests of Morocco and those of the major countries . . . in order to establish the sovereignty of the fatherland and preserve its honor."[151] The overall verdict was clear: "His Majesty had a triumphant stay in the United States."[152] The king had become his nation's sole legitimate representative on the world stage.

Even French observers showed themselves impressed by Mohammed V's visit to the United States. According to a report filed by the embassy in Washington, "The king's trip has been a success . . . [because] he gave his hosts the impression that he is their honest friend."[153] A "remarkable" public relations campaign had reached even "the American masses" by effectively portraying him as "faithful to national and religious traditions yet simultaneously open to the realities of the modern world, the most democratic [king] of the world, [who maintains] personal contacts with the man in the street."[154] The US media had particularly praised "the sovereign's . . . political maturity and moderation."[155] Even the legendary meeting during the Anfa Conference had been discussed by the press. In the eyes of his hosts, the king had become "one of the allies on which the United States can count as part of their plan . . . to make their policies acceptable to the Arab world."[156] The Moroccans had once again presented themselves in a very favorable light and introduced the American people to a kingdom previously unknown to the vast majority of them. This generally positive image of the Moroccan monarchy still exists today in the United States.

CONCLUSION

The formation of the postcolonial Moroccan state had reached an important milestone by the end of 1957. In less than two years after Morocco's independence, Mohammed V had skillfully dismantled the nationalists' global network of supporters. Many important Istiqlalis now worked directly for the monarch, who thereby weakened the political opposition. Because all of them had served as brokers within the larger network structure, the Istiqlal lost much of the social capital acquired throughout the years of the anticolonial struggle. As a result, only the king could bridge the structural hole between domestic and international politics. Moreover, the nationalists' former foreign supporters started to generate a positive image of the Alaoui dynasty abroad. Although the domestic power struggle would continue for a few more years, the monarch's co-optation campaign had contributed significantly to the dominance of the royal palace over the country's political parties.

Mohammed V's state visit to the United States strengthened his position as the kingdom's sole legitimate representative. Having replaced the members of the nationalist movement on the global stage, the monarch now spoke on behalf of the entire nation during his meetings with foreign leaders. Furthermore, the royal entourage had turned his trip into an impressive publicity success. Sidi Mohammed had used every opportunity available to personally thank the nationalist movement's former supporters in the name of the Moroccan people. These gestures of appreciation projected royal authority. Back home in Morocco, the pictures disseminated by the USIS enabled ordinary people to partake in their monarch's foreign adventures and to take pride in his enthusiastic reception by the most powerful nation on earth. Even the Istiqlal's chief strategist, Mehdi Ben Barka, had to admit that "the country's international prestige is growing as proven by our king's trip to the

United States and speech before the UN."[157] The royal voyage thus marked a triumphant finale to the fight for the interpretive dominance over post-independence Moroccan politics.

Studying the anticolonial movement's social network provides additional insights into the history of the North African kingdom. It becomes clear that the networked activism used by the nationalists had proven both uniquely efficient and extremely tenuous. The reason behind their success during the years of the independence struggle ultimately contributed to their demise. Success and defeat constituted two sides of the same coin. Moreover, by studying Moroccan anticolonialism through a relational framework, we discover a number of important historical actors who have previously gone unnoticed. These individuals not only made crucial contributions to Morocco's liberation from colonial rule but also shaped the formation of the postcolonial state. This does not diminish the roles played by the leaders of the four nationalist parties. But it makes us aware of numerous lesser-known activists whose biographies complicate existing notions about Morocco's decolonization as a top-down process with clearly defined hierarchies.

Ultimately, though, Mohammed V sidelined all potential competitors and institutionalized his dominance over the postcolonial state. The vast majority of his subjects venerated him as a benign father figure who would lead his people into a prosperous future. The nationalists had contributed to this outcome by presenting him as the embodiment of the Moroccan nation throughout the struggle for independence. His imagined centrality to Moroccan politics eventually turned into reality. Instead of forming an effective opposition to the monarch's increasingly dominant position, most nationalists went their separate ways after independence to pursue their own interests. "The Moroccan revolution has never been achieved. It was checked in mid-career by Mohammed V. Kings may be nationalist, but by nature they are never revolutionary," a disillusioned Istiqlali admitted in November 1957.[158] The outcome was an authoritarian monarchy that continues to dominate the country's political life well into the twenty-first century.

DECOLONIZATION RECONSIDERED

T HE HISTORY OF MOROCCAN anticolonial activism on the global stage offers us a new window into the process of decolonization. Horizontally fully integrated into the transnational anticolonial movements that emerged across Africa and Asia and vertically effective through their links to private citizens in Europe and the Americas, the Moroccans actively engaged with the post-1945 international order. They set the standards for years to come with regard to both scope and sophistication of their activities. Less than a decade after the nationalists had published their independence manifestos, diplomats at the United Nations began debating the future of Morocco for the first time. This remarkable achievement became possible only due to the Moroccans' countless foreign supporters, who helped them make the case abroad for the country's independence. Without their energetic assistance, the fate of the North African kingdom would undoubtedly have remained on the margins of public awareness at a time when global crises from Berlin to the Korean peninsula dominated the headlines.

It also enables us to reconceptualize this pivotal period of the twentieth century more generally. The Moroccans understood that the path to liberation laid on the exterior. Their comprehensive view of colonialism allowed them to engage directly with all three arenas in which the struggle for independence had to take place—colony, metropole, and the international arena constituted a single field of political action.[1] The ability to mobilize resources on all of these fronts concurrently constituted their formula for success. We also gain a better understanding of international relations in the aftermath of World War II. Global politics were not just the exclusive privilege of statesmen from London to New Delhi but also the domain of myriad nonstate actors who lobbied for their respective cases in the corridors of the nascent UN. An entire microcosm of activism existed just underneath the veneer of official diplomacy. The process of decolonization is thus best understood as consisting of different forms of politics unfolding on multiple levels simultaneously.

Another insight pertains to the logic of the early Cold War, which not only constrained anticolonialism but also offered unique opportunities for its success. With the US foreign policy establishment divided between the need to strengthen France as a NATO member and the need to undermine the appeal of communism across the region, the Moroccans could position themselves as potential allies. Neither the Truman nor the Eisenhower administration ever openly confronted the French government about its policies in North Africa. Therefore, it might initially appear as though the nationalists did not succeed. But the direct support they received from a large number of private citizens nonetheless enabled them to bring their case to worldwide attention. This would hardly have been possible outside the logic of the Cold War, which dramatically increased Western interest in world events. The general desire to find friends in what seemed like an increasingly hostile world played directly into the nationalists' hands. The tensions between Washington and Moscow could thus be highly productive.

The Moroccan campaign for independence also offers a new perspective on the UN during its early years. That the members of the MOID in New

York managed to gate-crash the meetings of the General Assembly before eventually obtaining official credentials from sympathetic delegations might seem like an entertaining anecdote. But this apparent lack of rigid protocol tells us a lot about the unregulated nature of the intergovernmental organization that facilitated the participation of outsiders. At a time when the divisions between the Western and the Eastern Blocs had not yet fully developed and the nonaligned world was just emerging, the fluidity of the global order enabled anticolonial activists to make their voices heard. And the Moroccans did their best to take advantage of this transitional moment. They skillfully positioned themselves as fully capable of self-rule by presenting themselves as pragmatic moderates. Whereas we often perceive the postwar period solely as a missed opportunity to accelerate the end of empires, it also offered great prospects for those willing to engage with international politics.

This was, of course, not a completely new development. Beginning in 1920, the League of Nations' mandates commission had emerged as the world's first platform for both members and independent experts to debate the practices of Western colonialism. The voices of the subject populations could sometimes be heard in Geneva, although usually indirectly via submitted petitions.[2] Beyond the confines of the world's first intergovernmental organization, both pro- and anticolonial actors sought to make their cases across Europe.[3] The Moroccan nationalists had also actively disseminated their message abroad during the interwar period. But Europe's moral bankruptcy became even more evident during the course of World War II. And the burgeoning international order of the early Cold War offered numerous additional possibilities. Their transnational anticolonial activism after 1945 thus differed in both scope and quality from anything previously seen.

Timing mattered. The Moroccan anticolonial struggle did not occur in a chronological vacuum but at a specific historical moment. And several pivotal world events served as the bookends. The end of World War II and the founding of the UN and the Arab League energized the nationalist campaign for independence. One decade later, the outbreak of the Algerian Revolution followed by the Bandung Conference demonstrated that the numerous local expressions of anticolonial activism across Africa and Asia had successfully morphed into a global movement. An increasingly hostile international environment exposed Western imperialism to attacks on multiple fronts. Seeking to preserve French rule over Algeria, their country's most important colonial possession, politicians in Paris ultimately realized the futility of maintaining their North African protectorates. That Moroccan independence suddenly seemed like a plausible option can be understood only within this matrix of world events.

The internationalization of the Moroccan struggle for independence subsequently inspired anticolonial activists from other countries to follow suit. Most prominently, the men and women of the FLN turned New York into another front line in their struggle against the French state. But whereas the Istiqlal and the PNR viewed the international arena as central to their efforts from the very beginning, the FLN embraced diplomacy while also engaging the French army on the battlefield. When an armed rebellion finally broke out in Morocco after the resident general had exiled Mohammed ben Youssef in August 1953, the party leadership did not control the predominantly rural guerrillas. The insurgency certainly increased the pressure on the French authorities, but it also threatened to undermine the nationalist movement's strategy of peaceful resistance. Because of their bourgeois backgrounds and partial integration into the French colonial apparatus, the nationalists eschewed revolutionary change.[4]

Liberation movements outside the Maghrib also recognized the necessity of engaging in international politics, since decolonization was a global process that went beyond political borders.[5] The Moroccans had provided direct assistance to the Algerians when the latter commenced their own campaign at the UN in 1955. And because of the FLN's connections to radical nationalists around the world, their method of interpersonal lobbying was transmitted to Palestinian and other revolutionaries. For example, the National Front for the Liberation of South Vietnam engaged in "guerrilla diplomacy" to discredit the regime in Saigon and thwart the US military campaign.[6] And the South African liberation struggle ultimately succeeded because the African National Congress created worldwide anti-Apartheid alliances during the 1960s that exerted considerable international pressure on the government in Pretoria to change its racist policies.[7] Numerous other anti-imperial movements subsequently adopted similar strategies.[8] The legacy of the Moroccan struggle for independence thus lived on long after the North African kingdom gained its sovereignty.

Still, such modes of transnational activism did not necessarily challenge the logic of the nation-state. Instead, they often reinforced it. The Moroccan nationalists are a case in point.[9] They understood all politics as global and therefore spent much of their energy propagating the case for Moroccan independence abroad. But whereas their campaign directly challenged European colonialism, they did not contest the underlying logic of an international order structured around formally sovereign nation-states that engaged one another through hierarchical institutions such as the UN. Their ultimate goal remained the establishment of an independent, constitutional monarchy fully recognized by other governments. Moreover, they actively sought an alliance with the United States and did not even oppose good relations with France once independence had been achieved. Although ambitious, their aims were certainly not radical.

Location was also significant.[10] The Moroccans established propaganda offices in cities that hosted intergovernmental organizations—the UN in New York and Paris as well as the Arab League in Cairo—in order to target their campaign at the world's leading diplomats, politicians, and journalists. Furthermore, these urban spaces contained an array of potential supporters, ranging from immigrant communities to anticolonial sympathizers. Many would ultimately assist the nationalists' efforts. Borders mattered too. Tangier's status as an international city made it an ideal nodal point permitting activists from both protectorates to operate semifreely and link Morocco to the wider world. The need for valid passports and visas shaped the Moroccans' decisions about where and when to travel. They did not operate in an abstract global space but within a multitude of distinct legal frameworks that both facilitated and inhibited their activities.

The structure of the Moroccans' social network also provides us with important insights into their conceptualization of politics. The extreme diversity of their associates was definitely the most impressive aspect of their global campaign. At times, they had to square the circle. One example can be found in the violent deaths of two outspoken allies. On 28 December 1948, a member of the Muslim Brotherhood shot Egyptian prime minister Mahmud Fahmi al-Nuqrashi, the same man with whom Mehdi Bennouna had worked closely during his visit to New York the previous year. Egyptian security forces then assassinated Hassan al-Banna, a fervent supporter of Maktab al-Maghrib al-'Arabi, six weeks later.[11] This anecdote highlights the complex—and occasionally outright contradictory—nature of the nationalists' network of supporters. Yet the activists' ability to create such a heterogeneous coalition in the first place reveals the skillfulness of the Moroccans, who grasped the importance of recruiting allies from across the political spectrum to make their case broadly appealing. And this pragmatism enabled them to defeat the colonial powers in the long run.

We must also keep in mind that the anticolonial activities on the exterior grew out of political parties with established hierarchies, clear membership rules, and a substantial level of ideological cohesiveness. By 1951, the Istiqlal had more than a hundred thousand dues-paying members, and the PNR had also recruited a significant following in the Spanish zone.[12] Both of these were broad-based social movements that effectively mobilized large sectors of the Moroccan population even though they remained present mainly only in the country's urban centers. Global networked and local institutionalized activism became intrinsically intertwined. Without the substantial financial resources provided by both parties, the diplomatic campaign would not have been possible. This hybrid form of social mobilization ultimately proved effective in winning the fight against the colonizers. Successful international appeals required a strong popular base at home.

REVISITING MOROCCO'S COLONIAL PAST

The nationalist movement's global activities reunited a politically divided country. Activists from both the French and the Spanish zones as well as Tangier worked hand in hand on the international stage, thus demonstrating the unity of the nationalist movement; the country's tripartite partition could not inhibit the rise of Moroccan anticolonialism. Of course, the inhabitants of the two protectorates experienced the age of foreign occupation quite differently. But the divisions artificially imposed by the Treaty of Fez did not limit their ability to imagine Morocco as a unified nation. The borders between the three legally distinct zones remained highly porous and failed to divide local society. Despite the methodological problems posed by its fragmented archival record, the history of colonial Morocco should be understood through a comprehensive framework of analysis that encompasses the entire territory nominally under the control of the Alaoui dynasty.

The continuing preeminence of the royal family also becomes easier to understand when studied in the context of the transnational liberation struggle. That the French authorities reinvigorated the moribund monarchy through the creation of a modern state apparatus, which they ultimately handed directly to Sidi Mohammed in 1956, remains a well-established fact, as is the notion that the sultan obtained the status of national icon due to his forced abdication and years in exile. But an analysis of how Mohammed ben Youssef skillfully co-opted the central nodes of the nationalist movement's advocacy network after independence demonstrates that he became an active participant in and not merely a passive beneficiary of this political process. The authoritarian monarchy that still dominates Morocco thus emerged out of the actions of both the colonizers and the colonized.

We also no longer perceive the events of March 1956 as a radical rupture in Moroccan history but as a gradual transformation of the political order. The two protectorates and the independent nation-state did not constitute two fundamentally distinct historical episodes. Many of the most important anticolonial activists occupied positions of great influence in postindependence Morocco, whether as state officials or pioneers of the country's burgeoning media landscape. Our understanding of the legacy of colonialism should thus move beyond a narrow focus on the institutions created by the French and Spanish authorities and needs to include the trajectories of the numerous individuals that straddled both sides of this chronological divide. The independent Moroccan nation-state was not built on top of the ruins of the protectorates but rather constructed out of the building materials left behind by the colonizers. The new age contained the residues of the old.

Another important task is the integration of Spanish colonialism into Moroccan historiography. The contradictory colonial policies pursued by the government in Madrid and the high commissioner in Tetouan provided openings that the Moroccans skillfully exploited. The Francoist dictatorship paradoxically proved much more willing to accommodate the local nationalist movement than were consecutive governments of the supposedly democratic French Fourth Republic. Spain's hope of escaping its international isolation through an alliance with the member states of the Arab League necessitated a seemingly benevolent attitude toward its colonial subjects. This desire for diplomatic recognition contributed to the relatively liberal political atmosphere inside the Spanish protectorate. As a result, nationalists and their publications continued to circulate in Tetouan long after the Residency in Rabat had banned them from the French zone in the wake of the Casablanca riots in December 1952.

Yet a focus on such pragmatic considerations tells only part of the story. Many Spaniards firmly believed in the existence of spiritual links between the two peoples on opposite sides of the Strait of Gibraltar. Moreover, the pivotal contributions made by Moroccan soldiers to Franco's rebellion had not been forgotten by the fascists and gave further impetus to the colonial ideology. The result was a political climate that provided numerous opportunities for the nationalists to send delegates abroad, smuggle illicit materials into French Morocco, and generally turn Tetouan into a hub for their global activities. The notion of brotherhood eventually even became an integral part of Moroccan national identity.[13] One might mistakenly assume that the Spanish protectorate remained marginal to the struggle for independence, because it rarely became the direct target of nationalist propaganda. In reality, however, Spanish politics played a pivotal role in the history of Morocco's decolonization.

POSTINDEPENDENCE FOREIGN POLICY

The relevance of this seemingly complicated nexus—Spanish and French empire, network and institution, local and global activism, party and palace, colonial and postcolonial state—becomes particularly evident with regard to the foreign policy pursued by the North African kingdom after independence. For example, Washington and Rabat developed extremely friendly relations in subsequent years as the United States and Morocco became unofficial allies during the Cold War.[14] Morocco received more than 400 million dollars in American aid between 1957 and 1963 and in 1966 became the fifth-largest recipient of US agricultural assistance;[15] the country had obtained more than $1 billion in military assistance and $1.3 billion in economic assistance by 1990, which amounted to more than one-fifth of the entire US aid to all African countries during this period.[16] In return, the Moroccan authorities signed a secret agreement permitting the Americans to maintain powerful radio transmitters near Tangier, which served as communication and spying tools in the western Mediterranean; the CIA and the NSA acted with impunity from Hassan II's regime in return for their assistance.[17] Driven by its twin interests in regional stability and the country's phosphate reserves, Washington continued to support the Moroccan regime for decades to come.[18] The excellent rapport between the two nations persists well into the twenty-first century. In the aftermath of 9/11, Morocco allowed the opening of a "black site" on the outskirts of Rabat, where US intelligence agents tortured suspected terrorists shielded from the public eye.[19] In 2004, the Bush administration elevated the country to the status of major non-NATO ally "in recognition of the close US-Morocco relationship."[20]

Meanwhile in Paris, successive French governments sought to create a global alliance centered on the former metropole by maintaining good relations with the former colonies.[21] Morocco played a crucial role within this larger strategic vision. Given that many of the former nationalists as well as Mohammed V's children had passed through the French education system, a Francophone culture continued to permeate the country's public life.[22] The administrative remnants of the colonial system—ranging from the judicial system to the Ministry of Agriculture—remained staffed by thousands of French civil servants, who trained the first generation of Moroccan technocrats who would eventually take over the state apparatus.[23] Combined with the kingdom's economic orientation toward the French market, these factors ensured that Rabat maintained close links to the former colonizer following independence.[24] France also served as Morocco's main trading partner for a long time and was the destination of 28 percent of all goods exported by the North African kingdom as late as 2008.[25]

Spain and Morocco, however, took much longer to develop the close links that characterize their bilateral relationship today. Because of the continuing presence of Spanish troops in Sidi Ifni until 1969 and in the Western Sahara until 1976, the rapport between the two states remained extremely delicate for more than two decades. But this diplomatic ice age eventually thawed. Beginning in 1979, the two kingdoms inaugurated an ambitious program of cultural cooperation that included regular academic exchanges.[26] Migration patterns have also been reversed since the end of the colonial era; citizens of the North African kingdom now constitute the largest non-European immigrant community in Spain.[27] Indeed, the contentious relationship between the two countries has been reversed so thoroughly that the Moroccan constitution adopted in 2011 explicitly mentions its "Andalusian" heritage as part of the kingdom's cultural legacy.[28] Moreover, by 2018, Spain had surpassed France as Morocco's main economic partner, having received 16.7 percent of all exports from the North African kingdom and having provided 16.8 percent of all imports by it.[29] The strong link between the two states also extends into the realm of security operations. What could better symbolize the often-surprising dynamics of Spanish-Moroccan relations than an article published in *El País* in 2015 that revealed that Moroccan antiterrorism agents operate freely inside Spain with the full cooperation of the local authorities?[30]

The relationship between Rabat and Cairo, by contrast, remained extremely chilly. The first foreign head of state to visit Morocco after independence was King Faisal II of Iraq, whom hundreds of thousands cheered on as he passed through the country's capital in May 1956. ("We do not forget the support of the Iraqi leaders at the [UN] . . . in the days of hardship," explained *al-ʿAlam*.)[31] But the Moroccan government refused to join the Arab League, thereby expressing its disapproval of the regional alliance widely regarded as Gamal Abdel Nasser's extended arm. French diplomats noted that Mohammed V viewed him as "his only serious rival" in North Africa.[32] While attending the Egyptian Independence Day celebrations in Cairo in June 1957, less than a year after the Suez War, Crown Prince Hassan irritated his hosts by remarking that his country would "naturally" remain a close ally of France.[33] It would take until October 1958 for Morocco to finally become a member of the League, primarily at the urging of the Iraqi government eager to create a counterweight to Egypt's regional hegemony. Furthermore, Mohammed V waited until January 1960 to accept Nasser's invitation to Cairo, and the Moroccan king combined the visit with trips to several other Arab capitals in order to downplay its significance.[34]

What motivated these diplomatic choices of the newly independent North African kingdom? Of course, the shared bourgeois background of the country's political class did not lend itself to the radical socialism propagated by the Third Worldist vanguard. Unlike the Free Officers in Egypt and their counterparts around the world, Morocco's leading politicians had not risen from the bottom of the social hierarchy but had been born into status and wealth. Moreover, matters of foreign policy always remained in the hands of the royal palace, and the king viewed Morocco's ambassadors as his personal representatives. The fact that Nasser's regime clandestinely sought to undermine the Moroccan monarchy obviously did not improve the situation either.[35] Yet these factors alone do not sufficiently explain why the country adopted such a nuanced, though ultimately pro-Western, attitude.

An equally important reason behind Morocco's foreign policy can be found in the legacy of the nationalist movement's global anticolonial campaign. The Moroccan statesmen had learned that little could be achieved against the explicit will of the United States. They had also received tremendous levels of support from private citizens in Europe and America, thus obtaining a positive view of the West in general. The unique socialization of the nationalists during their years abroad shaped Morocco's relatively homogenous political elites, providing them with a much more international outlook than most other postcolonial statesmen. These personal experiences laid the foundations for Morocco's foreign policy that has continued, with few adjustments, since independence. By contrast, their experiences in Cairo had been disheartening; the Free Officers' ascendance to power in July 1952 had proven particularly fatal to the nationalists' activities in the Middle East. Although the erroneous image of unwavering pan-Arab solidarity at the height of the anticolonial struggle still dominates popular imagination today, the Moroccan nationalists did not forget the failures of the revolutionary Egyptian regime to support their aspirations.[36] The turn toward Washington appears consequential only when viewed in this context.

Morocco become not an active member of the assertive anti-imperialist alliance of Third World states but rather a regional American junior partner. In 1961 it cofounded the Casablanca Group, which united various "progressive" countries in order to promote Pan-Africanism, and Hassan II personally led the Moroccan delegation that attended the founding meeting of the Non-Aligned Movement in Belgrade the same year. But the follow-up conference that took place in Cairo in October 1963 caused little excitement in Rabat.[37] According to a French diplomat, the Moroccans did not mind "proclaiming the general principles and repeating the slogan [of the Non-Aligned Movement], but they are always concerned about the national interests and maintaining good relations with the West."[38] The kingdom thus fulfilled its role as a client state and thereby secured Washington's unofficial approval for its occupation of the Western Sahara, which has been ongoing since 1975.[39]

The Moroccan government also actively participated in Cold War proxy wars on the African continent. When a border dispute between Morocco and Algeria erupted into full war in the fall of 1963, the revolutionary Cuban government saw Uncle Sam's hand behind the conflict and sent soldiers to support the Algerians against "Hassan who has become a trained bear" that "receives dollars and guns."[40] Moroccan troops even captured several Egyptian soldiers that had been sent by Nasser to support the Algerians, among them a certain Lieutenant Hosni Mubarak, the future fourth president of Egypt.[41] The rupture between Rabat and Cairo could not have been clearer. In the 1970s, Hassan II offered advisers to pro-Western rebels in Angola and even dispatched a military contingent to Zaire, where 1,500 soldiers successfully repelled two incursions by the Cuba-backed MPLA (People's Movement for the Liberation of Angola).[42]

Morocco's political class utilized the country's unique position to great benefit, obtaining aid from the United States while simultaneously maintaining economic relations with both Cuba and the Soviet Union; interestingly enough, the United States did not become Morocco's main supplier of weapons until two decades after independence.[43] An additional example can be found in Rabat's relationship with the PLO, which it supported not only verbally but also by sending soldiers to participate in the Six-Day War in 1967 and the Yom Kippur War in 1973.[44] Yet at the same time Morocco maintained good relations with the Mossad, facilitated the secret negotiations between Egypt and Israel that led to Anwar Sadat's visit to Jerusalem in 1977, invited Prime Minister Shimon Peres for talks in 1986, and initiated official diplomatic relations with the Jewish state in 1994.[45]

At a time when many Africans and Asians saw it as their mission to remake the world on the basis of justice and equality, the Moroccans positioned their country within the global hierarchies of the postcolonial era. Immediately prior to his travel to the United States in November 1957, Mohammed V proclaimed his desire to "make Morocco an intermediary between the Western and Eastern civilizations" due to its "geographic location."[46] His successor, Hassan II, described the same approach in more poetic language two decades later. "Morocco is like a tree nourished by roots deep in the soil of Africa, which breathes through foliage rustling to the winds of Europe. . . . Horizontally, it looks to the East, with which it is bound by ties of religion and culture," wrote the monarch in his autobiography.[47] This ability to find a midpoint served Morocco's elites well, even if it contributed little to anticolonial causes in other parts of the world. And it remained the basis of the country's foreign policy long after the Cold War had ended.

The North African kingdom also continues to be known for its sophisticated public relations activities abroad. This pertains particularly to the United States, where the country maintains, in the words of *Foreign Policy* magazine, "an army of flacks . . . capable of influencing American policy."[48] Many influential Washington-based think tanks habitually portray the country in an extremely favorable light on a whole range of issues.[49] Moreover, Moroccan officials continue to rely on prominent individuals, including high-ranking politicians, to promote their interests.[50] The same applies to France, where the Moroccan state maintains close relations with countless well-known public figures. By way of lavish gifts and complicated business arrangements, the royal palace has recruited innumerable advocates ranging from public intellectuals to former government ministers.[51] Seen in this light, the legacy of Maktab al-Maghrib al-'Arabi in Cairo, the Bureau de documentation et d'information du Parti de l'Istiqlal in Paris, and the Moroccan Office of Information and Documentation in New York continue to shape Moroccan politics today.

NETWORKED ACTIVISM: OPPORTUNITIES AND RISKS

A final insight we gain from studying the history of the Moroccan independence campaign pertains to the tenuousness of networked activism. Although their informal nature makes social networks effective tools for mobilization, they are prone to fragmentation in the transitional period following the initial protests. Therefore, they have proven less capable of withstanding well-organized political adversaries than have institutionalized forms of social organization such as political parties. The same structural logic that permits social networks to thrive in the short term simultaneously contributes to the long-term "fragility of networked protests."[52] Although their lack of clearly defined leadership roles enables their rapid expansion, the absence of a shared culture facilitates the co-optation of individual members by adversaries. The assumption that networked protests are inherently more capable of achieving desired policy changes does not seem warranted.

A similar dynamic unfolded in Morocco after the end of the two protectorates in the spring of 1956. As Mohammed ben Youssef co-opted the central nodes of the transnational advocacy network, he severely weakened the country's largest political party by drastically reducing the human and social capital at its disposal. The networked nature of the anticolonial campaign had proven both beneficial and detrimental to the Istiqlal as most of those previously active abroad gravitated into the orbit of the royal palace after independence. Beyond such external factors, the network's demise also resulted from its internal logic. By bringing together a wide range of individuals united solely by a shared aim—namely, the end of colonial rule—they created a very powerful yet unstable coalition. Once the anticolonial network had lost its *raison d'être*, little remained to hold the heterogeneous alliance of activists together. While perhaps not unavoidable, its demise must certainly be seen as consequential. We should thus keep in mind that "networking is not organization-building."[53] Although networked activism is undoubtedly a powerful type of political advocacy, its structure also has the potential to ultimately undermine its own achievements.

The flow of information within social networks poses another problem. By producing massive amounts of communications data, they enable surveillance on an unprecedented scale. This happened in colonial Morocco. As the archival record attests, the local agents of the French state operated a hyper-effective surveillance apparatus that recorded even the minutest details of the nationalists' activities. The anticolonial movement's transnational advocacy network facilitated this process since its very existence depended on the permanent exchange of information. Despite the nationalists' best attempts—including sending important information via coded messages or smuggling letters from Tangier to Gibraltar to be sent via British mail—the colonial authorities knew virtually everything about the Moroccans' efforts abroad. And they did so without the same resource-intensive levels of surveillance to which they resorted domestically. The networked nature of anticolonial activism thus exposed the nationalists to the prying eyes of the colonial state to an unprecedented degree.

The decolonization of Morocco thus offers both an encouraging example and a cautionary tale. On the one hand, the story of nationalists successfully appealing to global public opinion and thereby attaining their political objectives should serve as an inspiration for political activists around the world. Against great odds, the Moroccans overcame many obstacles—both domestic and foreign—to make their voices heard. If that could be done at a time when the transistor radio was just emerging as the most cutting-edge means of mass communication, today's tech-savvy social movements are doubtlessly better positioned to successfully make their cases on the global stage. But on the other hand, the collapse of the anticolonial coalition in the wake of Morocco's independence indicates the risks of social network–based activism. The same qualities that make this type of organization so powerful in the first place also endanger its longevity. The absence of hierarchies facilitates the recruitment of new supporters and adaptation to adverse circumstances, but that flexibility also undermines such a coalition's ability to withstand assaults by better-organized opponents. Short-term success can ultimately result in long-term defeat. Social networks thus should be powerful contributions to—rather than replacements of—institutionalized forms of political activism. Such hybrid structures seem most efficient. In this regard, the history of the Moroccan struggle for independence teaches us invaluable lessons that remain valid today.

NETWORK VISUALIZATIONS

Both the rise and fall of the Moroccan anticolonial advocacy network depended on the actions of several brokers. These individuals bridged the structural holes between the nationalist movement on the interior and the targets of its campaign on the exterior. By occupying important positions within the network structure, they acquired considerable social capital that secured them influential roles in postindependence Morocco. Their eventual co-optation by the monarch weakened the Istiqlal Party and thereby contributed to the hegemony of the royal palace over domestic politics. We can best understand the importance of these brokers within the nationalist movement's global social network by way of their "betweenness centrality."[1] This measure analyzes a node's structural significance by studying the number of shortest paths between other nodes that pass through it. Nodes with high betweenness centrality carry a significant amount of network traffic and thus have a disproportional influence on the flow of resources within the network's overall structure. In the Moroccan case, several individuals fit this description.

Following the end of World War II, the Moroccan nationalist movement adopted Tangier as a gateway that allowed it to bring its anticolonial mes-

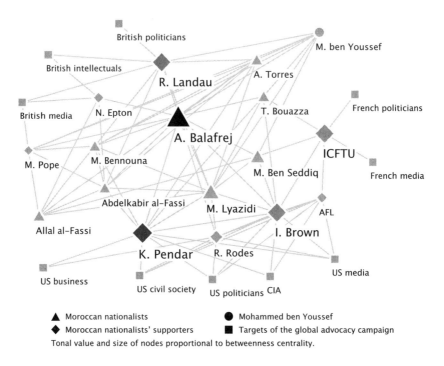

British politicians

M. ben Youssef

British intellectuals

R. Landau

A. Torres

British media   N. Epton

T. Bouazza   French politicians

A. Balafrej

ICFTU

M. Pope   M. Bennouna

M. Ben Seddiq   French media

Abdelkabir al-Fassi   M. Lyazidi

AFL

Allal al-Fassi

I. Brown

K. Pendar   R. Rodes

US media

US business   US civil society   US politicians   CIA

▲ Moroccan nationalists   ● Mohammed ben Youssef
◆ Moroccan nationalists' supporters   ■ Targets of the global advocacy campaign
Tonal value and size of nodes proportional to betweenness centrality.

FIGURE A.I. Tangier. (Based on figures created with Cytoscape.)

sage abroad. Because of the international zone's legal status outside the con-trol of the colonial powers, the activists turned it into a hub connecting the kingdom to the wider world. They took advantage of its geographical loca-tion by recruiting numerous foreigners that passed through the city, thereby creating a social network with a truly global reach. Because of the relatively large number of activists in Tangier, though, none of them gained a decisive structural advantage due to his work in the city. The acquired social capital was relatively widely dispersed. Even the leaders of both the Istiqlal and the PNR directly participated in the networked activism in and around the in-ternational zone.

Cairo became the second center of the Moroccans' transnational advo-cacy campaign following the arrival of the delegation representing Spanish Morocco at the Arab League's cultural committee in February 1946. The es-

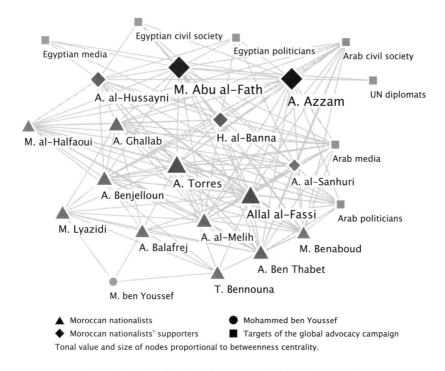

FIGURE A.2. Cairo in 1948. (Based on figures created with Cytoscape.)

tablishment of *Maktab al-Maghrib al-'Arabi* one year later institutionalized the anticolonial campaign in Egypt as a joint North African venture. Nonetheless, its Moroccan members proved particularly skilled at recruiting numerous prominent Arabs to publicly support their quest for independence. Eventually, their network of supporters extended across the entire Middle East. The city also offered an important venue for cooperation among nationalists from both protectorates; the nationalists then served as bridges between Morocco and the Arab world. Initially, these activists—mainly former students from French Morocco—played leading roles within the network structure.

In the wake of the military coup of 14 July 1952, however, the Moroccans' regional network quickly disintegrated as the new regime sidelined most of their former allies. The activists lost their contacts among the Egyptian elites

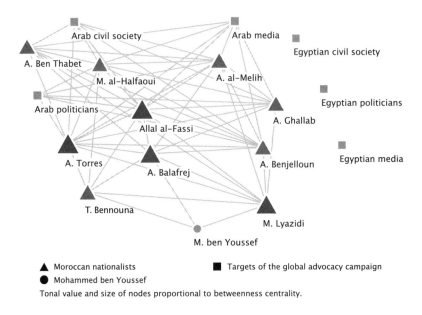

FIGURE A.3. Cairo after July 1952. (Based on figures created with Cytoscape.)

and experienced firsthand the downsides of networked activism. The Arab League also subsequently reduced its advocacy on behalf of Moroccan independence. Nonetheless, a few nationalists remained in Cairo until the eve of Morocco's independence in order to disseminate propaganda via Radio Cairo and network among Asian diplomats visiting the Egyptian capital. Yet although these nationalists continued their activities across the Middle East, they failed to regain the structural importance they had enjoyed in previous years. The fragility of the nationalist movement's social network of supporters had become apparent for the first time.

The end of World War II in Europe enabled the Moroccan nationalist movement to undertake an extensive outreach campaign in Paris. The members of the *Bureau de documentation et information du Parti de l'Istiqlal* successfully established contacts among the highest echelons of French society and brought the demands of the movement to public attention. By the fall of 1955, their unrelenting advocacy for Morocco's independence ultimately secured the support of the National Assembly to engage in negotiations with Sultan Mohammed ben Youssef. A small group of students played a pivotal role in the metropole by mobilizing the local Moroccan community and re-

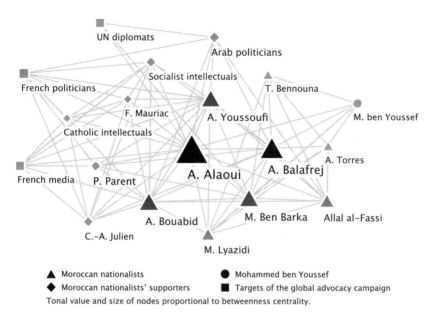

FIGURE A.4. Paris. (Based on figures created with Cytoscape.)

cruiting a diverse alliance of supporters. As a result of the group's efforts, they acquired considerable social capital. All of them would benefit from their activism in France after Morocco had obtained its independence.

New York became the most important site for the Moroccans' advocacy campaign after the arrival of the first delegate in the summer of 1947. As the home of the newly founded United Nations, the city enabled the nationalists to engage directly with diplomats from around the world in order to convince them of their cause. Beginning in 1952, the members of the Moroccan Office of Information and Documentation enlisted the support of numerous US citizens, who successfully presented the case of Morocco before the American public. Several nationalists dominated the activities in New York and therefore came to occupy central positions within the network structure. Because of the importance of the United States during the early Cold War, their acquired social capital was particularly valuable. Their brokerage roles increased their standing among their compatriots and laid the foundations for long and successful professional careers.

By the time Morocco finally obtained its independence in March 1956, the nationalists had established an impressive network of personal contacts, in-

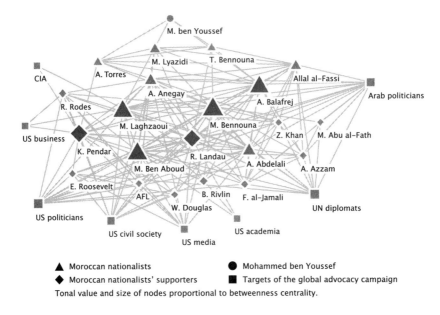

FIGURE A.5. New York. (Based on figures created with Cytoscape.)

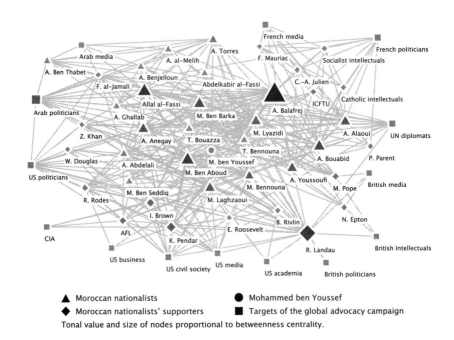

FIGURE A.6. Rabat in March 1956. (Based on figures created with Cytoscape.)

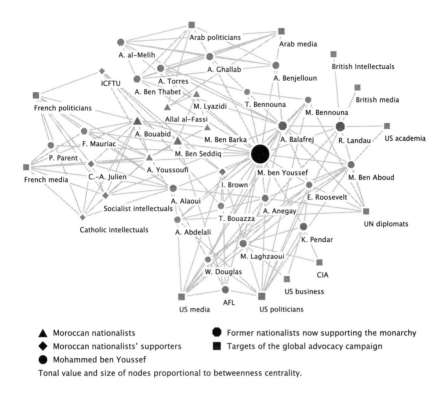

FIGURE A.7. Rabat in December 1957. (Based on figures created with Cytoscape.)

cluding numerous brokers connecting them to influential individuals and organizations around the world. Mohammed ben Youssef, by contrast, still appeared only on the network's periphery. It thus seemed as though the Istiqlal
would be able to solidify its position on the domestic political stage due to the
resources acquired throughout the liberation struggle. Those activists who
occupied central positions within the network structures appeared particularly preordained to become prominent politicians who would eventually
dominate Morocco's burgeoning party landscape. But this never happened.

Within just a few years following independence, Mohammed ben Youssef co-opted the central nodes of the nationalist movement's global advocacy
network. Many of the former anticolonial activists went to work directly for
the royal palace, thus strengthening the monarch while weakening the political opposition. By way of this strategy, Sidi Mohammed secured the social
and human capital they had acquired during their years abroad and sidelined

the remaining leaders of the Istiqlal. He thereby moved from the network's margins to its very center. From then on, all resources circulating between the interior and the exterior flowed directly through him. That the king had substantially increased his betweenness centrality contributed to his victory in the power struggle between party and palace. Understanding the structural importance of individual nodes within the nationalist movement's global advocacy network thus provides us with a better understanding of the processes that shaped the postcolonial Moroccan state.

NOTES

INTRODUCTION

1. "UN General Assembly Resolution A/RES/612(VII)—The Question of Morocco," 19 December 1952, http://research.un.org/en/docs/ga/quick/regular/7; and Leon Borden Blair, *Western Window in the Arab World* (Austin: University of Texas Press, 1970), 165.

2. "The Moroccan Question in the United Nations," *Moroccan News Bulletin*, 26 December 1952, 2.

3. Mohammed al-Khatib to Mehdi Bennouna, 21 October 1952, Mehdi Bennouna File, vol. 2, Bennouna Family Archive, Tetouan (hereafter BFA).

4. Tayeb Bennouna to Mehdi Bennouna, 10 November 1952, Mehdi Bennouna File, vol. 2, BFA.

5. PNR Communiqué No. 4, 7 March 1953, Mehdi Bennouna File, vol. 2, BFA.

6. See, for example, "Les reactions de l'opinion américaine," *al-Istiqlal*, 26 April 1952, 2; and "Les grands organs de la presse américaine critiquent sévèrement la politique française en Tunisie," *al-Istiqlal*, 24 May 1952, 4.

7. Tayeb Bennouna to Mehdi Bennouna, 10 November 1952, Mehdi Bennouna File, vol. 2, BFA.

8. Muhammad al-'Arabi al-Masari, *Al-Maghrib kharij siyaj al-himaya* (Rabat, MA: Manshurat 'Akath, 2012), 11–14.

9. Susan G. Miller, *A History of Modern Morocco* (New York: Cambridge University Press, 2012), 63–79.

10. "Protectorate Treaty between France and Morocco—March 30, 1912," *The American Journal of International Law* 6, no. 3 (1912): 207, 209.

11. Ibid., 207.

12. Ibid., 208.

13. "Treaty between France and Spain Regarding Morocco—November 27, 1912," *The American Journal of International Law* 7, no. 2 (1913): 81.

14. Miller, *A History of Modern Morocco*, 88.

15. The most important resistance movement was led by Mohammed b. Abdelkarim al-Khattabi in the northern Rif Mountains from 1920 until 1926. María Rosa de Madariaga, *Abd-el-Krim el Jatabi: La lucha por la independencia* (Madrid: Alianza Editorial, 2009); and C. Richard Pennell, *A Country with a Government and a Flag: The Rif War in Morocco, 1921–1926* (Boulder, CO: Lynne Rienner, 1986).

16. John P. Halstead, *Rebirth of a Nation: The Origins and Rise of Moroccan Nationalism, 1912–1944* (Cambridge, MA: Harvard Middle Eastern Monographs, 1967), 178–90.

17. Jan C. Jansen and Jürgen Osterhammel, *Dekolonisation—das Ender der Imperien* (Munich: Beck, 2013), 50–52. The relationship between Britain and its former white settler colonies underwent a very similar transformation within the framework of the Commonwealth during this period. See A. G. Hopkins, "Rethinking Decolonization," *Past & Present* 200 (2008).

18. Martin Thomas, *Fight or Flight: Britain, France, and Their Roads from Empire* (New York: Oxford University Press, 2014), 76.

19. "Recommendations adoptées par la conference," in *La Conférence africaine française, Brazzaville: 30 janvier 1944–8 février 1944* (Paris: Ministère des Colonies, 1945), 32.

20. Alistair Horne, *A Savage War of Peace: Algeria 1954–62* (New York: New York Review of Books, 2006), 23–28.

21. On the hierarchical nature of international relations during the Cold War, see Prasenjit Duara, "The Cold War as a Historical Period: An Interpretive Essay," *Journal of Global History* 6, no. 3 (2011).

22. Odd A. Westad, *The Global Cold War: Third World Interventions and the Making of Our Times* (New York: Cambridge University Press, 2005); Robert J. McMahon, ed., *The Cold War in the Third World* (New York: Oxford University Press, 2013); Tony Smith, "New Bottles for New Wine: A Pericentric Framework for the Study of the Cold War," *Diplomatic History* 24, no. 4 (2000); Piero Gleijeses, *Conflicting Missions: Havana, Washington, and Africa, 1959–1976* (Chapel Hill: University of North Carolina Press, 2002); and Piero Gleijeses, *Visions of Freedom: Havana, Washington, Pretoria, and the Struggle for Southern Africa, 1976–1991* (Chapel Hill: University of North Carolina Press, 2013).

23. Mark Mazower, *No Enchanted Palace: The End of Empire and the Ideological Origins of the United Nations* (Princeton, NJ: Princeton University Press, 2009).

24. Evan Luard, *A History of the United Nations*, vol. 2, *The Age of Decolonization, 1955–1965* (Palgrave: New York, 1989), 102.

25. "Charter of the United Nations," chapter 1, article 1, part 2, United Nations, accessed 7 February 2017, https://www.un.org/en/charter-united-nations; and "Universal Declaration of Human Rights," preamble, United Nations, accessed 7 February 2017, https://www.un.org/en/universal-declaration-human-rights/index.html. In the eyes of many anticolonial activists, however, the appeal of human rights did not lay in their protection of individuals against the authority of the state but rather in their ability to bring about the "threshold right of self-determination" that protected the "autonomy of the new nation" against foreign intervention. Samuel Moyn, *The Last Utopia—Human Rights in History* (Cambridge, MA: Belknap Press, 2010), 117.

26. Jessica Lynne Pearson, "Defending Empire at the United Nations: The Politics of International Colonial Oversight in the Era of Decolonisation," *The Journal of Imperial and Commonwealth History* 43, no. 3 (2017): 526.

27. Meredith Terretta, *Petitioning for Our Rights, Fighting for Our Nation: The History of the Democratic Union of Cameroonian Women, 1949–1960* (Bamenda, CM: Langaa Research & Publishing CIG, 2013); and Carol Anderson, *Eyes Off the Prize: The United Nations and the African American Struggle for Human Rights, 1944–1955* (New York: Cambridge University Press, 2003).

28. Meredith Terretta, "Anti-Colonial Lawyering, Postwar Human Rights, and Decolonization across Imperial Boundaries in Africa," *Canadian Journal of History* 52, no. 3 (2017); and Meredith Terretta, "'We Had Been Fooled into Thinking That the UN Watches over the Entire World': Human Rights, UN Trust Territories, and Africa's Decolonization," *Human Rights Quarterly* 34, no. 2 (2012).

29. Chris Saunders, "Namibian Solidarity: British Support for Namibian Independence," *Journal of Southern African Studies* 35, no. 2 (2009): 439.

30. Carol Anderson, *Bourgeois Radicals: The NAACP and the Struggle for Colonial Liberation, 1941–1960* (New York: Cambridge University Press, 2015).

31. André Mathiot, *Les territoires non autonomes et la charte des Nations Unies* (Paris: Librairie générale de droit et de jurisprudence, 1949), 62.

32. For a study of how the UN moved beyond serving as a mere platform for anticolonialism and became an active agent in the process of decolonization itself, see Eva-Maria Muschik, "Managing the World: The United Nations, Decolonization, and the Strange Triumph of State Sovereignty in the 1950s and 1960s," *Journal of Global History* 13, no. 1 (2018).

33. Vijay Prashad, *The Darker Nations: A People's History of the Third World* (New York: The New Press, 2007); and Christopher J. Lee, "At the Rendezvous of Decolonization: The Final Communiqué of the Asian-African Conference, Bandung, Indonesia, 18–24 April 1955," *Interventions* 11, no. 1 (2009).

34. Jeffrey James Byrne, "Beyond Continents, Colours, and the Cold War: Yugoslavia, Algeria, and the Struggle for Non-Alignment," *The International History Review* 37, no. 5 (2015).

35. Mark Philip Bradley, "Decolonization, Revolutionary Nationalism, and the Cold War, 1919–1962," in *The Cambridge History of the Cold War*, ed. Melvyn P. Leffler and Odd Arne Westad (New York: Cambridge University Press, 2009); and Samuel E. Crowl, "Indonesia's Diplomatic Revolution: Lining Up for Non-Alignment, 1945–1955," in *Connecting Histories: Decolonization and the Cold War in Southeast Asia, 1945–1962*, ed. Christopher E. Goscha and Christian F. Ostermann (Stanford, CA: Stanford University Press, 2009).

36. Janick Marina Schaufelbuehl et al., "Non-Alignment, the Third Force, or Fence-Sitting: Independent Pathways in the Cold War," *The International History Review* 37, no. 5 (2015).

37. Jason Parker, *Hearts, Minds, Voices: U.S. Cold War Public Diplomacy and the Formation of the Third World* (New York: Oxford University Press, 2016), 1; and Gerard McCann, "From Diaspora to Third Worldism and the United Nations: India and the Politics of Decolonizing Africa," *Past and Present* 218, suppl. 8 (2013): 260.

38. Mark T. Berger, "After the Third World? History, Destiny and the Fate of Third Worldism," *Third World Quarterly* 25, no. 1 (2004).

39. Genealogies of the term can be found in Leslie Wolf-Phillips, "Why 'Third World'?: Origin, Definition and Usage," *Third World Quarterly* 9, no. 4 (1987); and B. R. Tomlinson, "What Was the Third World?," *Journal of Contemporary History* 38, no. 2 (2003).

40. For an economic explanation of the "collapse" of Third Worldism, see Guy Laron, "Semi-Peripheral Countries and the Invention of the 'Third World,' 1955–65," *Third World Quarterly* 35, no. 9 (2014). Interesting studies of the impact of anticolonial nationalism on the Left in France and the United States, respectively, are Christoph Kalter, *The Discovery of the Third World: Decolonization and the Rise of the New Left in France, c. 1950–1976* (New York: Cambridge University Press,

2016); and Cynthia Young, *Soul Power: Culture, Radicalism, and the Making of a U.S. Third World Left* (Durham, NC: Duke University Press, 2006).

41. "Masaʿi al-quwwa al-thalitha fi haiʾat al-umam al-muttahida," *al-ʿAlam*, 10 February 1951, 2.

42. Richard H. Immermann and Petra Goedde, eds., introduction to *The Oxford Handbook of the Cold War* (New York: Oxford University Press, 2013), 7.

43. Robert Rézette, *Les partis politiques marocains* (Paris: A. Colin, 1955), 196.

44. I use the term *propaganda* as defined by *Merriam-Webster*: "Ideas, facts, or allegations spread deliberately to further one's cause or to damage an opposing cause." *Merriam-Webster*, s.v. "propaganda (*n.*)," accessed February 5, 2017, https://www.merriam-webster.com/dictionary /propaganda.

45. Allal al-Fassi to Azzam Pasha, 1 September 1948, dossier 2/folder 14, Allal al-Fassi Foundation, Rabat (hereafter AFF).

46. "Al-Zaʿim ʿAllal al-Fasi yusarrihu: Sanutalibu min haiʾat al-umam manh al-istiqlal ila al-Maghrib tibqan li-dusturiha," *al-ʿAlam*, 9 July 1952, 1.

47. Samuel Goldwyn, "World Challenge to Hollywood," *New York Times*, 31 August 1947, SM8.

48. Hizb al-Istiqlal, *Morocco under the Protectorate: Forty Years of French Administration. An Analysis of the Facts and Figures.* (New York: Moroccan Office of Information and Documentation, 1953).

49. "Franco-Moroccan Relations: Facts and Prospects," *Free Morocco*, 25 July 1953, 1.

50. "Nationalism, Independence and Democracy," *Free Morocco*, 25 June 1953, 1.

51. J. Clyde Mitchell, "Networks, Norms, and Institutions," in *Network Analysis*, ed. Jeremy Boissevain and J. Clyde Mitchell (The Hague: Mouton, 1973), 23–25; and Margaret E. Keck and Kathryn Sikkink, *Activists Beyond Borders—Advocacy Networks in International Politics* (Ithaca, NY: Cornell University Press, 1998), 3 & 12.

52. For an introduction to formalized social network analysis methods for humanities scholars, see Marten Düring et al., *Handbuch Historische Netzwerkforschung—Grundlagen und Anwendungen* (Berlin: LIT, 2016); Claire Lemercier, "Formal Network Methods in History: Why and How?," in *Social Networks, Political Institutions, and Rural Societies*, ed. Georg Fertig (Turnhout, BE: Brepols, 2015); Marten Düring and Linda Keyserlingk, "Netzwerkanalyse in den Geschichtswissenschaften. Historische Netzwerkanalyse als Methode für die Erforschung von historischen Prozessen," in *Prozesse—Formen, Dynamiken, Erklärungen*, ed. Rainer Schützeichel and Stefan Jordan (Wiesbaden, DE: VS Verlag für Sozialwissenschaften, 2012); Marten Düring et al., "VennMaker for Historians: Sources, Social Networks and Software," *REDES—Revista hispana para el análisis de redes sociales* 21, no. 2 (2011); Cristofoli Pascal, "Aux sources des grands réseaux d'interactions—Retour sur quelques propriétés déterminantes des réseaux sociaux issus de corpus documentaires," *Réseaux* 152 (2008); José María Imízcoz Beunza and Lara Arroyo Ruiz, "Redes sociales y correspondencia epistolar. Del análisis cualitativo de las relaciones personales a la reconstrucción de redes egocentradas," *REDES—Revista hispana para el análisis de redes sociales* 21, no. 2 (2011); and Christian Rollinger et al., "Editors Introduction," *Journal of Historical Network Research* 1 (2017). Successful examples of historical network analysis are Marten Düring, *Verdeckte Soziale Netzwerke im Nationalsozialismus. Berliner Hilfsnetzwerke Für Verfolgte Juden* (Berlin: De Gruyter, 2015); Daniel Iglesias, *Du pain et de la liberté: Socio-histoire des partis populaires apristes (Pérou, Venezuela, 1920–1962)* (Villeneuve d'Ascq, FR: Press Universitaires du Septentrion, 2015); Martin Stark, "Netzwerke in der Geschichtswissenschaft," in *Gläubiger, Schuldner, Arme. Netzwerke und die Rolle des Vertrauens*, ed. Curt W. Hergenröder (Wiesbaden, DE: VS Verlag für Sozialwissenschaften, 2010); and Romain Faure, *Netzwerke der Kulturdiplomatie—die internationale Schulbuch-*

revision in Europa 1945–1989 (Berlin: De Gruyter Oldenbourg, 2015). For an early example of the Moroccan nationalism's reliance on networked activism, see Franz Kogelmann, "Muhammad al-Makki an-Nasiri alias Sindbad der Seefahrer—Networking eines marokkanischen Nationalisten in den dreißiger Jahren des 20. Jahrhunderts," in *Die Islamische Welt als Netzwerk,* ed. Roman Loimeier (Würzburg, DE: Ergon, 2000).

53. On the concept of *embeddedness* within social networks, see Mark Granovetter, "Economic Action and Social Structure: The Problem of Embeddedness," *American Journal of Sociology* 91, no. 3 (1985). For a discussion of the methodological contributions made by network analysis, see Roman Loimeier and Stefan Reichmuth, "Zur Dynamik religiös-politischer Netzwerke in muslimischen Gesellschaften," *Die Welt des Islams* 36, no. 2 (1996): 151–52.

54. With regard to the relationship between activists and the political environment, see Charles Tilly, *From Mobilization to Revolution* (Reading, MA, Addison-Wesley, 1978); and Doug McAdam, *Political Process and the Development of Black Insurgency, 1930–1970* (Chicago: University of Chicago Press, 1999).

55. The methodological utility of network analysis for studying political activism on several levels simultaneously has been outlined by Cilja Harders, "Dimensionen des Netzwerkansatzes—Einführende theoretische Überlegungen," in *Die Islamische Welt als Netzwerk,* ed. Roman Loimeier (Würzburg, DE: Ergon, 2000).

56. Ronald S. Burt, *Structural Holes: The Social Structure of Competition* (Cambridge, MA: Harvard University Press, 1992); and Ronald S. Burt, "Structural Holes and Good Ideas," *American Journal of Sociology* 110, no. 2 (2004).

57. Ronald S. Burt, "The Network Structure of Social Capital," *Research in Organizational Studies* 22 (2000): 353; and Jeremy Boissevain, *Friends of Friends. Networks, Manipulators and Coalitions* (Oxford: Basil Blackwell, 1974), chap. 6.

58. Just like Georg Simmel's *tertius gaudens* ("the third who laughs"), brokers benefit from their location between two distinct groups that could no longer communicate in their absence. Georg Simmel, *Soziologie—Untersuchungen über die Formen der Vergesellschaftung* (Berlin: Duncker & Humblot, 1908), 82–89.

59. Nan Lin, "Building a Network Theory of Social Capital," *Connections* 22, no. 1 (1999).

60. Marisa von Bülow, "Brokers in Action: Transnational Coalitions and Trade Agreements in the Americas," *Mobilization: An International Quarterly* 16, no. 2 (2011): 168.

61. Mark S. Granovetter, "The Strength of Weak Ties," *American Journal of Sociology* 78, no. 6 (1973).

62. James S. Coleman, "Social Capital in the Creation of Human Capital," *American Journal of Sociology* 94, no. 1 (1988): S98, S118. The term was first defined by Pierre Bourdieu as the "aggregate of the actual or potential resources which are linked to the possession of a durable network of more or less institutionalized relationships of mutual acquaintance or recognition." Pierre Bourdieu, "The Forms of Capital," in *Handbook of Theory and Research for the Sociology of Education,* ed. John Richardson (New York: Greenwood, 1986), 249. But unlike scholars who subsequently developed his concept further, Bourdieu viewed social capital only in relation to, and not independent of, economic and cultural capital. In this book, I partially follow Bourdieu's approach: although I do not explicitly deal with economic and cultural capital, I do analyze social capital within the context of related variables, such as the status of individual actors within larger society and their ideological preferences.

63. Ronald S. Burt, *Brokerage and Closure* (New York: Oxford University Press, 2005), 4.

64. Nan Lin, *Social Capital—A Theory of Social Structure and Action* (New York: Cambridge University Press, 2001), 31–37.

65. Quoted from James Coleman, *Foundations of Social Theory* (Cambridge, MA: Belknap

Press, 1990), 312. For a study of actors strategically self-positioning within a network, see Vincent Buskens and Arnout van de Rijt, "Dynamics of Networks If Everyone Strives for Structural Holes," *American Journal of Sociology* 114, no. 2 (2009); and Roger Gould and Roberto Fernández, "Structures of Mediation: A Formal Approach to Brokerage in Transaction Network," *Social Methodology* 19 (1989): 104.

66. Ann Mische, *Partisan Publics: Communication and Contention across Brazilian Youth Activist Networks* (Princeton, NJ: Princeton University Press, 2009), 48–49.

67. David Easley and Jon Kleinberg, *Networks, Crowds, and Markets: Reasoning about a Highly Connected World* (New York: Cambridge University Press), 47–50.

68. Marisa von Bülow, *Building Transnational Networks—Civil Society and the Politics of Trade in the Americas* (New York: Cambridge University Press, 2010), 191.

69. For a study of leadership in social movements, see Mario Diani "'Leaders' or Brokers? Positions and Influence in Social Movement Networks," in *Social Movements and Networks: Relational Approaches to Collective Action*, ed. Mario Diani and Doug McAdam (New York: Oxford University Press, 2003), 117–18.

70. Matthew Connelly, *A Diplomatic Revolution—Algeria's Fight and the Origins of the Post–Cold War Era* (New York: Oxford University Press, 2002).

71. Jeffrey James Byrne, *Mecca of Revolution: Algeria, Decolonization, and the Third World Order* (New York: Oxford University Press, 2016).

72. Paul Thomas Chamberlin, *The Global Offensive: The United States, the Palestine Liberation Organization, and the Making of the Post–Cold War Order* (New York: Oxford University Press, 2012).

73. For a study of US president Woodrow Wilson's plan to spread the principle of self-determination in the aftermath of World War I, at least in Europe, as well as the global reception of this principle, see Erez Manela, *The Wilsonian Moment: Self-Determination and the International Origins of Anticolonial Nationalism* (New York: Oxford University Press, 2007).

CHAPTER I

1. Moroccan Parties to Moroccan and Arab Public Opinion, communiqué, 9 April 1951, Abdelkhaleq Torres File, vol. 2, BFA.

2. Ibid.

3. Intervención del Territorio de Yebala—Información: Expediente no. 266/Boletín 37, 26 April 1951, 15 (13.01), box 81/2161, Archivo General de la Administración, Alcalá de Henares (hereafter AGA).

4. Note de renseignements: Séjour des journalistes égyptiens, 9 April 1951, 1MA/200/266, Centre des archives diplomatiques, Nantes (hereafter CADN).

5. Ibid.

6. "Al-Ahzab al-wataniyya al-arb'a tuwahhidu sufufahum," *al-'Alam*, 11 April 1951, 1.

7. Rézette, *Les partis politiques marocains*, 190–91. The Arab League's founding members were Egypt, Syria, Lebanon, Iraq, Saudi Arabia, and Transjordan. Yemen joined the organization six weeks later. The League expanded in subsequent decades and currently has twenty-two member states.

8. Note de renseignements: Journalistes égyptiens, 11 April 1951, 1MA/200/266, CADN.

9. Intervención del Territorio de Yebala—Información, 12 April 1951, 15 (13.01), box 81/2161, AGA.

10. "Nadwa kubra yu'aqiduha al-sahafiyyun al-misriyyun bi-Tanja," *al-'Alam*, 10 April 1951, 1.

11. "Takrim ba'that al-sahafa al-misriyya al-'a'ida min al-Maghrib," *al-'Alam*, 28 April 1951, 1.

12. L'accord signé entre les partis marocains est remis à Azzam Pasha—extract du quotidien al-Misry, 27 April 1951, 1MA/200/266, CADN.

13. "La conjuration de Tanger," *Le Figaro*, 14/15 April 1951, Abdelkhaleq Torres File, vol. 2, BFA.

14. Reporte Union de los Partidos, 28 September 1949, 15 (13.01), box 81/2161, AGA.

15. Allal al-Fassi to Tayeb Bennouna, 23 August 1946, 15 (13.01), box 81/2157, AGA.

16. Reporte Union de los Partidos, 28 October 1949, 15 (13.01), box 81/2161, AGA; and Dificultades para la unión nacionalista, 12 April 1950, 15 (13.01), box 81/2161, AGA.

17. Rabat to Department of State, 13 April 1951, RG59/771.00/4-1451, United States National Archives, College Park, MD (hereafter USNA).

18. For a brief introduction to how the arrival of the US Army impacted Moroccan society, see Mohammed Kenbib, "L'impact américain sur ne nationalisme Marocain (1930–1947)," *Hespéris Tamuda* 26/27 (1988): 220–21.

19. Elizabeth Borgwardt, *A New Deal for the World: America's Vision for Human Rights* (Cambridge, MA: The Belknap Press, 2005), 34–35.

20. David Stenner, "Did Amrika Promise Morocco's Independence? The Nationalist Movement, the Sultan, and the Making of the 'Roosevelt Myth,'" *The Journal of North African Studies* 19, no. 4 (2014).

21. President Roosevelt to the Sultan of Morocco, 24 October 1947, RG59/881.00/10-2447, USNA.

22. Texto inédito sobre el nacionalismo de Tomás García Figueras, [n.d.], p. 162, 15 (13.01), box 81/2382, AGA.

23. "Dawr al-yaqaza al-maghribiyya," *al-ʿAlam*, 7 September 1947, 4.

24. *Maʿalamat al-Maghrib* (Encyclopédie du Maroc), ed. Mohammed Hajji (Salé, MA: Matabiʿa Sala, 2003), s.v. "ʿAbd al-Khaliq Turis."

25. Surat tabaq al-asl li-wathiqat al-mutalaba bi-l-istiqlal, 14 February 1943, Abdelkhaleq Torres File, vol. 2, BFA.

26. Halstead, *Rebirth of a Nation*, 262.

27. "The Independence Manifesto," in Hizb al-Istiqlal, *Morocco, Istiqlal Party Documents, 1944–1946* (Paris: Moroccan Office of Information and Documentation, 1946), 1–3.

28. ʿAllal al-Fasi, *Al-Harakat al-istiqlaliyya fi al-Maghrib al-ʿarabi* (Cairo: Maktab al-Maghrib al-ʿArabi, 1948), 283.

29. Hizb al-Istiqlal, *Morocco, Istiqlal Party Documents, 1944–1946*, 19–20.

30. "Al-Shuʿub al-qasira fi dustur al-umam al-muttahida," *al-ʿAlam*, 28 June 1947, 1.

31. David Stenner, "Centring the Periphery: Northern Morocco as a Hub of Transnational Anti-Colonial Activism, 1930–43," *Journal of Global History* 11, no. 3 (2016).

32. al-Fasi, *Al-Harakat al-istiqlaliyya*, 372.

33. Interview with M'hamid Zeghari, Kenitra, 1 June 1967, in Blair, *Western Window*, 101.

34. "Hurriyyat Arbaʿ," *al-ʿAlam*, 25 May 1947, 1.

35. "Sanat huquq al-insan (1948)," *al-ʿAlam*, 12 January 1949, 1.

36. "Hadith al-yawm," *al-ʿAlam*, 15 April 1949, 1.

37. "Taqrir istiʿmari gharib," *al-ʿAlam*, 7 July 1950, 4.

38. Andrew Buchanan, *American Grand Strategy in the Mediterranean during World War II* (New York: Cambridge University Press, 2013).

39. Martin Thomas, "Defending a Lost Cause? France and the United States Vision of Imperial Rule in French North Africa, 1946–1956," *Diplomatic History* 26, no. 2 (2002); and Samya El Machat, *Les Etats-Unis et le Maroc: Le choix stratégique, 1945–1959* (Paris: L'Harmattan, 1996).

40. Yahia H. Zoubir, "The United States, the Soviet Union and Decolonization of the Maghreb, 1945–1962," *Middle Eastern Studies* 31, no. 1 (1995).

41. Ministre des Affaires étrangères au Résident général, 25 July 1947, 1MA/5/976, CADN.

42. Arab Congratulations on November 8, 16 November 1944, RG59/881.00/11-1644, USNA.

43. Blair, *Western Window*, 98–99.

44. Lettre circulaire adressée par Sbihi dans les principales villes du Maroc, October 1945, 1MA/282/199, CADN.

45. Abdellatif Sbihi to Eleanor Roosevelt, telegram, 19 February 1946, 1MA/282/199, CADN; and Memorandum of Conversation: Henry Villard and Francis Lacoste, 11 March 1946, RG59/881.00/3-1146, USNA.

46. French Prohibit Formation of Roosevelt Club, 18 April 1946, RG59/881.00/4-1846, USNA.

47. Note sur le Club Roosevelt, 19 April 1946, 1MA/282/199, CADN.

48. Meeting in Commemoration of President Roosevelt, 18 April 1947, RG59/711.00/4-1847, USNA.

49. Ibid.

50. Alleged Views of the Sultan of Morocco, 5 June 1947, RG59/711.00/6-547, USNA.

51. Meeting in Commemoration of President Roosevelt, 18 April 1947, RG59/711.00/4-1847, USNA.

52. Ibid.

53. Mohammed Shahid Mathee and Ph.-J. Salazar, "Mohammed V: The Tangiers Speech," *African Yearbook of Rhetoric* 2, no. 3 (2011): 23.

54. Visit of the Sultan to Tangier, 30 April 1947, FO 371/67846A, United Kingdom National Archives, Kew (hereafter UKNA); and al-Fasi, *al-Harakat al-istiqlaliyya*, 388.

55. Visit to Tangier of His Majesty: Tangier to Department of State, 16 April 1947, RG59/881.001/4-1647, USNA.

56. Full Report on Sultan's Visit, 14 April 1947, FO 371/67846A, UKNA.

57. Tangier to Department of State, 13 April 1947, RG59/881.00/4-1347, USNA.

58. Tangier to Department of State, 11 April 1947, RG59/881.00/4-1147, USNA.

59. "Barnamaj al-rihla al-malakiyya," *al-'Alam*, 9 April 1947, 1.

60. Full Report on Sultan's Visit to Tangier, 11 April 1947, FO 371/67846A, UKNA.

61. al-Fasi, *Al-Harakat al-istiqlaliyya*, 357.

62. George Joffé, "The Moroccan Nationalist Movement: Istiqlal, the Sultan, and the Country," *Journal of African History* 26, no. 4 (1985): 306–7.

63. al-Fasi, *Al-Harakat al-istiqlaliyya*, 359.

64. "Yawm mashhud," *al-'Alam*, 12 April 1947, 1.

65. "Morocco's Sultan Perturbs France," *New York Times*, 11 April 1947, 11; and "Full Rights for Morocco," *The Times*, 15 April 1947, 4.

66. "Discours du Sultan à Tangier," *Le Monde*, 15 April 1947, 1; and al-Fasi, *Al-Harakat al-istiqlaliyya*, 368–69.

67. "Ta'liq Radiyu al-Qahira 'ala safar jallalat al-malik li-Tanja," *al-'Alam*, 18 April 1947, 1.

68. "Hadith li-sahafi misri 'an al-Maghrib wa kalimat al-malik," *al-'Alam*, 13 April 1947, 1.

69. al-Fasi, *Al-Harakat al-istiqlaliyya*, 352.

70. "Sada al-ziyara al-malakiyya li-Tanja," *al-'Alam*, 24 April 1947, 1.

71. Ibid.

72. "Al-Dhikra al-uwla," *al-'Alam*, 9 April 1948, 1.

73. William A. Hoisington, *The Casablanca Connection: French Colonial Policy, 1936–1943*

(Chapel Hill: University of North Carolina Press, 1984), 197; and Robin W. Winks, *Cloak & Gown: Scholars in the Secret War, 1939–1961* (New York: Morrow, 1987), 181–83.

74. US Office of Strategic Services, *Morocco*, vol. 2 (Washington, DC: Research and Analysis Branch, 1942), 114.

75. The US agents saw the small Jewish community as the antithesis to the allegedly pro-German Muslim population. The authors of the OSS dossier concluded that "they are suffering from anti-Jewish laws enacted by Vichy, which are popular with the Muslim population. There have been some anti-Jewish riots, but these are discouraged by the Sultan. Allied sympathy seems to be strong among the Jews. They have no political influence, however, only economic and financial." Ibid., vol. 1, 96–98.

76. Kenneth Pendar, *Adventure in Diplomacy: Our French Dilemma* (New York: Dodd & Mead, 1945), 11.

77. See, for example, memoranda prepared by Vice-Consul Kenneth Pendar, 19 March 1942, RG59/881.00/2141, USNA; and Conversation with Nationalist Leader Hajj Ahmed Balafrej, 26 August 1946, RG59/881.00/8-2646, USNA.

78. Carleton S. Coon, *A North Africa Story: The Anthropologist as OSS Agent, 1941–1943* (Ipswich, MA: Gambit, 1980), 23.

79. United Front of Moorish Nationalist Parties in Morocco, 15 June 1943, RG59/881.00/2571, USNA.

80. Returning Four Studies on Morocco with the Comments of the Legation, 11 September 1944, RG59/881.00/9-1144, USNA.

81. Note Sûreté régionale de Fès, 10 February 1930, 1MA/282/69, CADN.

82. Excerpt from Mr. Gordon Browne's Memorandum to Mr. Villard, 11 October 1943, RG59/881.00/2752, USNA.

83. Casablanca to Department of State, 22 November 1943, RG59/881.00/2700, USNA.

84. Renseignements de Gordon Browne, 27 September 1946, 1MA/282/69, CADN.

85. Note de renseignements, Casablanca, 25 September 1946, 1MA/282/69, CADN.

86. Richard Southgate to Jack D. Neal, 12 April 1945, RG226/OSS Personal Files/Entry 224/Walter B. Cline, USNA; and Le Cabinet militaire—619D, 23 March 1945, 1MA/5/980, CADN.

87. Donovan (OSS) to Berle (Department of State), 23 November 1944, RG226/OSS Personal Files/Entry 224/Walter B. Cline, USNA; Tangier to Department of State, no. 105, 25 April 1945, RG226/OSS Personal Files/Entry 224/Walter B. Cline, USNA; and Rabat to Department of State, no. 123, 13 October 1944, RG226/OSS Personal Files/Entry 224/Walter B. Cline, USNA. It is important to note that because the University of Minnesota had explicitly requested Cline's return to the United States, the protest by the French authorities was not the only reason for it.

88. Walter B. Cline, "Nationalism in Morocco," *Middle East Journal* 1 (1947): 28.

89. Note de renseignement concernant Walter Cline, 22 April 1949, 1MA/5/980, CADN.

90. Memorandum from Department of State to Rabat, 10 June 1949, RG59/881.00/4-2649, USNA.

91. "North Africa Recalls," *New York Times*, 9 November 1947, SM15.

92. Edward Toledano, "Young Man, Go to Casablanca," *Harper's Magazine*, September 1948, 109–11.

93. Brigitte Christine Maldidier, "The United States and Morocco, 1945–1953" (master's thesis, Stanford University, 1955), 19–20.

94. Egya N. Sangmuah, "Interest Groups and Decolonization: American Business and Labor in Morocco, 1948–1956," *The Maghreb Review* 13, nos. 3–4 (1988): 162.

95. "French Deny Discrimination," *New York Times*, 5 August 1949, 3.

96. Testimony Given before House Appropriations Sub-Committee, 19 May 1949, pp. 9, 11, Rodes Family Archive, Manchester, TN (hereafter RFA).

97. Testimony to Be Given before the Senate Appropriations Committee Hearings on Aid to Europe, 23 June 1949, p. 6, RFA.

98. Tangier to Department of State, 30 April 1947, RG59/711.81/4-3047, USNA.

99. Conversation with Resident General—Enclosure to Dispatch 30, 9 February 1949, RG59/881.008/2-949, USNA.

100. Maldidier, "The United States and Morocco, 1945–1953," 26.

101. US Department of State, *Foreign Relations of the United States, 1950*, vol. V, ed. Fredrick Aandahl and William Z. Slany (Washington, DC: US Government Printing Office, 1978), 1548–49.

102. Memo on Moroccan Trade Controls (preliminary draft), 20 February 1951, RG59/771.00/3-1351, USNA.

103. Note: Politique américaine au Maroc, [n.d.], 1MA/5/976, CADN.

104. Annie Lacroix-Riz, *Les protectorats d'Afrique du Nord, entre la France et Washington: Du débarquement à l'indépendance, Maroc et Tunisie 1942–1956* (Paris: L'Harmattan, 1988), 61.

105. Rights of Nationals of the United States of America in Morocco (Judgment France v. U.S.), 1952 I.C.J. 213 (27 August), *available at* http://www.worldcourts.com/icj/eng/decisions/1952.08.27_rights_of_nationals.htm.

106. "Morocco and The Hague Court," *New York Times*, 30 August 1952, 12.

107. "Al-Amrikun al-qatinun bi-l-Maghrib yabtahijun bi-qarar mahkamat Lahay," *al-ʿAlam*, 29 August 1952, 1.

108. "Masalat huriyyat al-jalb fi al-Maghrib amam majlis al-shuyukh al-amriki," *al-ʿAlam*, 7 August 1949, 1.

109. Conversation of McBride and Balafrej, 14 October 1949, enclosure no. 1 to Rabat to Department of State, 25 October 1949, RG59/881.00/10-2549, USNA.

110. Rabat to Department of State: Sultan Conveys Certain Information to Consulate, 12 January 1949, RG59/881.00/1-1249, USNA.

111. Rabat to Department of State: Further Evidences of Moroccan Dissatisfaction with US Policies, 31 March 1950, RG59/611.71/3-3150, USNA.

112. "Al-mudhakkira allati rafaʿatha jubhat al-ahzab al-wataniyya al-maghribiyya ila mahkamat Lahay," *al-ʿAlam*, 25 July 1949, 1.

113. Allal al-Fassi to the Egyptian Foreign Minister, 21 May 1952, dossier 2/folder 14, AFF.

114. Benjamin Rivlin, "The United States and Moroccan International Status, 1943–1956: A Contributory Factor in Morocco's Reassertion of Independence from France," *International Journal of African Historical Studies* 15, no. 1 (1982): 73.

115. "Al-Siyada al-maghribiyya takhruj muʿazzazatun al-janib min mahkamat Lahay," *al-ʿAlam*, 29 August 1952, 4.

116. "Haqiqat al-khilaf al-faransi al-amriki haula hurriyyat al-tijara bi-l-Maghrib," *al-ʿAlam*, 15 July 1952, 2.

117. Note de renseignements: Chambre de Commerce américaine du Maroc, 14 December 1954, 1MA/5/983, CADN.

118. C. D. Jackson to Henry Cabot Lodge, 10 November 1953, White House Central Files, Name File: Robert E. Rodes, Dwight D. Eisenhower Presidential Library, Abilene, KS (hereafter DDEPL).

119. J. C. Satterthwaite to Henry Cabot Lodge, 19 November 1953, White House Central Files, Name File: Robert E. Rodes, DDEPL.

120. Ibid.

121. H. A. Byroade to C. D. Jackson, 16 November 1953, White House Central Files, Name File: Robert E. Rodes, DDEPL.

122. Returning Four Studies on Morocco with the Comments of the Legation, 1 September 1944, RG59/881.00/9-1144, USNA.

123. "Mrs. Guinle Married—Argentinian Diplomat's Daughter Bride of Kenneth W. Pendar," *New York Times*, 21 March 1948, 59.

124. Ely J. Kahn, *The Big Drink: The Story of Coca-Cola* (New York: Random House, 1960), 38.

125. Blair, *Western Window*, 158.

126. For examples of events sponsored by Coca-Cola, see "Mablagh 150,000 frank min nuwwab Kuka Kula tabarruʿan ʿala al-mubara al-adabiyya al-thanya," *al-ʿAlam*, 4 November 1950, 1; and "Surat al-kaʾs alladhi ahdatahu dar Kuka Kula li-l-faʾiz fi al-sibaq," *al-ʿAlam*, 18 November 1951, 1. Quote taken from "Thirty-Thousand Americans Construct in Morocco Seven Giant Airfields" [English translation], *Paris-Press-Intransigeant*, 8 November 1951, RG59/611.71/11-2351, USNA.

127. Résident général au Ministre des Affaires étrangères Schuman, 3 December 1949, 1MA/200/892, CADN. See also Jonathan Wyrtzen, "Constructing Morocco: The Colonial Struggle to Define the Nation, 1912–56" (PhD diss., Georgetown University, 2009), 346–48.

128. Aide-mémoire de l'entretien de S. M. le Sultan et du Conseiller du gouvernement Chérifien, 15 November 1949, 1MA/200/889, CADN.

129. "Tadshin al-maʿmal al-jadid li-Kuka Kula bi-l-Dar al-Baida," *al-ʿAlam*, 20 January 1951, 4.

130. Estancia en Tánger de Kenneth Pendar, 25 January 1952, 15 (13.01), box 81/2121, AGA.

131. Informante: América, 8 February 1952, 15 (13.01), box 81/2166, AGA; and Asunto: Propósito de Taxistas de Tánger y Tetuán con motivo de la Próxima Marcha de Abdelkhalek Torres, 8 February 1952, 15 (13.01), box 81/2166, AGA.

132. Abdelkhaleq Torres to Azzam Pasha, 9 November 1951, Documents 1949–51, Abdelkhaleq Torres Foundation, Tetouan (hereafter ATF).

133. Ibid.

134. Richard F. Kuisel, "Coca-Cola and the Cold War: The French Face Americanization, 1948–1953," *French Historical Studies* 17, no. 1 (1991): 105.

135. Irwin M. Wall, *The United States and the Making of Postwar France, 1945–1954* (New York: Cambridge University Press, 1991), 124.

136. Ibid., 121, 185.

137. Kenneth Pendar to Senator William Benton, 1 May 1952, RFA.

138. Asunto: Campaña en los parises árabes contra el refrescante Coca-Cola e Pepsi-Cola—Boletín 923, Hoja 1, 28 September 1951, 15 (13.01), box 81/2167, AGA.

139. "Kuka kula halal," *al-ʿAlam*, 28 October 1951, 1; Reunión de Estudiantes en los Locales de Unidad Marroquí—Boletín 932, Hoja 2, 16 October 1951, 15 (13.01), box 81/2167, AGA.

140. "Fi tariq min Jidda ila Makka al-mukarrama," *al-ʿAlam*, 2 October 1951, 3.

141. "Fi salat al-jumʿa ams," *al-ʿAlam*, 20 October 1951, 1.

142. Kahn, *The Big Drink*, 37–38.

143. "US Faces Snares on Morocco Bases," *New York Times*, 2 October 1952, 9.

144. Retour de Mr. Kenneth Pendar aux USA, 23 November 1954, 91QO/560, Archives du ministère des Affaires étrangères, La Courneuve (hereafter AMAE).

145. Mr. Pendar's Views on the Current Situation, 6 February 1953, RG59/771.00/2-653, USNA.

146. Asunto: Comentarios—Boletín 210—Tánger, 17 September 1954, 15 (13.01), box 81/2167, AGA.

147. Undated Note, p. 4, 1MA/5/976, CADN.

148. "Thirty-Thousand Americans Construct in Morocco Seven Giant Airfields" [English translation], *Paris-Press-Intransigeant*, 8 November 1951, RG59/611.71/11-2351, USNA.

149. Résident général au Consul Dorman, 30 April 1952, 1MA/5/976, CADN.

150. Kenneth Pendar to US Ambassador Thomas Finletter, 28 October 1951, RFA.

151. Note pour le général Boyer de la Tour, 9 May 1951, 1MA/282/207, CADN.

152. Estancia en Tánger de Kenneth Pendar, 25 January 1952, 15 (13.01), box 81/2121, AGA.

153. Author Conversation with M'hamed Boucetta, 6 December 2012, Rabat (Morocco).

154. Rabat to Department of State, 30 April 1952, RG59/711.00/4-3052, USNA.

155. Hugh Wilford, *America's Great Game—The CIA's Secret Arabists and the Shaping of the Modern Middle East* (New York: Basic Books, 2013), xix–xxi.

156. John Prados, "The CIA and the Face of Decolonization," in *The Eisenhower Administration, the Third World, and the Globalization of the Cold War*, ed. Kathryn C. Statler (Lanham, MD: Rowman & Littlefield, 2006), 42.

157. The same discrepancy between the activities of the State Department and CIA could also be witnessed inside France. See Wall, *Making of Postwar France*, 96.

158. Mr. Rodes Apparently Champions Nationalist Aspirations, 20 May 1952, RG59/711.00/5-2052, USNA.

159. Albert Ayache, *Le mouvement syndical au Maroc*, vol. 2, *La marocanisation: 1943–1948* (Paris: L'Harmattan, 1982), 32–34, 173–75.

160. Rézette, *Les partis politiques marocains*, 37.

161. "Al-Tahrir al-ijtima'i," *al-'Alam*, 1 May 1951, 1.

162. Ayache, *Le Mouvement syndical au Maroc*, vol. 3, *Vers l'indépendance: 1949–1956*, 88–97.

163. As quoted in ibid., 129.

164. Istiqlal Celebrates May Day, 5 May 1949, p. 3, RG59/881.00/5-549, USNA.

165. Latest Developments in Union Labor Policy in Morocco, 25 August 1948, RG59/881.00/8-2548, USNA; and Union Rights and Possible Danger to War Effort and Morocco in Case of Conflict, 30 April 1948, RG59/881.00/4-3048, USNA.

166. See, for example, the conversation between Ali Bargach and Vice Consul Chase in Moroccan Concern over US Import Policy, Enclosure no. 2, 25 October 1949, RG59/881.00/10-2549, USNA.

167. Further Developments in the French, Nationalist, and Communist Positions Regarding Labor Unions in Morocco, 24 November 1948, RG59/881.00/11-2448, USNA.

168. Until their merger on 5 December 1955, the AFL and the CIO were two separate labor union federations. An overview of the international activities of the US labor movement after 1945 can be found in Geert Van Goethem and Robert Anthony Waters, eds., *American Labor's Global Ambassadors: The International History of the AFL-CIO during the Cold War* (New York: Palgrave Macmillan, 2013).

169. Sangmuah, "Interest Groups and Decolonization," 168–69. See also Willard A. Beling, "W.F.T.U. and Decolonisation: A Tunisian Case Study," *Journal of Modern African Studies* 2, no. 4 (1964): 561–63.

170. Sangmuah, "Interest Groups and Decolonization," 169; and "Tunisian Nationalist in Plea over 'Voice'; French Not Consulted, Ponder AFL," *New York Times*, 14 September 1951, 9.

171. Interview accordée par Mahjoub Ben Seddiq à un journaliste parisien, 14 April 1955, 1MA/200/479, CADN.

172. Rapport de la délégation de la CISL en Afrique du Nord, Maroc, 4 February 1951, RG18-07, box 9/13, George Meany Memorial AFL-CIO Archives at the University of Maryland University Libraries, College Park, MD (hereafter GMA).

173. Région de Fès: Note de Renseignements, 30 June 1952, 1MA/282/69, CADN.

174. The International Confederation of Free Trade Unions, *The ICFTU and the Workers of Morocco* (Brussels: ICFTU, 1956), pp. 18–19, RG18-07, box 11/19, GMA.

175. Communiqué de Presse, 26 August 1953, RG18-07, box 9/13, GMA.

176. The ICFTU and the Workers of Morocco, 1956, p. 20, RG18-07, box 11/19, GMA.

177. Ibid., p. 22.

178. Activités syndicales marocaines, 18 March 1955, 1MA/200/479, CADN.

179. Visite à la Direction de l'Intérieur de Ben Seddiq, Bouazza, Mohammed & Awab, 22 March 1955, 1MA/200/479, CADN.

180. Tayeb Bouazza to Irving Brown, 9 November 1954, RG18-05, box 31/2, GMA.

181. As quoted in Ayache, *Le Mouvement Syndical Au Maroc*, vol. 3, 182.

182. Some examples are Ronald Radosh, *American Labor and United States Foreign Policy* (New York: Random House, 1969); Michael Fichter, *Besatzungsmacht und Gewerkschaften: Zur Entwicklung und Anwendung der US-Gewerkschaftspolitik in Deutschland, 1944–1948* (Opladen, DE: Westdeutscher Verlag, 1982); and Annie Lacroix-Riz, "Autour d'Irving Brown: l'A.F.L., le Free Trade Union Committee le Département d'État et la scission syndicale française (1944–1947)," *Le Mouvement social* 151 (1990). An alternative story focusing on grassroots activism as a driving force behind the AFL's foreign policy can be found in Adam M. Howard, *Sewing the Fabric of Statehood: Garment Unions, American Labor, and the Establishment of the State of Israel* (Urbana: University of Illinois Press, 2018).

183. Ted Morgan, *A Covert Life: Jay Lovestone, Communist, Anti-Communist, and Spymaster* (New York: Random House, 1999), 285–86; and Wall, *Making of Postwar France*, 105.

184. See, for example, Région de Casablanca: Note de renseignements, 19 February 1951, 1MA/282/69, CADN.

185. Débats Parlementaires, *Journal Officiel de la République Française*, no. 29 (30 May 1956): 884. For a hagiographic portrayal of Irving Brown by the US media, see "Labor: The Most Dangerous Man," *Time*, 17 March 1952, http://content.time.com/time/magazine/article/0,9171,816103,00 .html.

186. El Ministro Plenipotenciario cargado del Consulado General a Rabat José Felipe Alcover al Señor Alto Comisario de España en Marruecos, 26 January 1955, 15 (13.01), box 81/2149, AGA.

187. Rabat to Department of State: Position of Istiqlal Party in Present French Moroccan Crisis, 21 February 1951, RG59/771.00/2-2151, USNA.

188. "L'accession des territoires non autonomes à l'indépendance: Preoccupation majeure de la CISL," *al-Istiqlal*, 18 October 1952, 3.

189. "Ittihad al-ʿummal al-amrikiyyin yahtaju ʿala siyasat al-ʿunf al-faransiyya," *al-Umma*, 28 November 1953, 2.

190. Notice Technique de Contre-Espionnage—Activités de Miss Epton en Afrique du Nord, 3 December 1947, 1MA/282/90, CADN.

191. "A Pretty Explorer Will Set Off Again," *The Sunday Herald* (Sydney), 5 July 1953, 24.

192. Nina Epton, *Journey under the Crescent Moon* (London: Victor Gollancz, 1949), 84.

193. Ambassadeur de France en Grande-Bretagne au Ministre des Affaires éntrangères Bidault, 13 October 1947, 1MA/282/90, CADN.

194. Epton, *Journey under the Crescent Moon*, 11.

195. Ibid., 39.

196. Ibid., 276.

197. 'Abd al-Majid bin Jalun, "Marrakush bidun hijab," *al-'Alam,* 10 May 1947, 1.

198. Ibid.

199. "Sawt yudafi'u 'an al-Maghrib," *al-Hurriyya,* 19 December 1946, 2.

200. Chef des brigades de surveillance du Maroc au Directeur des services de Sécurité publique, 19 August 1947, 1MA/282/90, CADN.

201. Notice Technique de Contre-Espionnage, 3 December 1947, 1MA/282/90, CADN.

202. Secretariat politique, 3 December 1946, 1MA/282/191, CADN.

203. Note de Renseignements, no. 160, 15 October 1951, 1MA/282/191, CADN; and Note sur Margaret Pope, 7 November 1951, 1MA/282/191, CADN.

204. Margaret Pope—journaliste anglaise, [n.d.], 1MA/282/191, CADN.

205. Note—Margaret Pope, 5 June 1951, 1MA/282/191, CADN.

206. Margaret Pope—journaliste anglaise, [n.d.], 1MA/282/191, CADN.

207. *Echo du Maroc*—Mise au point, 10 April 1951, 1MA/282/191, CADN.

208. Advice to answer a letter from Gen. Guillaume, 13 December 1951, FO 371/90242, UKNA.

209. Tangier to Foreign Office, 9 August 1951, FO 371/90269, UKNA; and Foreign Office to Tangier, 17 September 1951, FO 371/90269, UKNA.

210. Possibility of Visit to UK by Allal al-Fassi, 26 June 1951, RG59/771.00/6-2651, USNA.

211. Reported Desire of French Authorities to Request Expulsion of Legation's Scribe, 12 March 1951, RG59/771.00/3-1951, USNA.

212. Rom Landau, *Personalia* (London: Faber and Faber, 1949), 119–31.

213. Direction de l'Intérieur—a/s Landau, 17 June 1949, 1MA/282/125, CADN.

214. Rom Landau, *Morocco Independent under Mohammed V* (London: Allen & Unwin, 1961), 22.

215. M. E. Adeane to Rom Landau, 26 March 1951, MS 63, Rom Landau Collection, Department of Special Collections at the University of California–Santa Barbara (hereafter UCSB).

216. Allal al-Fassi to Rom Landau, 2 January 1950, MS68, series 1, box 1, Holt-Atherton Special Collections at the University of the Pacific, Stockton, CA (hereafter HASC).

217. Allal al-Fassi to Rom Landau, 26 October 1949, MS68, series 1, box 1, HASC.

218. Allal al-Fassi to Rom Landau, 29 January 1950, MS68, series 1, box 1, HASC.

219. Allal al-Fassi to Rom Landau, 12 June 1950, MS68, series 1, box 1, HASC.

220. Rom Landau to Morley Kennerley, 7 January 1950, Rom Landau Papers, box 1, Special Collections Research Center at Syracuse University, Syracuse, NY (hereafter SCRC).

221. Rom Landau to Morley Kennerley, 21 November 1950, Rom Landau Papers, box 1, SCRC; and "Al-Katib al-injlizi al-shahir Rum Landaw yusarrihu lana," *al-'Alam,* 16 November 1950, 1.

222. Rom Landau to Morley Kennerley, 16 November 1950, Rom Landau Papers, box 1, SCRC.

223. Rom Landau to Morley Kennerley, 22 February 1951, Rom Landau Papers, box 1, SCRC.

224. "Peace May Be in Moslem Hands," *New York Times,* 6 April 1952, SM14.

225. "Takrim al-brufasur Rum Landaw," *al-Anba',* 21 October 1969.

226. El nacionalismo norteafricano y sus aliados—Reporte para el Alto Comisario, 21 April 1947, 15 (13.01), box 81/1919, AGA.

227. Robert E. Rodes to Jay Lovestone, 2 December 1953, Jay Lovestone Files, RG18-03, box 55/21, GMA.

228. Robert E. Rodes to George Delaney, 12 September 1954, Jay Lovestone Files, RG18-03, box 55/21, GMA.

229. Mr. Rodes Apparently Champions Nationalist Aspirations, 20 May 1952, RG59/711.00/5-2052, USNA.

230. Allal al-Fassi to Rom Landau, 26 October 1949, MS68, series 1, box 1, HASC.

231. Texto inédito sobre el nacionalismo de Tomás García Figueras, [n.d.], pp. 211–12, 15 (13.01), box 81/2382, AGA.

232. US Department of State, *Foreign Relations, 1950*, vol. V, 1737, 1746.

CHAPTER 2

1. Ahmed Benaboud (son) to Ahmed Benaboud (father), 16 February 1946, 15 (13.01), box 81/2173, AGA; and The Delegation of Morocco to the Arab League [Spanish translation], 8 February 1946, *al-Hadaf* (Beirut), 15 (13.01), box 81/2173, AGA.

2. Commemorative Celebration of the Arab League in Cairo, 24 March 1946, M'hammad Benaboud File, BFA.

3. "Kalimat ra'is al-wafd al-marrakushi M'hammad bin 'Abbud fi ihtifal al-jama'a al-'arabiyya," *al-Ikhwan al-Muslimun*, 26 March 1946, p. 8, reproduced in M'hammad bin 'Abbud, *Al-Nidal al-watani li-l-shahid M'hammad bin 'Abbud fi-l-Mashriq: Shahadat wa watha'iq* (Tetouan, MA: Manshurat Jama'iyyat Titwan Asmir, 1997), 46.

4. M'hammad Benaboud and Mohammed al-Fassi al-Halfaoui to Tayeb Bennouna, 6 April 1946, M'hammad Benaboud File, BFA.

5. Nashrat al-akhbar al-wataniyya no. 8, 7 September 1946, M'hammad Benaboud File, BFA.

6. This chapter is based partly on the article by David Stenner, "'Bitterness towards Egypt'—The Moroccan Nationalist Movement, Revolutionary Cairo and the Limits of Anti-Colonial Solidarity," *Cold War History* 16, no. 2 (2015).

7. "Pact of the League of Arab States," 22 March 1945, in Anita L. P. Burdett, *Inauguration, 1944–1946*, vol. 4 of *The Arab League: British Documentary Sources, 1943–1963* (London: Archive Editions, 1995), 203.

8. Ahmed M. Gomaa, *The Foundation of the League of Arab States: Wartime Diplomacy and Inter-Arab Politics, 1941 to 1945* (London: Longman, 1977), 260.

9. "Pact of the League of Arab States," in Burdett, *Inauguration*, 206.

10. Rézette, *Les partis politiques marocains*, 151.

11. Mehdi Bennouna to Tayeb Bennouna, 15 September 1944, Mehdi Bennouna File, vol. 1, BFA.

12. Bulletin de renseignements—Maroc, 13 June 1945, série F60, box 885, Archives nationales, Pierrefitte-sur-Seine (hereafter ANF).

13. Nota del Alto Comisario, 1 September 1945, 15 (13.01), box 81/1901, AGA.

14. Khalifian dahir Appointing Benaboud and al-Fassi to Represent Morocco in Cairo, 30 November 1945, M'hammad Benaboud File, BFA.

15. "The Delegation of Morocco to the Arab League" [Spanish translation], *al-Hadaf* (Beirut), 8 February 1946, 15 (13.01), box 81/2173, AGA.

16. María Dolores Algora Weber, *Las relaciones hispano-árabes durante el régimen de Franco: La ruptura del aislamiento internacional (1946–1950)* (Madrid: Ministerio de Asuntos Exteriores, 1995), 303.

17. Department of State to Madrid, Paris, Rabat, and Tangier, 17 February 1954, RG59/771.00/2-1754, USNA.

18. Irene González González, "La 'hermandad hispano-árabe' en la política cultural del franquismo (1936–1956)," *Anales de Historia Contemporánea* 23 (2007): 193.

19. "UN General Assembly Resolution A/RES/39(I)—Relations of Members of the United Nations with Spain," 12 December 1946, accessed 8 March 2018, http://research.un.org/en/docs/ga/quick/regular/1.

20. Spain was permitted to open embassies in Iraq, Lebanon, and Jordan in 1953. Miguel Hernando de Larramendi Martínez et al., "El Ministerio de Asuntos Exteriores y la política exterior hacia el Magreb," in *La política interior Española hacia el Magreb: Actors e intereses*, ed. Miguel Hernando de Larramendi Martínez and Aurelia Mañé Estrada (Barcelona: Editorial Arual, 2009), 63.

21. Susan Martin-Márquez, *Disorientations: Spanish Colonialism in Africa and the Performance of Identity* (New Haven, CT: Yale University Press, 2008), chap. 1.

22. José Antonio González Alcantud, *El mito de al Ándalus: Orígenes y actualidad de un ideal cultural* (Córdoba, ES: Almuzara, 2014), 77–103.

23. Josep Lluís Mateo Dieste, *La "hermandad" hispano-marroquí: Política y religión bajo el Protectorado español en Marruecos, 1912–1956* (Barcelona: Edicions Bellaterra, 2003), 29.

24. Mimoun Aziza, *La sociedad rifeña frente al Protectorado español de Marruecos (1912–1956)* (Barcelona: Edicions Bellaterra, 2003), 259.

25. Tomás García Figueras, *Marruecos: La acción de España en el norte de Africa* (Madrid: Ediciones Fe, 1939), 290.

26. Mustapha el Merroun, *Las tropas marroquíes en la guerra civil española, 1936–1939* (Madrid: Almena, 2003); and María Rosa de Madariaga, *Los moros que trajo Franco: La intervención de tropas coloniales en la guerra civil española* (Barcelona: Ediciones Martínez Roca, 2002).

27. Mercè Solà Gussinyer, "L'organització del pelegrinatge a la Meca per Franco durant la Guerra Civil," *L'Avenç*, no. 256 (2001); and Ali Al Tuma, "Moros y Cristianos: Religious Aspects of the Participation of Moroccan Soldiers in the Spanish Civil War (1936–1939)," in *Muslims in Interwar Europe: A Transcultural Historical Perspective*, ed. Bekim Agai, Umar Ryad, and Mehdi Sajid (Leiden, NL: Brill, 2016), 154–55.

28. Eric Calderwood, "Franco's Hajj: Moroccan Pilgrims, Spanish Fascism, and the Unexpected Journeys of Modern Arabic Literature," *PMLA* 132, no. 5 (2017); and Fernando Valderrama Martínez, *Historia de la acción cultural de España en Marruecos (1912–1956)* (Tetouan, MA: Editora Marroquí, 1956), 814–32.

29. Texto inédito sobre el nacionalismo de Tomás García Figueras, [n.d.], p. 135, 15 (13.01), box 81/2382, AGA. For a critical analysis of how liberal ideas about age and maturity legitimized European imperialism, see Uday Singh Mehta, *Liberalism and Empire: A Study in Nineteenth Century British Liberal Thought* (Chicago: University of Chicago Press, 1999).

30. Stenner, "Centring the Periphery," 445–46.

31. Ministro de España en el Cairo al Alto Comisario en Tetuán, 29 March 1943, 15 (13.01), box 81/1902, AGA.

32. Bulletin no. 5 of the Central Committee of Hizb al-Islah, 7 April 1946, M'hammad Benaboud File, BFA.

33. El Alto Comisario de España en Marruecos Varela al Ministro de España en el Cairo Don Carlos de Miranda, 3 July 1946, 15 (13.01), box 81/2173, AGA.

34. Asunto: Actividades de Benaboud en Egipto—Información No. 3238, 8 July 1946, 15 (13.01), box 81/2173, AGA; and Departamento de Asuntos Indígenas—Información, 28 May 1946, 15 (13.01), box 81/2173, AGA.

35. Al-Akhbar al-Wataniyya Published by Hizb al-Islah, 5 August 1946, M'hammad Benaboud File, BFA.

36. M'hammad Benaboud to Tayeb Bennouna, 9 October 1946, reproduced in M'hammad bin 'Abbud, *Murasalat al-shahid M'hammad Ahmad bin 'Abbud, 1946–1949* (Tetouan, MA: Matba'at Titwan, 2016), 15–16.

37. M'hammad Benaboud to Driss Benaboud, 15 February 1946, 15 (13.01), box 81/2173, AGA.

38. La delegación marroquí en Egipto—Boletín clandestino de noticias de PNR, 5 August 1946, 15 (13.01), box 81/2173, AGA.

39. Hizb al-Islah to His Majesty the Sultan, 17 October 1946, M'hammad Benaboud File, BFA.

40. Ministero de España en el Cairo al Ministerio de Asuntos Exteriores, 27 March 1946, 15 (13.01), box 81/2173, AGA.

41. El Alto Comisario de España en Marruecos Varela al Ministro de España en el Cairo Don Carlos de Miranda, 3 July 1946, 15 (13.01), box 81/2173, AGA.

42. Texto inédito sobre el nacionalismo de Tomás García Figueras, [n.d.], p. 124, 15 (13.01), box 81/2382, AGA.

43. "Le gouvernement franquiste et la Ligue árabe," *La Dépêche Marocaine*, 20 December 1946, 15 (13.01), box 81/2173, AGA.

44. al-Fasi, *Al-Harakat al-istiqlaliyya*, 375–78.

45. Report of the First Conference of the Arab Maghrib Held in Cairo, 15–22 February 1947, M'hammad Benaboud File, BFA.

46. Idris al-Rashid, *Dhikriyat ʿan maktab al-maghrib al-ʿarabi fi al-Qahira* (Tunis, TN: Al-Dar al-ʿarabiyya li-l-kitab, 1981), 65–66.

47. ʿAbd al-Karim Ghallab, *Tarikh al-haraka al-wataniyya bi-l-Maghrib*, vol. 1 (Casablanca, MA: Matbaʿat al-najah al-jadida, 2000), 440–43.

48. For a detailed study of the same process in the context of Algerian nationalism, see James McDougall, *History and the Culture of Nationalism in Algeria* (New York: Cambridge University Press, 2006).

49. al-Fasi, *Al-Harakat al-istiqlaliyya*, 380.

50. One of the major hurdles faced by Moroccan nationalists was the widespread ignorance, even among the educated elite, about anything related to the Maghrib. The Moroccan nationalists routinely referred to their homeland as Marrakesh (*Marrakush*), since the ancient imperial capital remained the only location immediately recognized in Middle East. It was the French colonizers who created the political borders of the three distinct political entities called *al-Jazaʾir* (Algeria), *Tunis* (Tunisia), and *al-Maghrib* (Morocco) in the nineteenth and early twentieth centuries. Prior to the nineteenth century, Morocco was known as Marrakesh and the region of North Africa was referred to as *al-Maghrib al-Aqsa* (the Farthest West) in Arabic. Therefore, at the time the nationalists were pushing for independence, most Middle Easterners still associated the term *al-Maghrib* with all of North Africa rather than with the specific country of Morocco.

51. "Hadha Marrakush—taʾlif al-ustadh ʿAbd al-Majid bin Jallun," *al-ʿAlam*, 28 August 1949, 1.

52. Toumader Khatib, *Culture et politique dans le mouvement nationaliste marocain au Machreq* (Tetouan, MA: Association Tetouan-Asmir, 1996), 91.

53. Publication no. 66 by Maktab al-Maghrib al-ʿArabi: Honoring the Arab Delegations, 16 February 1948, M'hammad Benaboud File, BFA; and Khatib, *Culture et politique*, 72–77.

54. John Roy Carlson, *Cairo to Damascus* (New York: Knopf, 1951), 121.

55. Ambassadeur Arvengas au Ministre des Affaires étrangères Bidault, 16 April 1948, 1MA/200/338, CADN.

56. Pierre Frederix, "En el Cairo, centro de propaganda nacionalista norteafricana" [Spanish translation], [n.d.], 15 (13.01), box 81/1919, AGA.

57. B. M. 148-49, 11 February 1948, 1MA/200/338, CADN.

58. Allal al-Fassi to Mohammed Lyazidi, 4 June 1947, 1MA/200/338, CADN.

59. "Entretien avec Abdelkhaleq Torres" [French translation], *al-Ikhwan al-Muslimun*, 18 May 1947, série M/24QO/65, AMAE; and Ambassade au Caire au Ministre des Affaires étrangères, 16 June 1947, série M/24QO/65, AMAE.

60. For a detailed discussion of the influence of salafism on the emergence of the Moroccan nationalist movement, see Halstead, *Rebirth of a Nation*, 119–34.

61. Note de Renseignements, no. 39, 5 February 1948, 1MA/200/338, CADN; and Ambassadeur de France en Egypte Gilbert Arvengas au Ministre des Affaires étrangères Schuman, 6 August 1948, 1MA/200/338, CADN.

62. Photographie prise en 1947 au Caire à l'occasion de la Fête du Trône, 25 January 1949, 1MA/200/338, CADN.

63. Organisations d'Action de Propagande et d'Information Arabes, [n.d.], 1MA/200/338, CADN.

64. Note de renseignements: Moghreb Office au Cairo, 20 March 1948, 1MA/200/338, CADN.

65. Publication no. 66 by Maktab al-Maghrib al-'Arabi: Honoring the Arab Delegations, 16 February 1948, M'hammad Benaboud File, BFA.

66. "Samahat al-mufti," *al-'Alam*, 15 June 1947, 1.

67. Allal al-Fassi to Mohammed Lyazidi, 4 June 1947, 1MA/200/338, CADN.

68. Ambassadeur Arvengas au Ministre des Affaires étrangères Schuman, 11 January 1949, 1MA/200/338, CADN; and Charge d'Affaires de France au Ministre des Affaires étrangères Schuman, 4 September 1948, 1MA/200/338, CADN.

69. Communiqué by the Moroccan Parties to Moroccan and Arab Public Opinion, 9 April 1951, Abdelkhaleq Torres File, vol. 2, BFA.

70. Chargé d'Affaires de France au Ministre des Affaires étrangères Schuman, 4 September 1948, 1MA/200/338, CADN.

71. Ambassadeur Couve de Murville au Ministre des Affaires étrangères Schuman, 21 May 1951, 1MA/200/338, CADN.

72. "Al-duktur 'Azmi yughadir al-Maghrib," *al-'Alam*, 24 December 1946, 1.

73. "Al-duktur Mahmud 'Azmi yalqa muhadar 'an mushadatihi fi al-Maghrib al-'arabi," *al-'Alam*, 19 January 1947, 1.

74. "Wazir kharijiyyat Misr yaqtabilu al-duktur Mahmud 'Azmi ba'd 'udatihi min al-Maghrib," *al-'Alam*, 27 March 1951, 1; and Embassy Cairo to Department of State: Concluding Articles on Morocco by Dr. Mahmoud Azmi, Prominent Egyptian Journalist, 4 April 1951, RG59/771.00/4-451, USNA.

75. "Al-marhum al-duktur Mahmud 'Azmi wa-l-qadiya al-maghribiyya," *al-Umma*, 6 November 1954, 3.

76. Ambassade de France en Egypte au Ministre des Affaires Etrangères Pinay: Les voyages africains du Cheikh Bakoury, 10 January 1956, 213QONT/484, AMAE.

77. Le Ministre de France en Egypt au Ministre des Affaires étrangères, 19 September 1946, 1MA/200/338, CADN.

78. Minutes of Meeting of the Central Committee of the PNR, 21 May 1947, M'hammad Benaboud File, BFA.

79. Note sur Margaret Pope, 7 November 1951, 1MA/282/191, CADN.

80. Abdelkarim et la Ligue Arabe, 3 June 1946, 1MA/282/10, CADN.

81. "La nécessité de libérer immédiatement l'Emir et ses compagnons" [French translation], 7 May 1946, *al-Ikhwan al-Muslimun*, 10 (119.01), box 55/26929, AGA; and "El Heroe del Rif—El Emir Abd al-Karim" [Spanish translation], 10 October 1945, *al-Ahram*, 10 (119.01), box 55/26929, AGA.

82. M'hammad bin 'Abbud, *Maktab al-Maghrib al-'Arabi fi al-Qahira—Dirasat wa watha'iq* (Rabat, MA: Manshurat Ukaz, 1991), 48; and al-Fasi, *Al-Harakat al-istiqlaliyya*, 398–401.

83. Ghallab, *Tarikh al-haraka al-wataniyya*, vol. 1, 455–57.

84. Report of the Central Committee of Hizb al-Islah, 4 June 1947, M'hammad Benaboud File, BFA.

85. "Abd el Krim Jumps Ships in Egypt—Farouk Gives Riff Chief a Haven," *New York Times*, 1 June 1947, 1.

86. al-Fasi, *Al-Harakat al-istiqlaliyya*, 401.

87. Amir Mohammed b. Abdelkarim to Tayeb Bennouna, 9 December 1947, Tayeb Bennouna File, BFA.

88. Nacionalismo musulmán: Actividades de los emigrados en el Cairo, 9 January 1948, 15 (13.01), box 81/1910, AGA.

89. "Abdelkarim au Caire," *Le Monde*, 3 June 1947, 1.

90. Intervención Territorial del Rif: Interpretación, no. 509—Villa Sanjurjo, 28 July 1947, 15 (13.01), box 81/1724, AGA.

91. Ambassadeur de France en Egypte Arvengas au Ministre des Affaires étrangères Bidault, 30 June 1947, 1MA/200/338, CADN.

92. al-Fasi, *Al-Harakat al-istiqlaliyya*, 401.

93. "'Amal wa nata'ij," *al-'Alam*, 26 September 1947, 1.

94. Rouissi to Thameur, 18 August 1947, 1MA/200/338, CADN; and Rouissi to Thameur, 8 January 1948, 1MA/200/338, CADN.

95. "Al-Mufawwadiyya al-faransiyya fi Libnan tahtaju 'ala nishat al-za'im al-ustadh 'Allal al-Fasi," *al-'Alam*, 22 September, 1951, 1–2.

96. "Hafawat al-umma al-'iraqiyya bi-mumaththil al-wataniyya al-maghribiyya," *al-'Alam*, 12 October 1951, 1.

97. "Za'im Hizb al-Istiqlal fi al-'awasim al-'arabiyya," *al-'Alam*, 13 October 1951, 1–2.

98. "Nadwat za'im Hizb al-Istiqlal fi Dimashq," *al-'Alam*, 22 September 1951, 1–2.

99. Note confidential: 100 exemplaires de la brochure 'Arch Marrakouch' ont été saisis par Ben al-Melih du Caire à Fès, 17 September 1949, 1MA/200/338, CADN; and Renseignements—Secret, 12 August 1949, 1MA/200/338, CADN.

100. "Min brutukul al-Iskandariyya ila al-diman al-jama'i," *al-'Alam*, 14 December 1949, 1.

101. Tangier to Department of State, 23 March 1951, RG59/771.00/3-2351, USNA; "Al-Dhikra al-rabi'a li-jama'at al-duwal al-'arabiyya," *al-'Alam*, 22 March 1949, 1; and Renseignements—Secret, 12 August 1949, 1MA/200/338, CADN.

102. US Department of State, *Foreign Relations of the United States, 1947*, vol. V, ed. S. Everett and Rogers P. Churchill (Washington, DC: US Government Printing Office, 1971), 677–78.

103. "Jalalat al-malik yashruf haflat tamthiliyya min al-firqa al-misriyya," *al-'Alam*, 16 March 1950, 1.

104. "Arwa' yawm fi hiyat al-firqa al-misriyya bi-Fas," *al-'Alam*, 25 March 1950, 1–2.

105. "Hadith al-yawm," *al-'Alam*, 12 March 1950, 1.

106. "Rusul al-akhwa bayna Misr al-'aziza wa-l-Maghrib al-'arabi," *al-'Alam*, 29 October 1950, 1.

107. "Wa yawm min ayam al-'uruba bi-Fas," *al-'Alam*, 1 November 1950, 1.

108. Ambassadeur Couve de Murville au Ministre des Affaires étrangères Schuman, 10 August 1950, 1MA/200/338, CADN.

109. "Shuhada' al-Maghrib al-'arabi," *al-'Alam*, 21 December 1949, 1.

110. "Madinat Tanja taqtabilu riqqat al-ustadh Ibn 'Abbud fi mawkib rahib," *al-'Alam*, 4 Jan-

uary 1950, 1; and "Dhikra al-arbaʿin li-shuhada al-Maghrib al-ʿarabi bi-Tanja," *al-ʿAlam*, 2 February 1950, 1.

111. Maktab al-Maghrib al-ʿArabi, Bulletin No. 238, 7 January 1950, M'hammad Benaboud File, BFA.

112. El Alto Comisario de España en Marruecos al Ministerio de Asuntos Exteriores, 14 June 1950, 15 (13.01), box 81/1450, AGA.

113. Ambassadeur Arvengas au Ministre des Affaires étrangères Bidault, 1 December 1947, 1MA/200/338, CADN; Ambassadeur Couve de Murville au Ministre des Affaires étrangères Schuman, 8 January 1951, 1MA/200/338, CADN. Mohammed Lyazidi to Abdelkarim Ben Thabet, 5 October 1948, 1MA/200/217, CADN; Mohammed Lyazidi to Abdelkarim Ghallab, 30 September 1948, 1MA/200/217, CADN; and Allal al-Fassi to Mohammed Lyazidi, 10 October 1948, 1MA/200/217, CADN.

114. M'hammad Benaboud to Mehdi Bennouna, 11 May 1948, M'hammad Benaboud File, BFA.

115. Ambassadeur Couve de Murville au Ministre des Affaires étrangères Schuman, 5 December 1951, 1MA/200/338, CADN.

116. Ambassadeur Couve de Murville au Ministre des Affaires étrangères Schuman, 21 May 1951, 1MA/200/338, CADN. For a comment by US diplomats on the decline of Maktab al-Maghrib, see US Department of State, *Foreign Relations of the United States, 1949*, vol. VI, ed. Fredrick Aandahl and William Z. Slany (Washington, DC: US Government Printing Office, 1977), 1783–84.

117. Tayeb Bennouna to Mehdi Bennouna, 23 October 1952, 1MA/200/56, CADN.

118. M'hammad Benaboud to Mehdi Bennouna, 18 May 1948, M'hammad Benaboud File, BFA.

119. Charles-André Julien, *L'Afrique Du Nord en marche: Algérie-Tunisie-Maroc, 1880–1952* (Paris: Omnibus, 2002 [1953]), 319.

120. Union de los partidos, Amr-BJ, 19 March 1950, 15 (13.01), box 81/2161, AGA.

121. "Abd el-Karim rompt avec le Bureau du Maghreb," *Le Monde*, 20 June 1952, 2.

122. Les pays arabes et l'Afrique du Nord (Mai 1951–Mai 1952), 20 May 1952, 372QO/544, AMAE.

123. Azzam Pasha to M'hammad Benaboud, 18 August 1948, reproduced in M'hammad bin ʿAbbud , *Al-Nidal al-watani*, 64.

124. Ahmed Ben al-Melih to Mohammed Lyazidi, 25 January 1951, 1MA/200/338, CADN.

125. ʿIssam Gharib, *ʿAbd al-Rahman ʿAzzam: Al-Islam—Al-ʿUruba—Al-Wataniyya* (Cairo: Matbaʿat Dar al-kutub wa-l-wathaʾiq al-qawmiyya bi-l-Qahira, 2011), 212–16; Michel Laissy, *Du panarabisme à la Ligue Arabe* (Paris: G. P. Maisonneuve, 1948), 118.

126. US Department of State, *Foreign Relations, 1950*, vol. V, 1744.

127. G. H. Neville-Bagot, "Muslim Solidarity at the United Nations Organization in Support of Moroccan Independence," *The Islamic Review* (February 1952): 14.

128. Représentation de la France aux Nations-Unies à la Résidence générale à Rabat, 26 November 1952, 10POI/1/41, CADN.

129. Current Intelligence Bulletin, 17 November 1951, p. 5, Central Intelligence Agency Freedom of Information Act Electronic Reading Room (hereafter CIA-ERR).

130. Joel Gordon, *Nasser's Blessed Movement* (New York: Oxford University Press, 1992), 55.

131. Ahmad Abu al-Fath, *L'affaire Nasser* (Paris: Plon, 1962), 237; James P. Jankowski, *Nasser's Egypt, Arab Nationalism, and the United Arab Republic* (Boulder, CO: Lynne Rienner, 2002), 41; R. Hrair Dekmejian, *Egypt under Nasir* (Albany: SUNY Press, 1971), 111–13; Joel Gordon, *Nasser: Hero of the Arab Nation* (Oxford, UK: Oneworld, 2006), 6.

132. Reem Abou-el-Fadel, "Early Pan-Arabism in Egypt's July Revolution: The Free Officers' Political Formation and Policy-Making, 1946–54," *Nations and Nationalism* 21, no. 2 (2015).

133. Gamal Abdel Nasser, *The Philosophy of the Revolution* (Cairo: Mondiale Press, 1955 [1953]), 54.

134. Peter Woodward, *Nasser* (New York: Longman, 1992), 43; Jean Lacouture, *Gamal Abdel Nasser* (Paris: Bayard, 2005), 187; Anthony Nutting, *Nasser* (London: Constable, 1972), 76; Jankowski, *Nasser's Egypt*, 55.

135. "Al-Jamaʿa al-ʿarabiyya fi ʿahd jadid," *al-ʿAlam*, 16 September 1952, 2.

136. "Jamaʿat al-duwal al-ʿarabiyya fi ʿahdiha al-jadid," *al-ʿAlam*, 29 September 1952, 1, 4.

137. "Al-Ustadh Ahmad al-Malih yatahaddith ila qurraʾ al-ʿAlam," *al-ʿAlam*, 20 September 1952, 2.

138. Mohammad Iqbal Ansari, *The Arab League, 1945–1955* (Aligarh, IN: Institute of Islamic Studies, Aligarh Muslim University, 1968), 80–86. For an analysis of the Arab League's reluctance to support North Africa before the UN, see Samya el-Mechat, "L'improbable 'Nation arabe.' La Ligue des États arabes et l'indépendance du Maghreb (1945–1956)," *Vingtième Siècle* 82 (2004).

139. Les pays arabes et l'Afrique du Nord, 12 May 1953, 214QONT/647, AMAE.

140. Richard P. Mitchell, *The Society of the Muslim Brothers* (London: Oxford University Press, 1969), 109, 127; and Gordon, *Nasser's Blessed Movement*, 98–108.

141. Sonia Dabous, "Nasser and the Egyptian Press," in *Contemporary Egypt: Through Egyptian Eyes*, ed. Charles Tripp (New York: Routledge, 1993), 104–5; Gordon, *Nasser's Blessed Movement*, 140; and Abu al-Fath, *L'affaire Nasser*, 239–40.

142. Ilan Pappé, *The Rise and Fall of a Palestinian Dynasty: The Husaynis, 1700–1948* (Berkeley: University of California Press, 2010), 346. On Nasser's contribution to the founding of the PLO, see Laurie Brand, "Nasir's Egypt and the Reemergence of the Palestinian National Movement," *Journal of Palestine Studies* 17, no. 2 (winter 1988): 41–43.

143. Direction générale: Les relations franco-égyptiennes et leurs incidences sur le problème marocain, 18 May 1955, série M/24QO/65, AMAE.

144. New York au Résident général à Rabat, 17 December 1954, 372QO/580, AMAE.

145. Ambassadeur de France en Egypte Maurice Couve de Murville au Ministre des Affaires étrangères Georges Bidault, 5 September 1953, 214QONT/647, AMAE.

146. Allal al-Fassi to Istiqlal Party, 2 May 1953, dossier 2/folder 14, AFF.

147. Ibid.

148. Allal al-Fassi to Istiqlal Party, 3 August 1953, dossier 2/folder 14, AFF.

149. Stéphane Bernard, *Le conflit franco-marocain, 1943–1956*, vol. 1, *Historique* (Brussels: Institut de sociologie Université libre de Bruxelles, 1963), 177–85.

150. Communiqué Issued by Hizb al-Islah al-Watani, 22 September 1953, Mehdi Bennouna File, vol. 2, BFA.

151. Current Intelligence Bulletin, 21 August 1953, p. 7, CIA-ERR.

152. Fathi Dib, *Abdel Nasser et la révolution algérienne* (Paris: L'Harmattan, 1985), 12.

153. Campagne de la Radio du Caire contre la politique française en Afrique du Nord, 16 October 1953, 213QONT/484, AMAE.

154. Traduction d'une émission radiophonique de langue arabe No. 260—Voix des arabes, 21 August 1954, 1MA/282/50, CADN.

155. Les voyages africains du Cheikh Bakoury—futures relations de l'Egypte avec les pays d'Afrique du Nord, 10 January 1956, 213QONT/484, AMAE.

156. Abdelkabir al-Fassi to Allal al-Fassi, 24 September 1954, reproduced in ʿAllal al-Fasi, *Nida al-Qahira* (Morocco, 1959), 10.

157. "Voice of Arab Stirs Mideast: Broadcasts Are Now Most Potent," *New York Times*, 15 January 1956, E5.

158. Note sur les ingérences égyptiennes en Afrique du Nord, 20 October 1956, p. 5, 213QONT/485, AMAE.

159. Dib, *Abdel Nasser et la révolution algérienne*, 17.

160. Note sur les ingérences égyptiennes en Afrique du Nord, 20 October 1956, p. 3, 213QONT/485, AMAE.

161. Zaki Mbarek, *Résistance et armée de libération: Portée politique, liquidation, 1953–1958* (Casablanca, MA: MBC, 1987), 18, 53.

162. Rézette, *Les partis politiques marocains*, 234.

163. Boubker Bennouna to Mohammed Castillo, [n.d.], 15 (13.01), box 81/2083, AGA.

164. al-Masari, *al-Maghrib kharij siyaj al-himaya*, 13.

165. Department of State to Madrid, Paris, Rabat, and Tangier, 17 February 1954, RG59/771.00/2-1754, USNA.

166. Le consul général de France à Tetouan au Ministre des Affaires étrangères, 14 December 1954, 257QO/20, AMAE.

167. Ibid.

168. Emission du Caire, 12 April 1954, 213QONT/484, AMAE.

169. L'Egypte et l'Afrique du Nord, 2 September 1955, 213QONT/485, AMAE.

170. Les relations franco-égyptiennes et leurs incidences sur le problème marocain, 18 May 1955, série M/24QO/71, AMAE.

171. Boletín no. 266: Comentarios, 29 November 1954, 15 (13.01), box 81/2161, AGA.

172. Malcolm H. Kerr, *The Arab Cold War: Gamal Abd al-Nasir and His Rivals, 1958–1970* (New York: Oxford University Press, 1971), 6; and Adeed Dawisha, "Egypt," in *The Cold War and the Middle East*, ed. Yezid Sayigh and Avi Shlaim (Oxford: Clarendon Press, 1997), 29.

173. James P. Jankowski, "Arab Nationalism in 'Nasserism' and Egyptian State Policy, 1952–1958," in *Rethinking Nationalism in the Arab Middle East*, ed. James Jankowski and Israel Gershoni (New York: Columbia University Press, 1997), 156–57.

174. Dib, *Abdel Nasser et la révolution algérienne*, 12–13.

175. Ambassadeur de France en Egypte Maurice Couve de Murville au Ministre des Affaires étrangères Georges Bidault, 4 December 1953, 213QONT/485, AMAE.

176. Télégramme de New York à Rabat No. 2838, 5 October 1953, 10POI/1/41, CADN.

177. Laura M. James, "Whose Voice? Nasser, the Arabs, and 'Sawt al-Arab' Radio," *Transnational Broadcasting Journal* 16 (2006): 3.

178. Ambassadeur de France en Egypte Maurice Couve de Murville au Ministre des Affaires étrangères Georges Bidault, 14 May 1953, 214QONT/647, AMAE.

179. Embassy Baghdad to Department of State, 2 February 1954, RG59/771.00/2-254, USNA.

180. Ibid.

181. Ambassadeur de France au Liban Georges Balaÿ au Ministre des Affaires étrangères Georges Bidault, 15 September 1953, 214QONT/647, AMAE.

182. Ambassade au Baghdad au Ministère des Affaires étrangères, 20 October 1952, 372QO/576, AMAE.

183. Note sur les ingérences égyptiennes en Afrique du Nord, 20 October 1956, 213QONT/485, AMAE.

184. Télégramme de New York à Paris No. 2569, 22 October 1954, 10POI/1/41, CADN.

185. Télégramme de New York à Paris No. 2434, 14 October 1954, 10POI/1/41, CADN.

186. Martin Thomas, "France Accused: French North Africa before the United Nations, 1952–1962," *Contemporary European History* 10, no. 1 (2001): 102.

187. Télégramme de New York à Rabat No. 149-154, 24 November 1952, 10POI/1/41, CADN.

188. US Department of State, *Foreign Relations of the United States, 1952–54*, vol. XI, pt. 1, ed. John P. Glennon (Washington, DC: US Government Printing Office, 1983), 654–55.

189. Kerr, *The Arab Cold War*, 2–6; Patrick Seale, *The Struggle for Syria: A Study of Post-War Arab Politics, 1945–1958* (London: I. B. Tauris, 1986), 186–237; P. J. Vatikiotis, *Arab Regional Politics in the Middle East* (New York: St Martin's Press 1984), 83; Elie Podeh, *The Quest for Hegemony in the Arab World* (Leiden, NL: E. J. Brill, 1995), 243; Cyrus Schayegh, "1958 Reconsidered: State Formation and the Cold War in the Early Postcolonial Arab Middle East," *International Journal of Middle East Studies* 45, no. 3 (2013); and Mohammed Fadhel Jamali, *Inside the Arab Nationalist Struggle: Memoirs of an Iraqi Statesman* (New York: I. B. Tauris, 2012), 253–60.

190. Michael Eppel, "The Elite, the Effendiyya, and the Growth of Nationalism and Pan-Arabism in Hashemite Iraq, 1921–1958," *International Journal of Middle East Studies* 30, no. 2 (1998): 245–47.

191. Charles Tripp, *A History of Iraq* (New York: Cambridge University Press, 2002), 134.

192. Samira Haj, *The Making of Iraq, 1900–1963: Capital, Power, and Ideology* (Albany: State University of New York Press, 1997), 102–7; and Peter Sluglett and Marion Farouk-Sluglett, *Iraq Since 1958: From Revolution to Dictatorship* (New York: I. B. Tauris, 1996), 43.

193. Adeed Dawisha, *Iraq: A Political History from Independence to Occupation* (Princeton, NJ: Princeton University Press, 2009), 115.

194. Ambassadeur de France en Egypte Armand du Chayla au Ministre des Affaires étrangères Antoine Pinay, 29 August 1955, 213QONT/485, AMAE.

195. "Final Communique of the Asian African Conference," in *Asia-Africa Speaks from Bandung* (Djakarta: Ministry of Foreign Affairs of the Republic of Indonesia, 1955), 161.

196. Allal al-Fassi to Tayeb Bennouna, 19 November 1954, dossier 2/folder 14, AFF.

197. Ahmed Balafrej to Rom Landau, 14 April 1955, MS68, series 1, box 1, HASC.

198. Ministère des affaires étrangères: Conférence de Bandung, July 1955, pp. 1–2, 214QONT/553, AMAE.

199. "Al-Maghrib al-'arabi fi Bandung," *al-Umma*, 18 April 1955, 1.

200. Ibid.

201. Ibid.

202. Ibid.

203. "Al-'Iraq tutalib bi-tahrir al-Maghrib al-'arabi fi mu'tamar al-duwal al-ifriqa [sic] al-asiyawiyya," *al-Umma*, 12 April 1955, 2.

204. "L'Égypte fera appel à la neutralité et à la lutte contre le colonialisme au congres africano-asiatique" [French translation], *al-Ahram*, 21 March 1955, 214QONT/553, AMAE.

205. *Asia-Africa Speaks from Bandung*, 166.

206. Ministère des Affaires étrangères: Conférence de Bandung, July 1955, p. 22, 214QONT/553, AMAE.

207. "Al-Maghrib al-'arabi yakun jubha muttahida," *al-Umma*, 20 April 1955, 4.

208. Tánger: Boletín no. 92, 26 April 1955, 15 (13.01), box 81/2150, AGA.

209. al-Fasi, *Nida al-Qahira*, foreword.

210. Julien, *L'Afrique Du Nord en marche: Algérie-Tunisie-Maroc, 1880–1952*, 319.

CHAPTER 3

1. Le Général Guillaume visite le lieu des émeutes, *AFP Spécial Outre-mer*, no. 1907, 10 December 1952, Archives Paret, carton 2, Institut d'histoire du temps présent, Paris (hereafter IHTP).

2. Daniel Rivet, "Conscientes inquiètes, militants politiques et experts coloniaux: Des intel-

lectuels face à la crise franco-marocaine (décembre 1952–fin 1954)," in *Le Comité France-Maghreb: Réseaux intellectuels et d'influence face à la crise marocaine (1952–1955)*, ed. Daniel Rivet (Paris: Les Cahiers de l'IHTP, 1997), 20.

3. "La vocation des chrétiens dans l'Union française," *Le Figaro*, 17 January 1953, 1.

4. Serge Berstein and Pierre Milza, *Histoire de la France au XXe siècle*, vol. 3, *1945–1958* (Brussels: Editions Complexe, 1991), 14.

5. Richard Vinen, *France, 1934–1970* (New York: St. Martin's Press, 1996), 101.

6. Jeremy D. Popkin, *A History of Modern France* (Upper Saddle River, NJ: Prentice Hall, 2006), 285.

7. Ibid., 280.

8. French Press and Information Service, *Toward a Federal Union: The French Solution of the Colonial Problem* (New York: St. Martin's Press, 1945), 12; and Hubert Jules Deschamps, *The French Union: History, Institutions, Economy, Countries and Peoples, Social and Political Changes* (Paris: Berger-Levrault, 1956), 247. For a nuanced analysis of the French Union as an arena of mediation between imperial France and the aspirations of its colonized subjects, see Frederick Cooper, *Citizenship between Empire and Nation: Remaking France and French Africa, 1945–1960* (Princeton, NJ: Princeton University Press, 2014).

9. Popkin, *A History of Modern France*, 282.

10. Charles Sowerwine, *France Since 1870: Culture, Politics and Society* (New York: Palgrave, 2001), 270.

11. Philippe Dewitte, "Intellectuels et étudiants africains à Paris à la veille des indépendances (1945–1960)," in *Le Paris des étrangers depuis 1945*, ed. Antoine Marès and Pierre Milza (Paris: Publications de la Sorbonne, 1994); Samir Amin, *A Life Looking Forward* (New York: Zed Books, 2006), 57–75; and Amady Aly Dieng, *Histoire des organisations d'étudiants africains en France (1900–1950)* (Dakar: L'Harmattan-Sénégal, 2011).

12. Lt. Colonel P. Devillars, "L'immigration marocaine en France, Vol. I," 1952, p. 44, série 3H, box 1418, Service historique de l'Armée de terre, Vincennes (hereafter SHAT). By comparison, the number of Algerian residents had already surpassed 150,000.

13. Cpt. Roger Maneville, "De l'évolution sociale et politique des marocains en France," December 1946, p. 12, série 3H, box 1418, SHAT.

14. Ibid., 11.

15. Ibid., 13.

16. Mohammed Bekraoui, "Les étudiants marocains en France à l'époque du protectorat, 1927–1939," in *Présences et images franco-marocaines au temps du protectorat*, ed. Jean-Claude Allain (Paris: L'Harmattan, 2003), 102; and Charles-Robert Ageron, "L'association des étudiants musulmans nord-africains en France durant l'entre-deux-guerres," *Revue française d'histoire d'outre-mer* 70, no. 258 (1983): 32.

17. Ibid., 23.

18. Résident général Puaux au Ministère des Affaires étrangères Bidault, 11 February 1946, série M/24QO/65, AMAE; and Pierre Vermeren, *La formation des élites marocaines et tunisiennes: Des nationalistes aux islamistes, 1920–2000* (Paris: La Découverte, 2002), 117.

19. Note de renseignements: Mehdi Ben Aboud, 23 October 1952, Ha23, Archives de la Préfecture de la Police de Paris (hereafter APP).

20. Fiche de renseignements sur Abderrahman Youssoufi, [no date], 1MA/282/14, CADN.

21. Note de renseignements: Abderrahim Bouabid, 3 April 1951, 1MA/282/14, CADN.

22. Charles-André Julien, *Le Maroc face aux impérialismes: 1415–1956* (Paris: Les éditions du Jaguar, 2011 [1978]), 196.

23. Note de renseignements: Ahmed Alaoui al-Fassi, [no date], 1MA/282/21, CADN; and Fiche de renseignements de l'étudiant Ahmed Alaoui, 5 July 1945, 1MA/282/21, CADN.

24. Séjour à Paris de Balafrej, 19 February 1947, Ha23, APP.

25. Cpt. Roger Maneville, "De l'évolution sociale et politique des marocains en France," December 1946, pp. 19–20, série 3H, box 1418, SHAT.

26. L'Office du Maroc au Préfet de Police: Al-Hajj Diouri, 17 February 1954, Ha23, APP.

27. "Hadith al-yawm," al-Hurriyya, 17 October 1946, 1.

28. Ibid.

29. Cpt. Roger Maneville, "De l'évolution sociale et politique des marocains en France," December 1946, p. 32, série 3H, box 1418, SHAT.

30. Report: Les marocains en France, June 1959, série F7, box 15352, ANF.

31. Activité communiste dans les milieux marocains, 12 November 1952, Ha23, APP.

32. "Al-'ummal al-magharba bi-Faransa," al-'Alam, 8 February 1951, 2.

33. "Al-Yad al-'amila al-maghribiyya bi-Urubba wa wujub al-ihtimam biha," al-'Alam, 9 August 1950, 2.

34. "Hawla qadiyat al-jama'iyya al-khayriyya al-islamiyya bi-Baris," al-'Alam, 13 October 1951, 2.

35. L'Office du Maroc au Préfet de Police: Driss al-Fallah, 17 February 1954, Ha23, APP.

36. "Hadith ma' al-katib al-'amm li-l-jama'iyya al-khayriyya bi-Faransa," al-'Alam, 12 July 1952, 2.

37. "Qadiyat al-jama'iyya al-khayriyya al-islamiyya bi-Baris," al-'Alam, 4 February 1952, 2.

38. Directeur générale de la Sûreté nationale au Préfet de Police: Ahmed Snoussi, 2 June 1955, Ha23, APP.

39. Activité de la délégation de l'Istiqlal, 2 April 1947, Ha23, APP.

40. Rapport sur l'administration française au Maroc—Bureau d'Information et de documentation du parti de l'Istiqlal à Paris, 1947, p. 4, Fonds Julien, IHTP.

41. "Al-Talaba al-magharba bi-Faransa," al-'Alam, 11 September 1948, 5.

42. R.G.8—no. 1381, 20 November 1953, Ha23, APP.

43. Direction des renseignements généraux: Manifestation des étudiants marocains, 20 November 1947, série M/24QO/581, AMAE.

44. "Tullab Baris yahtafilun bi-ikhwanihim al-qadimin min al-dakhil," al-'Alam, 29 July 1951, 2.

45. "Al-Magharba bi-Baris yahtafilun bi-'aid al-'arsh," al-'Alam, 18 November 1946, 1.

46. "Aid al-'arsh bi-Baris," al-'Alam, 20 November 1946, 2, 4.

47. Hizb al-Istiqlal, XIXe anniversaire de l'accession au trône de Sa Majesté Mohammed V Roi du Maroc, 1927–1946 (Paris: Bureau de Documentation et d'Information du Parti de l'Istiqlal, 1946), 10, 15.

48. Manifesto du Parti de l'Istiqlal, 11 May 1945, série M/24QO/65, AMAE.

49. Au peuple de France, 11 January 1946, série M/24QO/65, AMAE.

50. Une délégation de Marocains à Monsieur le député, 3 February 1946, série M/24QO/65, AMAE.

51. Résident général Puaux au Ministre des Affaires étrangères Bidault, 11 February 1946, série M/24QO/65, AMAE.

52. Télégramme: Rabat au Ministère des Affaires étrangères, 11 August 1946, série M/24QO/65, AMAE.

53. Note sur le séjour à Paris d'une délégation de l'Istiqlal, 14 October 1946, série M/24QO/65, AMAE.

54. See, for example, Hizb al-Istiqlal, *Le mouvement national marocain—bref aperçu historique* (Paris: Bureau de Documentation et d'Information du Parti de l'Istiqlal, 1946).

55. Hizb al-Istiqlal, *Documents, 1944–46* (Paris: Bureau de Documentation et d'Information du Parti de l'Istiqlal, September 1946), 28.

56. Note sur le séjour à Paris d'une délégation de l'Istiqlal, 14 October 1946, série M/24QO/65, AMAE; and Télégramme: Ministère des Affaires étrangères à Rabat, 1 February 1947, série M/24QO/65, AMAE.

57. Déclaration faite par la délégation de l'Istiqlal, 30 August 1946, série M/24QO/65, AMAE.

58. Hizb al-Istiqlal, *Conférence de presse donnée par la délégation du Parti de l'Istiqlal à Paris le 30 août 1946* (Paris: Bureau de Documentation et d'Information du Parti de l'Istiqlal, 1946), pp. 8, 13; and Déclaration faite par la délégation du Parti de l'Istiqlal à l'issue de la conférence de Presse donné à Paris le 30 aôut 1946, dossier Istiqlal, Centre d'Etudes et de Recherches Mohammed Bensaid Aït Idder, Casablanca (hereafter CERMBAI).

59. US Embassy in Paris to Department of State, 31 August 1946, RG59/881.00/8-3146, USNA.

60. "Ta'liq sahifa biljikiyya 'ala 'amal al-wafd al-maghribi bi-Baris," *al-Hurriyya*, 8 October 1946, 2.

61. "Al-za'im 'Allal al-Fasi ya'umm Baris," *al-'Alam*, 22 April 1947, 1.

62. "Nadi al-fikr al-faransi yahtafil bi-l-za'im Muhammad 'Allal al-Fasi," *al-'Alam*, 20 May 1947, 1.

63. Activité générale du leader nationaliste marocain Allal el Fassi, 3 May 1947, série M/24QO/65, AMAE; and "Al-Za'im 'Allal al-Fasi bi-Baris," *al-'Alam*, 29 April 1947, 1.

64. Séjour à Paris de el-Fassi, 27 April 1947, Ha23, APP; and "al-Za'im 'Allal bi-madinat Liyun," *al-'Alam*, 3 May 1947, 1.

65. Réception d'Allal al-Fassi à Gennevilliers, 27 April 1947, série M/24QO/65, AMAE.

66. Réception organisé en l'honneur de el Fassi, 29 April 1947, série M/24QO/65, AMAE.

67. Activité communiste dans les milieux marocains, 12 November 1952, Ha23, APP.

68. Mémoire presenté au gouvernement français par le Parti de l'Istiqlal, 31 January 1947, série M/24QO/65, AMAE.

69. Résident général au Ministère des Affaires étrangères, 2 February 1947, série M/24QO/65, AMAE.

70. "'Aid al-'arsh bi-Baris," *al-'Alam*, 20 November 1946, 4.

71. "Sahib al-sumuw al-malaki waliy al-'ahd al-amir mawlaya al-Hassan fi Baris," *al-'Alam*, 7 August 1949, 1.

72. "Ihtifal al-jaliyya al-maghribiyya fi Baris bi-sahib al-jalala al-malik al-mu'azzam," *al-'Alam*, 5 November 1950, 2.

73. "Waliy 'ahd al-mamlaka al-maghribiyya yuballighu tahiyat sahib al-jalala," *al-'Alam*, 10 August 1949, 1.

74. "Al-mudhakarat al-siyasiyya la tazalu mustamirra bayna sahib al-jalala wa-l-hukuma al-faransiyya," *al-'Alam*, 20 October 1950, 1.

75. Directeur des Services de sécurite publique au Préfet de Police: Abdalkarim Khatib, 27 July 1955, Ha23, APP.

76. "Ihtifal al-jaliyya al-maghribiyya fi Baris bi-sahib al-jalala al-malik al-mu'azzam," *al-'Alam*, 5 November 1950, 2.

77. US Department of State, *Foreign Relations, 1950*, vol. V, 1762.

78. Le Préfet de la Police au Ministre de la Défense nationale, 12 April 1955, Ha23, APP.

79. "Haflat 'aid al-'arsh fi al-kharij," *al-'Alam*, 23 November 1950, 2; and "Jama'iyyat talabat shimal ifriqiyya al-muslimun bi-Tuluz," *al-'Alam*, 2 January 1951, 1, 4.

80. "Taliban maghribiyyan amam al-qada al-faransi bi-Burdu," *al-ʿAlam*, 2 May 1951, 1.

81. Office du Maroc au Résident générale, 1 June 1951, 1MA/282/14, CADN.

82. Fiche de renseignements concernant Ahmed Alaoui, 20 August 1954, 1MA/282/21, CADN.

83. Directeur des Offices du Maroc en France au Résidence générale à Rabat, 24 May 1951, 1MA/282/21, CADN.

84. Note de renseignements sur Ahmed Alaoui, 7 April 1951, 1MA/282/21, CADN.

85. Bulletin de renseignements concernant Ahmed Alaoui, 20 March 1951, 1MA/282/21, CADN.

86. Note de renseignements sur Ahmed Alaoui, 7 April 1951, 1MA/282/21, CADN.

87. Fiche de renseignements concernant Temsamani, 25 July 1955, 1MA/282/207, CADN.

88. Note: Mission de Temsamani à Paris, 20 May 1951, 1MA/282/207, CADN.

89. Note pour le général Boyer de la Tour, 9 May 1951, 1MA/282/207, CADN.

90. Note pour le général Boyer de la Tour, 16 May 1951, 1MA/282/207, CADN.

91. Note a Monsieur le Directeur de l'Intérieur, 2 June 1951, 1MA/282/207, CADN.

92. Note de Renseignements, 12 July 1951, 1MA/282/56, CADN.

93. L'Ambassadeur de France en Grand-Bretagne au Résident général Guillaume, 14 December 1951, 1MA/282/207, CADN.

94. Note a Monsieur le Directeur de l'Intérieur, 1 June 1951, 1MA/282/207, CADN; and Note a Monsieur le Directeur de l'Intérieur, 23 May 1951, 1MA/282/207, CADN.

95. It was only after the construction of its official headquarters on the east side of Midtown Manhattan had been completed in October 1952 that the United Nations permanently moved to New York.

96. Zakya Daoud and Maâti Monjib, *Ben Barka* (Paris: Editions Michalon, 1996), 106.

97. Allal al-Fassi to Azzam Pasha, 1 September 1948, dossier 2/folder 14, AFF.

98. Déclaration par l'Istiqlal, le MTLD et le Destour tunisien, 2 November 1948, dossier Paris, CERMBAI.

99. Les pays arabes et l'Afrique du Nord (Mai 1951–Mai 1952), 20 May 1952, 372QO/544, AMAE.

100. "Conférence de presse d'Allal al-Fassi," 21 September 1951, carton JU24, Centre d'histoire de Sciences-Po, Paris (hereafter CHSP).

101. Allal al-Fassi to Azzam Pasha, 9 August 1951, dossier 2/folder 14, AFF.

102. "Duwal al-jamaʿa al-ʿarabiyya tusajjilu al-qadiya al-maghribiyya fi jadwal ʿamal haiʾat al-umam al-muttahida," *al-ʿAlam*, 6 October 1951, 1.

103. Résident général au Ministère des Affaires étrangères, 5 December 1951, série M/24QO/582, AMAE.

104. "Al-qadiya al-maghribiyya ʿala ʿatabat haiʾat al-umam," *al-ʿAlam*, 5 September 1951, 1.

105. "Naʿam fi al-Maghrib azma," *al-ʿAlam*, 6 October 1951, 1.

106. "Maktab haiʾat al-umam yadaʿu qadiyat al-Maghrib amam al-raʾi al-ʿamm al-ʿalami," *al-ʿAlam*, 11 November 1951, 1.

107. "A la commission de tutelle de l'ONU, M. Pignon sort en claquant la porte," *L'Humanité*, 24 November 1951, Ha1, APP.

108. Subject: Morocco—from Mr. Perkins to Mr. Bonbright, 9 October 1951, RG59/771.00/10-951, USNA.

109. "Fi haflat ʿaid al-ʿarsh Baris," *al-ʿAlam*, 21 November 1951, 1.

110. "Barqiyat ila haiʾat al-umam," *al-ʿAlam*, 13 December 1951, 1; and Texto inédito sobre el nacionalismo de Tomás García Figueras, [n.d.], p. 236, 15 (13.01), box 81/2382, AGA.

111. "Mandub al-ʿIraq yuthiru qadiyat al-Maghrib fi munazzamat al-umam," *al-ʿAlam*, 14 November 1951, 1.

112. "Al-mandub al-amriki al-mukallaf bi-dars al-qadiya al-magribiyya yasruhu li-jaridat al-ʿAlam," *al-ʿAlam*, 10 November 1951, 1.

113. US Department of State, *Foreign Relations of the United States, 1951*, vol. V, ed. William Z. Slany (Washington, DC: US Government Printing Office, 1982), 1384.

114. Ibid., 1394.

115. Ibid.

116. Ibid.

117. "ʿAllal al-Fasi yubriqu ila haiʾat al-umam, 20 November 1951," *al-ʿAlam*, 20 November 1951, 1.

118. "Tadamun al-shuʿub al-ʿarabiyya wa-l-islamiyya fi mukafahat al-istiʿmar," *al-ʿAlam*, 15 December 1951, 1.

119. "Baʿd qarar haiʾat al-umam al-muttahida fi qadiyat al-Maghrib," *al-ʿAlam*, 16 December 1951, 1.

120. Allal al-Fassi to Egyptian Minister of Justice Kamil Mursi, 21 June 1952, dossier 2/folder 15, AFF.

121. "Résultats complets du Maroc," *La Vigie Marocaine*, 23 October 1945, 1MA/282/190, CADN; Renseignements: Pierre Parent, 16 January 1953, 1MA/282/190, CADN; and "Pierre Parent," Assemblée nationale—les députés de la IVe République, accessed 17 April 2018, http://www2.assemblee-nationale.fr/sycomore/fiche/(num_dept)/5680.

122. Memo on New Fédération de la Résistance française du Maroc, 20 December 1943, RG59/881.00/2711, USNA.

123. Pierre Parent, *Les Marocains et nous* (Rabat, MA: Imprimerie nouvelle, 1933), 14; and Renseignements: Pierre Parent, 16 January 1953, 1MA/282/190, CADN.

124. See, for example, *La politique indigène au Maroc* (Rabat, MA: Imprimerie nouvelle, n.d.); *Le problème marocain en 1949* (Toulouse, FR: Imprimerie régionale, 1949); *Maroc 1948* (Toulouse, FR: Imprimerie regionale, 1948); *Causerie sur le Maroc de 1951* (Toulouse, FR: Imprimerie régionale, 1951); and *Expolsé du Maroc* (Toulouse, FR: Imprimerie regionale, 1955).

125. Note de Renseignements, No. 856, 16 February 1951, 1MA/282/190, CADN.

126. Rapport au Directeur de l'Intérieur, 1 June 1951, 1MA/282/207, CADN.

127. Rapport du chef du Bureau du Maroc sur la réunion à la Maison du commerce à Lille, 4 May 1953, 1MA/282/190, CADN.

128. "Les problèmes de l'heure," *al-Istiqlal*, 24 November 1951, 1.

129. Jamaa Baïda, "Charles-André Julien et le nationalisme marocain," in *Empreintes, mélanges offerts à Jacques Levrat*, ed. Sylviane Noubecourt-El Kohen (Rabat, MA: Al-Asas/La Source, 2000).

130. As quoted in Georges Oved, *La gauche française et le nationalisme marocain, 1905–1955*, vol. 2, *Tentations et limites du réformisme colonial* (Paris: L'Harmattan, 1984), 245.

131. Charles-André Julien au Président de la République Vincent Auriol, 20 May 1952, Fonds Julien, IHTP.

132. Julien, *L'Afrique du Nord en marche*, 338.

133. Abdelmajid Benjelloun, *Le nord du Maroc—l'indépendance avant l'indépendance (Jean Rous et le Maroc, 1953–1956)* (Paris: L'Harmattan, 1996), 217.

134. "Après le voyage du Sultan—la question du Maroc," *Le Figaro*, 15 November 1950, 5; and "Hadith al-yawm," *al-ʿAlam*, 17 November 1950, 1.

135. Rivet, "Conscientes inquiètes," 12–14.

136. Office du Maroc au Résident général à Rabat, 23 May 1955, 1MA/282/21, CADN.

137. US Department of State, *Foreign Relations of the United States, 1949*, vol. VI, 1782.

138. Treize professeurs du Lycée Lyautey aux directeurs de journaux, 18 December 1952, Dossiers Malagar 14, Centre François Mauriac, Saint-Maixant (hereafter CFMSM).

139. Jean Lacouture, *François Mauriac* (Paris: Editions du Seuil, 1980), 446, 455.

140. Rivet, "Conscientes inquiètes," 20.

141. "La vocation des chrétiens dans l'Union française," *Le Figaro*, 17 January 1953, 1.

142. "Pour une nouvelle alliance entre la France et l'Islam," *Le Figaro*, 24 March 1953, 1.

143. "Le drame marocain devant la conscience chrétienne," *Cahiers du Témoignage Chrétien XXXV*, no. 4 (1953), Archives Paret, carton 2, IHTP.

144. Georgette Elgey, *Histoire de la IVe République: La république des contradictions (1951–1954)* (Paris: Fayard, 1993), 460.

145. Lacouture, *François Mauriac*, 458.

146. "Du complot à la répression," *Le Figaro*, 13 March 1953, 13.

147. Alexander Werth, *France, 1940–1955* (New York: Henry Holt, 1956), 618.

148. Robert Baudoy to François Mauriac, 17 January 1953, Dossiers Malagar 14, CFMSM; and Maurice Eonnet (Le Mas) to François Mauriac, 20 January 1953, Dossiers Malagar 14, CFMSM.

149. Odette Pannetier to François Mauriac, 2 April 1953, Dossiers Malagar 14, CFMSM.

150. Pierre Rousselot to François Mauriac, 26 March 1953, Dossiers Malagar 14, CFMSM.

151. "Nous n'acceptons pas que la page soit tournée—réponse à François Mauriac," *Paris*, 23 January 1953, 1, Archives Paret, carton 3, IHTP; "Il est difficile de prendre au sérieux M. François Mauriac," *La Vigie marocaine*, 26 March 1953, p. 1, Archives Paret, carton 3, IHTP; "Pour François Mauriac, Champion de l'Istiqlal," *Aspects de la France*, 10 April 1953, p. 6, Archives Paret, carton 3, IHTP; and "Les ennemis de la présence française en Afrique vont chercher leurs chiffres et leurs références dans le Figarro," *Aspects de la France*, 19 June 1953, Archives Paret, carton 3, IHTP.

152. Paul Chaignaud to François Mauriac, 30 January 1953, Dossiers Malagar 14, CFMSM.

153. Friar René to François Mauriac, 1 May 1953, Dossiers Malagar 14, CFMSM.

154. R. Blachère to François Mauriac, 15 January 1953, Dossiers Malagar 14, CFMSM.

155. "Un humble marocain" to François Mauriac, 25 March 1953, Dossiers Malagar 14, CFMSM; and "Un jeune Istiqlalien" to François Mauriac, 26 March 1953, Dossiers Malagar 14, CFMSM.

156. "Étudiant marocain" to François Mauriac, 17 February 1953, Dossiers Malagar 14, CFMSM; Ramdan Lahlimi to François Mauriac, 10 February 1953, Dossiers Malagar 14, CFMSM; and Mohammed ben Gelloun to François Mauriac, 10 March 1953, Dossiers Malagar 14, CFMSM.

157. Photo of Mohammed ben Youssef dedicated to François Mauriac, March 1953, Dossiers Malagar 14, CFMSM.

158. André Le Gall, *Mauriac politique* (Paris: L'Harmattan, 2017), chap. 4.

159. Rom Landau, *Moroccan Drama, 1900–1955* (Gateshead on Tyne, UK: Northumberland Press Ltd., 1956), 289.

160. Mohammed al-Khatib to Mehdi Bennouna, 29 January 1953, Mehdi Bennouna File, vol. 1, BFA.

161. Rabat to Department of State: French Press Review, 25 March 1953, RG59/971.61/3-2553, USNA.

162. "La Verité sur la tuerie de Casablanca comme la dévoile Mauriac le plus grand des écrivains français" [French translation], *Falastin*, 5 February 1953, Dossiers Malagar 14, CFMSM.

163. Paul Clay Sorum, *Intellectuals and Decolonization in France* (Chapel Hill: University of North Carolina Press, 1977), 51–53.

164. Rivet, "Conscientes inquiètes," 23.

165. Communiqué—Comité France-Maghreb, 8 June 1953, Archives Charles-André Julien, carton JU13, CHSP.

166. Communiqué—Comité France-Maghreb, 4 December 1954, Archives Paret, carton 16, IHTP; and Convocation: Veillée de prières pour l'amnistie Outre-mer en l'église cathédrale Notre Dame de Paris, 12 June 1954, Dossiers Malagar 14, CFMSM.

167. France-Maghreb—Bulletin mensuel d'information, no. 1, March 1954, p. 3, Archives Paret, carton 16, IHTP.

168. Rivet, "Conscientes inquiètes," 40.

169. CIA Report: Ex-Sultan of Morocco Falsely Accused of Being German Agent, 20 January 1954, p. 1, CIA-ERR.

170. "Avant la visite de François Mitterand Président de la République française au Roi du Maroc—Interview avec C.-A. Julien," *Radio France Internationale*, January 1982, Dossiers Malagar 14, CFMSM.

171. *Ma'alamat al-Maghrib* (Encyclopédie du Maroc), ed. M. Hajji (Salé, MA: Matabi'a Sala, 2003), s.v. "Robert Barrat."

172. Robert Barrat, *Justice pour le Maroc* (Paris: Editions du Seuil, 1953), 7.

173. Robert Schuman, "Nécessité d'une politique," *Maroc et Tunisie, le problème du protectorat* (Paris: Cahier No. 2—La Nef, March 1953), 9.

174. Guy Delanoë, *La résistance marocaine et le mouvement "conscience française"* (Paris: L'Harmattan, 1991), 87, 141.

175. Hervé Bleuchot, *Les libéraux français au Maroc, 1947–1955* (Aix-en-Provence: Editions de l'Université de Provence, 1973), 80, 133.

176. Delanoë, *La résistance marocaine et le mouvement*, 110.

177. Rivet, "Conscientes inquiètes," 30.

178. Direction générale de l'interieur: Fiche de renseignements sur Abderrahmane Yousfi, [n.d.], 1MA/282/14, CADN.

179. Mohammed al-Khatib to Mehdi Bennouna, 29 January 1953, Mehdi Bennouna File, vol. 1, BFA.

180. Fiche de renseignements concernant Ahmed Alaoui, 20 August 1954, 1MA/282/21, CADN.

181. Abdelkabir al-Fassi to Roger Paret, 27 March 1954, Fonds Paret, carton 2, IHTP.

182. Estimation, après enquête, du nombre des victimes des événements de Décembre 1952, Dossiers Malagar 14, CFMSM.

183. Noms des victimes des derniers évènements des 7 & 8 décembre 1952—fournis par l'Istiqlal, Fonds Paret, carton 2, IHTP.

184. Barrat, *Justice pour le Maroc*, 246.

185. "Al-Maghrib la yaqbalu ansaf al-hulul li-qadiyatihi," *al-Umma*, 26 August 1954, 1.

186. "Al-Hizb al-Ishtiraki al-Faransi yutalibu bi-istiqlal al-Maghrib wa siyadatihi," *al-Umma*, 6 July 1954, 1.

187. Oved, *La gauche française*, 279–81.

188. Boletín no. 275: Comentarios, 10 December 1954, 15 (13.01), box 81/2161, AGA.

189. Organisation, implantation et activités des partis nationalistes marocains dans la métropole, 30 June 1955, série 24QO/71, AMAE.

190. Ibid.

191. Ibid.

192. Ibid.

193. Ibid.

194. Ibid.

195. Ibid.

196. Ibid.

197. Office du Maroc: Note au sujet de l'expulsion de Youssoufi, 1 June 1951, 1MA/282/14, CADN.

198. Objet: Congrès de Zagreb, Ahmed Alaoui, 4 January 1951, 1MA/282/14, CADN.

199. Office du Maroc à Rabat, 4 June 1951, 1MA/282/14, CADN.

200. Directeur des Offices du Maroc en France au Résident général à Rabat, 5 February 1952, 1MA/282/21, CADN.

201. Office du Maroc à Rabat, 4 June 1951, 1MA/282/14, CADN.

202. Oved, *La gauche française*, 282.

203. André de Laubadère, "Le statut international du Maroc depuis 1955," *Annuaire français de droit international* 2 (1956): 124.

204. Lacouture, *François Mauriac*, 456.

205. The Algerian-born Berque went on to become an influential sociologist of the Arab world, and his book *Le Maghreb entre deux guerres* (Paris: Edition du Seuil, 1962) is still considered one of the most important analyses of French colonialism in North Africa.

206. Rivet, "Consciences inquiètes," 18–20.

207. Numerous scholars have written on the historical relationship between liberalism and imperialism, analyzing how its ideological commitment to "progress" and "development" provided an important intellectual justification for Western expansion in Africa and Asia. See, for example, Karuna Mantena, "The Crisis of Liberal Imperialism," *histoire@politique* 11 (2010); Domenico Losurdo, *Liberalism: A Counter History* (New York: Verso, 2011); and Jennifer Pitts, *A Turn to Empire: The Rise of Imperial Liberalism in Britain and France* (Princeton, NJ: Princeton University Press, 2005).

208. Sorum, *Intellectuals and Decolonization in France*, 73–79.

209. Todd Shepard, *The Invention of Decolonization: The Algerian War and the Remaking of France* (Ithaca, NY: Cornell University Press, 2006), 6.

CHAPTER 4

1. Diary Entry, 14 July 1947, Mehdi Bennouna File, vol. 1, BFA.

2. Ibid.

3. Ibid.

4. Ibid.

5. Ibid.

6. Carta del Presidente de la Universidad Americana de El Cairo acerca del aprovachamiento del estudiante Mehdi Bennouna, 25 February 1943, 10 (119.04), box 55/27193, AGA.

7. Mehdi Bennouna to Tayeb Bennouna, 15 September 1944, Mehdi Bennouna File, vol. 1, BFA.

8. His Highness the Khalifa Moulay Hassan ben al-Mehdi to His Highness the Sultan, 12 May 1947, Mehdi Bennouna File, vol. 1, BFA.

9. Entry visa for the United States for Mehdi Bennouna, 31 May 1947, Mehdi Bennouna File, vol. 1, BFA.

10. Notice Technique de Contre-Espionnage: M. Bennouna, 29 January 1948, 1MA/282/56, CADN.

11. US Consul Alling au Consul général de Beauverger, 10 June 1947, 1MA/282/56, CADN.

12. Abdelkhaleq Torres to Tayeb Bennouna, 6 June 1947, Mehdi Bennouna File, vol. 1, BFA.

13. Introductory letter by the Secretary General of Hizb al-Islah to the representatives of the Arab countries, 5 June 1947, Mehdi Bennouna File, vol. 1, BFA.

14. For an introduction to the history of Arab-American activism on behalf of Palestine during the post–World War II years, see Denise Laszewski Jenison, "'American Citizens of Arabic-Speaking Stock': The Institute of Arab-American Affairs and Questions of Identity in the Debate over Palestine," in *New Horizons of Muslim Diaspora in North America and Europe,* ed. Moha Ennaji (New York: Palgrave Macmillan, 2016).

15. Diary entry, 26 June 1947, Mehdi Bennouna File, vol. 1, BFA.

16. Mehdi Bennouna to Tayeb Bennouna, 11 June 1947, Mehdi Bennouna File, vol. 1, BFA.

17. Rory Miller, "Sinning? The Case of the Arab Office, Washington, 1945–1948," *Diplomacy & Statecraft* 15 (2004): 318.

18. Diary entry, 12 June 1947, Mehdi Bennouna File, vol. 1, BFA.

19. Diary entry, 11 July 1947, Mehdi Bennouna File, vol. 1, BFA.

20. Ambassadeur Bonnet au Ministre des Affaires étrangères Bidault, 16 July 1947, 1MA/282/56, CADN; El Abed Bouhafa al Embajador de España en Washington, 3 July 1953, 10 (26.2), box 54/12747, AGA; and Embajada de España en Washington al Ministerio de Asuntos Exteriores, 19 March 1951, 10 (26.2), box 54/12747, AGA.

21. Diary entry, 2 July 1947, Mehdi Bennouna File, vol. 1, BFA; and Diary Entry, 10 July 1947, Mehdi Bennouna File, vol. 1, BFA.

22. Notice Technique de Contre-Espionnage: M. Bennouna, 29 January 1948, 1MA/282/56, CADN.

23. Diary entry, 3 September 1947, Mehdi Bennouna File, vol. 1, BFA.

24. "'Aid al-'arsh bi-Nyuyurk," *al-'Alam,* 30 November 1946, 1; and Diary entry, 10 July 1947, Mehdi Bennouna File, vol. 1, BFA.

25. Diary entry, 18 July 1947, Mehdi Bennouna File, vol. 1, BFA.

26. Diary entry, 2 August 1947, Mehdi Bennouna File, vol. 1, BFA; and Notice Technique de Contre Espionnage: M. Bennouna, 29 January 1948, 1MA/282/56, CADN.

27. Diary entry, 16 September 1947, Mehdi Bennouna File, vol. 1, BFA.

28. Diary entry, 23 July 1947, Mehdi Bennouna File, vol. 1, BFA.

29. Diary entry, 11 June 1947, Mehdi Bennouna File, vol. 1, BFA.

30. Diary entry, 6 August 1947, Mehdi Bennouna File, vol. 1, BFA.

31. Arthur Goldschmidt and Robert Johnston, *Historical Dictionary of Egypt* (Lanham, MD: Scarecrow Press, 2003), s.v. "Abu al-Fath, Mahmud (1893–1958)."

32. Diary entry, 16 July 1947, Mehdi Bennouna File, vol. 1, BFA.

33. Diary entry, 11 August 1947, Mehdi Bennouna File, vol. 1, BFA; and Diary entry, 2 September 1947, Mehdi Bennouna File, vol. 1, BFA.

34. Chargé d'Affaires de France au Ministre des Affaires étrangères Schuman, 18 September 1948, 1MA/200/338, CADN.

35. Diary Entry, 21 July 1947, Mehdi Bennouna File, vol. 1, BFA.

36. Fortnightly Club Flushing: Notice to Club Members, [n.d.], Mehdi Bennouna File, vol. 2, BFA.

37. "Moroccos [*sic*] Seek Aid of US for Liberty," *New York Times,* 8 July 1947, 8.

38. Mehdi Bennouna to Trygve Lie, 12 July 1947, Mehdi Bennouna File, vol. 1, BFA; and Diary entry, 14 July 1947, Mehdi Bennouna File, vol. 1, BFA.

39. Embassy Paris to Department of State, 14 July 1947, RG59/881.00/7-747, USNA.

40. Diary entry, 14 July 1947, Mehdi Bennouna File, vol. 1, BFA.

41. US Department of State, *Foreign Relations of the United States, 1947*, vol. V, 698–99.

42. Ibid., 700–701.

43. Secret memorandum, 11 July 1947, RG59/881.00/6-1147, USNA.

44. Ministre des Affaires étrangères à Paris au Résident général à Rabat, 20 June 1947, série M/24QO/645, AMAE.

45. Diary entry, 15 September 1947, Mehdi Bennouna File, vol. 1, BFA.

46. Diary entry, 29 November 1947, Mehdi Bennouna File, vol. 1, BFA.

47. Diary entry, 16 September 1947, Mehdi Bennouna File, vol. 1, BFA.

48. Diary entry, 21 September 1947, Mehdi Bennouna File, vol. 1, BFA.

49. Diary entry, 16 September 1947, Mehdi Bennouna File, vol. 1, BFA.

50. Mehdi Bennouna to Driss Bennouna and Abdelkarim Bennouna, 2 January 1948, Mehdi Bennouna File, vol. 1, BFA.

51. Publication No. 64 of Maktab al-Maghrib al-ʿArabi in Cairo, 11 February 1948, M'hammad Benaboud File, BFA.

52. Mehdi A. Bennouna, *Our Morocco: The True Story of a Just Cause* (Morocco: 1951), vi.

53. "Maghribuna: Al-tarikh al-haqiqi li-qadiya ʿadila," 17 December 1951, *al-ʿAlam*, 2.

54. Ambassadeur Parodi au Ministre des Affaires étrangères Bidault, 28 July 1947, 1MA/282/56, CADN.

55. Comité de Propaganda y Difusion—Partido Reformista Nacional, no. 23, 10 December 1947, 15 (13.01), box 81/2161, AGA.

56. Paris contre-espionage: Lettre de Abdelkhaleq Torres à Tayeb Bennouna, 26 November 1947, 1MA/200/338, CADN.

57. Ibid.

58. Ibid.

59. Rom Landau to Morley Kennerley, 27 October 1951, Rom Landau Papers, box 1, SCRC.

60. Leaflet: American Sailors, Rom Landau Middle East Collection, MS68, series 1, box 4, HASC.

61. Libro de Mehdi Bennouna 'Our Morocco,' 21 December 1952, 15 (13.01), box 81/2157, AGA.

62. Landau, *Morocco Independent under Mohammed V*, 23.

63. Rom Landau to Morley Kennerley, 16 December 1951, Rom Landau Papers, box 1, SCRC.

64. Tangier to Department of State, 18 December 1951, RG59/771.00/12-1851, USNA.

65. Ibid.

66. Ibid.

67. Landau, *Morocco Independent under Mohammed V*, 103–10.

68. Résident général au Ministre des Affaires étrangères Schuman, 7 March 1952, 1MA/5/976, CADN.

69. Rézette, *Les partis politiques marocains*, 219.

70. Landau, *Morocco Independent under Mohammed V*, 24.

71. Rom Landau to Morley Kennerley, 15 February 1952, Rom Landau Papers, box 1, SCRC.

72. Rom Landau, "Morocco," *International Conciliation*, no. 477 (January 1952): 356.

73. Ambassadeur de France au Résident général à Rabat, 17 January 1953, 1MA/282/125, CADN.

74. Note de Renseignements, no. 46.027, 13 October 1952, 1MA/282/125, CADN.

75. "Kitab jadid li-mistir Rum Landaw ʿan al-Maghrib," *al-ʿAlam*, 27 October 1952, 2.

76. "Quwwa al-raʾi al-ʿamm fi al-duwal al-dimuqratiyya," *al-ʿAlam*, 19 June 1952, 1.

77. "Risalat Amrika," *al-ʿAlam*, 19 September 1952, 2.

78. "Wa ʿayn al-rida . . . ," *al-ʿAlam*, 29 December 1949, 1.

79. "Majlis al-amn, khatar ʿala al-amn," *al-ʿAlam*, 16 January 1949, 1.

80. "Baʿd khamas sanawat," *al-ʿAlam,* 24 October 1950, 1.

81. "Moroccan Reports Increase," *New York Times*, 27 January 1952, 26.

82. Mehdi Bennouna, "In the United States" (presentation, From Anfa to Aix-Les-Bains, 1943–1956: First International Conference Association for the Study of Moroccan-American Relations, Tangier, MA, 25–26 April 1978).

83. "Morocco Unrest Is Echoed in US," *New York Times*, 25 December 1951, 17.

84. Mehdi Ben Aboud, "American Policy and Moroccan Independence as Seen through the Moroccan Office in New York" (podium discussion, From Anfa to Aix-Les-Bains, 1943–1956, Tangier, Morocco, 25–26 April 1978).

85. Résident général au Ministre des Affaires étrangères Schuman, 7 March 1952, 1MA/5/976, CADN.

86. Ben Aboud, "American Policy and Moroccan Independence."

87. "Apartment Rentals," *New York Times*, 23 October 1952, 55.

88. "Morocco and the United States," *Free Morocco*, 25 December 1953, 1.

89. Rom Landau to Morley Kennerley, 12 July 1952, Rom Landau Papers, box 1, SCRC.

90. Proposal Prepared by Mehdi Bennouna to Organize the Work Inside the Morocco Office, [n.d.], Mehdi Bennouna File, vol. 2, BFA.

91. Mehdi Ben Aboud, letter to the editor, *Washington Post*, 31 December 1951, 6.

92. Some of the publications of the MOID are Hizb al-Istiqlal, *Morocco, before the Protectorate, under the Protectorate, Failure of the Protectorate* (New York: Moroccan Office of Information and Documentation, 1951); *Mohammed Ben Youssef, the Popular King of Morocco* (New York: Moroccan Office of Information and Documentation, 1952); *Morocco, Istiqlal Party Documents, 1944–1946*; *Some Guiding Facts on the Problem of Morocco* (Washington, DC: Moroccan Office of Information and Documentation, 1951); and *Morocco under the Protectorate: Forty Years of French Administration*.

93. Représentation de la France aux Nations-Unies à la Résidence générale au Maroc, 2 November 1953, 10POI/1/41, CADN.

94. "Maktab Marrakush bi-l-Wilayat al-Muttahida," *al-Umma*, 16 November 1953, 2.

95. Depeche du Consul général de San Francisco à l'Ambassadeur de France à Washington, 8 January 1954, 1MA/282/125, CADN.

96. "Kitab jadid li-Mistar Landaw ʿan al-Maghrib," *al-ʿAlam,* 27 October 1952, 2.

97. Rom Landau, "The Lobby that Runs North Africa," *America* 88, no. 14 (3 January 1953); and Rom Landau, *France and the Arabs* (Toronto: Canadian Institute of International Affairs, 1954), 15.

98. Rom Landau, "The Problem of Morocco," *America* 87, no. 2 (12 April 1952): 40.

99. "Al-Maghrib fi ʿamm 1955," *al-Umma*, 14 April 1955, 2.

100. "Morocco and the United States," *Free Morocco*, 25 May 1953, 1.

101. "Morocco and the United Nations," *Free Morocco*, 25 December 1953, 1; "Welcome to Our Readers," *Free Morocco*, 20 April 1953, 1; and "Sultan Deplores French Policy that Drives Moroccan Workers into Communist CGT," *Moroccan News Bulletin*, 3 April 1953, 2.

102. "Liberty and Freedom Will Come," *Free Morocco*, 25 May 1953, 3; and "Morocco Held Explosive," *Free Morocco*, 25 September 1954, 5.

103. Représentation de la France aux Nations-Unies à la Résidence générale au Maroc, 3 November 1954, 10POI/1/41, CADN.

104. Rézette, *Les partis politiques marocains*, 219.

105. Irene to Mehdi Bennouna, 1 May 1953, Mehdi Bennouna File, vol. 2, BFA.

106. Summary of the Most Important Things Mentioned in the Letters of Mehdi Bennouna during November 1952, 17 November 1952, Mehdi Bennouna File, vol. 2, BFA.

107. Rom Landau, *The Sultan of Morocco* (London: R. Hale, 1951), 36.

108. "Katib shahir yuthni 'ala mawqif Isbaniya," *al-Umma*, 22 December 1954, 1.

109. J. Winterbottom (Labor MP) to Robert Hale Ltd., 15 November 1951, Rom Landau Papers, box 1, SCRC.

110. Landau, *Morocco Independent under Mohammed V*, 25.

111. Eulalie Heakes (of the Women's Vancouver Branch of the Canadian Institute of International Affairs) to Rom Landau, 24 February 1954, Rom Landau Papers, box 3, SCRC.

112. Letter to the members of the Service Bureau for Women's Organizations, 19 November 1952, Rom Landau Papers, box 22, SCRC.

113. Mrs. George Dunsmoor (President of the Friday Morning Club) to Rom Landau, 17 May 1954, Rom Landau Papers, box 3, SCRC.

114. Betty Coan (Assistant Secretary of the City Club of Portland) to Rom Landau, 20 June 1955, Rom Landau Papers, box 3, SCRC.

115. Byron E. Eshelman (Chaplain of the California state prison San Quentin) to Rom Landau, 1 January 1956, Rom Landau Papers, box 3, SCRC.

116. Note au sujet Rom Landau, [n.d.], 1MA/282/125, CADN.

117. "Le Maréchal de France et l'agent de l'Antifrance," *Aspects de la France*, 3 July 1953, 2; and "Les bailleurs de fonds de l'Istiqlal démasqués," *Paris*, 9 January 1953, 1.

118. Robert Montagne, *Révolution au Maroc* (Paris: Editions France Empire, 1953), 227.

119. "Al-Za'im 'Allal al-Fasi yasarrihu: Sanutalibu min hai'at al-umam manh al-istiqlal ila al-Maghrib," *al-'Alam*, 9 July 1952, 1.

120. "Al-za'im 'Allal al-Fasi fi al-Suwid," *al-'Alam*, 22 July 1952, 1.

121. "La Suède votera-t-elle oui?" [French translation], *Aftonbladet*, 1 August 1952, 1MA/5/980, CADN; and British Embassy Stockholm to the Foreign Office, 31 July 1952, FO 371/97125, UKNA.

122. Allal al-Fassi to Abdelmajid Benjelloun and Ahmed Balafrej, 11 August 1952, dossier 2/folder 14, AFF.

123. "L'appui de l'Amérique Latine—La presse brésilienne fait echo aux déclarations d'Allal el Fassi," *al-Istiqlal*, 18 October 1952, 2.

124. Ambassadeur Jacques Baeyens au Ministre des Affaires étrangères Robert Schuman: Voyage au Chili d'Allal el Fassi, 23 October 1952, 1MA/282/33, CADN.

125. Allal al-Fassi to Abdelmajid Benjelloun, 23 October 1952, dossier 2/folder 14, AFF.

126. "Nishat al-za'im 'Allal fi Amrika," *al-'Alam*, 16 October 1952, 1; "Le colonialism est contraire au droit sacré du l'homme" [French translation], *Ultima Hora*, 27 September 1952, 1MA/282/33, CADN; and Embassy Santiago de Chile to Department of State: Moroccan Independence Leader in Chile, 24 October 1952, RG59/771.00/10-2452, USNA.

127. "Shata za'im Hizb al-Istiqlal 'Allal al-Fasi li-l-da'wa ila al-qadiya al-maghribiyya fi Shili," *al-'Alam*, 13 November 1952, 1.

128. Ambassadeur Jacques Baeyens au Ministre des Affaires étrangères Robert Schuman: Voyage de Si Allal el Fassi, 4 November 1952, 1MA/282/33, CADN.

129. "Wusul al-za'im 'Allal al-Fasi ila Nyu Yurk," *al-'Alam*, 30 October 1952, 1.

130. Landau, *Morocco Independent under Mohammed V*, 27.

131. "Min mahkamat al-'adl al-duwaliyya ila hai'at al-umam al-muttahida," *al-'Alam*, 3 September 1952, 1.

132. "Fi hafla 'aid al-'arsh bi-Nyu Yurk," *al-'Alam*, 21 November 1952, 1.

133. Summary of the most important things mentioned in the letters of Mehdi Bennouna

during November 1952, 17 November 1952, Mehdi Bennouna File, vol. 2, BFA. One of the books distributed was Pierre Parent, *Dissertation on Morocco of 1951* (Flushing, NY: Moroccan Office of Information and Documentation, 1952).

134. Ahmed Balafrej to Rom Landau, 11 December 1965, MS68, series 1, box 1, HASC.

135. "Risalat Amrika," *al-ʿAlam*, 16 September 1952, 1.

136. "Al-kutla al-ʿarabiyya al-asiyawiyya tabhathu wasaʾil al-ʿamal fi ʿard al-qadiyatayn al-maghribiyya wa-l-tunisiyya," *al-ʿAlam*, 4 October 1952, 1.

137. "Wazir kharijiyyat al-ʿIraq yaktabu li-zaʿim Hizb al-Istiqlal," *al-ʿAlam*, 26 August 1952, 1.

138. "Manifestación de la colonia marroquí en Nueva York" [Spanish translation], *al-Shaʿb*, 17 December 1952, Press Bulletin 257, 15 (13.01), box 81/2161, AGA.

139. "Nadwat al-zaʿim ʿAllal al-Fasi haula al-qadiya al-maghribiyya," *al-ʿAlam*, 3 June 1952, 4.

140. "Qadiyat al-Maghrib fi haiʾat al-umam bayna al-ams wa-l-yawm," *al-ʿAlam*, 24 October 1952, 2.

141. US Department of State, *Foreign Relations of the United States, 1952–54*, vol. IX, pt. 1, ed. John P. Glennon (Washington, DC: US Government Printing Office, 1986), 258.

142. US Department of State, *Foreign Relations of the United States, 1952–54*, vol. III, ed. William Z. Slany (Washington, DC: US Government Printing Office, 1979), 1143.

143. Ibid.

144. "Qadiyat al-Maghrib fi haiʾat al-umam," *al-ʿAlam*, 14 October 1952, 1.

145. Ibid.

146. Copia del escrito dirigio por la oficina de enlace del Frente Nacionalista a los jefes de los partidos, 12 October 1952, 15 (13.01), box 81/12710, AGA.

147. Tayeb Bennouna to Mehdi Bennouna, 2 November 1952, Mehdi Bennouna File, vol. 2, BFA.

148. Tayeb Bennouna to Mehdi Bennouna, 6 October 1952, 15 (13.01), box 81/12710, AGA.

149. Mohammed al-Khatib to Mehdi Bennouna, 21 October 1952, Mehdi Bennouna File, vol. 2, BFA.

150. "UN General Assembly Resolution A/RES/612(VII)—The Question of Morocco," 19 December 1952, http://research.un.org/en/docs/ga/quick/regular/7; and Blair, *Western Window in the Arab World*, 165.

151. Mehdi Bennouna to US Ambassador Philip C. Jessup, 18 December 1952, Mehdi Bennouna File, vol. 2, BFA.

152. Tayeb Bennouna to Mehdi Bennouna, 23 December 1952, Mehdi Bennouna File, vol. 2, BFA.

153. Dorothy Brandon, "Moroccans Eager for Hearing in UN," *Washington Post,* 30 December 1952, 35.

154. Landau, *Moroccan Drama*, 352–53.

155. Ibid.

156. Thomas, "France Accused," 100.

157. "Moroccan Nationalist Quits UN for Cairo," *New York Times*, 6 January 1953, 10; La Policia Internacional da ordenes a la 'Iberia' para que no de pasaje a varios nacionalistas, 5 February 1953, 15 (13.01), box 81/2083, AGA.

158. Ahmed Balafrej to Rom Landau, 28 January 1966, MS68, series 1, box 1, HASC.

159. Department of State to Embassy in Paris, 15 January 1953, RG59/771.00/1-1553, USNA; and Memo of conversation with Ben Aboud, 13 August 1953, RG59/771.00/8-1353, USNA.

160. Telegram from Islah Party to President Eisenhower, 19 August 1953, RG59/771.00/8-1953, USNA.

161. Driss Bennouna to Tayeb Bennouna, 3 September 1953, 15 (13.01), box 81/2083, AGA.

162. Kenneth J. Perkins, "North African Propaganda and the United States, 1946–1956," *African Studies Review* 19, no. 3 (1976): 77.

163. El-Mostafa Azzou, "La propagande des nationalistes marocains aux Etats-Unis (1945–1956)," *Guerres mondiales et conflits contemporains* 230, no. 2 (2008): 95.

164. Gilbert Jonas, "The Student Federalist Movement," in *American Students Organize: Founding the National Student Association after World War II*, ed. Eugene G. Schwartz (Westport, CT: American Council on Education/Praeger, 2006), 774.

165. "Gilbert Jonas, 76, N.A.A.C.P. Fund-Raiser, Dies," *New York Times*, 27 November 2006, C15.

166. William Welsh et al., "Covert U.S. Government Funding of NSA International Programs," in *American Students Organize—Founding the National Student Association after World War II,* ed. Eugene G. Schwartz (Westport, CT: American Council on Education/Praeger, 2006), 565.

167. Benjamin Rivlin, "Unity and Nationalism in Libya," *The Middle East Journal* 3, no. 1 (1949); "The Tunisian Nationalist Movement: Four Decades of Evolution," *The Middle East Journal* 6, no. 2 (1952); "Morocco, Domestic or World Issue," *Foreign Policy Bulletin* 33, no. 4 (1953); and "Context and Sources of Political Tensions in French North Africa," *The Annals of the American Academy of Political and Social Science* 298 (1955).

168. Benjamin Rivlin, "An American Point of View," *Free Morocco*, 25 May 1953, 4.

169. The Asia Institute Invites You to a Symposium on The Moroccan Problem on Thursday, 11 December 1952, at 8 p.m., [n.d.], 1MA/282/207, CADN.

170. Représentation de la France aux Nations-Unies à la Résidence générale au Maroc, 12 December 1952, 10POI/1/41, CADN.

171. Ahmed Balafrej to Rom Landau, [n.d.], MS68, series 1, box 1, HASC.

172. Memorandum on AJC meetings with Istiqlal Party leaders, October 1954, American Jewish Committee Information Center and Digital Archives.

173. Ibid.

174. "Nashrat al-wafd al-maghribi bi-hai'at al-umam," *al-ʿAlam,* 4 December 1952, 4.

175. Activités des nationalistes nord-africains aux Etats-Unis, 23 April 1954, 91QO/560, AMAE.

176. Rom Landau, *Among the Americans* (London: Hale, 1953), 99.

177. Eleanor Roosevelt, "My Day, January 3, 1953," *The Eleanor Roosevelt Papers Digital Edition* (2017), https://www2.gwu.edu/~erpapers/myday/displaydoc.cfm?_y=1953&_f=md002422.

178. Ibid.

179. Eleanor Roosevelt to Rom Landau, 2 March 1953, MS63, Rom Landau Collection, UCSB; and Eleanor Roosevelt to Rom Landau, 25 February 1954, MS63, Rom Landau Collection, UCSB.

180. Note: Activités nationalistes marocains, 18 November 1952, 10POI/1/41, CADN.

181. US Department of State, *Foreign Relations of the United States, 1952–54,* vol. XI, pt. 1, 717.

182. Rom Landau to William O. Douglas, 14 November 1953, William O. Douglas Collection, box 1725, folder 2, Library of Congress, Washington, DC (hereafter LOC); and Mehdi Ben Aboud to William O. Douglas, 29 June 1952, William O. Douglas Collection, box 1725, folder 2, LOC.

183. William O. Douglas to Mehdi Ben Aboud, 6 October 1954, William O. Douglas Collection, box 1725, folder 2, LOC.

184. William O. Douglas, "The French Are Facing Disaster Again in Morocco," *Look* 18, no. 21 (19 October 1954): 36.

185. US Department of State, *Foreign Relations of the United States, 1952–54,* vol. XI, pt. 1, 656.

186. Bruce Murphy, *Wild Bill: The Legend and Life of William O. Douglas* (New York: Random House, 2003), 336.

187. Ambassade de France, *Answer to Article by Justice William O. Douglas Published in Look Magazine, October 19, 1954* (New York: Service de Press et d'Information, October 1954), 14, 15a.

188. Télégramme de New York à Paris No. 3510/14, 11 December 1954, 372QO/580, AMAE.

189. See, for example, "La Question marocaine devant l'assemblée des Nations Unies," *al-Istiqlal*, 27 September 1952, 1; "La Question de la violation des droits syndicaux au Maroc et en Tunisie," *al-Istiqlal*, 30 September 1952, 1; "La France, les Etats-Unis et le problème Nord Africain," *al-Istiqlal*, 25 October 1952, 1; "Au Maroc la discrimination raciale existe dans tous les domaines," *al-Istiqlal*, 1 November 1952, 1; and "Tahlil daqiq li-mawqif Amrika bayna al-tiyarat al-mukhtalifa min qadiyatay al-Maghrib wa Tunis," *al-'Alam*, 28 October 1952, 1.

190. Représentation de la France aux Nations-Unies à la Résidence générale au Maroc, 24 September 1953, 10POI/1/41, CADN.

191. US Department of State, *Foreign Relations of the United States, 1952–54*, vol. XI, pt. 1, 643–44.

192. Wilford, *America's Great Game*, 119–31.

193. "L'Afrique du Nord a le sentiment d'avoir été injustement traitée par les nations occidentales," *al-Istiqlal*, 1 November 1952, 1.

194. Communiqué of Hizb al-Islah, 7 March 1953, Mehdi Bennouna File, vol. 2, BFA.

195. "Jama'iyya jadida li-ta'ziz al-'alaqat al-thaqafiyya bayna al-Amrikiyyin wa shu'ub al-Sharq al-Awsat," *al-'Alam*, 1 July 1951, 2.

196. Compte-rendu de la mission aux Etats-Unis de Temsamani, January 1955, p. 7, 1MA/282/207, CADN.

197. Conférence annuelle des American Friends of the Middle East, 13 February 1953, 91QO/560, AMAE.

198. Walther Reuther to Ahmed Balafrej and Bahi Ladgham, 24 September 1953, RG18-05, box 13/12, GMA; and Justice for People of Morocco, [n.d.], RG18-05, box 11/19, GMA.

199. Free Trade Union Committee of the AFL, "Fair Play for the People of Morocco," 2 September 1953, RG59/771.00/9-253, USNA.

200. American Federation of Labor, "Report of Proceedings of the Annual Convention of the American Federation of Labor" (Los Angeles, 1954), 600.

201. Press and Information Service of the French Embassy in New York, 2 July 1953, série M/24QO/160, AMAE.

202. As quoted in Morgan, *A Covert Life*, 290.

203. Jay Lovestone to Robert E. Rodes, 28 June 1953, Jay Lovestone Files, RG18-03, box 55/21, GMA.

204. Robert E. Rodes to Jay Lovestone, 16 December 1953, Jay Lovestone Files, RG18-03, box 55/21, GMA.

205. Robert E. Rodes, "Treaty Rights in Morocco," *Free Morocco*, 25 April 1955, 7.

206. Marjorie Rodes, *The United States and the French-Moroccan Problem: The Other Side* (New York: Free Trade Union Committee of the American Federation of Labor, 1954); and *The Real Ruler of Morocco* (New York: Johnnie Walker Press, 1954).

207. Extrait d'une letter de l'Ambassade de France aux Etats-Unis, 14 March 1952, 1MA/5/976, CADN.

208. Abdelmajid Benjelloun, *Approches du colonialisme espagnol et du mouvement nationaliste marocain dans l'ex-Maroc Khalifien* (Rabat, MA: Okad, 1988), 247–48.

209. Note de renseignements: Kenneth Pendar, 5 September 1951, 1MA/5/980, CADN.

210. Kenneth Pendar to William O. Douglas, 16 June 1954, box 363, folder 7, LOC.

211. William O. Douglas to Gardner Cowles Jr., 9 November 1954, box 363, folder 7, LOC.

212. Kenneth Pendar to William O. Douglas, 26 October 1954, box 363, folder 7, LOC.

213. William O. Douglas to Kenneth Pendar, 13 December 1955, box 363, folder 7, LOC.

214. Kenneth Pendar to Eleanor Roosevelt, 25 July 1954, box 363, folder 7, LOC.

215. Ibid.

216. Kenneth Pendar to William O. Douglas, 10 September 1954, box 363, folder 7, LOC.

217. "Nous avons poursuive et détruit les mensonges de l'Istiqlal partout où ils se manifestaient," *La Vigie Marocaine*, 28 December 1952, p. 1, 1MA/282/207, CADN.

218. Compte-rendu de la mission aux Etats-Unis de Temsamani, 7 January 1954, pp. 2–3, 15, 1MA/282/207, CADN.

219. Resultats et conséquences d'une tournée de conférences dans le Middle West, November 1953, p. 1, 1MA/282/207, CADN; and Compte-rendu de la mission aux Etats-Unis de Temsamani, January 1955, p. 2, 1MA/282/207, CADN.

220. "Nous avons poursuive et détruit les mensonges de l'Istiqlal partout où ils se manifestaient," *La Vigie Marocaine*, 28 December 1952, p. 1, 1MA/282/207, CADN; and "La situation politique au Maroc—notions générals," [n.d.], 1MA/282/207, CADN.

221. La Depeche Marocaine, 4 October 1953—Noticias de Prensa, Boletín 209, 5 October 1953, 15 (13.01), box 81/2161, AGA.

222. Activités de l'Istiqlal, 6 November 1952, 1MA/282/207, CADN.

223. Représentation de la France aux Nations-Unies à la Résidence générale au Maroc, 14 October 1953, 10POI/1/41, CADN.

224. Mohammed Temsamani à André Noel (Résidence générale, Rabat), [n.d.], 1MA/282/207, CADN.

225. Compte-rendu de la mission accomplie aux Etats-Unis, 7 January 1954, pp. 3, 15, 1MA/282/207, CADN.

226. Mohammed Temsamani to Résident Général Augustin Guillaume, 27 January 1954, 1MA/282/207, CADN.

227. Egya N. Sangmuah, "The United States and the French Empire in North Africa, 1946–1956: Decolonization in the Age of Containment" (PhD diss., University of Toronto, 1989).

228. US Department of State, *Foreign Relations of the United States, 1952–54*, vol. XI, pt. 1, 63, 631.

229. French Embassy in Washington to the Ministry of Foreign Affairs, 2 November 1953, 372QO/579, AMAE.

230. US Department of State, *Foreign Relations of the United States, 1952–54*, vol. XI, pt. 1, 655.

231. Ibid.

232. French Embassy in Baghdad to the Ministry of Foreign Affairs, 26 June 1954, 372QO/580, AMAE.

233. Ahmed Balafrej to Rom Landau, 12 November 1954, MS68, series 1, box 1, HASC.

234. "Al-Qadiya al-maghribiyya fi-l-umam al-muttahida," *al-Umma*, 24 January 1955, 2.

235. United Nations General Assembly Resolution A/RES/812(IX), "The Morocco Question," 17 December 1954, accessed 9 January 2018, http://www.un.org/en/ga/search/view_doc.asp?symbol=A/RES/812(IX).

236. Rivlin, "The United States and Moroccan International Status, 1943–1956," 79.

237. Secretary of State Dulles to Embassy in London, 15 October 1953, RG59/771.00/10-1553, USNA.

238. La délégation de France aux Nations unies à New York au Ministre des Affaires étrangères, 13 November 1954, 372QO/580, AMAE.

239. La délégation de France aux Nations unies à New York au Ministre des Affaires étrangères, 21 September 1955, 372QO/579, AMAE.

240. Hector (of The Reader's Digest Association in Pleasantville, New York) to Ahmed Benaboud, 12 September 1955, 15 (13.01), box 81/2167, AGA.

241. Rodman Wilson to Ahmed Benaboud, [n.d.], 15 (13.01), box 81/2167, AGA.

242. The aid provided by the Moroccans to the Algerians included the printing and distribution of the first publications of the FLN. See, for example, Jabhat al-Tahrir al-Qawmi, *The Peaceful Settlement of the Algerian Question* (The Algerian Delegation c/o Moroccan Office of Information and Documentation, 75-18 Woodside Ave., Elmhurst 73, New York, 1955). In addition to financing the MOID, Mohammed Laghzaoui also provided financial contributions to the FLN activists in New York. Morgan, *A Covert Life*, 294.

243. Burt, "The Network Structure of Social Capital," 353.

244. Aram Bakshian Jr., "The Unlikely Rise of Al Jazeera," *The Atlantic*, 25 November 2012.

245. Ernest Gellner, "Review: Morocco Independent under Mohammed V," *Middle East Journal* 17, no. 1/2 (1963): 175.

246. Ahmed Balafrej to Rom Landau, 27 April 1953, MS68, series 1, box 1, HASC.

CHAPTER 5

1. "Morocco Sultan Returns in Triumph from Exile," *New York Times*, 17 November 1955, 1.

2. "Sultan Gets Big Welcome on Return to Morocco," *Los Angeles Times*, 17 November 1955, 7.

3. "Ruju' al-amal," *al-'Alam*, 18 November 1955, 1.

4. Miller, *A History of Modern Morocco*, 151–54; Bernard, *Le conflit franco-marocain*, vol. 1, chs. 7–8; and Charles-Robert Ageron, *La décolonisation française* (Paris: Armand Colin Éditeur, 1991), 98–99.

5. As quoted in Bernard, *Le conflit franco-marocain*, vol. 1, 336.

6. Ibid.

7. Martin Thomas, "From French North Africa to Maghreb Independence: Decolonization in Morocco, Tunisia and Algeria, 1945–1956," in *Crisis of Empire: Decolonization and Europe's Imperial States, 1918–1975*, ed. Martin Thomas, Bob Moore, and L. J. Butler (London: Hodder Education, 2008), 217.

8. Laubadere, "Le statut international du Maroc depuis 1955," 124–26.

9. Ryo Ikeda, *The Imperialism of French Decolonization—French Policy and the Anglo-American Response in Tunisia and Morocco* (New York: Palgrave Macmillan, 2015), 164–78.

10. "Al-Sha'b yahtifu b-ism malakihi Muhammad bin Yusif akthar min alf milyun marra," *al-Umma*, 17 November 1955, 1.

11. In his autobiographical account of the inner workings of the Moroccan monarchy, Moulay Hicham el-Alaoui identified the "merciless struggle for spoils" as the major characteristic of royal politics. *Journal d'un prince banni—demain, le Maroc* (Paris: Bernard Grasset, 2014), 119.

12. Maâti Monjib, *La monarchie marocaine et la lutte pour le pouvoir: Hassan II face à l'opposition nationale, de l'indépendance à l'état d'exception* (Paris: L'Harmattan, 1992), 27.

13. "10,000 mawatin yastaqbilun zu'ama' Hizb al-Istiqlal bi-Tanja," *al-Umma*, 22 November 1955, 1; and "'Ashrat al-alaf min al-muwatinin yahtashidun fi matar Titwan wa mayadiniha l-istiqbal 'Allal al-Fasi," *al-Umma*, 28 November 1955, 1.

14. "Ba'd ada' salat al-jum'a al-mubaraka inha jalalat al-malik al-mu'azzam ziyaratahu al-maymuna li-l-Dar al-Baida," *al-Umma*, 11 February 1956, 1.

15. "Al-Watan kulluhu yajtama'u fi sa'id Titwan li-yastqabilu jalalat al-malik za'im al-istilqlal wa-l-wahda," *al-Umma*, 9 April 1956, 1.

16. "Bahth ta'awun fi al-shu'un al-fanniyya wa-l-idariyya," *al-'Alam*, 30 March 1956, 1.

17. "Tawhid al-watan," *al-'Alam*, 4 April 1956, 1.

18. Jonathan Wyrtzen, *Making Morocco: Colonial Intervention and the Politics of Identity* (Ithaca, NY: Cornell University Press, 2015), 275–81; and Michel Abitbol, *Histoire du Maroc* (Paris: Editions Perrin, 2009), 553–55.

19. "Kilmat sumuw ra'is arkan al-quwwat al-malakiyya al-musallaha amam jalalat al-malik," *al-'Alam*, 14 May 1956, 1.

20. "Fi haflat al-dhubbat allati aqamaha jalalat al-malik," *al-'Alam*, 17 May 1956, 1.

21. "Al-Maghrib fi hai'at al-umam al-muttahida: Khitab jalalat al-malik," *al-Umma*, 23 July 1956, 1.

22. Interestingly enough, the nationalists had already been referring to him by that name and title for over a decade.

23. Remy Leveau, *Le fellah marocain, défenseur du trône* (Paris: PFNSP, 1985), 7–25.

24. John Waterbury, *The Commander of the Faithful: The Moroccan Political Elite—a Study in Segmented Politics* (New York: Columbia University Press, 1970), 144.

25. "Hizb al-Islah al-watani yu'linu indimajahu fi Hizb al-Istiqlal tamhidan li-tahqiq wahdat al-bilad," *al-Umma*, 17 March 1956, 1; and Hajji, *Ma'alamat al-Maghrib*, s.v. "'Abd al-Khaliq Turris."

26. Jean Lacouture and Simonne Lacouture, *Le Maroc à l'épreuve* (Paris: Editions du Seuil, 1958), 145–55.

27. Monjib, *La monarchie marocaine*, 18.

28. "Ad: Unclaimed Accounts—Chase Manhattan Bank," *New York Times*, 23 October 1976, 17. This anecdote also hints at the immense wealth Laghzaoui must have possessed at that time.

29. "Al-Mudir al-'amm li-l-amn al-watani al-sayyid Muhammad al-Aghzawi yastalimu maqalid wazifihi," *al-'Alam*, 28 April 1956, 1.

30. "Darurat istitbab al-aman," *al-'Alam*, 29 April 1956, 1.

31. Pierre Vermeren, *Histoire du Maroc depuis l'indépendance* (Paris: La Découverte, 2002), 25; and Monjib, *La monarchie marocaine*, 33.

32. Landau, *Morocco Independent under Mohammed V*, 110.

33. Omar Brousky, *La république de Sa Majesté: France-Maroc, liaisons dangereuses* (Paris: Nouveau Monde Editions, 2017), 84.

34. Morgan, *A Covert Life*, 294.

35. Stuart H. Schaar, *The Mass Media in Morocco: In Morocco Information Still Travels Best by Word of Mouth* (New York: American Universities Field Staff, 1968), 2–3.

36. "Sahib al-jalala yusallimu li-l-duktur Ibn 'Abbud awraq i'timadihi," *al-'Alam*, 29 July 1956, 1.

37. William O. Douglas to Mehdi Ben Aboud, 9 October 1956, William O Douglas Collection, box 1725, folder 2, LOC.

38. Fiche: Abderrahman Ben Abdelali, [n.d.], 1MA/282/14, CADN.

39. Note de *Petit Marocain*, 10 March 1964, 1MA/282/14, CADN.

40. Department of State Memo of Conversation: Ambassador Mehdi Ben Aboud, 20 August 1957, RG59/Entry# P294/Visits by Heads of Government, 1928–76, box 82, USNA.

41. "Pretty Moroccan Fights Fallacies: Brunette U.N. Delegate, 24, Gives U.S. a New View of Moslem Women," *New York Times*, 13 December 1959, 131.

42. Ahmed Balafrej to Rom Landau, 28 November 1963, MS68, series 1, box 1, HASC.

43. Monjib, *La monarchie marocaine*, 30.

44. Rabat to Department of State, 13 August 1957, RG59/Entry# P294/Visits by Heads of Government, 1928–76, box 82, USNA.

45. "Décret royal no 555-67 du 8 chaabane 1387 (11 novembre 1967) relatif à la composition et à l'organisation du Gouvernement," *Bulletin official du Royaume du Maroc*, no. 2872 (15 Novembre 1967): 1332–33.

46. Assia Bensalah Alaoui, *Moulay Ahmed Alaoui: La passion et le verbe* (Rabat, MA: Marsam, 2010), 15.

47. Rabat to Department of State: Biographies of Aides Accompanying King of Morocco to US, 13 November 1957, RG59/Entry# P294/Visits by Heads of Government, 1928–76, box 82, USNA.

48. Ibid.

49. Hajji, *Maʿalamat al-Maghrib*, s.v. "ʿAbd al-Majid bin Jalun."

50. Ibid., s.v. "ʿAbd al-Karim Ghallab."

51. Ibid., s.v. "ʿAbd al-Kabir al-Fasi," "Tayib Binnuna," "ʿAbd al-Majid bin Jalun," "ʿAbd al-Khaliq Turris," "ʿAbd al-Rahim Bu ʿAbid," and "ʿAbd al-Latif Sbihi"; and "Jalalat al-malik yusallim li-l-zaʿim al-Turays wa-l-ustadh ʿAbd al-Rahim Bu ʿAbid awraq iʿtimadihim safirayn bi-Madrid wa Baris," *al-Umma*, 20 June 1956, 1.

52. Postes diplomatiques du Maroc à l'étranger et représentations étrangères au Maroc, 2 June 1959, série M/130SUP/70, AMAE.

53. Miller, *A History of Modern Morocco*, 154.

54. Invitation de S. M. Sidi Mohammed ben Youssef à François Mauriac de vouloir bien venir dîner le 5 novembre à 20 heures, Dossiers Malagar 14, CFMSM.

55. "Avant la visite de François Mitterand Président de la République Française au Roi du Maroc—Interview avec C.-A. Julien," *Radio France Internationale*, January 1982, Dossiers Malagar 14, CFMSM.

56. Ambassador Zeghari to François Mauriac, 14 November 1957, Dossiers Malagar 14, CFMSM.

57. Lettre Pierre Parent au Chargé d'affaires de France à Rabat, 11 July 1957, 1MA/282/190, CADN.

58. "Pierre Parent," Assemblée nationale—les députés de la IVe République, accessed 17 April 2018, http://www2.assemblee-nationale.fr/sycomore/fiche/(num_dept)/5680.

59. "Un home libre disparait," *al-Istiqlal,* 23 November 1957, 4.

60. "Le courier des lecteurs: À la mémoire de M. Parent," *al-Istiqlal*, 30 November 1957, 2.

61. Robert E. Rodes to the director of the Department of Arts and Craft, 25 June 1968, RFA.

62. Robert E. Rodes to William R. Poage, 7 July 1967, RFA.

63. Robert E. Rodes to Mustapha Alaoui, 4 November 1968, RFA.

64. Ahmed Balafrej to Rom Landau, 12 April 1956, Rom Landau Middle East Collection, MS68, series 1, box 1, HASC.

65. Landau, *Morocco Independent under Mohammed V*, 30–33.

66. "Maʿ al-katib al-britani al-kabir mistir Rum Landaw," *al-ʿAlam*, 22 September 1956, 1.

67. Ambassade du Royaume du Maroc en France, *Bulletin Quotidien d'information*, no. 305 (New York: Service de Presse et d'Infromation, 26 July 1962), 2.

68. Mehdi Bennani to Rom Landau, 30 September 1963, MS68, series 1, box 1, HASC.

69. Rom Landau to Mohammed al-Fassi, 4 September 1958, MS68, series 1, box 1, HASC; and Mohammed al-Fassi to Rom Landau, 16 March 1959, MS68, series 1, box 1, HASC.

70. Rom Landau to Robert Burns, 29 September 1962, MS68, series 1, box 1, HASC.

71. Ahmed Balafrej to Rom Landau, 28 November 1963, MS68, series 1, box 1, HASC.

72. John F. Kennedy to Rom Landau, 29 July 1957, Rom Landau Papers, box 1, SCRC.

73. John F. Kennedy to Rom Landau, 23 August 1957, Rom Landau Papers, box 1, SCRC.

74. John F. Kennedy to Rom Landau, 29 July 1957, Rom Landau Papers, box 1, SCRC.

75. Blair, *Western Window in the Arab World*, 311.

76. Wizarat al-Tarbiyya al-Wataniyya, *Al-Jadid fi al-tarikh: Al-sanna al-thaniya min suluk bakaluriya* (Rabat, MA: Dar nashr al-maʿrifa, 2007), 56. I would like to thank Kate Maye-Saidi for providing this reference.

77. Charles-André Julien to Ahmed Balafrej, 21 November 1962, Archives Charles-André Julien, carton JU27, CHSP.

78. "La société moderne a besoin d'ingénieurs et de techniciens," *al-Istiqlal*, 21 December 1957, 6–7.

79. Ahmed Bennani to Charles-André Julien, 10 January 1958, Archives Charles-André Julien, carton JU27, CHSP; Mohammed al-Fassi to Charles-André Julien, 22 November 1957, Archives Charles-André Julien, carton JU27, CHSP; and Mbarek Bekkai to Charles-André Julien, 4 January 1958, Archives Charles-André Julien, carton JU27, CHSP.

80. Biographie de C. A. Julien: Un homme dans le siècle, [n.d.], p. 6, Fonds Julien, IHTP.

81. Julien, *L'Afrique Du Nord en marche*, 312.

82. Mahjoub Ben Seddiq to George Meany, 24 December 1956, Brown Files, RG18-04, box 31/3, GMA.

83. Tayeb Bouazza to Irving Brown, 1 November 1956, Brown Files, RG18-05, box 31/2, GMA.

84. Tayeb Bouazza to Irving Brown, 18 April 1957, RG18-05, box 31/2, GMA.

85. US Ambassador Yost to Irving Brown, 8 September 1958, RG18-004, box 31/3, GMA.

86. Postes diplomatiques du Maroc à l'étranger et représentations étrangères au Maroc, 2 June 1959, série M/130SUP/70, AMAE.

87. "Jalalat al-Malik al-muʿazzam yaqtabilu maktab al-Ittihad al-Maghribi li-l-Shughl," *al-ʿAlam*, 13 December 1955, 1; and "Sumuw al-ʿahd al-mahbub yazuru markaz al-Ittihad al-Maghribi li-l-Shughl wa yakhtabu fi al-ʿummal," *al-ʿAlam*, 16 December 1955, 1.

88. "Muzahara ʿummaliyya kubra fi maqarr al-malik bi-Baris," *al-Umma*, 12 November 1955, 1.

89. Robert D. Forst, "The Origins and Early Development of the Union Marocaine Du Travail," *International Journal of Middle East Studies* 7, no. 2 (1976): 282.

90. US Consul Schaufele (Casablanca) to Irving Brown, 10 August 1960, RG18-004, box 31/3, GMA.

91. Irving Brown to Col. Ahmed Dlimi, 28 March 1975, RG18-004, box 31/3, GMA.

92. Kahn, *The Big Drink*, 38.

93. "Tahni'at Kuka Kula bi-munasibat Ramadan," *al-ʿAlam*, 12 April 1956, 3.

94. "Kenneth Pendar, Ex-Vice Consul, Aide in North Africa, Dies," *New York Times*, 8 December 1972, 48.

95. "Casablanca, base avancée de Coca-Cola," *Afrik.com*, 9 March 2001, http://www.afrik.com/article2368.html.

96. Abdelaziz Tazi and Marc Thiollier, *Les relations comerciales entre le Maroc et les Etats Unis* (New York: Sociètè gènèrale pour favoriser le dèveloppement du commerce et de l'industrie en France, 1963), 14.

97. Eleanor Roosevelt, *On My Own* (New York: First Da Capo Press, 1992), 365.

98. Ibid., 364–66; and "Mrs. Roosevelt in Morocco," *New York Times*, 18 March 1957, 2.

99. "Mrs. Kennedy visits Bazaar in Morocco," *New York Times*, 15 October 1963, 5.

100. "Mrs. Kennedy given a home in Morocco," *New York Times*, 27 December 1963, 28.

101. "Edward Kennedy in Morocco," *New York Times*, 20 November 1966, 4.

102. See, for example, Visit to Tangier of His Majesty: Tangier to Department of State, 16 April 1947, RG59/881.001/4-1647, USNA.

103. Rabat to Department of State, 16 October 1956, RG59/Entry# P294/Visits by Heads of Government, 1928–76, box 82, USNA.

104. Rabat to Department of State, 14 February 1957, RG59/Entry# P294/Visits by Heads of Government, 1928–76, box 82, USNA.

105. "Al-Sha'b yastaqbilu na'ib al-ra'is al-amriki istiqbalan ra'i'an," *al-'Alam*, 2 March 1957, 1; and "Al-Baida yastqabilu bi-hamas kabir khalifat al-ra'is al-amriki," *al-'Alam*, 3 March 1957, 1.

106. "Nixon Shakes Hands, Pats Babies, and Crowds in Morocco Love It," *New York Times*, 2 March 1957, 1.

107. Visit of the King of Morocco, 19 November 1957, RG59/Entry# P294/Visits by Heads of Government, 1928–76, box 82, USNA.

108. Ibid.

109. Salim Yaqub, *Containing Arab Nationalism: The Eisenhower Doctrine and the Middle East* (Chapel Hill: University of North Carolina Press, 2004), 3.

110. Rabat to Department of State, 13 August 1957, RG59/Entry# P294/Visits by Heads of Government, 1928–76, box 82, USNA.

111. Rabat to Department of State, 21 August 1957, RG59/Entry# P294/Visits by Heads of Government, 1928–76, box 82, USNA.

112. Memo: Public Relations Aspect of Visit of Mohammed V, 23 October 1957, RG59/Entry# P294/Visits by Heads of Government, 1928–76, box 81, USNA.

113. "En marge du voyage de Sa Majesté aux USA," *al-Istiqlal*, 30 November 1957, 13.

114. Blair, *Western Window in the Arab World*, xii.

115. Ibid., 221.

116. USIS Rabat to USIA Washington, 28 August 1957, RG59/Entry# P294/Visits by Heads of Government, 1928–76, box 82, USNA; and Blair, *Western Window in the Arab World*, 221.

117. William M. Rountree to Secretary of State, 4 November 1957, RG59/Entry# P294/Visits by Heads of Government, 1928–76, box 82, USNA.

118. Rabat to Department of State, 1 November 1957, RG59/Entry# P294/Visits by Heads of Government, 1928–76, box 82, USNA.

119. Rabat to Department of State, 11 May 1957, RG59/Entry# P294/Visits by Heads of Government, 1928–76, box 82, USNA.

120. "Safara jalalat al-malik ila Amrika," *al-'Alam*, 25 November 1957, 1.

121. Rabat to Department of State, 25 November 1957, RG59/Entry# P294/Visits by Heads of Government, 1928–76, box 82, USNA.

122. White House Press Release, 25 November 1957, RG59/Entry# P294/Visits by Heads of Government, 1928–76, box 81, USNA.

123. Secretary of State's Dinner—Menu, [n.d.], RG59/Entry# P294/Visits by Heads of Government, 1928–76, box 81, USNA.

124. Proposed Guests for President's Dinner at the White House, 25 November 1957, RG59/Entry# P294/Visits by Heads of Government, 1928–76, box 81, USNA.

125. Memorandum for Mr. Buchanan, 15 November 1957, RG59/Entry# P294/Visits by Heads of Government, 1928–76, box 81, USNA.

126. "Jalalat al-malik yushidu bi-l-sadaqa al-maghribiyya al-amrikiyya," *al-'Alam*, 26 November 1957, 1.

127. Arrangements for the Visit of HM Mohammed V to Niagara Falls, 7 December 1957, RG59/Entry# P294/Visits by Heads of Government, 1928–76, box 81, USNA.

128. Blair, *Western Window in the Arab World*, 219.

129. Memorandum for Mr. Buchanan, 15 November 1957, RG59/Entry# P294/Visits by Heads of Government, 1928–76, box 81, USNA.

130. "Dulles and King Confer on Bases," *New York Times*, 27 November 1957, 1.

131. Secretary of State's Dinner—Guest List: Other Departments and Agencies, [n.d.], RG59/Entry# P294/Visits by Heads of Government, 1928–76, box 81, USNA.

132. Rabat to Department of State, 13 October 1957, RG59/Entry# P294/Visits by Heads of Government, 1928–76, box 82, USNA.

133. University of the Pacific, *The State Visit of His Majesty, King Mohammed V of Morocco to the College of the Pacific* (San Francisco: 1957), 9.

134. "King Mohammed Invites L.A. Hosts to Morocco," *Los Angeles Times*, 3 December 1957, 25.

135. "Jawharat al-Basifik tahtafilu bi-jalalat al-malik," *al-ʿAlam*, 6 December 1957, 1.

136. "4 Daughters Join King on Visit," *New York Times*, 9 December 1957, 3.

137. "Mohammed Visits the Zoo, Pets a Potto, Acquires Chimpanzee, Shies at Python," *New York Times*, 13 December 1957, 2.

138. "3 Princesses Find Folks Polite Here," *New York Times*, 12 December 1957, 3.

139. "Diplomatie: Le messager des nations émergeants," *al-Istiqlal*, 14 December 1957, 3.

140. "UN Head Is Host to Moroccan King," 11 December 1957, *New York Times*, 19.

141. Eleanor Roosevelt, "My Day, December 12, 1957," *The Eleanor Roosevelt Papers Digital Edition* (2017), https://www2.gwu.edu/~erpapers/myday/displaydoc.cfm?_y=1957&_f=md003984.

142. "Diplomatie: Le messager des nations émergeants," *al-Istiqlal*, 14 December 1957, 3.

143. William M. Rountree (State Department) to Mr. Wiley T. Buchanan (White House), 24 March 1958, RG59/Entry# P294/Visits by Heads of Government, 1928–76, box 81, USNA.

144. "Visitor from Morocco," *New York Times*, 25 November 1957, 30.

145. "Westernmost Arab King—Mohammed V," *New York Times*, 26 November 1957, 5.

146. "An Understanding Visitor," *Washington Post*, 26 November 1957, A15.

147. "Dashing Moroccan Heir," *New York Times*, 29 November 1957, 15.

148. "Diplomatie—Le voyage de Sa Majesté un éclatant succès," *al-Istiqlal*, 30 November 1957, 3.

149. "Chaleureux accueil des USA à S M le Roi," *al-Istiqlal*, 30 November 1957, 16; and "Sa Majesté aux USA," *al-Istiqlal*, 7 December 1957, 20.

150. "Najah," *al-ʿAlam*, 28 November 1957, 1.

151. Ibid.

152. "En un clin d'oeuil," *al-Istiqlal*, 21 December 1957, 2.

153. Ambassade de France à Washington au Ministre des Affaires étrangères, 3 December 1957, 91QO/437, AMAE.

154. Ibid.

155. Ibid.

156. Ibid.

157. "La politique des faux semblants," *al-Istiqlal*, 28 December 1957, 3.

158. "Westernmost Arab King—Mohammed V," *New York Times*, 26 November 1957, 5.

CONCLUSION

1. A brief discussion of the importance of all three levels to the history of decolonization can be found in John Darwin, "Decolonization and the End of Empire," in *The Oxford History of the British Empire*, eds. Robin W. Winks and Alaine Low, vol. 5 (New York: Oxford University Press, 1999), 556.

2. Susan Pedersen, *The Guardians: The League of Nations and the Crisis of Empire* (New York: Oxford University Press, 2015), 94; and Arthur Asseraf, "Making Their Own Internationalism: Algerian Media and a Few Others the League of Nations Ignored, 1919–1943," in *International Organizations and the Media in the Nineteenth and Twentieth Centuries: Exorbitant Expectations*, eds. Jonas Brendebach, Martin Herzer, and Heidi J. S. Tworek (London: Routledge, 2018).

3. Cyrus Schayegh, "The Expanding Overlap of Imperial, International, and Transnational Political Activities, 1920s–1930s: A Belgian Case Study," *International Politics* (2017).

4. A brief theorization of the conditions under which anticolonial movements engaged in armed struggle can be found in Tony Smith, "Patterns in the Transfer of Power: A Comparative Study of French and British Decolonization," in *The Transfer of Power in Africa. Decolonization, 1940–60*, ed. Prosser Gifford and William Roger Louis (New Haven, CT: Yale University Press, 1982), 109–10.

5. See, for example, Nico Slate, *Colored Cosmopolitanism: The Shared Struggle for Freedom in the United States and India* (Cambridge, MA: Harvard University Press, 2012).

6. Robert K. Brigham, *Guerrilla Diplomacy—The NFL's Foreign Relations and the Viet Nam War* (Ithaca, NY: Cornell University Press, 1999).

7. Rob Skinner, *The Foundations of Anti-Apartheid: Liberal Humanitarians and Transnational Activists in Britain and the United States, c. 1919–64* (New York: Palgrave Macmillan, 2010), 185; Ryan M. Irwin, *Gordian Knot: Apartheid and the Unmaking of the Liberal World Order* (New York: Oxford University Press, 2012), 42, 130, 154, and 173; and Scott Thomas, *The Diplomacy of Liberation: The Foreign Relations of the ANC since 1960* (London: I. B. Tauris, 1996).

8. For a study of the role played by cinematography in the formation of transnational anti-imperial alliances, see R. Joseph Parrott, "A Luta Continua: Radical Filmmaking, Pan-African Liberation and Communal Empowerment," *Race & Class* 57, no. 1 (2015).

9. That even globally active anticolonial movements such as the Algerian FLN did not seek to abolish the international system of nation-states has been argued by Byrne, *Mecca of Revolution*, 291–93.

10. The importance of urban spaces in the creation of links between nationalists around the globe has been emphasized by Michael Goebel, *Anti-Imperial Metropolis: Interwar Paris and the Seeds of Third World Nationalism* (New York: Cambridge University Press, 2017), 5.

11. Goldschmidt and Johnston, *Historical Dictionary of Egypt*, s.v. "Al-Banna, Hasan (1906–1949)" and s.v. "Al-Nuqrashi, Mahmud Fahmi (1988–1948)."

12. Rézette, *Les partis politiques marocains*, 306.

13. Eric Calderwood, *Colonial al-Andalus: Spain and the Making of Modern Moroccan Culture* (Cambridge, MA: Harvard University Press, 2018).

14. Yahia H. Zoubir, "Les États-Unis et le Maghreb: Primauté de la sécurité et marginalité de la démocratie," *L'Année du Maghreb* 2 (2005/6).

15. "Études et notes: Les États-Unis et le Maghreb," *Maghreb*, March–April 1965, 40–41.

16. Yahia H. Zoubir, "The United States and Morocco: The Long-Lasting Alliance," in *Handbook on US–Middle East Relations*, ed. Robert E. Looney (New York: Routledge, 2009), 238.

17. Bob Woodward, *Veil: The Secret Wars of the CIA, 1981–1987* (New York: Simon and Schuster, 2007), 299.

18. El-Mostafa Azzou, "Les relations entre le Maroc et Les Etats-Unis: Regards sur la période 1943–1970," *Guerres mondiales et conflits contemporains* 221 (2006): 113.

19. "Mapping the Black Sites," *PBS Frontline*, accessed 15 November 2013, http://www.pbs.org/frontlineworld/stories/rendition701/map; and "Morocco Attacked on US Rendition," *BBC News Online*, 28 September 2006, http://news.bbc.co.uk/2/hi/africa/5390646.stm.

20. "US Rewards Morocco for Terror Aid," BBC News, accessed 5 May 2018, http://news.bbc.co.uk/2/hi/africa/3776413.stm.

21. Jean-Pierre Bat, *La fabrique des barbouzes: Histoire des réseaux Foccart en Afrique* (Paris: Nouveau monde, 2015); and Pierre Pascalon, "Les aspects économiques de la politique tiers-mondiste du Général De Gaulle de 1962 à 1969," in *De Gaulle et le Tiers Monde: Actes Du Colloque*, ed. Institut Charles de Gaulle (Paris: A. Pedone, 1984), 189.

22. Vermeren, *La formation des élites marocaines et tunisiennes*, 101–220. Moreover, not only did Morocco request to join the European Union in 1987, but Mohammed VI even wrote a PhD thesis on the relationship between Europe and Morocco. Mohammed Ben El Hassan Alaoui [King Mohammed VI], *La Coopération entre l'Union Européenne et les Pays du Maghreb* (Paris: Editions Nathan, 1994).

23. Leveau, *Le fellah marocain*, 7.

24. Michael Willis and Nizar Messari, "Analyzing Moroccan Foreign Policy and Relations with Europe," *Review of International Affairs* 3, no. 2 (2003): 162–63.

25. The Economist Intelligence Unit, *Morocco: Country Profile 2008* (London: The Economist Intelligence Unit, 2008), 48.

26. Rocío Velasco de Castro. "Las relaciones hispano-marroquíes: Fronteras geográficas e ideológicas y su ambivalente papel en la Historia," in *Conflictos y cicatrices: Fronteras y migraciones en el mundo hispánico*, ed. A. Delgado Larios (Madrid: Dykinson, 2014), 197–98.

27. "Population Figures at 1 January 2015," Instituto Nacional de Estadística, 25 June 2015, http://www.ine.es/en/prensa/np917_en.pdf; Bernabé García López, "La evolución de la inmigración marroquí en España (1991–2003)," in *Atlas de la inmigración magrebí en España*, eds. B. García López and M. Berriane (Madrid: Ministerio de Trabajo y Asuntos Sociales & Universidad Autónoma de Madrid, 2004).

28. Kingdom of Morocco, "La constitution: Edition 2011," accessed 7 May 2018, http://www.sgg.gov.ma/Portals/0/constitution/constitution_2011_Fr.pdf.

29. The Economist Intelligence Unit, *Morocco: Country Report March 2018* (London: The Economist Intelligence Unit, 2018), 14.

30. "Agentes secretos marroquíes combaten a la yihad en España," *El País*, 4 January 2015, http://politica.elpais.com/politica/2014/12/29/actualidad/1419876499_947344.html.

31. "Tadshin ʿahd min al-tadamun wa-l-taʿawun," *al-ʿAlam*, 25 May 1956, 1.

32. Note pour le directeur général: Vues du Prince Moulay Hassan sur la situation actuelle en Méditerranée, summer 1956, 130SUP/239, AMAE.

33. Note sur les rélations entre le Maroc et l'Égypte de Nasser, 27 July 1957, 130SUP/239, AMAE.

34. Philippe Herreman, "Mohammed V au Moyen-Orient—une mission de bonne volonté," *Le Monde Diplomatique*, February 1960, 5; and Embassy Rabat to Department of State, 7 December 1959, RG 59/771.11/12-759, USNA.

35. US Department of State, *Foreign Relations of the United States, 1958–60*, vol. XIII, ed. John P. Glennon (Washington, DC: US Government Printing Office, 1992), 464.

36. For an example of the erroneous narrative of Moroccan-Egyptian solidarity throughout the anticolonial struggle, see "Maroc-Égypte: Nuage d'été," *Jeune Afrique*, 25 January 2015, 42–43.

37. For a study of Morocco's foreign policy toward sub-Saharan Africa during this period, see El Mellouki Riffi Bouhout, "La politique marocaine de coopération avec l'Afrique subsaharienne: 1960–1994," in *Le Maroc et l'Afrique après l'indépendance*, ed. Abdellah Saaf (Rabat, MA: Publications de l'Institut des Etudes Africaines—Université Mohammed V, 1996), 66–68.

38. Ambassadeur Pierre de Leusse à Rabat au Ministre des Affaires étrangères, 9 November 1964, 130SUP/240, AMAE.

39. George Joffé, "Sovereignty and the Western Sahara," *The Journal of North African Studies* 15, no. 3 (2010); and Stephen Zunes, "The United States and Morocco: The Sahara War and Regional Interests," *Arab Studies Quarterly* 9, no. 4 (1987).

40. A high-ranking Cuban official quoted in Piero Gleijeses, *Conflicting Missions: Havana, Washington, and Africa, 1959–1976* (Chapel Hill: University of North Carolina Press, 2003), 41.

41. Ambassadeur Pierre de Leusse à Rabat au Ministre des Affaires étrangères, 13 April 1964, 130SUP/240, AMAE; and "Salih Hishad . . . muhawalat inqilab Ufqir wa sijn tazmamart," *al-Jazeera*, 6 May 2009, https://www.youtube.com/watch?v=7eE3bBB6sjk.

42. John Damis, "Les relations des États-Unis avec le Maroc," *Maghreb-Machrek* 111 (January 1986): 10.

43. C. Richard Pennell, *Morocco Since 1830: A History* (New York: New York University Press, 2000), 343.

44. Werner K. Ruf, "La politique étrangère des états maghrébins," *Maghreb-Machrek* 59 (1973): 29.

45. Bruce Maddy-Weitzman, "Israel and Morocco: A Special Relationship," *The Maghreb Review* 21, nos. 1–2 (1996): 36–48. According to recent revelations, the Mossad even played a central role in the kidnapping and murder of Ben Barka in October 1965. "Révélations en Israël sur l'implication du Mossad dans l'affaire Ben Barka," *Le Monde*, 23 March 2015, http://www.lemonde.fr/international/article/2015/03/23/revelations-en-israel-sur-l-implication-dans-l-affaire-ben-Barka_4599477_3210.html#IAKGe4cVko4APVjz.99.

46. "Notre objectif: Établir une monarchie constitutionelle," *al-Istiqlal*, 23 November 1957, 10.

47. Hassan II, *The Challenge* (London: Macmillan, 1978), 169.

48. "The $20 Million Case for Morocco," *Foreign Affairs*, 25 February 2015, http://foreignpolicy.com/2014/02/25/the-20-million-case-for-morocco.

49. See, for example, Ann Marie Wainscott, *Bureaucratizing Islam: Morocco and the War on Terror* (New York: Cambridge University Press, 2017), 233; and Yassine Majdi et al., "Maroc vs. Polisario—la guerre souterraine," *Tel Quel*, 6 May 2016, 28–34.

50. "Notre diplomatie est-elle défaillante?—Interview avec Abderrahmane Mekkaoui et Bernabé Lopez García," *Zamane*, May 2013, 37.

51. Brousky, *La république de Sa Majesté*, 71–88.

52. Zeynep Tufekci, *Twitter and Tear Gas: The Power and Fragility of Networked Protest* (New Haven, CT: Yale University Press, 2017), xxvii.

53. Francis Fukuyama, "The Failures of the Facebook Generation in the Arab Spring," *The Daily Beast*, 21 May 2012, https://www.thedailybeast.com/the-failures-of-the-facebook-generation-in-the-arab-spring.

APPENDIX

1. Easley and Kleinberg, *Networks, Crowds, and Markets*, 73–78; and Lipton C. Freeman, "A Set of Measures of Centrality Based on Betweenness," *Sociometry* 40, no. 1 (1977).

BIBLIOGRAPHY

ARCHIVES
Morocco
Abdelkhaleq Torres Foundation, Tetouan (ATF)
Allal al-Fassi Foundation, Rabat (AFF)
Bennouna Family Archive, Tetouan (BFA)
Centre d'Etudes et de Recherches Mohamed Bensaid Aït Idder, Casablanca (CERMBAI)

France
Archives de la Préfecture de la Police, Paris (APP)
Archives du ministère des Affaires étrangères, La Courneuve (AMAE)
Archives nationales, Pierrefitte-sur-Seine (ANF)
Centre des archives diplomatiques, Nantes (CADN)
Centre François Mauriac, St-Maixant (CFMSM)
Centre d'histoire de Sciences-Po, Paris (CHSP)
Institut d'histoire du temps présent, Paris (IHTP)
Service historique de l'Armée de terre, Vincennes (SHAT)

Spain
Archivo General de la Administración, Alcalá de Henares (AGA)

United States
American Jewish Committee Information Center and Digital Archives
Central Intelligence Agency Freedom of Information Act Electronic Reading Room (CIA-ERR)
Dwight D. Eisenhower Presidential Library, Abilene, KS (DDEPL)

George Meany Memorial AFL-CIO Archives at the University of Maryland University Libraries, College Park, MD (GMA)
Holt-Atherton Special Collections at the University of the Pacific, Stockton, CA (HASC)
Special Collections Research Center at Syracuse University, Syracuse, NY (SCRC)
Library of Congress, Washington, DC (LOC)
Rodes Family Archive, Manchester, TN (RFA)
Department of Special Collections at the University of California–Santa Barbara, Santa Barbara, CA (UCSB)
United States National Archives, College Park, MD (USNA)

United Kingdom
United Kingdom National Archives, Kew (UKNA)

MAGAZINES AND NEWSPAPERS
al-'Alam (Rabat)
al-Hurriyya (Tetouan)
al-Istiqlal (Rabat)
al-Umma (Tetouan)
Aspects de la France (Paris)
Free Morocco (New York)
Harper's Magazine (New York)
Jeune Afrique (Paris)
Le Figaro (Paris)
Le Monde (Paris)
Le Monde diplomatique (Paris)
Los Angeles Times
Moroccan News Bulletin (New York)
New York Times
Paris (Casablanca)
Tel Quel (Casablanca)
The Sunday Herald (Sydney)
The Times (London)
Washington Post
Zamane (Casablanca)

PUBLISHED SOURCES
Ambassade de France. *Answer to Article by Justice William O. Douglas Published in Look Magazine, October 19, 1954*. New York: Service de Press et d'Information, October 1954.
Ambassade du Royaume du Maroc en France. *Bulletin Quotidien d'information*, no. 305. New York: Service de Presse et d'Infromation, 26 July 1962.
American Federation of Labor. "Report of Proceedings of the Annual Convention of the American Federation of Labor." Los Angeles, 1954.
Asia-Africa Speaks from Bandung. Djakarta: Ministry of Foreign Affairs of the Republic of Indonesia, 1955.
A.S.M.A.R. Conference "From Anfa to Aix-Les-Bains, 1943–1956: First International Conference Association for the Study of Moroccan-American Relations," Tangier, Morocco, 25–26 April 1978.

Burdett, Anita L. P. *Inauguration, 1944–1946*. Vol. 4 of *The Arab League: British Documentary Sources, 1943–1963*. London: Archive Editions, 1995.

Débats Parlementaires. *Journal Officiel de la République Française*, no. 29 (30 May 1956).

"Décret royal no 555-67 du 8 chaabane 1387 (11 novembre 1967) relatif à la composition et à l'organisation du Gouvernement," *Bulletin official du Royaume du Maroc*, no. 2872 (15 Novembre 1967).

The Economist Intelligence Unit. *Morocco: Country Profile 2008*. London: The Economist Intelligence Unit, 2008.

————. *Morocco: Country Report March 2018*. London: The Economist Intelligence Unit, 2018.

French Press and Information Service. *Toward a Federal Union: The French Solution of the Colonial Problem*. New York: St. Martin's Press, 1945.

Hizb al-Istiqlal. *Conférence de presse donnée par la délégation du Parti de l'Istiqlal à Paris le 30 août 1946*. Paris: Bureau de Documentation et d'Information du Parti de l'Istiqlal, 1946.

————. *Documents, 1944–46*. Paris: Bureau de Documentation et d'Information du Parti de l'Istiqlal, September 1946.

————. *Le mouvement national marocain—bref aperçu historique*. Paris: Bureau de Documentation et d'Information du Parti de l'Istiqlal, 1946.

————. *Mohammed Ben Youssef, the Popular King of Morocco*. New York: Moroccan Office of Information and Documentation, 1952.

————. *Morocco, before the Protectorate, under the Protectorate, Failure of the Protectorate*. New York: Moroccan Office of Information and Documentation, 1951.

————. *Morocco, Istiqlal Party Documents, 1944–1946*. Paris: Moroccan Office of Information and Documentation, 1946.

————. *Morocco under the Protectorate: Forty Years of French Administration. An Analysis of the Facts and Figures*. New York: Moroccan Office of Information and Documentation, 1953.

————. *XIXe anniversaire de l'accession au trône de Sa Majesté Mohammed V Roi du Maroc, 1927–1946*. Paris: Bureau de Documentation et d'Information du Parti de l'Istiqlal, 1946.

————. *Some Guiding Facts on the Problem of Morocco*. Washington, DC: Moroccan Office of Information and Documentation, 1951.

Jabhat al-Tahrir al-Qawmi. *The Peaceful Settlement of the Algerian Question*. The Algerian Delegation c/o Moroccan Office of Information and Documentation, 1955.

La Conférence africaine française, Brazzaville: 30 janvier 1944–8 février 1944. Paris: Ministère des Colonies, 1945.

Mathee, Mohamed Shahid, and Ph.-J. Salazar. "Mohammed V: The Tangiers Speech." *African Yearbook of Rhetoric* 2, no. 3 (2011): 19–25.

"Protectorate Treaty between France and Morocco—March 30, 1912," *The American Journal of International Law* 6, no. 3 (1912): 207–9.

"Treaty between France and Spain Regarding Morocco—November 27, 1912," *The American Journal of International Law* 7, no. 2 (1913): 81–99.

University of the Pacific. *The State Visit of His Majesty, King Mohammed V of Morocco to the College of the Pacific*. San Francisco: University of the Pacific, 1957.

US Department of State. *Foreign Relations of the United States, 1947*, vol. V, edited by S. Everett and Rogers P. Churchill. Washington, DC: US Government Printing Office, 1971.

————. *Foreign Relations of the United States, 1949*, volume VI, edited by Fredrick Aandahl and William Z. Slany. Washington, DC: US Government Printing Office, 1977.

————. *Foreign Relations of the United States, 1950*, vol. V, edited by Fredrick Aandahl and William Z. Slany. Washington, DC: US Government Printing Office, 1978.

———. *Foreign Relations of the United States, 1951*, vol. V, edited by William Z. Slany. Washington, DC: US Government Printing Office, 1982.

———. *Foreign Relations of the United States, 1952–54*, vol. III, edited by William Z. Slany. Washington, DC: US Government Printing Office, 1979.

———. *Foreign Relations of the United States, 1952–54*, vol. IX, pt. 1, edited by John P. Glennon. Washington, DC: US Government Printing Office, 1986.

———. *Foreign Relations of the United States, 1952–54*, vol. XI, pt. 1, edited by John P. Glennon. Washington, DC: US Government Printing Office, 1983.

———. *Foreign Relations of the United States, 1958–60*, vol. XIII, edited by John P. Glennon. Washington, DC: US Government Printing Office, 1992.

US Office of Strategic Services. *Morocco.* 2 vols. Washington, DC: Research and Analysis Branch, 1942.

Wizarat al-Tarbiyya al-Wataniyya [Ministry of National Education]. *Al-Jadid fi al-tarikh: Al-sanna al-thaniya min suluk bakaluriya.* Rabat, MA: Dar nashr al-maʻrifa, 2007.

BOOKS AND ARTICLES

Abitbol, Michel. *Histoire du Maroc.* Paris: Editions Perrin, 2009.

Abou-el-Fadel, Reem. "Early Pan-Arabism in Egypt's July Revolution: The Free Officers' Political Formation and Policy-Making, 1946–54." *Nations and Nationalism* 21, no. 2 (2015): 289–308.

Abu al-Fath, Ahmad. *L'affaire Nasser.* Paris: Plon, 1962.

Ageron, Charles-Robert. *La décolonisation française.* Paris: Armand Colin Éditeur, 1991.

———. "L'association des étudiants musulmans nord-africains en France durant l'entre-deux-guerres." *Revue française d'histoire d'outre-mer* 70, no. 258 (1983): 25–56.

Alaoui, Mohamed Ben El Hassan [King Mohamed VI]. *La Coopération entre l'Union Européenne et les Pays du Maghreb.* Paris: Editions Nathan, 1994.

Alaoui, Moulay Hicham el-. *Journal d'un prince banni—demain, le Maroc.* Paris: Bernard Grasset, 2014.

Algora Weber, María Dolores. *Las relaciones hispano-árabes durante el régimen de Franco: La ruptura del aislamiento internacional (1946–1950).* Madrid: Ministerio de Asuntos Exteriores, 1995.

Al Tuma, Ali. "Moros y Cristianos: Religious Aspects of the Participation of Moroccan Soldiers in the Spanish Civil War (1936–1939)." In *Muslims in Interwar Europe: A Transcultural Historical Perspective,* edited by Bekim Agai, Umar Ryad, and Mehdi Sajid, 151–77. Leiden, NL: Brill, 2016.

Aly Dieng, Amady. *Histoire des organisations d'étudiants africains en France (1900–1950).* Dakar: L'Harmattan-Sénégal, 2011.

Amin, Samir. *A Life Looking Forward.* New York: Zed Books, 2006.

Anderson, Carol. *Bourgeois Radicals: The NAACP and the Struggle for Colonial Liberation, 1941–1960.* New York: Cambridge University Press, 2015.

———. *Eyes Off the Prize: The United Nations and the African American Struggle for Human Rights, 1944–1955.* New York: Cambridge University Press, 2003.

Ansari, Mohammad Iqbal. *The Arab League, 1945–1955.* Aligarh, IN: Institute of Islamic Studies, Aligarh Muslim University, 1968.

Asseraf, Arthur. "Making Their Own Internationalism: Algerian Media and a Few Others the League of Nations Ignored, 1919–1943." In *International Organizations and the Media in the Nineteenth and Twentieth Centuries: Exorbitant Expectations,* edited by Jonas Brendebach, Martin Herzer, and Heidi J. S. Tworek, 117–37. London: Routledge, 2018.

Ayache, Albert. *Le mouvement syndical au Maroc.* 3 vols. Paris: L'Harmattan, 1982.

Aziza, Mimoun. *La sociedad rifeña frente al Protectorado español de Marruecos (1912–1956)*. Barcelona: Edicions Bellaterra, 2003.

Azzou, El-Mostafa. "La propagande des nationalistes marocains aux Etats-Unis (1945–1956)." *Guerres mondiales et conflits contemporains* 230, no. 2 (2008): 89–98.

———. "Les relations entre le Maroc et Les Etats-Unis: Regards sur la période 1943–1970." *Guerres mondiales et conflits contemporains* 221 (2006): 105–16.

Baïda, Jamaa. "Charles-Andre Julien et le nationalisme marocain." In *Empreintes, mélanges offerts à Jacques Levrat*, edited by Sylviane Noubecourt-El Kohen, 57–68. Rabat, MA: Al-Asas/La Source, 2000.

Barrat, Robert. *Justice pour le Maroc*. Paris: Editions du Seuil, 1953.

Bat, Jean-Pierre. *La fabrique des barbouzes : Histoire des réseaux Foccart en Afrique*. Paris: Nouveau monde, 2015.

Bekraoui, Mohammed. "Les étudiants marocains en France à l'époque du protectorat, 1927–1939." In *Présences et images franco-marocaines au temps du protectorat*, edited by Jean-Claude Allain, 89–111. Paris: L'Harmattan, 2003.

Beling, Willard A. "W.F.T.U. and Decolonisation: A Tunisian Case Study." *Journal of Modern African Studies* 2, no. 4 (1964): 551–64.

Ben Aboud, Mehdi. "American Policy and Moroccan Independence as Seen through the Moroccan Office in New York." Podium discussion, From Anfa to Aix-Les-Bains, 1943–1956, Tangier, Morocco, 25–26 April 1978.

Benjelloun, Abdelmajid. *Approches du colonialisme espagnol et du mouvement nationaliste marocain dans l'ex-Maroc Khalifien*. Rabat, MA: Okad, 1988.

———. *Le nord du Maroc—l'indépendance avant l'indépendance (Jean Rous et le Maroc, 1953–1956)*. Paris: L'Harmattan, 1996.

Bennouna, Mehdi A. "In the United States." Presentation at From Anfa to Aix-Les-Bains, 1943–1956: First International Conference Association for the Study of Moroccan-American Relations, Tangier, MA, 25–26 April, 1978.

———. *Our Morocco: The True Story of a Just Cause*. Morocco: 1951.

Bensalah Alaoui, Assia. *Moulay Ahmed Alaoui: La passion et le verbe*. Rabat, MA: Marsam, 2010.

Berger, Mark T. "After the Third World? History, Destiny and the Fate of Third Worldism." *Third World Quarterly* 25, no. 1 (2004): 9–39.

Bernard, Stéphane. *Le conflit franco-marocain, 1943–1956*, vol. 1, *Historique*. Bruxelles: Institut de sociologie, Université libre de Bruxelles, 1963.

Berque, Jacques. *Le Maghreb entre deux guerres*. Paris: Edition du Seuil, 1962.

Berstein, Serge, and Pierre Milza. *Histoire de la France au XXe siècle*, vol. 3, *1945–1958*. Bruxelles: Editions Complexe, 1991.

Beunza, José María Imízcoz, and Lara Arroyo Ruiz. "Redes sociales y correspondencia epistolar. Del análisis cualitativo de las relaciones personales a la reconstrucción de redes egocentradas." *REDES—Revista hispana para el análisis de redes sociales* 21, no. 2 (2011): 98–138.

Blair, Leon Borden. *Western Window in the Arab World*. Austin: University of Texas Press, 1970.

Bleuchot, Hervé. *Les libéraux français au Maroc, 1947–1955*. Aix-en-Provence, FR: Editions de l'Université de Provence, 1973.

Boissevain, Jeremy. *Friends of Friends. Networks, Manipulators and Coalitions*. Oxford: Basil Blackwell, 1974.

Borgwardt, Elizabeth. *A New Deal for the World: America's Vision for Human Rights*. Cambridge, MA: The Belknap Press, 2005.

Bouhout, El Mellouki Riffi. "La politique marocaine de coopération avec l'Afrique subsaharienne:

1960–1994." In *Le Maroc et l'Afrique après l'indépendance*, edited by Abdellah Saaf, 57–86. Rabat, MA: Publications de l'Institut des Etudes Africaines—Université Mohammed V, 1996.

Bourdieu, Pierre. "The Forms of Capital." In *Handbook of Theory and Research for the Sociology of Education*, edited by John Richardson, 241–58. New York: Greenwood, 1986.

Bradley, Mark Philip. "Decolonization, Revolutionary Nationalism, and the Cold War, 1919–1962." In *The Cambridge History of the Cold War*, edited by Melvyn P. Leffler and Odd Arne Westad, 464–85. New York: Cambridge University Press, 2009.

Brand, Laurie. "Nasir's Egypt and the Reemergence of the Palestinian National Movement." *Journal of Palestine Studies* 17, no. 2 (winter 1988): 29–45.

Brigham, Robert K. *Guerrilla Diplomacy—The NFL's Foreign Relations and the Viet Nam War*. Ithaca, NY: Cornell University Press, 1999.

Brousky, Omar. *La république de Sa Majesté: France-Maroc, liaisons dangereuses*. Paris: Nouveau Monde Editions, 2017.

Buchanan, Andrew. *American Grand Strategy in the Mediterranean during World War II*. New York: Cambridge University Press, 2013.

Burt, Ronald S. *Brokerage and Closure*. New York: Oxford University Press, 2005.

———. "The Network Structure of Social Capital." *Research in Organizational Studies* 22 (2000): 345–423.

———. "Structural Holes and Good Ideas." *American Journal of Sociology* 110, no. 2 (2004): 349–99.

———. *Structural Holes: The Social Structure of Competition*. Cambridge, MA: Harvard University Press, 1992.

Buskens, Vincent, and Arnout van de Rijt. "Dynamics of Networks If Everyone Strives for Structural Holes." *American Journal of Sociology* 114, no. 2 (2009): 371–407.

Byrne, Jeffrey James. "Beyond Continents, Colours, and the Cold War: Yugoslavia, Algeria, and the Struggle for Non-Alignment." *The International History Review* 37, no. 5 (2015): 912–32.

———. *Mecca of Revolution: Algeria, Decolonization, and the Third World Order*. New York: Oxford University Press, 2016.

Calderwood, Eric. *Colonial al-Andalus: Spain and the Making of Modern Moroccan Culture*. Cambridge, MA: Harvard University Press, 2018.

———. "Franco's Hajj: Moroccan Pilgrims, Spanish Fascism, and the Unexpected Journeys of Modern Arabic Literature." *PMLA* 132, no. 5 (2017): 1097–116.

Carlson, John Roy. *Cairo to Damascus*. New York: Knopf, 1951.

Chamberlin, Paul Thomas. *The Global Offensive: The United States, the Palestine Liberation Organization, and the Making of the Post–Cold War Order*. New York: Oxford University Press, 2012.

Cline, Walter B. "Nationalism in Morocco." *Middle East Journal* 1 (1947): 18–28.

Coleman, James S. *Foundations of Social Theory*. Cambridge, MA: Belknap Press, 1990.

———. "Social Capital in the Creation of Human Capital." *American Journal of Sociology* 94, no. 1 (1988): 95–120.

Connelly, Matthew. *A Diplomatic Revolution—Algeria's Fight and the Origins of the Post–Cold War Era*. New York: Oxford University Press, 2002.

Coon, Carleton S. *A North Africa Story: The Anthropologist as OSS Agent, 1941–1943*. Ipswich, MA: Gambit, 1980.

Cooper, Frederick. *Citizenship between Empire and Nation: Remaking France and French Africa, 1945–1960*. Princeton, NJ: Princeton University Press, 2014.

Crowl, Samuel E. "Indonesia's Diplomatic Revolution: Lining Up for Non-Alignment, 1945–1955." In *Connecting Histories: Decolonization and the Cold War in Southeast Asia, 1945–1962*, edited by Christopher E. Goscha and Christian F. Ostermann, 238–57. Stanford, CA: Stanford University Press, 2009.

Dabous, Sonia. "Nasser and the Egyptian Press." In *Contemporary Egypt: Through Egyptian Eyes*, edited by Charles Tripp, 100–121. New York: Routledge, 1993.

Damis, John. "Les relations des États-Unis avec le Maroc." *Maghreb-Machrek* 111 (January 1986): 5–23.

Daoud, Zakya, and Maâti Monjib. *Ben Barka*. Paris: Editions Michalon, 1996.

Darwin, John. "Decolonization and the End of Empire." In *The Oxford History of the British Empire*, edited by Robin W. Winks and Alaine Low, vol. 5, 541–77. New York: Oxford University Press, 1999.

Dawisha, Adeed. "Egypt." In *The Cold War and the Middle East*, edited by Yezid Sayigh and Avi Shlaim, 27–47. Oxford: Clarendon Press, 1997.

———. *Iraq: A Political History from Independence to Occupation*. Princeton, NJ: Princeton University Press, 2009.

Dekmejian, R. Hrair. *Egypt under Nasir*. Albany: SUNY Press, 1971.

Delanoë, Guy. *La résistance marocaine et le mouvement "conscience française."* Paris: L'Harmattan, 1991.

Deschamps, Hubert Jules. *The French Union: History, Institutions, Economy, Countries and Peoples, Social and Political Changes*. Paris: Berger-Levrault, 1956.

Dewitte, Philippe. "Intellectuels et étudiants africains à Paris à la veille des indépendances (1945–1960)." In *Le Paris des étrangèrs depuis 1945*, edited by Antoine Marès and Pierre Milza, 319–42. Paris: Publications de la Sorbonne, 1994.

Diani, Mario. "'Leaders' or Brokers? Positions and Influence in Social Movement Networks." In *Social Movements and Networks: Relational Approaches to Collective Action*, edited by Mario Diani and Doug McAdam, 105–22. New York: Oxford University Press, 2003.

Dib, Fathi. *Abdel Nasser et la révolution algérienne*. Paris: L'Harmattan, 1985.

Douglas, William O. "The French Are Facing Disaster Again in Morocco." *Look* 18, no. 21 (19 October 1954): 33–37.

Duara, Prasenjit. "The Cold War as a Historical Period: An Interpretive Essay." *Journal of Global History* 6, no. 3 (2011): 457–80.

Düring, Marten. *Verdeckte Soziale Netzwerke im Nationalsozialismus. Berliner Hilfsnetzwerke Für Verfolgte Juden*. Berlin: De Gruyter, 2015.

Düring, Marten, Matthias Bixler, Michael Kronenwett, and Martin Stark. "VennMaker for Historians: Sources, Social Networks and Software." *REDES—Revista hispana para el análisis de redes sociales* 21, no. 2 (2011): 388–452.

Düring, Marten, Ulrich Eumann, Martin Stark, and Linda von Keyserlingk, eds. *Handbuch Historische Netzwerkforschung—Grundlagen und Anwendungen*. Berlin: LIT, 2016.

Düring, Marten, and Linda Keyserlingk. "Netzwerkanalyse in den Geschichtswissenschaften. Historische Netzwerkanalyse als Methode für die Erforschung von historischen Prozessen." In *Prozesse—Formen, Dynamiken, Erklärungen*, edited by Rainer Schützeichel and Stefan Jordan, 337–50. Wiesbaden, DE: VS Verlag für Sozialwissenschaften, 2012.

Easley, David, and Jon Kleinberg. *Networks, Crowds, and Markets: Reasoning about a Highly Connected World*. New York: Cambridge University Press, 2010.

Elgey, Georgette. *Histoire de la IVe République: La république des contradictions (1951–1954)*. Paris: Fayard, 1993.

El Machat, Samya. *Les Etats-Unis et le Maroc: Le choix stratégique, 1945–1959*. Paris: L'Harmattan, 1996.

———. "L'improbable 'Nation arabe.' La Ligue des États arabes et l'indépendance du Maghreb (1945–1956)." *Vingtième Siècle* 82 (2004): 57–68.

el Merroun, Mustapha. *Las tropas marroquíes en la guerra civil española, 1936–1939.* Madrid: Almena, 2003.

Eppel, Michael. "The Elite, the Effendiyya, and the Growth of Nationalism and Pan-Arabism in Hashemite Iraq, 1921–1958." *International Journal of Middle East Studies* 30, no. 2 (1998): 227–50.

Epton, Nina. *Journey under the Crescent Moon.* London: Victor Gollancz, 1949.

al-Fasi, 'Allal. *Al-Harakat al-istiqlaliyya fi al-Maghrib al-'arabi.* Cairo: Maktab al-Maghrib al-'Arabi, 1948.

———. *Nida al-Qahira.* Morocco, 1959.

al-Fassi, Allal. See al-Fasi, 'Allal.

Faure, Romain. *Netzwerke der Kulturdiplomatie—die internationale Schulbuchrevision in Europa 1945–1989.* Berlin: De Gruyter Oldenbourg, 2015.

Fichter, Michael. *Besatzungsmacht und Gewerkschaften: Zur Entwicklung und Anwendung der US-Gewerkschaftspolitik in Deutschland, 1944–1948.* Opladen, DE: Westdeutscher Verlag, 1982.

Figueras, Tomás García. *Marruecos: La acción de España en el norte de Africa.* Madrid: Ediciones Fe, 1939.

Forst, Robert D. "The Origins and Early Development of the Union Marocaine Du Travail." *International Journal of Middle East Studies* 7, no. 2 (1976): 271–87.

Freeman, Linton C. "A Set of Measures of Centrality Based on Betweenness." *Sociometry* 40, no. 1 (1977): 35–41.

García López, Bernabé. "La evolución de la inmigración marroquí en España (1991–2003)." In *Atlas de la inmigración magrebí en España,* edited by B. García López and M. Berriane, 213–21. Madrid: Ministerio de Trabajo y Asuntos Sociales & Universidad Autónoma de Madrid, 2004.

Gellner, Ernest. "Review: Morocco Independent under Mohammed V." *Middle East Journal* 17, no. 1/2 (1963): 174–75.

Ghallab, 'Abd al-Karim. *Tarikh al-haraka al-wataniyya bi-l-Maghrib.* Vol. 1. Casablanca, MA: Matba'at al-najah al-jadida, 2000.

Ghallab, Abdelkarim. See Ghallab, 'Abd al-Karim

Gharib, 'Issam. *'Abd al-Rahman 'Azzam: Al-Islam—Al-'Uruba—Al-Wataniyya.* Cairo: Matba'at Dar al-kutub wa-l-watha'iq al-qawmiyya bi-l-Qahira, 2011.

Gleijeses, Piero. *Conflicting Missions: Havana, Washington, and Africa, 1959–1976.* Chapel Hill: University of North Carolina Press, 2003.

———. *Visions of Freedom: Havana, Washington, Pretoria, and the Struggle for Southern Africa, 1976–1991.* Chapel Hill: University of North Carolina Press, 2013.

Goebel, Michael. *Anti-Imperial Metropolis: Interwar Paris and the Seeds of Third World Nationalism.* New York: Cambridge University Press, 2017.

Goethem, Geert Van, and Robert Anthony Waters, eds. *American Labor's Global Ambassadors: The International History of the AFL-CIO during the Cold War.* New York: Palgrave Macmillan, 2013.

Goldschmidt, Arthur, and Robert Johnston. *Historical Dictionary of Egypt.* Lanham, MD: Scarecrow Press, 2003.

Gomaa, Ahmed M. *The Foundation of the League of Arab States: Wartime Diplomacy and Inter-Arab Politics, 1941 to 1945.* London: Longman, 1977.

González Alcantud, José Antonio. *El mito de al Ándalus: Orígenes y actualidad de un ideal cultural.* Córdoba: Almuzara, 2014.

González González, Irene. "La 'hermandad hispano-árabe' en la política cultural del franquismo (1936–1956)." *Anales de Historia Contemporánea* 23 (2007): 183–97.

Gordon, Joel. *Nasser: Hero of the Arab Nation.* Oxford, UK: Oneworld, 2006.

———. *Nasser's Blessed Movement.* New York: Oxford University Press, 1992.

Gould, Roger, and Roberto Fernández. "Structures of Mediation: A Formal Approach to Brokerage in Transaction Networks." *Social Methodology* 19 (1989): 89–126.

Granovetter, Mark S. "Economic Action and Social Structure: The Problem of Embeddedness." *American Journal of Sociology* 91, no. 3 (1985): 481–510.

———. "The Strength of Weak Ties." *American Journal of Sociology* 78, no. 6 (1973): 1360–80.

Haj, Samira. *The Making of Iraq, 1900–1963: Capital, Power, and Ideology.* Albany: State University of New York Press, 1997.

Hajji, Muhammad, ed. *Maʿalamat al-Maghrib* (Encyclopédie du Maroc). Salé, MA: Matabiʿa Sala, 2003.

Halstead, John P. *Rebirth of a Nation: The Origins and Rise of Moroccan Nationalism, 1912–1944.* Cambridge, MA: Harvard Middle Eastern Monographs, 1967.

Harders, Cilja. "Dimensionen des Netzwerkansatzes—Einführende theoretische Überlegungen." In *Die Islamische Welt als Netzwerk,* edited by Roman Loimeier, 17–52. Würzburg, DE: Ergon, 2000.

Hassan II. *The Challenge.* London: Macmillan, 1978.

Hoisington, William A. *The Casablanca Connection: French Colonial Policy, 1936–1943.* Chapel Hill: University of North Carolina Press, 1984.

Hopkins, A. G. "Rethinking Decolonization." *Past & Present* 200 (2008): 211–47.

Horne, Alistair. *A Savage War of Peace: Algeria 1954–62.* New York: New York Review of Books, 2006.

Howard, Adam M. *Sewing the Fabric of Statehood: Garment Unions, American Labor, and the Establishment of the State of Israel.* Urbana: University of Illinois Press, 2018.

Ibn ʿAbbud, Mʾhammad. *Al-Nidal al-watani li-l-shahid Mʾhammad bin ʿAbbud fi al-Mashriq: Shahadat wa wathaʾiq.* Tetouan, MA: Manshurat jamaʿiyyat Titwan Asmir, 1997.

———. *Maktab al-Maghrib al-ʿArabi fi al-Qahira—Dirasat wa wathaʾiq.* Rabat, MA: Manshurat Ukaz, 1991.

———. *Murasalat al-shahid Mʾhammad Ahmad bin ʿAbbud, 1946–1949.* Tetouan, MA: Matbaʿat Titwan, 2016.

Iglesias, Daniel. *Du pain et de la liberté: Socio-histoire des partis populaires apristes (Pérou, Venezuela, 1920–1962).* Villeneuve d'Ascq, FR: Press Universitaires du Septentrion, 2015.

Ikeda, Ryo. *The Imperialism of French Decolonization—French Policy and the Anglo-American Response in Tunisia and Morocco.* New York: Palgrave Macmillan, 2015.

Immermann, Richard H., and Petra Goedde, eds. Introduction to *The Oxford Handbook of the Cold War,* 1–13. New York: Oxford University Press, 2013.

Irwin, Ryan M. *Gordian Knot: Apartheid and the Unmaking of the Liberal World Order.* New York: Oxford University Press, 2012.

Jamali, Mohammed Fadhel. *Inside the Arab Nationalist Struggle: Memoirs of an Iraqi Statesman.* New York: I. B. Tauris, 2012.

James, Laura M. "Whose Voice? Nasser, the Arabs, and 'Sawt al-Arab' Radio." *Transnational Broadcasting Journal* 16 (2006).

Jankowski, James P. "Arab Nationalism in 'Nasserism' and Egyptian State Policy, 1952–1958." In *Rethinking Nationalism in the Arab Middle East,* edited by James Jankowski and Israel Gershoni, 150–68. New York: Columbia University Press, 1997.

———. *Nasser's Egypt, Arab Nationalism, and the United Arab Republic.* Boulder, CO: Lynne Rienner, 2002.

Jansen, Jan C., and Jürgen Osterhammel. *Dekolonisation—das Ender der Imperien.* München: Beck, 2013.

Joffé, George. "The Moroccan Nationalist Movement: Istiqlal, the Sultan, and the Country." *Journal of African History* 26, no. 4 (1985): 289–308.

———. "Sovereignty and the Western Sahara." *The Journal of North African Studies* 15, no. 3 (2010): 375–84.

Jonas, Gilbert. "The Student Federalist Movement." In *American Students Organize: Founding the National Student Association after World War II*, edited by Eugene G. Schwartz, 761–76. Westport, CT: American Council on Education/Praeger, 2006.

Julien, Charles-André. *L'Afrique Du Nord en marche: Algérie-Tunisie-Maroc, 1880–1952.* Paris: Omnibus, 2002 [1953].

———. *Le Maroc face aux impérialismes: 1415–1956.* Paris: Les éditions du Jaguar, 2011 [1978].

Kahn, Ely J. *The Big Drink: The Story of Coca-Cola.* New York: Random House, 1960.

Kalter, Christoph. *The Discovery of the Third World: Decolonization and the Rise of the New Left in France, c. 1950–1976.* New York: Cambridge University Press, 2016.

Keck, Margaret E., and Kathryn Sikkink. *Activists Beyond Borders—Advocacy Networks in International Politics.* Ithaca, NY: Cornell University Press, 1998.

Kenbib, Mohammed. "L'impact américain sur le nationalisme Marocain (1930–1947)." *Hespéris Tamuda* 26/27 (1988): 202–23.

Kerr, Malcolm H. *The Arab Cold War: Gamal Abd al-Nasir and His Rivals, 1958–1970.* New York: Oxford University Press, 1971.

Khatib, Toumader. *Culture et politique dans le mouvement nationaliste marocain au Machreq.* Tetouan, MA: Association Tetouan-Asmir, 1996.

Kogelmann, Franz. "Muhammad al-Makki an-Nasiri alias Sindbad der Seefahrer—Networking eines marokkanischen Nationalisten in den dreißiger Jahren des 20. Jahrhunderts." In *Die Islamische Welt als Netzwerk,* edited by Roman Loimeier, 257–86. Würzburg, DE: Ergon, 2000.

Kuisel, Richard F. "Coca-Cola and the Cold War: The French Face Americanization, 1948–1953." *French Historical Studies* 17, no. 1 (1991): 96–116.

Lacouture, Jean. *François Mauriac.* Paris: Editions du Seuil, 1980.

———. *Gamal Abdel Nasser.* Paris: Bayard, 2005.

Lacouture, Jean, and Simonne Lacouture. *Le Maroc à l'épreuve.* Paris: Editions du Seuil, 1958.

Lacroix-Riz, Annie. "Autour d'Irving Brown: l'A.F.L., le Free Trade Union Committee le Département d'État et la scission syndicale française (1944–1947)." *Le Mouvement social* 151 (1990): 79–118.

———. *Les protectorats d'Afrique du Nord, entre la France et Washington: Du débarquement à l'indépendance, Maroc et Tunisie 1942–1956.* Paris: L'Harmattan, 1988.

Laissy, Michel. *Du panarabisme à la Ligue Arabe.* Paris: G. P. Maisonneuve, 1948.

Landau, Rom. *Among the Americans.* London: Hale, 1953.

———. *France and the Arabs.* Toronto: Canadian Institute of International Affairs, 1954.

———. *Invitation to Morocco.* London: Faber and Faber, 1950.

———. "The Lobby that Runs North Africa." *America* 88, no. 14 (3 January 1953): 371–72.

———. *Moroccan Drama, 1900–1955* (Gateshead on Tyne, UK: Northumberland Press Ltd., 1956).

———. "Morocco." *International Conciliation,* no. 477 (January 1952): 311–59.

———. *Morocco Independent under Mohammed V.* London: Allen & Unwin, 1961.

———. *Personalia.* London: Faber and Faber, 1949.

———. "The Problem of Morocco." *America* 87, no. 2 (12 April 1952): 39–41.

———. *The Sultan of Morocco*. London: R. Hale, 1951.

Laron, Guy. "Semi-Peripheral Countries and the Invention of the 'Third World,' 1955–65." *Third World Quarterly* 35, no. 9 (2014): 1547–65.

Larramendi Martínez, Miguel Hernando de, Irene González, and Bárbara Azaola Piazza et al., "El Ministerio de Asuntos Exteriores y la política exterior hacia el Magreb." In *La política interior Española hacia el Magreb: Actors e intereses*, edited by Miguel Hernando de Larramendi Martínez and Aurelia Mañé Estrada, 61–87. Barcelona: Editorial Arual, 2009.

Laszewski Jenison, Denise. "'American Citizens of Arabic-Speaking Stock': The Institute of Arab-American Affairs and Questions of Identity in the Debate over Palestine." In *New Horizons of Muslim Diaspora in North America and Europe,* edited by Moha Ennaji, 35–51. New York: Palgrave Macmillan, 2016.

Laubadère, André de. "Le statut international du Maroc depuis 1955." *Annuaire français de droit international* 2 (1956): 122–49.

Lee, Christopher J. "At the Rendezvous of Decolonization: The Final Communiqué of the Asian-African Conference, Bandung, Indonesia, 18–24 April 1955." *Interventions* 11, no. 1 (2009): 81–93.

Le Gall, André. *Mauriac politique*. Paris: L'Harmattan, 2017.

Lemercier, Claire. "Formal Network Methods in History: Why and How?" In *Social Networks, Political Institutions, and Rural Societies*, edited by Georg Fertig, 281–310. Turnhout, BE: Brepols, 2015.

Leveau, Remy. *Le fellah marocain, défenseur du trône*. Paris: PFNSP, 1985.

Lin, Nan. "Building a Network Theory of Social Capital." *Connections* 22, no. 1 (1999): 28–51.

———. *Social Capital—A Theory of Social Structure and Action*. New York: Cambridge University Press, 2001.

Loimeier, Roman, and Stefan Reichmuth. "Zur Dynamik religiös-politischer Netzwerke in muslimischen Gesellschaften." *Die Welt des Islams* 36, no. 2 (1996): 145–85.

Losurdo, Domenico. *Liberalism: A Counter History*. New York: Verso, 2011.

Luard, Evan. *A History of the United Nations*, vol. 2, *The Age of Decolonization, 1955–1965*. Palgrave: New York, 1989.

Madariaga, María Rosa de. *Abd-el-Krim el Jatabi: La lucha por la independencia*. Madrid: Alianza Editorial, 2009.

———. *Los moros que trajo Franco: La intervención de tropas coloniales en la guerra civil española*. Barcelona: Ediciones Martínez Roca, 2002.

Maddy-Weitzman, Bruce. "Israel and Morocco: A Special Relationship." *The Maghreb Review* 21, nos. 1–2 (1996): 36–48.

Maldidier, Brigitte Christine. "The United States and Morocco, 1945–1953." Master's thesis, Stanford University, 1955.

Manela, Erez. *The Wilsonian Moment: Self-Determination and the International Origins of Anticolonial Nationalism*. New York: Oxford University Press, 2007.

Mantena, Karuna. "The Crisis of Liberal Imperialism." *histoirepolitique* 11 (2010): 1–24.

Martin-Márquez, Susan. *Disorientations: Spanish Colonialism in Africa and the Performance of Identity*. New Haven, CT: Yale University Press, 2008.

al-Masari, Muhammad al-ʿArabi. *Al-Maghrib kharij siyaj al-himaya*. Rabat, MA: Manshurat ʿAkath, 2012.

Mateo Dieste, Josep Lluís. *La "hermandad" hispano-marroquí: Política y religión bajo el Protectorado español en Marruecos, 1912–1956*. Barcelona: Edicions Bellaterra, 2003.

Mathiot, André. *Les Territoires non autonomes et la charte des Nations Unies*. Paris: Librairie générale de droit et de jurisprudence, 1949.

Mazower, Mark. *No Enchanted Palace: The End of Empire and the Ideological Origins of the United Nations*. Princeton, NJ: Princeton University Press, 2009.

Mbarek, Zaki. *Résistance et armée de libération: Portée politique, liquidation, 1953–1958*. Casablanca, MA: MBC, 1987.

McAdam, Doug. *Political Process and the Development of Black Insurgency, 1930–1970*. Chicago: University of Chicago Press, 1999.

McCann, Gerard. "From Diaspora to Third Worldism and the United Nations: India and the Politics of Decolonizing Africa." *Past and Present* 218, suppl. 8 (2013): 258–80.

McDougall, James. *History and the Culture of Nationalism in Algeria*. New York: Cambridge University Press, 2006.

McMahon, Robert J., ed. *The Cold War in the Third World*. New York: Oxford University Press, 2013.

Mehta, Uday Singh. *Liberalism and Empire: A Study in Nineteenth Century British Liberal Thought*. Chicago: University of Chicago Press, 1999.

Miller, Rory. "Sinning? The Case of the Arab Office, Washington, 1945–1948." *Diplomacy & Statecraft* 15 (2004): 303–25.

Miller, Susan G. *A History of Modern Morocco*. New York: Cambridge University Press, 2013.

Mische, Ann. *Partisan Publics: Communication and Contention across Brazilian Youth Activist Networks*. Princeton, NJ: Princeton University Press, 2009.

Mitchell, J. Clyde. "Networks, Norms, and Institutions." In *Network Analysis*, edited by Jeremy Boissevain and J. Clyde Mitchell, 15–35. The Hague: Mouton, 1973.

Mitchell, Richard P. *The Society of the Muslim Brothers*. London: Oxford University Press, 1969.

Monjib, Maâti. *La monarchie marocaine et la lutte pour le pouvoir: Hassan II face à l'opposition nationale, de l'indépendance à l'état d'exception*. Paris: L'Harmattan, 1992.

Montagne, Robert. *Révolution au Maroc*. Paris: Editions France Empire, 1953.

Morgan, Ted. *A Covert Life: Jay Lovestone, Communist, Anti-Communist, and Spymaster*. New York: Random House, 1999.

Moyn, Samuel. *The Last Utopia—Human Rights in History*. Cambridge, MA: Belknap Press, 2010.

Murphy, Bruce. *Wild Bill: The Legend and Life of William O. Douglas*. New York: Random House, 2003.

Muschik, Eva-Maria. "Managing the World: The United Nations, Decolonization, and the Strange Triumph of State Sovereignty in the 1950s and 1960s." *Journal of Global History* 13, no. 1 (2018): 121–44.

Nasser, Gamal Abdel. *The Philosophy of the Revolution*. Cairo: Mondiale Press, 1955 [1953].

Neville-Bagot, G. H. "Muslim Solidarity at the United Nations Organization in Support of Moroccan Independence." *The Islamic Review* (February 1952): 14–18.

Nutting, Anthony. *Nasser*. London: Constable, 1972.

Oved, Georges. *La gauche française et le nationalisme marocain, 1905–1955*, vol. 2, *Tentations et limites du réformisme colonial*. Paris: L'Harmattan, 1984.

Pappé, Ilan. *The Rise and Fall of a Palestinian Dynasty: The Husaynis, 1700–1948*. Berkeley: University of California Press, 2010.

Parent, Pierre. *Causerie sur le Maroc de 1951*. Toulouse, FR: Imprimerie regionale, 1951.

———. *Dissertation on Morocco of 1951*. Flushing, NY: Moroccan Office of Information and Documentation, 1952.

———. *Expolsé du Maroc*. Toulouse, FR: Imprimerie régionale, 1955.

———. *La politique indigène au Maroc*. Rabat, MA: Imprimerie nouvelle, n.d.

———. *Le problème marocain en 1949*. Toulouse, FR: Imprimerie régionale, 1949.

———. *Les Marocains et nous*. Rabat, MA: Imprimerie nouvelle, 1933.

———. *Maroc 1948*. Toulouse, FR: Imprimerie régionale, 1948.

Parker, Jason. *Hearts, Minds, Voices: U.S. Cold War Public Diplomacy and the Formation of the Third World*. New York: Oxford University Press, 2016.

Parrott, R. Joseph. "A Luta Continua: Radical Filmmaking, Pan-African Liberation and Communal Empowerment." *Race & Class* 57, no. 1 (2015): 20–38.

Pascal, Cristofoli. "Aux sources des grands réseaux d'interactions—Retour sur quelques propriétés déterminantes des réseaux sociaux issus de corpus documentaires." *Réseaux* 152 (2008): 21–58.

Pascalon, Pierre. "Les aspects économiques de la politique tiers-mondiste du Général De Gaulle de 1962 à 1969." In *De Gaulle et le Tiers Monde: Actes Du Colloque*, edited by Institut Charles de Gaulle, 167–99. Paris: A. Pedone, 1984.

Pearson, Jessica Lynne. "Defending Empire at the United Nations: The Politics of International Colonial Oversight in the Era of Decolonisation." *The Journal of Imperial and Commonwealth History* 45, no. 3 (2017): 525–49.

Pedersen, Susan. *The Guardians: The League of Nations and the Crisis of Empire*. New York: Oxford University Press, 2015.

Pendar, Kenneth. *Adventure in Diplomacy: Our French Dilemma*. New York: Dodd & Mead, 1945.

Pennell, C. Richard. *A Country with a Government and a Flag: The Rif War in Morocco, 1921–1926*. Boulder, CO: Lynne Rienner, 1986.

———. *Morocco Since 1830: A History*. New York: New York University Press, 2000.

Perkins, Kenneth J. "North African Propaganda and the United States, 1946–1956." *African Studies Review* 19, no. 3 (1976): 65–77.

Pitts, Jennifer. *A Turn to Empire: The Rise of Imperial Liberalism in Britain and France*. Princeton, NJ: Princeton University Press, 2005.

Podeh, Elie. *The Quest for Hegemony in the Arab World*. Leiden, NL: E. J. Brill, 1995.

Popkin, Jeremy D. *A History of Modern France*. Upper Saddle River, NJ: Prentice Hall, 2006.

Prados, John. "The CIA and the Face of Decolonization." In *The Eisenhower Administration, the Third World, and the Globalization of the Cold War*, edited by Kathryn C. Statler, 27–46. Lanham, MD: Rowman & Littlefield, 2006.

Prashad, Vijay. *The Darker Nations: A People's History of the Third World*. New York: The New Press, 2007.

Radosh, Ronald. *American Labor and United States Foreign Policy*. New York: Random House, 1969.

al-Rashid. Idris. *Dhikriyat 'an Maktab al-Maghrib al-'Arabi fi al-Qahira*. Tunis, TN: Al-Dar al-'arabiyya li-l-kitab, 1981.

Rézette, Robert. *Les partis politiques marocains*. Paris: A. Colin, 1955.

Rivet, Daniel. "Conscientes inquiètes, militants politiques et experts coloniaux: Des intellectuels face à la crise franco-marocaine (décembre 1952–fin 1954)." In *Le Comité France-Maghreb: Réseaux intellectuels et d'influence face à la crise marocaine (1952–1955)*, edited by Daniel Rivet, 11–43. Paris: Les Cahiers de l'IHTP, 1997.

Rivlin, Benjamin. "Context and Sources of Political Tensions in French North Africa." *The Annals of the American Academy of Political and Social Science* 298 (1955): 109–16.

———. "Morocco, Domestic or World Issue." *Foreign Policy Bulletin* 33, no. 4 (1953): 1–3.

———. "The Tunisian Nationalist Movement: Four Decades of Evolution." *The Middle East Journal* 6, no. 2 (1952): 167–93.

———. "The United States and Moroccan International Status, 1943–1956: A Contributory Factor in Morocco's Reassertion of Independence from France." *International Journal of African Historical Studies* 15, no. 1 (1982): 64–82.

———. "Unity and Nationalism in Libya." *The Middle East Journal* 3, no. 1 (1949): 31–44.

Rodes, Marjorie. *The Real Ruler of Morocco*. New York: Johnnie Walker Press, 1954.

———. *The United States and the French-Moroccan Problem: The Other Side*. New York: Free Trade Union Committee of the American Federation of Labor, 1954.

Rollinger, Christian, Marten Düring, Robert Gramsch-Stehfest, and Martin Stark. "Editors Introduction," *Journal of Historical Network Research* 1 (2017): i–vii.

Roosevelt, Eleanor. *On My Own*. New York: First Da Capo Press, 1992.

Ruf, Werner K. "La politique étrangère des états maghrébins." *Maghreb-Machrek* 59 (1973): 22–33.

Sangmuah, Egya N. "Interest Groups and Decolonization: American Business and Labor in Morocco, 1948–1956." *The Maghreb Review* 13, nos. 3–4 (1988): 161–74.

———. "The United States and the French Empire in North Africa, 1946–1956: Decolonization in the Age of Containment." PhD diss., University of Toronto, 1989.

Saunders, Chris. "Namibian Solidarity: British Support for Namibian Independence." *Journal of Southern African Studies* 35, no. 2 (2009): 437–54.

Schaar, Stuart H. *The Mass Media in Morocco: In Morocco Information Still Travels Best by Word of Mouth*. New York: American Universities Field Staff, 1968.

Schaufelbuehl, Janick Marina, Sandra Bott, Jussi Hanhimäki, and Marco Wyss. "Non-Alignment, the Third Force, or Fence-Sitting: Independent Pathways in the Cold War." *The International History Review* 37, no. 5 (2015): 901–11.

Schayegh, Cyrus. "The Expanding Overlap of Imperial, International, and Transnational Political Activities, 1920s–1930s: A Belgian Case Study." *International Politics* (2017): 1–21.

———. "1958 Reconsidered: State Formation and the Cold War in the Early Postcolonial Arab Middle East." *International Journal of Middle East Studies* 45, no. 3 (2013): 421–43.

Schuman, Robert. "Nécessité d'une politique," *Maroc et Tunisie, le problème du protectorat*. Paris: Cahier No. 2—La Nef, March 1953.

Seale, Patrick. *The Struggle for Syria: A Study of Post-War Arab Politics, 1945–1958*. London: I. B. Tauris, 1986.

Shepard, Todd. *The Invention of Decolonization: The Algerian War and the Remaking of France*. Ithaca, NY: Cornell University Press, 2006.

Simmel, Georg. *Soziologie—Untersuchungen über die Formen der Vergesellschaftung*. Berlin: Duncker & Humblot, 1908.

Skinner, Rob. *The Foundations of Anti-Apartheid: Liberal Humanitarians and Transnational Activists in Britain and the United States, c. 1919–64*. New York: Palgrave Macmillan, 2010.

Slate, Nico. *Colored Cosmopolitanism: The Shared Struggle for Freedom in the United States and India*. Cambridge, MA: Harvard University Press, 2012.

Sluglett, Peter, and Marion Farouk-Sluglett. *Iraq Since 1958: From Revolution to Dictatorship*. New York: I. B. Tauris, 1996.

Smith, Tony. "New Bottles for New Wine: A Pericentric Framework for the Study of the Cold War." *Diplomatic History* 24, no. 4 (2000): 567–91.

———. "Patterns in the Transfer of Power: A Comparative Study of French and British Decolonization." In *The Transfer of Power in Africa. Decolonization, 1940–60*, edited by Prosser Gifford and William Roger Louis, 87–115. New Haven, CT: Yale University Press, 1982.

Solà Gussinyer, Mercè. "L'organització del pelegrinatge a la Meca per Franco durant la Guerra Civil." *L'Avenç*, no. 256 (2001): 56–61.

Sorum, Paul Clay. *Intellectuals and Decolonization in France.* Chapel Hill: University of North Carolina Press, 1977.

Sowerwine, Charles. *France Since 1870: Culture, Politics and Society.* New York: Palgrave, 2001.

Stark, Martin. "Netzwerke in der Geschichtswissenschaft." In *Gläubiger, Schuldner, Arme. Netzwerke und die Rolle des Vertrauens,* edited by Curt W. Hergenröder, 187–90. Wiesbaden, DE: VS Verlag für Sozialwissenschaften, 2010.

Stenner, David. "'Bitterness towards Egypt'—The Moroccan Nationalist Movement, Revolutionary Cairo and the Limits of Anti-Colonial Solidarity." *Cold War History* 16, no. 2 (2015): 159–75.

———. "Centring the Periphery: Northern Morocco as a Hub of Transnational Anti-Colonial Activism, 1930–43." *Journal of Global History* 11, no. 3 (2016): 430–50.

———. "Did Amrika Promise Morocco's Independence? The Nationalist Movement, the Sultan, and the Making of the 'Roosevelt Myth.'" *The Journal of North African Studies* 19, no. 4 (2014): 524–39.

Tazi, Abdelaziz, and Marc Thiollier. *Les relations comerciales entre le Maroc et les Etats Unis.* New York: Société générale pour favoriser le développement du commerce et de l'industrie en France, 1963.

Terretta, Meredith. "Anti-Colonial Lawyering, Postwar Human Rights, and Decolonization across Imperial Boundaries in Africa." *Canadian Journal of History* 52, no. 3 (2017): 448–78.

———. *Petitioning for Our Rights, Fighting for Our Nation: The History of the Democratic Union of Cameroonian Women, 1949–1960.* Bamenda, CM: Langaa Research & Publishing CIG, 2013.

———. "'We Had Been Fooled into Thinking That the UN Watches over the Entire World': Human Rights, UN Trust Territories, and Africa's Decolonization." *Human Rights Quarterly* 34, no. 2 (2012): 329–60.

Thomas, Martin. "Defending a Lost Cause? France and the United States Vision of Imperial Rule in French North Africa, 1946–1956." *Diplomatic History* 26, no. 2 (2002): 215–47.

———. *Fight or Flight: Britain, France, and Their Roads from Empire.* New York: Oxford University Press, 2014.

———. "France Accused: French North Africa before the United Nations, 1952–1962." *Contemporary European History* 10, no. 1 (2001): 91–121.

———. "From French North Africa to Maghreb Independence: Decolonization in Morocco, Tunisia and Algeria, 1945–1956." In *Crisis of Empire: Decolonization and Europe's Imperial States, 1918–1975,* edited by Martin Thomas, Bob Moore, and L. J. Butler, 209–27. London: Hodder Education, 2008.

Thomas, Scott. *The Diplomacy of Liberation: The Foreign Relations of the ANC since 1960.* London: I. B. Tauris, 1996.

Tilly, Charles. *From Mobilization to Revolution.* Reading, MA: Addison-Wesley, 1978.

———. *Social Movements, 1768–2012.* Boulder, CO: Paradigm Publishers, 2013.

Tomlinson, B. R. "What Was the Third World?" *Journal of Contemporary History* 38, no. 2 (2003): 307–21.

Tripp, Charles. *A History of Iraq.* New York: Cambridge University Press, 2002.

Tufekci, Zeynep. *Twitter and Tear Gas: The Power and Fragility of Networked Protest.* New Haven, CT: Yale University Press, 2017.

Valderrama Martínez, Fernando. *Historia de la acción cultural de España en Marruecos (1912–1956).* Tetouan, MA: Editora Marroquí, 1956.

Vatikiotis, P. J. *Arab Regional Politics in the Middle East.* New York: St Martin's Press, 1984.

Velasco de Castro, Rocío. "Las relaciones hispano-marroquíes: Fronteras geográficas e ideológicas y su ambivalente papel en la Historia." In *Conflictos y cicatrices: Fronteras y migraciones en el mundo hispánico*, edited by A. Delgado Larios, 183–204. Madrid: Dykinson, 2014.

Vermeren, Pierre. *Histoire du Maroc depuis l'indépendance*. Paris: La Découverte, 2002.

———. *La formation des élites marocaines et tunisiennes: Des nationalistes aux islamistes, 1920–2000*. Paris: La Découverte, 2002.

Vinen, Richard. *France, 1934–1970*. New York: St. Martin's Press, 1996.

von Bülow, Marisa. "Brokers in Action: Transnational Coalitions and Trade Agreements in the Americas." *Mobilization: An International Quarterly* 16, no. 2 (2011): 165–80.

———. *Building Transnational Networks—Civil Society and the Politics of Trade in the Americas*. New York: Cambridge University Press, 2010.

Wainscott, Ann Marie. *Bureaucratizing Islam: Morocco and the War on Terror*. New York: Cambridge University Press, 2017.

Wall, Irwin M. *The United States and the Making of Postwar France, 1945–1954*. New York: Cambridge University Press, 1991.

Waterbury, John. *The Commander of the Faithful: The Moroccan Political Elite—a Study in Segmented Politics*. New York: Columbia University Press, 1970.

Welsh, William, et al. "Covert U.S. Government Funding of NSA International Programs." In *American Students Organize—Founding the National Student Association after World War II*, edited by Eugene G. Schwartz, 565–74. Westport, CT: American Council on Education/Praeger, 2006.

Werth, Alexander. *France, 1940–1955*. New York: Henry Holt, 1956.

Westad, Odd A. *The Global Cold War: Third World Interventions and the Making of Our Times*. New York: Cambridge University Press, 2005.

Wilford, Hugh. *America's Great Game—The CIA's Secret Arabists and the Shaping of the Modern Middle East*. New York: Basic Books, 2013.

Willis, Michael, and Nizar Messari. "Analyzing Moroccan Foreign Policy and Relations with Europe." *Review of International Affairs* 3, no. 2 (2003): 152–72.

Winks, Robin W. *Cloak & Gown: Scholars in the Secret War, 1939–1961*. New York: Morrow, 1987.

Wolf-Phillips, Leslie. "Why 'Third World'?: Origin, Definition and Usage." *Third World Quarterly* 9, no. 4 (1987): 1311–27.

Woodward, Bob. *Veil: The Secret Wars of the CIA, 1981–1987*. New York: Simon and Schuster, 2007.

Woodward, Peter. *Nasser*. New York: Longman, 1992.

Wyrtzen, Jonathan. "Constructing Morocco: The Colonial Struggle to Define the Nation, 1912–56." PhD diss., Georgetown University, 2009.

———. *Making Morocco: Colonial Intervention and the Politics of Identity*. Ithaca, NY: Cornell University Press, 2015.

Yaqub, Salim. *Containing Arab Nationalism: The Eisenhower Doctrine and the Middle East*. Chapel Hill: University of North Carolina Press, 2004.

Young, Cynthia. *Soul Power: Culture, Radicalism, and the Making of a U.S. Third World Left*. Durham, NC: Duke University Press, 2006.

Zoubir, Yahia H. "Les États-Unis et le Maghreb: Primauté de la sécurité et marginalité de la démocratie." *L'Année du Maghreb* 2 (2005/6): 563–84.

———. "The United States and Morocco: The Long-Lasting Alliance." In *Handbook on US–Middle East Relations*, edited by Robert E. Looney, 237–48. New York: Routledge, 2009.

———. "The United States, the Soviet Union and Decolonization of the Maghreb, 1945–1962." *Middle Eastern Studies* 31, no. 1 (1995): 58–84.

Zunes, Stephen. "The United States and Morocco: The Sahara War and Regional Interests." *Arab Studies Quarterly* 9, no. 4 (1987): 422–41.

INDEX

Page numbers in italic indicate material in figures.